HONEYBEE FLORA OF ETHIOPIA

Reinhard Fichtl and Admasu Adi

D1662947

Reinhard Fichtl and Admasu Adi

HONEYBEE FLORA OF ETHIOPIA

This book is the result of the cooperation between the German Development Service (DED) and the Ministry of Agriculture – Livestock & Fishery Resources Main Department, Addis Ababa, Ethiopia.

CIP-Titelaufnahme der Deutschen Bibliothek

Fichtl, Reinhard:
Honeybee flora of Ethiopia / Reinhard Fichtl and Admasu Adi. DED. – Weikersheim : Margraf, 1994
  ISBN 3-8236-1234-4
NE: Admasu Adi:

Authors:

Reinhard Fichtl
Böhmerbrunnenstr. 2
92345 Dietfurt
Germany

Admasu Adi
Ministry of Agriculture
Holetta Bee Research & Training Centre
P.O. Box 62181
Addis Ababa, Ethiopia

Editors:

Sue Edwards
National Herbarium
Addis Ababa, Ethiopia

Ensermu Kelbessa
National Herbarium
Addis Ababa, Ethiopia

Photos:

Reinhard Fichtl

Printing and Binding:

Vier-Türme-Verlag
Benedict Press
Münsterschwarzach, Germany

ISBN 3-8236-1234-4

Traditional backyard beekeeping in Ambo: note the range of bee baskets and other containers for bees

HONEYBEE FLORA OF ETHIOPIA

CONTENTS

Foreword

Ethiopia's wide climatic and edaphic variability have endowed this country with diverse and unique flowering plants thus making it highly suitable for sustaining large numbers of bee colonies and the long-established practice of beekeeping. Nevertheless, the bees and the plants they depend on, like all renewable natural resources, are constantly under threat from lack of knowledge and appreciation of these endowments.

Beekeeping is an important activity for many rural people - both men and women - and is also carried out in homegardens and even houses in all parts of the country. There is no nationality in Ethiopia which does not have beekeepers and for some beekeeping and the collection and selling of honey and other bee products is a major economic activitiy.

At a world level, Ethiopia is fourth in beeswax and tenth in honey production. Honey and beeswax also play a big role in the cultural and religious life of the peoples of the country.

Beekeeping is one of the major branches of agriculture because bees are the pollinating agents for many crops. Pollination increases not only the quantity but also the quality of fruits and seeds for many oilcrops, legumes, fruits and vegetables. The single pollinating potential of a honeybee colony becomes evident when it is realized that the bees of a single bee colony visit about 400 million flowers per year.

This book, which describes and illustrates 500 honey plants, both indigenous and introduced, is believed to be an invaluable reference to all interested and involved in beekeeping. It is also believed that it will be of value to environmentalists, conservationists, foresters, agriculturalists, and others by creating and increasing awareness of the importance of our highly diverse natural resources. I trust this book sets the ground for a better appreciation as well as more detailed studies of apiculture and honey plants.

Ethiopia has now launched an economic policy which favours and promotes peasant agriculture on a sustainable basis. The timely appearance of this work will contribute immensely to this cause.

I hereby express recognition to all involved of the intense efforts that went into the preparation and publication of this highly esteemed book with a special appreciation of its contribution to the greening of Ethiopia.

Congratulation!

Teketel Forsido
A/Minister of Agriculture

ACKNOWLEDGEMENTS

Most of the manifold research work would not have been accomplished without the support given by the staff members of the Holetta Bee Research & Training Centre. We would like to thank the following: Ato Ayalew Kassaye (Senior Beekeeping Expert), Ato Gezahegne Tadesse (Senior Beekeeping Expert, MoA), Ato Amsallu Bezabeh (Centre Manager), Ato Nuru Adgaba, W/t Serawit Kassa, W/t Hadas G/Marriam, W/t Enani Beshwerde, Ato Dereji Woltedji, Ato Woldu Berhane and Ato Faris Surur for their assistance in plant collection.

We particularly wish to thank the German Agency for Technical Co-operation (GTZ) for the constant understanding and the provision of financial support, particularly Dr Thomas Labahn, Mr Peter Buri and Dr George Conn.

We also are grateful to the German Development Service (DED) for logistic and financial support, particularly Eberhard Jennerjahn (DED-Country Representative), for his support and encouragement. In addition we would like to thank the DED staff for cooperation and assistance. W/t Yealemwork Berhanu, W/t Tifsehet Workneh, Ato Salomon Admassu and Mr Manfred Drewes (former DED-Country Representative)

For support during field-trips and hospitality we wish to acknowledge the following institutions and individuals: Dr Zerbini and wife, IAR at Holetta, the staff of the Research Stations of ILCA at Debre Zeyit and at Debre Berhan, the Catholic Mission at Addo - Dembi Dollo, Hermannsburger Mission at Challia - Wellega, the Blue Nile Children Home at Bahir Dar and the many beekeepers from whom we have enjoyed great hospitality and are too numerous to acknowledge individually.

We appreciate the contribution of many beekeepers and individuals, particularly Mr Adolf Spitzer (DED), Mr Rainer Schäfer (Apiculturist-DED), Ato Mamush Asfaw, Ato Getenet Negussie and Ato Molla Eshete for their assistance in plant collection and support in data collection. Mr Cristoph Ermer and Mr Gerald Rummler for cooperation and assistance sending colour slides, Ato Desta G/Michael for valuable information in tej preparation, Mr Bernd Willutzki (Apiculturist-DED) for providing photos of a flowering Baobab tree, Ato Solomon Tilahun for checking text layout, Ato Asebe Abdena (ILCA) for valuable information on fodder legumes, and particularly Dr Tsedeke Abate (IAR) for very valuable information on honeydew-producing insects and identification.

It would not have been possible to have completed this book without the support, expertise, professionalism and dedication of the staff of the National Herbarium of Addis Ababa University. All plant specimens have been identified in the National Herbarium and the descriptions for the book have been prepared in consultation with the staff of the National Herbarium as well as from data from the Herbarium Collections and supporting literature, including that prepared for the Flora of Ethiopia.

We would like to thank the following: Dr Tewolde Berhan G. Egziabher (Keeper, National Herbarium & Leader Ethiopian Flora Project), Dr Sebsebe Demissew, Dr Mesfin Tadesse, Dr Getachew Aweke, Dr Zemede Asfaw (Asst. Dean of Sience Faculty), Dr Tamrat Bekele, Ato Mirutse Giday (assistance in vernacular names), Ato Tekle Haimanot Haile Selassie, Ato Yilma Tesfaye (assistance in glossary), W/ro Asselefetch Ketsela, W/ro Emebet Getnet, Ato Berhanu Lemma, Ato Melaku Wendafrash, W/t Atsede Bekele, W/t Eyerusalem Nebiyu.

The contribution and leadership of the editors Ms Sue Edwards and Dr Ensermu Kelbessa to the completion of the book was most substantial. It is not only their advice, guidance and criticism of the text, but also the contribution of much valuable information and the encouragement and their spirit which made this book project come alive.

In addition the editors prepared the camera-ready copy for the printers.

Reinhard Fichtl

Addis Ababa
May 1994

INTRODUCTION

What is in this book

This book has the title "Honeybee Flora of Ethiopia". The word Flora with a capital letter is used for a book about the plants - flora with a small letter - of a particular geographical area. The complete flora of Ethiopia has between six and seven thousand species of flowering plant. This book has restricted itself to five hundred species which have been observed by the authors and their beekeeping friends as particularly important for honeybees and whose portraits have been captured through the expert eye of Reinhard Fichtl's camera. This does not mean, however, that these are the only plants important to honeybees. Far from it.

The five hundred species have also been chosen to show the wide range of plants in Ethiopia which are important to bees. There are the beautiful indigenous trees of the remaining forests, such as *Aningeria altissima*, KARARO, which provides a particularly delicately-flavoured golden honey, as well as very important introduced species such as the eucalypts which are widely grown by farmers and which also provide very valuable honey. The chapter on shrubs and herbs also includes some important crop plants such as the oil crop *Guizotia abyssinica*, as well as maize and sorghum which have a surprising importance for honeybees.

Shrubs and herbs are often considered as "weeds"; plants where more useful species such as trees or crops could be grown. This book shows that many of these plants are very valuable, not only for bees but in many other ways, providing forage, or cover against erosion, or some medicinal and culturally important products. Even plants of wetlands such as *Nymphaea nouchali* and *Rotala repens* have been included. And all these plants provide pollen and/or nectar for honeybees making Ethiopia one of the most honey-rich countries in the world. If you have ever drunk a cup of Ethiopian coffee sweetened with honey, you should know why it took such a long time for sugar cane to come into the country. And coffee sweetened with honey is considered a very good settler for mild stomach upsets.

Last, but not least, the book contains as many vernacular names as it was possible for the authors and the specialist in the National Herbarium to collect in the time available.

How to use this book

This book can be used both to identify a plant visited by honeybees, as well as to find out what plants are valuable to beekeepers. The plants are presented in two chapters: one for herbs and shrubs, and the other for trees. Thus one should look in the chapter according to the type of plant one is interested in. However, he/she may have to check both sections for shrubs and small trees as sometimes a small tree can be found growing as a shrub, and vice versa.

If one knows the vernacular name of the plant, he/she can look it up in the index at the end of the book. But do not be disappointed if the name cannot be found in this index. There are more than 70 languages with 200 dialects in Ethiopia. Common English and German names have also been included.

The key to identifying a plant is to look at the pictures. In each chapter of the book, the plants have been arranged alphabetically according to their family and then alphabetically by name within the family. In many cases, pictures from plants in the same family appear together on the same page. This should be particularly useful for important groups like the CLOVERS, *Trifolium* spp. and *Plectranthus* spp. where there are many species important for honeybees. Once one has found a picture which seems to match the plant he/she is interested in, then the short description should be read through to confirm this. It is also useful to check on the habitat and altitudinal range of the plant as this is important in getting a correct identification. For example, the two subspecies of *Guizotia scabra* have different habitats.

Also just open the book to enjoy the pictures and learn more about the plants that support an almost invisible hoard of busy workers which provide people with one of the oldest and most enjoyable foods, honey.

Sue Edwards &
Ensermu Kelbessa

APICULTURE

From the very earliest times man has been associated with honeybees as can be seen in the role which honey, wax, and bees play in mythology and in the rituals of ancient man, even nowadays. The beginning of beekeeping was, no doubt, the chance to find and rob the honey from wild bee colonies more than ten thousand years ago. This is still practiced in many parts of Africa.

Of all the countries in the world, probably none has a longer tradition of beekeeping than Ethiopia. The hieroglyphs of ancient Egypt refer to this land as the source for honey and beeswax. It is thus assumed that the keeping of bees in baskets may have started about five thousand years ago in the northern regions along with the early settlements.

Since the fourth century, during the time of king Ezana, Christianity with a strong emphasis on a monastic culture contributed a lot to the intensive growth of beekeeping because of the need for wax for religious ceremonies. In addition the farming community had to supply the nobility and the social elites with honey for making traditional beverages.

According to some estimates, Ethiopia, with about three to five million bee colonies, is the country with the highest bee density in Africa. As in many other African countries beeswax is a very important product of beekeeping. Thus, after China, Mexico and Turkey, Ethiopia is the fourth largest wax producing country with an estimated two thousand one hundred tonnes per year. She is one of the five biggest wax exporters to the world market. According to FAO's estimation, the production of honey amounts also to twenty-one thousand tonnes per year. With this amount, Ethiopia is the largest honey producing country in Africa and world-wide it stands in tenth place.

Honey, or rather its further treatment, plays a big role in the cultural and religious life of the peoples of Ethiopia. No birth or burial, no wedding or other social event can be imagined without the honeybeer TEJ, which has long been the national beverage. This honeybeer is brewed by female homeowners and shopkeepers using their own facilities. In order to enhance the fermentation process, it is best to brew this beverage using not only honey, but also pollen, wax and sometimes brood, the combination of ingredients obtained from the traditional honey harvest. Additionally, crude honey is widely used for different medical treatments in the rural communities. The high portion of pollen found in crude honey, in honeybeer and other honey drinks contributes a fixed amount of protein in people's diet. In regions where cattle breeding is limited because of the Tsetse fly and other problems, the bee brood, which is rich in vitamins and protein, is highly respected.

In western Wellega there are beekeepers who own up to one thousand bee colonies. They do not count the number of hives any more, but only the number of trees on which the hives are hanging.

The Bees

In Ethiopia at least three geographical races are confirmed to be present. The Ethiopian bees are *Apis mellifera scutellata*, *Apis m. monticola* and *Apis m. yemenitica*.

Generally, *Apis m. scutellata* is regarded as the African bee occurring in altitudes between 500 and more than 2400 m. Sample collections have clearly shown the occurrence of *Apis m. scutellata* in Ethiopia, Kenya, Tanzania, Rwanda, Burundi, Zimbabwe, Botswana, and South Africa.

The gentle race *Apis m. monticola* of the Afro-alpine zone which occurs between altitudes of 2400 up to 3400m in Ethiopia, is also present in Kenya, Tanzania, Malawi, Rwanda, Burundi and Cameroon.

The drought resistant lowland bee *Apis m. yemenitica* is found on the south-eastern escarpment and in the southeastern lowlands. It also occurs in Sudan, Chad, Uganda, Kenya, Somalia and Djibouti.

Beside the *Apis mellifera* races, stingless bees (*Trigona* spp.) are commonly found in medium altitudes up to 2300 m a.s.l. This bee produces a special honey called TAZMA.

The TAZMA bee is a small bee, about 10 mm long, having the nest built in cavities in the ground about 1 m deep. It has many characteristics in common with honeybees like storing of honey, using wax for building combs, building up of larger colonies and the division of labour.

The TAZMA honey is a liquid with a strong acid flavour. It is widely prized as a panacea for many ills.

The finding of underground nests is the special duty of shepherds or so-called TAZMA experts. Nectar foraging TAZMA bees are carefully caught from the flowers and a thin cotton thread is fixed between thorax and abdomen. The so-obstructed bee can be observed flying back to the nest. The entrance will be marked and ownership of the nest is shown. If necessary the nest will be guarded. At harvesting time a small tunnel is dug from the side to reach the wax combs inside the cavity. The digging is done very carefully and in most cases the colony can abscond to settle down elsewhere.

Behaviour

Apis m. scutellata is a typical African honeybee, more involved in brood rearing, swarming and wax production and less in honey production. It has a high swarming rate, rapid colony development and a strong tendency to abscond and migrate. This behaviour is a reflection of their ecology.

A women selling freshly-harvested comb honey in the highlands.

The African honeybees do not need to store large amounts of honey to survive the winter and thus do not require the large colonies typical of temperate evolved bees. Additionally, predation on honey bees is much more intense in tropical habitats and nests in small cavities are easily defended. Also, if a predator succeeds in destroying a nest, much less is lost by the colony in a small nest. After a disaster the queen can leave the site and begin a new nest elsewhere.

Due to the many enemies of bees: honey hunters, bee eating birds (*Merops* spp.), honey badger (*Mellivora capensis*), wasps and particularly ants, the bees have developed a very strong defense behaviour. Even after small disturbances thousands of bees will leave the nest to attack everything which is moving.

If the bees do not succeed in driving away potential predators they will immediately leave the nest and try to settle elsewhere in more convenient surroundings. The same is true if there is a serious scarcity of bee feed.

They will settle in rock crevices, in cavities in the ground, in termite mounds, in holes of trees, in empty containers and barrels, and generously in empty bee baskets and log hives hanging in trees, under roofs of houses or even just lie on the ground.

Beside their aggressiveness, a considerably high reproduction rate is a further strategy of survival. The African honeybees do not produce more swarm cells compared with temperate evolved bees, but because of the favourable climate and the rich honeybee flora in tropical African habitats, even very small bee swarms with only two to three thousand bees have a good chance to survive and to develop into big colonies within a short time. This high rate in reproduction is a reasonable biological quality in their struggle for survival.

Traditional beekeeping

Traditional beekeeping has the oldest and richest practices which have been carried out by the people for thousands of years. In Ethiopia, beekeeping is one of the oldest agricultural activities having been passed from generation to generation without being modified up to present times. Several million bee colonies are managed with the same old traditional beekeeping methods in almost all parts of the country. Beekeeping has been and still is very widespread and economically important for the farming community of the country.

The farmers, in order to produce their bee baskets, use cheap local materials like clay, straw, bamboo, false banana leaves, bark of trees, logs and animal dung. Like in the other branches of agriculture, they do not need to invest and they use very few tools, mostly a knife. Almost all methods are based on the concept of minimal management. They fix up the bee hives and hang them on certain trees. They hope for a swarm to move in and then they will wait for the time in which the honey harvest is possible. For harvesting, they have to climb up the trees to reach the baskets which were placed in the upper branches, then use a flaming torch to clear the basket and allow the honey to be collected. During the harvesting, the colony will often be destroyed or at least damaged because the honey comb together with the brood and the pollen is cut out with a knife.

4

Numerous bee baskets of a Wellega bee keeper hanging in a tree.

A traditional queen cage made from bamboo.

Traditional Equipment

The beekeepers are using very little equipment for their job. A simple knife and home-made traditional baskets are enough.

The traditional bee hives are simple cylindrical containers for the bees and their combs. The following variants on this basic design are found throughout the country.

Log hives are hollowed logs, made of different timber, hung up in the trees.

Bark hives are made from the bark of big trees, plastered with animal dung, and hung up in the trees.

Bamboo hives are one of the most commonly used hives; the bamboo is woven and leaves of *Ensete ventricosum* are added together with animal dung and hung up in the trees.

Woven straw hives are woven with a rope and then plastered with animal dung and hung up in the trees.

Clay hives are cylindrical hives made of clay, plastered with animal dung inside and are used more in the Northern regions and placed beside the houses or sometimes even inside the houses

Animal dung hives are cylindrical hives made of cowdung. They are used more in the Northern areas and placed beside the houses.

Twig hives are made with twigs which are woven together with other twigs and climbers and then plastered with animal dung and hung up in the trees.

False banana hives are made with the leaves of *Ensete ventricosum* and are commonly used in the South and Southwest of the country.

Pot Hives are made from loamy clay soil and commonly used for carrying water are also widespread in southern parts of the country.

Traditional smokers are widely used, made of clay or cowdung. These are commonly small containers with one or two openings and the smoke of glowing cowdung is carefully blown towards the bees during harvesting. Because beekeepers usually work with bees during the night, a flaming torch is used.

Hive Preparation

Traditional beekeeping is entirely dependent on the occupation of baskets by wild swarms. Thus the beekeeping community has developed various methods to make empty hives attractive to swarms. First the baskets will be smeared inside with a layer of fresh cowdung which is considered to prevent diseases and provide better insulation. After drying the hive will be smoked inside with selected herbs and shrubs. The smoking materials vary from region to region. Most commonly the bark of *Otostegia integrifolia*, *Olea europaea* subsp. *cuspidata*, *Olea capensis* subsp. *welwitchii* and *Ekebergia capensis* are used. Many beekeepers prefer to bait the hives inside with the fresh leaves of *Ocimum basilicum* and in western parts the hive will be baited with the endemic *Echinops longisetus.*

Afterwards the baskets will be closed on both sides with woven straw discs. A small hole is left for the bee entrance.

Beekeeping Knowledge

Skills and knowledge are transferred from one generation to the next, improved by "trial and error" only.

The biological knowledge is confined to immediate observations and repeated experience. The beekeeper hardly knows anything about bee biology. Ethiopian cultures and traditions explain to him the division of labour inside a hive and the bee behaviour.

For him the queen is a king and the worker bees are aggressive honey makers. Due to the round abdomen which reminds one of a traditional clay-pot, the drones are considered to be responsible for carrying water.

Advanced practical skills are widely found within the beekeeping community. Many beekeepers are used to cutting part of the wing of the queen to reduce absconding. During swarming seasons young queens will be caged in bamboo queen-cages or cages made of grass and other different materials to guide the swarm tendency of the colony. Inspection or management at critical times for bees are restricted with taboos. It is, therefore, strictly forbidden to disturb the bees at the end of the rainy season because "worms" would spoil the colony. This is a drastic warning to prevent wax moths from entering the hives during times when colonies are very weak.

In some parts of the country the splitting of strong colonies is widely used. The whole basket will be divided into two parts without harming the colony and the queenless part reproduces a new queen. Mainly animal dung hives and clay hives are very appropriate for this practices as they can be divided simply with a machete.

The beekeepers have an intensive knowledge of herbs, shrubs and trees growing in their surroundings. They identify most of the plants, giving detailed descriptions of their various applications. They know their use as bee plants as well as their use for human or veterinary medicine and health care. Their knowledge of application ranges from plants as insecticides or pesticides, to seasonings and condiments, perfume and aromatic plants, to areas where plants are used for religious and magic rites.

Hive Management

Hive management with baskets is confined to handling bees and cropping honey. It also includes the baiting of hives and siting them.

After the small rains at the end of April and after the big rainy season sometime in September, the beekeepers fix the baskets in the upper branches of selected trees. Commonly trees are selected which bear flowers to attract wild swarms. The baskets will be hung up horizontally to avoid accumulating heat. In areas where the tree cover is already scarce, the hives will be placed under the roofs of houses.

Since the baskets have a relatively small volume the swarming tendency will be supported and many swarms will be produced. Therefore it is easy for the

Since the baskets have a relatively small volume the swarming tendency will be supported and many swarms will be produced. Therefore it is easy for the beekeeper to expand his apiary by displaying empty hives. In times of reproduction they will soon attract swarms.

The fixing of bee hives in upper branches of tall trees protects against theft as well as preventing predators like lizards, honey badger and ants from having access to the hive.

Handling Bees

Experienced beekeepers are very aware of their bees and have a certain liking or respect for bees. Bees are carefully smoked and the hives are always watched. Many women are found among the beekeepers who fearless apply a patient approach particularly in harvesting the colonies.

The respect for bees and the strong intensive defense reaction of the bees determines the beekeeper's attitude towards the bees. The normal beekeeper first smokes all the bees to protect himself, instead of giving priority to controlling the bees by careful and purposeful smoking.

Swarm Treatment

African bees do not have a strong tendency to eliminate young virgin queens during the swarming process. Often quite a number of queens are found within one swarm. The experienced beekeeper will try to catch the swarm and push it onto the ground where he will carefully look for the queens. If several are found he will cage them in small bamboo cages and place the cage inside a mature colony. The small slits of the cage will allow the nurse bees to feed the queen but the narrowness of the cage prevents the queens eliminating each other. Queens are even sometimes sold or used for colonies where a queen has been lost due to an attack by ants. Some beekeepers who are used to splitting strong colonies are able to use these queens.

Feeding

During harvesting times experienced beekeepers leave some proportion of honey to the bees to avoid starving and absconding.

In some regions the beekeepers feed their bees with freshly slaughtered meat scraps placed near the hive or put fresh animal blood at their disposal. This might be related to the bees' behaviour to obtain essential chemical substances or minerals from liquids like blood, urine and other body liquids, and from decaying plant materials.

Many beekeepers feed their bees with ground beans, chick peas and peas which are placed either inside or outside the entrance of the baskets.

Bee baskets being moved in the migratory bee keeping practiced in Gojjam.

A lone *Acacia albida* tree with its lonely bee basket above the Blue Nile gorge.

Honey Hunting

Honey hunting is quite popular in some regions of Ethiopia. The honey hunters spend most of their time tracing and robbing any wild colony. If he finds a wild colony he will immediately exploit it, because nobody can claim ownership.

In western and southwestern Ethiopia, even from prehistoric times, cultures have developed which had a complete value system depending on honey hunting. There the respect for a person depended not on the size of cultivated land owned nor on the number of trees, but on honey. For social respect, the quantity of bee hives one managed is used as a measurement. Thus, the Mesengo differ from the Anuak, Murle and Nuer in that their God WAKAYO gave them honey in order to make them rich.

The honey hunter roams through the forests and mountainous areas watching out for holes in trees and noisy bees. With wooden sticks he will beat against promising trees to agitate bees in nests and he will try to follow the honey guide (*Indicator indicator*). This bee eating bird tries to lure the honey badger or the hunter towards the bee nests in order to be provided with brood.

If bees are found they will be pushed away using excessive fire and smoke. When the colony is out of reach of the honey hunter, the tree is felled to extract the contents of the bees nest.

Migratory beekeeping

In some regions of Ethiopia, for example in Gojjam, simple migratory beekeeping is widely used. This is not done to ensure better pollination of nearby crops like *Guizotia abyssinica* but to get additional income through honey production. The baskets are closed with fresh cowdung and the following day they are carried on the shoulder to the selected fields. Since the wings of the queen have been cut, absconding does not occur.

Hive Products

Honey is a seasonal crop and not stored for a long time. Fresh comb honey is highly esteemed near urban centres, particularly near Addis Ababa. Most of the honey harvested is a mixture of pollen, wax and honey, which is widely used for honeybeer brewing which is mainly brewed by women. Honey is also used extensively in local medicine as a panacea and to strengthen the body.

Pollen is harvested together with honey. It is rich in protein and is essential to enhance the development of the right yeasts in the honeybeer.

Bee brood is also harvested as a high quality protein food. It is sucked or chewed out from freshly harvested combs and eaten just after harvesting the baskets. It is distributed within the family and highly prized by children.

Beeswax is of little practical value for the beekeepers. Occasionally it is used to grease the baking plate METAD of the INJERA stove. Otherwise, it is simply thrown away. All the wax traded within Ethiopia is collected from the honey beer breweries

Traditional honey harvesting taking place at night.

as a waste-product of brewing crude honey which contains wax, pollen and brood. This wax is used extensively to make various types of tapers and candles for the Orthodox church. It is this wax which also enters the international trade.

In most cases propolis is not harvested and therefore not used.

Honey Harvest

After a certain time when honey can be expected, the beekeeper will climb up the trees during night to examine the weight of the baskets. This is a very risky job and sometimes serious accidents take place. If the basket is considered to yield quite a good amount of honey it will be carefully let down using hand woven strings. A smoky camp fire will be made to keep the bees calm. In most cases beekeepers don't have any protective clothing and harvesting is more or less a painful matter. To avoid too many bee stings the beekeeper often removes his clothes because the bees are less able to sting on sweaty skin.

With a simple knife the rear cover lid of the basket will be carefully opened and a lot of smoke is driven in. The irritated bees will draw back inside the hive and the honey and pollen combs will be cut off with the knife. In many cases all the combs will be removed, particularly in regions where bee colonies are plentiful. The beekeeper works very carefully and deliberately and removes bees from the comb with the finger tip. Brood combs and pollen and honey combs will be sorted out later on. After the basket is harvested it will not be hung up in the tree but cleaned and prepared for the next season.

During this operation quite a number of irritated bees buzzes around and clusters on the grass. Often the whole colony will die. If the queen survives the colony will occupy an empty basket in the following day or two.

Thus, the promotion of the bees' swarming tendency by using small volume baskets must be seen as an exceptional cultural effort because otherwise the bee population of Ethiopia would not have any chance to survive.

Conclusion

Traditional beekeeping, despite its antiquated appearance, is a very efficient undertaking. No investments are necessary to obtain sufficient honey yields. If the harvest must be increased, additional baskets will be prepared and hung up in trees. The biology of the bees does not require sophisticated managements methods like nucleus making and queen rearing. The volume of baskets ensures that sufficient swarms will be produced to replace the bee colonies spoiled during traditional harvesting.

The provision of sufficient nectar and pollen sources, and a better knowledge of the importance of pollination and environmental protection will safeguard one of the richest and oldest agricultural practices of the world.

400 HERBS AND SHRUBS
FOR BEES

Introduction

For far too long, the absence of a honey plant guide has been acutely felt by beekeepers and agricultural extension experts, by educators in institutions, and by many readers interested in the Ethiopian flora.

Since time immemorial the Ethiopian Highlands have been used for agriculture. Located within the tropics, the climate in these areas is moderate to warm. The favourable weather conditions with mostly sufficient rainfall have created a complex and extensive rural culture, which has produced an unbelievable multitude of varieties in wheat, barley, TEFF, ENSET and many other cultivated plants.

The northern and central parts of the country were initially much more extensively covered with forests forming a mosaic with grassland and wetlands. This provided habitats for a high diversity of trees, shrubs and herbs. Nowadays with the expansion of agriculture and a very rapid population growth the forests have dwindled to tiny remnants, such as are found around churches, and the vegetation is dominated by shrubs, cultivated plants and herbs which have largely replaced the former forest vegetation.

After the heavy rains between July and September, known as KREMT, vast areas of the highlands are coloured golden-yellow because of the abundance of *Bidens* species ADEY-ABEBA, indigenous oil crops like *Guizotia abyssinica* NUG, and red-violet with very many CLOVERS. Along paths, forest edges, river banks and swampy meadows, a multitude of herbs are found growing and flowering, many of them not found elsewhere in the world: that is, they are endemic.

Apiculture is deeply rooted in Ethiopian rural life and is basic to many cultural activities. Traditional knowledge by Ethiopian beekeepers and others of their botanical surroundings is large but largely unrecorded.

This section of the "Honeybee Flora of Ethiopia" draws attention to some of the herbs and shrubs of importance to Ethiopian beekeepers. It provides the reader with pictures and descriptions to demonstrate the very rich diversity of the Ethiopian flora. This is accompanied by valuable information which has been gathered from the farming community itself and which can be used to stimulate respect for this knowledge and contribute to rehabilitating the Ethiopian environment in partnership with the rural people.

Acanthus eminens C.B. Clarke /
Acanthaceae
CHOCHA (Kem)

A woody herb or shrub to 4 m high. Leaves large, up to 30 cm long, thistle-like, shiny green above, deeply pinnatifid with spiny margins. Flowers are deep blue-violet.

Commonly growing in evergreen montane forests, under partial shade of trees, along roadsides and streams, at altitudes between 1500 and 2500 m.

Flowering almost all year round, fairly frequently visited by carpenter bees as well as *honeybees especially when other major sources of nectar and pollen are scarce.*

Acanthus sennii Chiov. /
Acanthaceae
KOSHESHLA (Amh); KOSORU, SOKORU (Or); OKOLE (Sid)

An erect and very prickly perennial herb, growing to 2 m high; sometimes a low shrub or even undershrub. Stem branching from the base. Leaves are dry and stiff, simple, and deeply lobed. Flowers produced in a cluster at the end of the stem; pink, cadmium red, crimson, scarlet or vermilion and very showy.

Endemic to the highlands of Ethiopia. This sometimes hedge-forming plant grows in dry habitats, at margins of forests, in open land, along roadsides, stream and riverbanks, at altitudes between 1500 and 3200 m.

In local medicine the whole plant is used against HOT SIRAY and SHINT MAT.

Flowering almost throughout the year. Pollinated by birds, *honeybees also collect pollen and nectar from the flowers.*

Asystasia gangetica (L.)
T.Anders. / Acanthaceae
GRBIA (Tya)

A straggling or sometimes creeping herb with ascending flowering stems up to 2 m tall. Leaves ovate, cordate at the base. Flowers almost white, arranged in one-sided racemes which have purple/violet nectar guides.

Growing along forest margins, in grassland and bushland, usually in shade of hedges and trees at altitudes between 600 and 2200 m. Sometimes found as a weed of cultivation and along roadsides.

Flowering from July to March, *honeybees forage for the abundant nectar and pollen all day round. The plant is a very important honey source.*

Barleria grandis Nees. /
Acanthaceae

A subshrub or shrub growing to 1.5 m high. Leaves large, bluish green above and paler below. Flowers large, white to yellowish-white are born in racemes in leaf-axils and at the end of branches.

Endemic to Ethiopia and found only in the Takazze, Abbay and Gibe river systems. It grows on rocky hillsides, in open woodland and scrub, at altitudes between 1600 and 1800 m.

Flowering from October to November, *bees forage for pollen and nectar from the flowers that open towards late afternoon.*

Barleria ventricosa Hochst. ex Nees / Acanthaceae

A scandent perennial herb with sub-sessile elliptic leaves. The light blue flowers are borne in the upper leaf-axils and at the end of stems/branches.

Common in dry bushland, thickets and forest edges, in wooded grassland and along paths at altitudes between 1200 and 2900 m.

Flowering from September to December, *honeybees collect pollen and nectar from the flowers frequently.*

Brillantaisia madagascariensis Lindau / Acanthaceae

DARGU (Or)

An erect, branched, perennial herb growing to 2 m. The leaves are broadly ovate with toothed margins. The pink to purple flowers are arranged in terminal spikes with broadly cordate bracts.

Growing in shade, along margins of evergreen forests, along waterways and roadsides, mainly in western parts of the country at altitudes up to 2200 m.

Flowering after the big rains, *honeybees forage for nectar and pollen.*

Dicliptera maculata Nees. / Acanthaceae

A perennial herb growing to 1 m tall. Leaves ovate-lanceolate. Flowers pink, borne in cymes.

Growing mostly under the shade of large trees in montane forest, beside rivers and other waterways, and forest margins at altitudes between 1000 and 2200 m.

Flowering mostly from September to January, *honeybees collect pollen and nectar from the flowers.*

Hygrophila auriculata (Schum.) Heine / Acanthaceae

YESIET-MLAS, AMEKIELA (Amh); KORATTI-SARE (Or); E'SHOCH'-GUASSA (Tya)

An erect sparingly branched perennial or annual herb with square stems and elliptic leaves. Stem with long brown spines beneath each set of leaves which are arranged in whorls. Flowers pinkish to purplish, but sometimes white.

Growing at altitudes as low as 500 m in areas waterlogged for part of the year, and up to 2800 m in grassland and along paths and forest edges.

It is eaten by cattle and the seeds can produce a semi-drying oil. The fleshy root has a cooling, slimy taste and a marshy smell.

Flowering from August to February, *honeybees collect pollen and nectar from the flowers frequently. The plant is an important honey source in lower parts of the country.*

Hypoestes forskaolii *(Vahl)*
R.Sch. / Acanthaceae
DARGU (Or)

A perennial herb or subshrub with ascending branches growing to 1 m high. Leaves dark green, paler beneath, ovate to lanceolate and entire. Flowers white, with purple nectar guides, arranged in erect racemes.

Growing in open woodland, disturbed montane forest, grassland and is common along roadsides at altitudes between 500 and 2700 m.

Flowering throughout the year, *honeybees forage for the abundant pollen and nectar. The plant is an important honey source.*

Hypoestes triflora *(Forssk.)*
Roem. & Schult. / Acanthaceae
TQUR-T'ELENG (Amh); DARGU (Or)

A straggling annual, variable in size, but often growing to a height of 50 cm. Leaves elliptic and flowers pink or white.

Very widespread throughout the country, found in the shade of forests, growing in woodland and along roadsides and waterways at altitudes between 1200 and 2900 m.

This herb is used as a wound dressing for animals.

Flowering from July to February, *honeybees collect pollen and nectar from the flowers frequently. It is a prolific producer of nectar at lower altitudes where the herb is growing under shade of Acacia spp. The stimulating nectar supplies strengthen the bee colonies after harvesting in November.*

Isoglossa laxa *Oliv.* /
Acanthaceae
DARGU (Or)

An erect annual or perennial herb growing to 70 cm high. Leaves ovate, entire and flowers white.

Very widespread throughout the country, found in the forest shade, woodland and along roadsides at altitudes between 1300 and 2700 m.

Flowering from September to December the *honeybees collect pollen and nectar from the flowers.*

Isoglossa somalensis *Lindau* /
Acanthaceae
DARGU (Or)

An erect annual or perennial herb growing to 60 cm high. Leaves entire. Flowers white to pale pink, in cymes.

Common in dry evergreen woodland and at forest edges, in evergreen montane forest and in partial shade of trees and widespread as a roadside plant at altitudes between 1600 and 3000 m.

Flowering from September to February, *honeybees collect pollen and nectar from the flowers frequently.*

Justicia heterocarpa T.Anders. subsp. vallicola Hedren / Acanthaceae

A pubescent perennial herb with ascending to erect stems growing to 1 m high, and with ovate leaves. Flowers pale purple-red (magenta).

Growing under shade of woody plants in scrub, wooded grassland and woodland, commonly in degraded Acacia woodland and in sandy soils at altitudes between 500 and 1900 m.

This subspecies is endemic to central and southern Ethiopia.

Flowering all year round, but more profusely after the big rains up to January. In dry areas *honeybees visit the flowers the whole day to collect pollen and nectar.*

Justitia ladanoides Lam. / Acanthaceae

AKADE (Anu); TELENGE, CHINGERCH (Amh)

A much-branched erect or sometimes prostrate perennial or annual growing to 2 m high under favourable conditions, with ascending hairy stems. Leaves lanceolate to ovate, dark green. Flowers large pinkish to purple with white nectar guides, in the axils or at ends of stems.

Found in the forest shade, woodland and bushland, on rocky hillsides and eroded soils, sometimes as a weed and commonly as a roadside plant at altitudes between 500 and 2800 m.

Flowering almost all year round, *honeybees collect pollen and nectar from the flowers very frequently.*

Justitia schimperana (Hochst. ex Nees) T.Anders. / Acanthaceae (syn. Adhatoda schimperiana)

SENSEL (Amh); TUMOGA (Kef); T/DUMUGA (Or); SODA, SHIMFA (Tya)

An erect much-branched shrub growing to 5 m high with woody stems and large elliptic leaves. Flowers white, in dense cylindrical, terminal spikes.

Growing in scrub, montane forests, at the edges of evergreen forests and bushland and is a very common hedge-forming plant at altitudes between 1400 and 2600 m.

Used as a hedge around houses in many districts, it has many uses. The crushed, strong-smelling leaves are used to clean pots for TELA. It has many medicinal uses: leaves for the treatment of malaria and relieving asthma, roots against Leishmaniasis. Twigs are used as a tooth-brush.

Flowering throughout the year, but more profusely after the big rains. *Honeybees collect pollen and nectar from the flowers and the plant is reported as a honey source.*

Phaulopsis imbricata (Forssk.) Sweet. / Acanthaceae

DARGU (Or)

A pubescent annual or short-lived perennial with creeping-ascending stems to 30 cm high and elliptic leaves. Flowers small white in dense axillary and terminal cymes.

Growing in woodland, dry and wet evergreen forests, bushland and on drier parts of the plateau, at altitudes between 600 and 2500 m.

Flowering almost all year round, but more profusely from October to January. *Honeybees collect pollen and nectar from the flowers.*

Ruttya speciosa *Engler /*
Acanthaceae

A much branched shrub which grows to 4 m tall. It has entire leaves and dark-centred orange-red flowers in short axillary cymes.

Commonly found in bushland, along riverbanks, in partial shade of trees at altitudes between 1600 and 2400 m.

The flowers are very rich in nectar and they are visited by birds, carpenter bees, *honeybees.* Flowering from October to December, *honeybees collect pollen and nectar.*

Agave americana *L. /*
Agavaceae

QA'CHA (Amh); AMERICAN ALOE, CENTURY PLANT (Eng); HUNDERTJÄHRIGE ALOE (German)

A plant with large leaves borne in a rosette, each up to 1.5 m long, dark green with yellow strips or all grey-green, with widely-spaced teeth along the margin. Flowers are yellowish to greenish-white, arranged on large stalks to 5 m tall.

Found as an ornamental and as a hedge forming plant in drier parts of the country at altitudes up to 2400 m. Fibre is extracted from the leaves and old flowering stems are used as fuel.

Flowering plants are found throughout the year, honeybees collect pollen and abundant nectar from the flowers frequently. It is a valuable bee plant because of its irregular and long lasting flowering periods and is of enormous attraction especially during times of pollen scarcity. It provides sufficient nectar for stimulating brood rearing. The flavour of honey, if obtained, is strong and poor.

Agave sisalana *Perr. ex Eng. /*
Agavaceae

YA-A (Afar); KACHA (Amh & Ade); E'QA (Tya); KACHIYA (Wel); SISAL (Eng); SISALAGAVE (German)

A robust perennial with a rosette of thick fleshy leaves up to 2 m long. The tips and thick margins bear sharp spines. Flowers yellowish-green and borne on many-branched panicles on flowering stalks to 4 m tall.

Widely cultivated for fibre production in plantations near Awasa town. Commonly planted and regenerating naturally to form an impenetrable hedge around homesteads and cultivated fields and to stabilize terraces at altitudes between 1600 to 2400 m.

Fibre is extracted from the leaves and the flower stalks are used to make fences as well as for fuel when they dry up.

Flowering and use for honeybees the same as for Agave americana.

Aloe berhana *Reynolds /*
Aloaceae

IRET (Amh); ORGEESA (Or); IRE (Tya)

A usually stemless herb which may have a thick prostrate stem when old. Leaves arranged in a very dense rosette, spreading and recurved up to 60 cm long with toothed margins. They are dull dark green, drying brown when old. Flowers red, arranged in branched racemes up to 1 m tall.

This endemic is very common on rocky hillsides and in grassland where thin soil overlies basalt stones at altitudes between 2000 and 2700 m.

Flowering from November to March the *honeybees are foraging pollen and nectar.*

Achyranthes aspera L. /
Amaranthaceae

T'ELENJ, ATTUCH (Amh); KACHABA
(Had); DARGU, MATANNE (Or);
MATENEH (Sid); DODET, ME'CHELO,
MUTCHULO RODUT (Tya); DEVIL'S
HORSEWHIP (Eng)

A scrambling annual or perennial herb
growing to 3 m tall, with opposite,
simple leaves. Flowers small, pale pink
or green, reddish or whitish, in
terminal spikes.

Widespread and sometimes a
troublesome weed, it occurs in
hedges, thickets and shaded habitats,
bushland and riverine forest
throughout the country at altitudes
between 700 and 3500 m.

Flowering all year round, *honeybees
collect pollen and nectar from the
flowers frequently. The long flowering
period makes this species very
valuable for bee colony maintenance.*

Celosia argentea L. /
Amaranthaceae

BELBELTO (Amh); ABABO (Or)

An erect annual herb growing to 2 m
tall with lanceolate-elliptic leaves.
Flowers in dense terminal, spikes, first
pink then white and shining.

Found as a weed of cultivation,
especially in maize, and along
irrigation ditches, also by roadsides, in
bushland and riverine forest, at
altitudes between 600 and 1900 m. It is
cultivated in the Gibe river system
area.

Flowering from September to May,
*honeybees forage for pollen and
nectar from the flowers. The
prolonged flowering period helps
maintain bee colonies during periods
when other bee feed is scarce.*

Crinum abyssinicum Hochst. ex
A.Rich / Amaryllidaceae

A herb with long narrowly lanceolate
leaf blades which have a distinct
midrib. The deeply-buried
underground bulb is up to 15 cm
across. The plant often propagates
vegetatively to form dense clusters.
Flowers sweetly scented, large white,
trumpet-shaped, in clusters.

Found in waterlogged valley grassland
and swampy depressions, along
stream banks and sometimes in
cultivated fields and on rocky slopes,
at altitudes between 1650 and 3100 m.

Flowering is mainly at the start of the
main rains in June and July.
*Honeybees are foraging pollen and
mainly nectar.*

Scadoxus multiflorus (Martyn)
Raf. / Amaryllidaceae

YEDJIB AGEDA (Amh); FIHISO (Ge'ez);
ABRASA (Or); INBOBA ANBESA (Tre)

A herb growing to 70 cm high with a
tuberous base and stems which have
reddish to brownish spotted markings.
Leaves lanceolate, glossy dark green,
appearing mostly after the flowers.
Flowers conspicuous deep reddish
and forming a large ball.

Found in forests under shade of trees
and in bushland, in deciduous
woodland and riverine forests, at
altitudes between 700 and 3000 m.

In traditional medicine the roots are
used against Leishmaniasis.

Flowering is mainly between the small
and large rains - February to May.
*Honeybees collect abundant pollen
from the flowers.*

Alepedia longifolia *E.Mey.* /
Apiaceae

A plant growing to 125 cm high with large spoon-like toothed leaves. Flowers greenish-white, in conspicuous triangular-shaped dense umbels looking like a single flower.

Found in grassland, dry evergreen woodland and on rocky slopes at altitudes between 1800 and 2600 m.

Flowering from July to November, *honeybees forage for pollen and nectar.*

Anethum foeniculum *L.* /
Apiaceae

KAMUN (Amh) 'NSLAL (Amh & Tya); KAMUNI (Or); FENNEL (Eng); FENCHEL (German)

An erect perennial herb growing to 2 m high. Stems blue-green stems and profusely branched. Leaves blue-green with sheathed bases and bipinnately divided. Flowers yellow, arranged in compound umbels.

A perennial herb of the highlands, found on rocky land, in mountain pasture and along paths at altitudes between 1500 and 2500 m.

The plant is used for flavouring sauces and preparing alcoholic beverages. It has a high value in local medicine being used against gonorrhoea and stomach ache. The roots are applied to the umbilical cord of newborn babies and against SHINT MAT.

Flowering from September to November, *honeybees are visiting the plant very frequently.*

Anethum graveolens *L.* /
Apiaceae

'NSLAL, SELAN (Amh); KAMUNI (Or); SANDAN-SHOA, SHILAN (Tya); DILL (Eng); GURKENKRAUT (German)

An erect, annual herb with a strong characteristic smell growing to 150 cm tall with finely grooved stems and finely divided leaves. Flowers yellowish, arranged in numerous compound umbels.

Cultivated and also found occasionally as an escape on degraded mountain slopes and as a weed in cultivation at altitudes between 1500 and 2000 m.

The dried fruits and flowers are used as flavouring agents in sauces and in the preparation of KATIKALA.

Flowering almost all year round, *honeybees are important pollinators and visit the flowers for pollen and nectar.*

Coriandrum sativum *L.* /
Apiaceae

DMBLAL (Amh); DEBO, SHUCAR (Or); TSAGHA, ZAGDA (Tya); CORIANDER (Eng); KORIANDER (German)

An erect, annual, glabrous, branching herb growing to 130 cm tall. Leaves variable in shape and size, pinnately divided into many leaflets. Flowers white to pale-pink, arranged in compound umbels.

Native to the Mediterranean this is the oldest known spice. In Ethiopia it is grown in homegardens and as a crop at altitudes between 1500 to 2500 m.

In Ethiopia the fruits are used in the preparation of BERBERE and as a flavouring agent in WOT, and INJERA.

Flowering almost all year round it is *frequently visited by honeybees for pollen and nectar.*

Ferula communis L. / Apiaceae

'NSLAL, DOG (Amh & Tya)

A robust perennial herb growing to 2 m, occasionally 4 m high. Leaves trifoliate with very conspicuous sheathing bases, 3 to 4 pinnae and long fine linear leaf lobes. Flowers yellow, without petals.

Found in upland grassland, sometimes as a weed of cultivation at altitudes between 1700 and 2800 m.

Widely used for flavouring local alcohol ARAKE. In local medicine the roots are used against haemorrhage and NEKERSA.

In Sicily dried stems of *Ferula* were used to produce horizontal bee hives, very similar to the African baskets.

Flowering is after the big rains. *Honeybees collect pollen and nectar from the flowers.*

Steganotaenia araliaceae

Hochst. / Apiaceae

SHUNKWORI (Amh); JIRMA-JALESA (Or); ANTROKOHELA, ENDUGOKHILLA, MOAD (Tya)

A deciduous shrub or tree growing to 5 m tall with ascending branches and grey brown, thick corky bark. Leaves crowded near the end of branches, each with 5-9 leaflets which are toothed. Flowers white, in compound umbels clustered at the end of twigs, usually appear before the leaves.

Found in open woodland, along riverbanks and near villages at altitudes between 1300 and 1900 m.

In traditional medicine the roots are used against diabetes mellitus and elephantiasis.

Flowering time is from after rains, *honeybees are foraging pollen and nectar.*

Trachyspermum ammi *(L.)*

Sprague ex Turrill / Apiaceae

NECH'-AZMUD (Amh); AZMUD-ADDI, KAMON, KAMUNI (Or); GUMMUR-HURTUI (Som) AZMUD, CAMUN (Tya)

An erect herb growing to 1.6 m high, with oblong leaves, which are divided into linear segments. Flowers white, in showy umbels.

Often cultivated with barley and teff at altitudes between 1700 and 2200 m.

The dried, roasted and ground fruits are an important spice in sauces and for a special kind of bread. Fruits and roots are used against stomach complaints.

Flowering from October to December, *honeybees collect nectar and pollen very frequently and the plant is an important honey source.*

Carissa edulis *(Forssk.)* Vahl / Apocynaceae

AGAM (Amh); AGAMSA (Or); AGAMSA (Tya)

A thorny, much-branched shrub or scrambling climber growing to 5 m high, all parts exude a milky latex when cut. Leaves simple, glabrous and opposite. Flowers pinkish white and strongly scented. Fruits edible, small and dark purple to black when ripe.

Found in montane bushland, at forest margins and along roadsides and river banks and on rocky slopes at altitudes from 550 to 2600 m.

The roots are used against snake-bites, toothache and stomach ache. The dried branches are commonly used for fencing.

Flowering almost all year round, *honeybees collect pollen and nectar from the flowers frequently*

Arisaema enneaphyllum

Hochst. ex A.Rich / Araceae

YELREGNOCH TILA (Amh); FUGI-BATCHAW (Kem); ABUTAYE (Or); HAMBAGWITA (Tya); JACK-IN-THE-PULPIT (Eng)

An erect herb growing to 1.4 m high with palmate leaves. A green and white striped sheath surrounds the flower-mass which is joined directly to the stem.

The underground tuber is a common food of the FUGAZ people of the Kembata area.

Commonly found in wetter forests and upland grassland at altitudes above 2000 m.

Flowering from April to June, the *honeybees visit the plants very frequently for their nectar and abundant pollen.*

Zantedeschia aethiopica *(L.)*

Spreng. / Araceae

YET'RUMBA-ABEBA (Amh) LILY OF THE NILE (Eng)

A perennial rhizomatous herb growing to 80 cm high, with heart- or arrow-shaped tough leaves. The big white long-stalked flower is funnel-shaped and consists of a yellow spike, clasped by a white petal-like sheath.

The roots are poisonous.

Widely cultivated and growing easily from seed, it is found also in seasonal waterlogged places, and swampy areas.

Flowering after the rains, profusely from September to December. *Honeybees collect pollen and nectar from the flowers.*

Calotropis procera *(Ait.) Ait.f.* /
Asclepiadaceae

TOBBIYA (Amh); KIMBO (Or); GEEDA'I (Tya); DEAD SEA FRUIT (Eng)

A poisonous erect shrub or small tree with soft wood growing to 5.5 m. Leaves large, elliptic or ovate and clasping the stem at their base. Flowers purple, violet and white, arranged in dense masses at the ends of branches. Fruits very large, green and filled with loose cotton-like fibres.

When cut all parts exude a poisonous caustic, milky juice.

Growing in dry areas where water accumulates beside roads, in scrub and semi-desert areas from 500 to 1700 m.

The shrub is an indicator of ground water in dry areas.

Flowering throughout the year it is much visited by sunbirds, carpenter bees, *honeybees.* The honey is said to be poisonous.

Gymnema sylvestre *R.Br.* /
Asclepiadaceae

A woody, softly hairy climber with stems growing to 3 m long. Leaves light green, ovate and softly hairy. Flowers pale yellow, borne in axillary umbels.

It is found in deciduous woodland and montane forests at altitudes between 500 and 1900 m.

Flowering from November to August, *honeybees very frequently forage for the nectar.*

Acmella caulirhiza *Del.* /
Asteraceae

(syn. *Spilanthes mauritiana*)

YEMDR-BERBERIE, DAME (Amh);
BERBERE-ABAKTA (Tya)

A creeping, stoloniferous perennial herb, with ascending stems to 40 cm long. Leaves opposite, ovate, and toothed. Flower heads yellow, solitary about 1 cm across and terminal.

A common plant of usually wet places, on grassy slopes, forest floors and along stream banks and occasionally a weed of cultivation at altitudes between 600 and 2600 m.

In local medicine the whole herb is used as an analgesic.

Individuals of the species flower almost all year round, *honeybees collect pollen and nectar from the flowers.*

Ageratum conyzoides *L.* /
Asteraceae

AREMA (Amh); GUNYATO (Gur); ADDA, TUFO (Or)

An erect, branching, softly hairy annual herb growing to 100 cm high. Leaves ovate, opposite with regularly serrated margins. Flower heads pale blue or lilac, purplish or whitish or yellowish-green, arranged in flat-topped clusters.

This pantropical weed is common in wetter areas, under shade of trees, on eroded soils, in grassland, along waterways and paths at altitudes between 1000 and 2400 m.

In local medicine the herb is used for wound dressing.

Flowering throughout the year, *honeybees gather pollen and nectar very frequently.*

Anthemis tigreensis *A.Rich.* /
Asteraceae

A prostrate or sometimes erect annual herb growing to 30 cm high. Leaves grey-green, alternate and divided into rounded segments. Flower heads white, attractive, on long stalks.

A common plant of higher altitudes and sometimes locally dominant in fallow fields. It grows on degraded mountain slopes, in grassland and seasonally waterlogged soils, at altitudes between 1200 and 4400 m.

In local medicine the roots are used against wet eczema.

Flowering throughout the year, but especially in masses after the short rains. *Honeybees collect pollen and nectar from the flowers.*

Aspilia africana *(Pers.) C.Adams* /
Asteraceae

A woody perennial herb or shrub growing to 100 cm high, usually much-branched. Leaves alternate, elliptic-lanceolate. Flower heads large yellow.

Growing in wetter places, in meadows and swamps, on eroded rocky slopes and in *Acacia* woodland at altitudes between 900 and 2900 m.

Flowering from September to November, *honeybees collect abundant pollen and nectar from the flowers frequently.*

Aspilia mossambicensis *(Oliv.) Wild* / Asteraceae

A scandent shrub growing to 3 m high, rarely an erect woody perennial herb 1 m high. Stems and branches are sometimes reddish brown. Leaves rough sessile, often ovate, sometimes narrowly elliptic or ovate-lanceolate with entire or toothed margins. Flower heads yellow, arranged in loose paniculate corymbs.

This polymorphic species is found in wooded grassland and dry woodland, along waterways and forest edges, at altitudes between 900 and 2400 m.

Individual plants can be found in flower from July to December. *Honeybees frequently gather abundant pollen and nectar from the flowers.*

Berkheya spekeana *Oliv.* / Asteraceae

An erect thistle-like annual herb growing to 2.5 m high. The stem is erect and branching above, with lanceolate to oblong spiny leaves and large yellow flower heads.

Growing along roadsides, in open land, scrub and evergreen bushland, in burnt savanna and pastures, at altitudes between 1700 and 2800 m.

Flowering after the rains from September to November, *honeybees collect pollen and nectar from the flowers very frequently.*

Bidens ghedoensis *Mesfin* / Asteraceae

KELO (Or)

An erect bushy, annual herb, to 3m high with much-branched stem. Leaves pinnate or three-times pinnatisect. Flower heads small, yellow clustered in a flat-topped panicle.

Endemic in southern Ethiopia where it grows on bushy hillside slopes, in dry evergreen woodland, along roadsides and at forest edges, at altitudes from 1380 to 2600 m.

Flowering after the big rains up to December, *honeybees collect pollen and nectar from the flowers very frequently and the plant is a honey source.*

Bidens macroptera *(Sch.-Bip. ex Chiov.) Mesfin* / Asteraceae

ADEY-ABEBA (Amh); KELO (Or); GELGELLE-MESKEL (Tya)

A perennial herb with several stems arising from a woody rootstock to 60 cm high. Leaves broadly ovate, pinnatisect or rarely lobed. Flowers heads yellow, clustered in erect panicles.

Endemic, found only in Ethiopia in rocky or stony places on mountain slopes and in grassland, along forest margins, in open places in ericaceous scrub and sometimes also along roadside cliffs, at altitudes between 1800 and 3700 m, common above 2500 m. It is one of the few species of *Bidens* that occurs at altitudes up to 3700 m.

Flowering from September to December, *honeybees collect pollen and nectar from the flowers frequently and the plant is a honey source.*

Bidens pachyloma *(Oliv. & Hiern)*
Cuf. / Asteraceae

YEMESKEL-ABEBA, ADEY-ABEBA (Amh); ADELA (Kem); KELO (Or); GELGELE-MESKEL (Tya); MESKEL FLOWER (Eng)

An annual herb growing to 2 m high. Leaves pinnately divided. Flower heads conspicuous yellow and erect.

Endemic to the highlands of Ethiopia, this is a common plant in fallow fields, highland grassland, on mountain slopes with low shrubs and trees, along river banks, margins of arable land and roadsides, at altitudes between 2200 and 3300 m.

Flowering in September and October, *honeybees collect nectar and pollen and the plant is a honey source.*

Bidens pilosa *L.* / Asteraceae

CHEGOGIT, YSATAN-MERFY (Amh); MUTE (Had); SAMIE, ABARE (Or); ZAGOGO, QATTATO (Tya)

An erect annual herb, often branched, growing to 1 m high, with pinnately 3-5-lobed opposite leaves. Flower heads with or without the white or creamy-white ray florets.

A bad weed of fields and gardens, it grows in open places, along roadsides, in waste land and on poor and exhausted soils, at altitudes between 1600 and 2400 m.

In local medicine the leaves are used against intestinal inflammations and, together with the roots, against conjunctivitis and snake-bites.

It usually flowers after the main rains in September and October. *Honeybees collect small amounts of nectar and abundant salmon-yellow pollen very frequently.*

Bidens prestinaria *(Sch.-Bip.)*
Cuf. / Asteraceae

YEMESKEL-ABEBA, ADEY-ABEBA (Amh); ADELA (Kem); KELO (Or); GELGELE MESKEL (Tya); MESKEL FLOWER (Eng)

An erect polymorphic annual herb growing to 1.5 m, often branching above, with pinnate leaves. Flower heads yellow, clustered in showy panicles at the end of branches.

Growing at forest edges, on dry rocky slopes and in evergreen woodland, it is a common weed of the Central Highlands of Ethiopia at altitudes between 1300 and 2900 m.

It has medicinal properties and has been reported to have been used to control bleeding.

It flowers profusely in September and October. *Honeybees collect nectar and pollen and the plant is an important honey source.*

Bothriocline schimperi *Oliv. & Hiern.* / Asteraceae

SHETTO (Kef)

A much-branched erect perennial herb to 2 m tall with a woody base. Leaves lanceolate and toothed, dull dark green above, paler beneath. Flowers heads pale to dark lilac, arranged in terminal panicles.

Commonly found in evergreen woodland and scrub, eroded places and along paths, at forest edges at altitudes between 1600 and 2800 m.

Pulverized leaves smell and the flowers are said to be dangerous for the eyes.

Flowering from September to May, *honeybees are foraging abundant nectar and pollen from the flowers. This species is a very important bee plant.*

Carduus camaecephalus

(Vatke.) Oliv. & Hiern / Asteraceae

KOSHESHLA (Amh)

A spiny stemless rosette plant, with thick fleshy tap-roots. Leaves pinnatisect lying flat on the ground, elliptic or oblanceolate in outline. Flower heads whitish to pinkish or violet, sweet-scented, sessile in the centre of the rosettes, usually solitary.

Growing along roadsides, and very common in montane grassland and overgrazed areas, also in secondary scrub at altitudes between 2000 and 4300 m.

It has a long flowering period from August to February. *Honeybees collect pollen and nectar from the flowers frequently.*

Carduus nyassanus *R.E.Fries* /

Asteraceae

KOSHESHLA (Amh); DANDER (Tya); THISTLE (Eng)

An erect perennial herb, attaining a height of 2 m. Stems erect, with spinescent wings. Leaves sessile, elliptic to oblong, highly dissected with spines on the margins. Flower heads spiny, red to pale violet, in clusters at ends of branches.

Growing in forests, as a weed in fallow land, along roads, in pastures where the soil has been waterlogged during the rainy season, and bamboo thickets at altitudes between 2000 and 3500 m.

Flowering from October to February, *honeybees collect abundant pale-yellow pollen and copious nectar from the flowers frequently.*

Carthamus lanatus *L.* /

Asteraceae

YE-AHIYA-SUF (Amh); SEKENDER, AF-A'NSTI, DANDER-BEITA (Tya)

A thistle-like annual herb growing to 1 m high with an erect stem. Leaves usually green to greyish-green, ovate-lanceolate to ovate, with spines on the margins. Flower heads are solitary, lemmon-yellow with spiny bracts.

Growing in fallow ground, as a weed of *Erragrostis tef* and other crops and along roadsides at altitudes between 1000 and 2400 m.

Flowering after the big rains from November to January, the plant *provides pollen and some amount of nectar.*

Carthamus tinctorius *L.* /

Asteraceae

YAHYA-SUF, SUF (Amh); SUFI (Or); SUF (Tya); SAFFLOWER (Eng)

An annual herb with much-branched stiff stem, growing to 75 cm high. Leaves ovate to linear with finely spine-toothed margins. Flower heads yellow to orange or reddish-orange, thistle-like in terminal heads.

Cultivated for the edible oil-producing seeds and in former times for the orange-red dye. It is often mixed with *Eragrostis te*f, or grown in strips beside others crops, sometimes found as an escape at altitudes between 1000 and 2400 m.

Lightly roasted and crushed seeds are mixed with water to produce a milk-like fasting drink or made into FITFIT with INJERA.

Flowering from November to February, *honeybees collect pollen and nectar from the flowers frequently.*

Centaurea melitensis L. / Asteraceae

An annual herb growing up 70 cm high with narrowly winged stems, provided with coarse hairs. Basal leaves oblanceolate and pinnatisect; upper leaves lanceolate. Flowers heads yellow, solitary or arranged in cymes surrounded by spines.

A native of southern Europe now found as a weed of cultivation and in roadside ditches at altitudes between 2000 and 2400 m.

Individual plants flower from October to January. *Honeybees gather copious pollen and some nectar from the flowers. Nectar supply is affected by humidity.*

Cichorium intybus L. / Asteraceae

CHICORY (Eng); WEGWARTE (German)

A perennial herb with tough stem growing to 60 cm or sometimes more, erect and much-branched. Basal leaves are pinnatifid, while upper ones are lanceolate. Flower heads sky-blue and sessile.

A recent invader on black soils now found in masses after crops are harvested at altitudes of 1800 to 2000 m.

The young roots are edible like carrots and can be used as fodder. Elsewhere, used as a coffee substitute or admixture.

Flowering profusely during the dry seasons from November to January when it provides abundant pollen and some nectar. *Honeybees collect pollen and nectar from the flowers very frequently.*

Cirsium dender Friis. / Asteraceae

DANDER (Amh & Tya)

An erect perennial herb growing to 5 m high. Stem hollow and branched with spiny wings in upper parts. Leaves very large, alternate, divided with spines on margins and veins, with light green upper surface and white-woolly beneath. Flowers heads white, drooping and arranged in terminal or axillary heads which are surrounded by spines.

Endemic herb found in evergreen scrub, degraded woodlands and along paths at altitudes between 2300 and 2800 m.

Flowering from November to February, *honeybees forage on abundant pollen and nectar.*

Cirsium englerianum DiHoffm. / Asteraceae

KOSHESHLA (Amh)

An erect perennial herb growing to 4 m high, branched at the top. The spiny wings on the stem are interrupted. The bipinnatisect leaves are alternately arranged and end in spines. The pink flowers form a large head on erect terminal stems.

Endemic herb found along forest margins and in damp wooded grassland at altitudes between 1760 and 2260 m.

Individual plants found flowering at any time of the year, but most profusely from September to January. *Honeybees visit the flowers for pollen and nectar and where there are many plants of this species they are a good honey source.*

Cirsium schimperi *(Vatke) Cuf.* / Asteraceae

KOSHESHLA (Amh)

A very prickly, erect and bushy perennial herb growing to 2 m high. Leaves dark green, sessile, much divided, yellowish-green with spines at the margins. Flower heads purple or pale pink, arranged in terminal solitary heads.

Endemic species found among boulders in streams or on river banks, in grassy areas, open woodland and along paths at altitudes between 2000 and 3100 m.

Individual plants can be found in flower at any time of the year but most profusely from August to December. *This species provides useful food supplies for bees which collect pollen and nectar from the flowers frequently.*

Cosmos bipinnatus *Cav.* / Asteraceae

COSMEA (Eng); SCHMUCKKÖRBCHEN (German)

An erect, annual herb, to 2 m high. Stem densely branched with erect or ascending branches. Leaves bipinnately divided with narrowly linear segments. Flower heads red, purple, pink or white, solitary or clustered in erect terminal panicles.

This ornamental plant is native to tropical America. It has been cultivated in public and private gardens, and has escaped in waste ground in Sidamo, southern Ethiopia, at altitudes between 1350 and 2450 m.

Flowering throughout the year, *honeybees forage for nectar and pollen very frequently.*

Conyza steudelli *Sch.-Bip.* / Asteraceae

A stiff, erect much-branched herb growing to 80 cm high. Leaves broadly-ovate and toothed. Flower heads pale dirty yellow to white, arranged in loose terminal corymbs.

Growing in disturbed and eroded places, evergreen woodland and sometimes as a weed at altitudes between 2400 and 3600 m.

In local medicine the leaves are used against syphilitic chancre.

Flowering from December to May, *honeybees frequently visit the flowers for pollen and nectar.*

Cotula abyssinica *Sch.-Bip. ex A.Rich.* / Asteraceae

A small herb growing to 15 cm high. Leaves divided with flat segments. Flower heads pale yellow, button-shaped without ray florets, about 1 cm across.

A common plant of higher altitudes and sometimes found as a weed of cultivation. It grows in rocky ground, degraded mountain slopes, grassland and seasonally waterlogged soils and also in overgrazed areas at altitudes between 2400 and 4200 m.

Flowering from October to January, it is visited by *honeybees for pollen and nectar.*

Crassocephalum sarcobasis

(DC) S.Moor / Asteraceae

A hairy erect annual herb growing to 80 cm high. Leaves ovate to elliptic, entire or toothed. Flower heads dull dark red, erect.

Growing in meadows, disturbed and cultivated land, under trees, along roadsides and at forest edges. It is fairly widespread at altitudes between 1700 and 2100 m.

Flowering from September to December, *honeybees collect pollen and nectar from the flowers frequently.*

Crassocephalum vitellinum

(Benth.) Moore / Asteraceae

JEGALLATIIT, LT'-MAREFYA (Amh)

A trailing woolly, weak-stemmed perennial herb with stems growing to 1.5 m long. Leaves ovate. Flower heads yellow, solitary.

Growing along edges of damp areas and waterways, on rocky slopes, in grassland and upland woodland at altitudes from 500 to 3300 m.

In local medicine the flower is used for wound dressing.

The nodding flower heads can be seen throughout the year, but more profusely after the rains.

Honeybees collect pollen and nectar from the flowers frequently and the long flowering period is very helpful for strengthening bee colonies. It is a good honey source.

Crepis rueppellii *Sch.-Bip.* / Asteraceae

YEFYEL-WETET (Amh)

A small herb with a rosette of leaves lying flat on the ground and a long tap-root. Flower heads yellow, solitary, born on erect stems. All parts when cut bleed a milky juice.

Growing on rocky slopes, in upper montane forest, overgrazed areas and on degraded soils at altitudes between 2000 and 3700 m.

In local medicine the roots are used against LIB DIKAM.

Flowering at any time of the year, but more profusely from December to March, *honeybees collect pollen and nectar from the flowers.*

Cynara scolymus *L.* / Asteraceae

ARTICHOKE (Eng); ARTISCHOKE (German)

A thistle-like perennial herb growing to 2 m high. Leaves soft, glabrescent above and greyish beneath with wide, spineless segments. Flower heads very large, violet, terminal and solitary.

The species is native to the Mediterranean, but nowadays widely cultivated for the edible immature flower heads which are eaten as a vegetable. The leaves make good forage. Grown in and around towns mostly where there are expatriates at altitudes between 1800 and 2300 m.

Flowering from September to January, *honeybees forage on abundant nectar and pollen. Where there are many plants of this species they can provide a honey flow.*

Dahlia pinnata *Cav.* / Asteraceae

DAHLIA (Eng & German)

An erect perennial herb growing to 1.8 m high. Leaves simple, or pinnatisect or bipinnate with 3-5 leaflets and toothed margins. Flower heads are more or less erect, light to dark-purple, often with yellowish or rosy spots at the base of the petals.

A native of Mexico, but nowadays widely grown as an ornamental in many public and private gardens between 1600 and 2500 m.

There are many cultivated hybrids and varieties with many strong flower colours.

Flowering all year round, *honeybees collect pollen and nectar frequently.*

Echinops ellenbeckii *D.Hoffm.* / Asteraceae

KOILO, KOSHESHLA (Amh)

A gregarious shrub growing to 4 m high. Stem grey, woody below and much-branched with a cracking corky bark. Leaves light blue-green and twice pinnatisect, elliptic or oblanceolate, terminating in sharp spines. Flower heads large, globose, red, solitary and raised well above the leaves on long stalks.

Endemic species which grows along roadsides forming hedges, and in forest and wooded grassland at altitudes between 2200 to 2950 m.

In local medicine the flowers are used against headache and haemorrhoids.

Flowering from November to May. The flowers are *very frequently visited by honeybees for nectar and pollen. Where the plants grow gregariously they can provide a honey flow and valuable pollen supplies over a long period.*

Echinops giganteus *A.Rich.* / Asteraceae

KOSHESHLA, SHOK' (Amh); KANKAMO (Wel)

An erect herbaceous plant growing to 2 m high. Leaves are very large and sharply toothed, green above and greyish below. Flower heads form a ball and are big white to pale-bluish, on erect spiny stems which branch above.

Growing in open forests and degraded bushland, along forest edges and roadsides at altitudes between 1600 and 2400 m.

Flowering from October to February, *honeybees collect nectar and pollen very frequently and the plant is a honey source where it grows in masses.*

Echinops hispidus *Fresen.* / Asteraceae

KOSHESHLA (Amh); DANDER (Tya); GLOBE THISTLE (Eng)

A robust woody, perennial herb growing to 50 cm high. It is provided with stiff hairs and it has tuberous roots. Leaves large, oblanceolate and pinnatisect with terminal sharp spines. Flower heads whitish to bluish, solitary and up to 10 cm across.

Commonly growing on dry hillsides, in open short grassland, on grassy slopes with scattered trees and shrubs and sometimes as a weed at altitudes between 1700 and 2800 m.

Flowering from September to February, *honeybees gather abundant pollen and nectar, and in dense stands the plant is a honey source.*

Echinops longisetus A. Rich. / Asteraceae

HALUTA (Had); KOMBORRE, SEKORU, KOSORU (Or), KORE-ADI (Or-Harerge); ANGAFO (Or-Bale)

An erect shrub or woody perennial herb growing to 6 m high. The stem is often unbranched with many large deeply-lobed to pinnatisect leaves. Flower heads terminal, deep red, pink or crimson.

Endemic which grows in rocky areas, open woodland, closely grazed pastures, *Erica arborea* bushland, along margins of evergreen forests, in secondary *Acacia* scrub on slopes, and along roadsides at altitudes between 2000 and 4000 m.

In Wellega it is used for smoking bee baskets to attract *honeybees*.

Flowering from September to January. *Honeybees collect pollen and nectar from the flowers frequently and the plant is a honey source when growing in dense stands.*

Echinops macrochaetus Fresen. / Asteraceae

KOSHESHLA (Amh)

An erect spiny perennial herb or shrublet, with much-branched stems up to 3 m high and a woody rootstock. Leaves sessile and pinnatisect. Flower heads small balls, pale blue or white and raised conspicuously above the leaves.

This plant is very drought resistant and grows around houses, beside roads, on hillsides and rocky places, in disturbed ground at altitudes from 1400 up to 3600 m.

Flowering from October to March. *Honeybees collect nectar and pollen and the plant is an important honey source.*

Eclipta prostrata (L.) L. / Asteraceae

A tough erect or prostrate herb with ascending stems to 60 cm high. Leaves lanceolate to narrowly elliptic and narrowed at both ends. Flower heads small, white, found in clusters of 1-3 terminally or in leaf axils.

This cosmopolitan weed is found on mountain slopes, under shade of trees at altitudes between 600 and 2000 m.

Flowering from February to August. *The flowers are visited by honeybees for pollen and nectar.*

Emilia discifolia DC. / Asteraceae

A small branched herb growing to 60 cm high. Leaves alternate, obovate with toothed leaf margins. Flower heads yellow, arranged on long terminal and axillary flower stalks.

Growing in burned savanna, on dry hillsides, in open bush and woodland and along roadsides at altitudes between 600 and 2100 m.

Flowering from September to March, *honeybees forage for nectar and pollen.*

Ethulia gracilis *Del.* / Asteraceae

An erect, branched annual growing to 60 cm or more with linear-lanceolate to elliptic leaves. Flower heads white to violet, in panicles.

Found in grassland, woodland, often in partial shade of hedges and bushes and even as a weed throughout the plateau between 1700 and 2300 m.

This plant flowers from October to February. *Honeybees collect pollen and nectar from the flowers frequently.*

Ethulia sfr *DC* / Asteraceae

A small erect, sometimes weak-stemmed annual herb growing to 30 cm high. Leaves sessile, lanceolate with entire to toothed margins. Flower heads purple, found in open erect or drooping panicles.

Found in evergreen bushland and meadows, along forest edges and waterways, in disturbed ground and sometimes as a weed of cultivation at altitudes between 2000 and 2400 m.

Flowering from May to October, *honeybees frequently gather pollen and nectar.*

Galinsoga parviflora *Cav.* / Asteraceae

BALCHA, GOROSITU, DHA-NEQAY, NEKELKEGNE, YEMDR-BERHERU, ABADABO, YESHEWA-AREM (Amh); AKSHET (Gur); ABATABO (Or); DKA-NEQEL (Tya); GALLANT SOLDIER (Eng); FRANZOSENKRAUT (German)

A soft erect herb, with a branched stem up to 20 cm tall. Leaves opposite, simple, ovate, soft and slightly hairy. The leaf margin is slightly toothed. Flower heads small, with white rays and yellow centres.

Native to S America, but now distributed world-wide as a weed. In Ethiopia it is very common, and grows as a weed of cultivation and disturbed areas, particularly under shade of trees and bushes at altitudes between 1600 and 2400 m.

The herb is used for wound dressing.

Flowering all year round, *honeybees collect pollen and nectar.*

Flaveria trinervia *(Spreng.)* C.Mohr / Asteraceae

GOROSEZA (Or); D'KA-NEKEL (Tya)

An erect annual herb growing to 0.5 m tall. It is much-branched with opposite leaves which are distinctly 3-nerved from the base. Flower heads yellow, very small, arranged in dense axillary clusters.

Growing in eroded places, on silt deposited from flooding beside rivers, along paths and as a weed of cultivation particularly in irrigated farms, sometimes becoming dominant, at altitudes between 800 and 2100 m.

Flowering from October to January, *honeybees collect pollen and nectar.*

Gnaphalium rubriflorum *Hilliard*
/ Asteraceae

A small herb with erect stems, up to 30 cm tall, with ascending branches from the base. Leaves entire, alternate, greyish lanceolate. Flower heads small, white to violet in terminal clusters.

Growing in wet or damp places, along streams, in cultivated field and in wet evergreen forests, at altitudes between 2000 and 2700 m.

Flowering almost all year round, *honeybees collect pollen and nectar from the flowers.*

Guizotia abyssinica *(L.f.) Cassini*
/ Asteraceae

NUGI (Afar & Or); NUG (Amh); NUGA (Had & Kem); NUGHIO (Kef); NUHUK (Tre); NIHUG (Tya); ANUGA (Wel); NIGER-SEED (Eng); GINGELLIKRAUT (German)

An erect leafy annual herb growing to 2 m high. Leaves opposite, simple, oblong, toothed or entire. Flower heads large, yellow in terminal panicles.

A crop plant native to the Ethiopian highlands and the most important oil crop in the country. It is grown on both better and poorer soils between 1500 and 2450 m.

The seeds are used in local medicine against cold. Leaves and fruits are used against leprosy.

Roasted and pounded seeds in boiled water are drunk during fasting periods.

Flowering from September to October, *honeybees collect nectar and pollen and the plant is one of the most important honey sources of the country.*

Guizotia scabra *(Vis.) Chiov.*
subsp. **scabra** *Baagoe* / Asteraceae

HADA, TUFO (Or)

An erect perennial herb growing to 1.3 m high. Leaves simple, sticky, narrowly lanceolate to broadly oblanceolate or ovate, toothed or entire. Flower heads conspicuous yellow, arranged in several compound panicles.

Found in short grassland, meadows, along forest margins, roadside ditches and waterways at altitudes between 1300 and 2900 m.

Flowering all year round, *bees work on the flowers throughout the day and gather significant quantities of pollen and nectar.*

Guizotia scabra *(Vis.) Chiov.*
subsp. **schimperi** *(Sch.-Bip.) Baagoe* / Asteraceae

MECH' (Amh); JELA (Had); SESHA-A (Kem); HADE (Or); NEHUKAS (Tya)

An erect and fast growing annual herb with stems up to 3 m tall. Leaves and flowers similar to subsp. *scabra*.

One of the most important broad-leaved weeds in Ethiopia, widely distributed throughout the plateau at altitudes from 1300 up to 2600 m.

It is recognized as a "weed cleaner" by the farmers as it suppresses the growth of other broadleaved herbs. It also grows in bushland and open wasteland among shrubs, along roadside ditches and river banks.

Flowering from August to February, *honeybees collect nectar and pollen very frequently and the plant is a very important honey source.*

Haplocarpha schimperi *(Sch.-Bip.) Beauv.* / Asteraceae
GETIN (Amh)

A herb with hollow stems which are sometimes up to 30 cm high (if present) and a rosette of leaves pressed to the ground. Leaves dark green above and white below, with waved or lobed margins. Flower heads, large, yellow, solitary, usually sessile in the centre of the leaf rosette.

Growing in damp waterlogged areas and cold montane forest at altitudes between 2400 and 3700 m.

Getin flowers from November to June, *honeybees collect pollen and nectar from the flowers very frequently. The long flowering period is very helpful for providing abundant pollen and nectar during times where bee food is scarce.*

Helianthus annuus *L.* / Asteraceae
YEFERENJ-SUF, SUF (Amh); DUBI, SUFI-FERENJI, NUGI ADI (Or); FARANJA-SHUFIYA (Wel)

An annual herb growing to 3 m high, with unbranched to much-branched stems. Leaves alternate, ovate-lanceolate to ovate, with large blunt teeth. Flower heads very large, yellow, consisting of 1000-2000 florets up to 30 cm in diameter.

A native of North America and Mexico, in Ethiopia it is cultivated in home-gardens in many places at altitudes between 1700 and 2450 m.

It is a grown for food, fodder and oil.

Dried green stems and leaves are recommended to be used for smoker fuel. It has also extrafloral nectaries. *Honeybees collect nectar and pollen and the plant is a honey source.*

Helichrysum formosissimum *(Sch.-Bip.) A.Rich.* var.**formosissimum** / Asteraceae
EVERLASTING FLOWER (Eng)

A perennial erect herb or weak shrub up to 1.5 m tall. Leaves oblong-lanceolate with bases clasping the stem. Flower heads red to pink or white papery and shining, arranged in dense or loose terminal corymbs.

One of the commonest and most beautiful *Helichrysum* species of the alpine zone.

Commonly growing in montane forest, upland bushland, along waterways and on grassy hillsides at altitudes between 2500 and 3900 m.

Flowering almost all year round but more abundantly from October to January, *honeybees forage for pollen and small amounts of nectar.*

Helichrysum formosissimum *(Sch.-Bip.) A.Rich.* var. **guilelmii** *(Engl.) Mesfin* / Asteraceae
EVERLASTING FLOWER (Eng)

A large weak-stemmed shrub growing to 2 m tall with pale greyish-white sessile hairy leaves which are lanceolate-oblong. Flower heads large, conspicuous, white or red, arranged in terminal corymbs.

Uncommon, found in the upper alpine zone, and degraded woodland, on rocky slopes and along paths at altitudes between 2500 and 3700 m.

Flowering from January to June, *honeybees forage on pollen and small amounts of nectar.*

Helichrysum splendidum

(Thumb.) Less. / Asteraceae

STRAW-FLOWER (Eng)

A much-branched annual, growing to
1.4 m high. Leaves alternate, entire,
grey-green and covered with white
hairs. Flower heads bright yellow,
small, many crowded together in
terminal corymbs.

Found in grassland and scrub on
slopes and along forest edges in drier
areas at altitudes between 2500 and
3900 m.

Flowering all year round, *honeybees
collect pollen and nectar.*

Helminthotheca echioides *(L.)*

Holub. / Asteraceae

An annual plant growing to 50 cm high
or sometimes more. The stems are
thick and forked with oblong-
lanceolate and entire leaves. Flower
heads yellow, in a terminal cluster.

Growing in meadows, along roadside
ditches and in disturbed areas at
altitudes between 2000 and 2500 m.

Flowering from October to February,
*honeybees collect pollen and nectar
from the flowers frequently.*

Inula confertiflora *A.Rich.* /
Asteraceae

An erect hairy annual herb growing to
2 m high. The stem comes from a
rosette of large simple basal leaves.
Stem leaves alternate, simple and
sessile. Flower heads big yellow, in
flat-topped groups.

Found in rocky places, along forest
edges, paths, waterways and in
evergreen woodland at altitudes
between 2400 and 3700 m.

In rural areas the roots of the plant are
dried and smoked as a fumigant
during child birth and a solution of
leaves pounded in water is applied to
diseased eyes of cattle. The roots are
used against leprosy.

Flowering from August to March,
*honeybees collect pollen and nectar
from the flowers.*

Lactuca inermis *Forssk.* /
Asteraceae

An erect herb, much-branched above,
growing to 1 m high. Leaves pinnatifid,
toothed or entire. Flower heads pale
pink to pale violet, arranged in dense
erect panicles.

The whole plant excudes a milky latex
if cut.

Found in grassland, bushland, open
woodland, degraded remnant forests
and as a weed of cultivation at
altitudes between 1600 and 3100 m.

It is said to have medicinal value.

Flowering throughout the year,
*honeybees frequently gather pollen
and nectar.*

Laggera pterodonata *(DC.)*
Sch.-Bip. / Asteraceae

KES-KESA (Amh); ZAGEZELA (Tya)

A large erect, single-stemmed, thistle-like annual growing to 3 m high. The stems have toothed wings and the leaves are oblanceolate. Flower heads dirty-pink, arranged in loose terminal corymbs.

Commonly found in bushland, waste ground, along forest edges and roadsides at altitudes between 1900 and 2600 m.

The herb is used as a disinfectant.

Flowering from November to February, *honeybees collect pollen and nectar from the flowers frequently.*

Launaea cornuta *(Oliv. & Hiern.)*
C.Jeffrey / Asteraceae

YE'SEY'TAN-GOMEN, WATATE (Tya); WILD LETTUCE (Eng)

A tall perennial herb up to 1.2 m high. The erect stem arises from a basal rosette. Lower leaves at ground level are lobed and the upper ones are sessile and alternate with toothed margins. Flower heads yellow in much-branched terminal panicles.

All parts exude milky latex when cut.

Growing as a weed commonly on black soils at altitudes between 1000 and 1900 m.

Flowering from October to December, *honeybees gather both nectar and pollen.*

Microglossa pyrifolia *(Lam.)*
O.Kuntze / Asteraceae

HAREG (Amh)

A scrambling shrub up to 2 m tall. Leaves narrowly ovate and acuminate. Flower heads pale to dark yellow, arranged in often drooping corymbs.

Found at forest margins, in wooded grassland and bushland and along paths at altitudes between 1600 and 2900 m.

In local medicine the flowers and leaves are used against conjunctivitis.

Flowering from October to April, *honeybees frequently gather pollen and nectar. Because of the long flowering period this plant is important for beekeepers to strengthen colonies during times where bee feed is scarce.*

Mikaniopsis clematoides
(A.Rich) M.Redh. Asteraceae

HAREG (Amh)

A strong woody climber with stems up to 4 m long and ovate dentate leaves. Flower heads cream to white, in axillary or terminal clusters.

A common climber of the more humid highlands, growing in montane forests, hedges, along forest margins and paths, and on degraded slopes at altitudes between 2400 and 3200 m.

Flowering from November to March, *honeybees frequently forage on pollen and nectar.*

Plectocephalus varians
(A.Rich.) Jeffrey / Asteraceae

ETSE-YOHANNES (Ge'ez);
FUGAZERARO (Had)

A perennial erect herb growing to 50 cm high. Basal leaves are sessile and rough. Flower heads sweetly-scented, large, white to pale pink, produced at the end of erect stems.

Endemic, growing in seasonally flooded meadows, open grassy mountain slopes, shaded moist grassy ravines along perennial streams, at altitudes between 1900 and 3600 m.

Flowering from September to December, *honeybees collect pollen and nectar from the flowers frequently.*

Senecio hadiensis *Forssk.* /
Asteraceae

TAIFARETH (Tya)

A robust, semi-succulent perennial trailing climber, with stems up to 5 m long. Leaves entire, ovate to elliptic. Flowers heads yellow, in large numbers in dense corymbs.

Growing in *Acacia* woodland, dry evergreen woodland and ground-water forests at altitudes between 1300 and 2400 m. It is often cultivated for ornament and making decorations.

Flowering from October to March, *honeybees collect pollen and nectar from the flowers frequently.*

Senecio fresenii *Sch.-Bip. ex Oliv. & Hiern.* / Asteraceae

A tough much-branched greyish herb up to 1 m high. Leaves sessile, grey-green, alternate, linear, entire and covered in long white hairs. Flower heads yellow, arranged in dense erect corymbs.

Common at the upper limit of montane forest and at the lower part of Sub-Afroalpine vegetation, growing on rocky slopes and along paths, at altitudes between 3000 and 3500 m.

Flowering from December to June, *honeybees forage for nectar and pollen.*

Senecio lyratus *Forssk.* /
Asteraceae

A soft-stemmed, branched annual with stems growing to 100 cm high. Leaves smooth and palmately lobed. Flower heads yellow, clustered together in erect corymbs.

Growing in forest and at forest margins, under shade of trees, in swamps, degraded bushland, on dry mountain slopes and along paths, at altitudes between 1700 and 3000 m.

Flowering almost all year round, *honeybees forage on nectar and pollen.fs*

Senecio myriocephalum *Sch.-Bip. ex A.Rich.* / Asteraceae

An erect tough herb growing to 3 m high. with a light green, unbranched stem. Leaves sessile, green above and whitish beneath, narrowly lanceolate and toothed along the margins. Flower heads yellow, arranged in dense erect corymbs.

Found in heavily disturbed *Juniperus* forests, open degraded woodland and on rocky slopes, at altitudes between 2200 and 3300 m.

Flowering almost all year round, *honeybees forage on pollen and nectar.*

Senecio ochrocarpus *Oliv. & Hiern* / Asteraceae

DIFU (Or)

A robust glabrous herb growing to 1 m high. Leaves alternate, simple and elliptic. Flower heads yellow in dense corymbs.

Growing in upland grassland and along rivers in marshy places, especially around springs even in forests at altitudes between 2400 and 3000 m.

Flowering from August to November, *honeybees collect pollen and nectar from the flowers very frequently.*

Senecio steudelii *Sch.-Bip. ex A.Rich.* / Asteraceae

An erect herb up to 50 cm high. Leaves ascending, alternate, almost sessile, narrowly lanceolate and slightly toothed along the margins. Flower heads yellow, arranged in erect terminal corymbs.

Growing in swamps, along waterways and in water at altitudes of about 2800 to 3000 m.

Flowering from April to June, *honeybees forage for pollen and nectar.*

Silybum marianum *(L.) Gaertn.* / Asteraceae

MILK THISTLE, HOLY THISTLE (Eng); MARIENDISTEL (German)

An erect annual up to 2 m high, with a basal rosette of obovate spiny leaves which are white-veined. Flower heads purple, large and borne singly on long stems with bracts ending in sharp spines.

Found along roadside ditches, in wasteland and fallow land, at altitudes between 2400 and 2500 m.

This introduced weed from Southern Europe is toxic to animals. The flower part is edible at flowering stage like the artichoke. An edible oil can be extracted from the seeds.

Elsewhere it is also a medicinal plant which contains an active substance "silymarin".

Flowering from August to December, *honeybees collect pollen and nectar from the flowers frequently.*

Solanecio angelatus *(Vahl)*
C.Jeffrey / Asteraceae

HAREG (Amh)

A climbing annual herb growing to 2.5 m high. Leaves opposite and petiolate with palmate venation and lobed margins. Flower heads creamy-white in dense erect corymbs.

Found in evergreen bushland and along fences around houses in altitudes from 1300 to 2500 m.

Flowering almost all year round, *honeybees collect pollen and nectar from the flowers frequently. The plant is very valuable for strengthening bee colonies at times when other bee food is scarce.*

Solanecio gigas *(Vatke) C.Jeffrey*
(syn. *Senecio gigas*) / Asteraceae

YESKKOKO-GOMEN (Amh); NOBE (Kef)

A giant herb or shrub with soft woody stems growing to 4 m high. The bark is whitish-grey. Leaves large and shallowly lobed. Flower heads dull yellow, numerous, clustered in large terminal panicles.

All parts of the plant, but especially the flowers, have an unpleasant or mushy odour.

Endemic found along stream banks in wet evergreen forests at altitudes between 1750 and 2800 m. It also grows as a hedge-plant and in church compounds and house-gardens in villages and is very common throughout the highlands.

In traditional medicine the roots are used against typhoid fever.

Flowering is from October to March, when *honeybees forage for pollen and nectar.*

Solanecio mannii *(Hook.f.)*
C.Jeffrey / Asteraceae

DOMBRECCO (Kef)

A much-branched, soft wooded shrub with green stems which grow to 4 m high. Leaves large, oblong-elliptic and toothed at the margins. Flower heads small yellow, have an unpleasant odour, and are arranged in dense cymes.

Commonly found in the humid western and southwestern parts of the country, growing along forest edges and paths at altitudes up to 2400 m.

Commonly used as a live fence planted from cuttings.

Flowering from November to February, *bee visits have been reported.*

Sonchus asper *(L.) Hill* /
Asteraceae

FOSI-MOSKOJEW (Tya); SPINY SOW THISTLE (Eng)

An erect, unbranched, bluish-green annual, up to 1.2 m high, with a rather thick hollow stem which has milky latex when cut. Leaves spirally arranged with pinnate lobes which are toothed and prickly. Flower heads yellow, in small erect panicles.

A cosmopolitan weed frequently found in irrigated farmland, particularly on black cotton soil, also along roadsides, in eroded and fallow ground. It also grows in open forest, and along rivers at altitudes between 1000 and 2500 m.

Flowering almost all year round, *honeybees collect pollen and nectar from the flowers frequently.*

Sonchus bipontini *Aschers /* Asteraceae

An annual herb, erect or trailing, growing up to 1.5 m tall. Leaves linear, white woolly below, sessile and clasping the stem. Flower heads yellow, arranged in terminal clusters.

Growing along roadsides, at forest edges, in scrub and wooded grassland, at altitudes from 1000 to 3300 m.

Flowering from August to May, *honeybees forage on abundant pollen and nectar very frequently.*

Sphaeranthus suaveolens
(Forrsk.) D.C.
Asteraceae

ARASHADIYE, HOLAGABIS, ALA-SHIEN (Gur); HOLAGABIS (Or); KARAMUT (Tya)

A weak-stemmed, trailing annual herb with elliptic, serrate leaves. Flower heads dull red-purple, spherical, terminal on ascending stems.

This common herb is found along waterways, roadside ditches, in swamps, seasonal waterlogged places and sometimes as a weed of cultivation, at altitudes from 1000 to 2500 m.

It is used as a condiment for local butter. In local medicine the whole plant is used against coughs, headache, severe colds, skin disease and as a laxative.

Flowering from September to June and flowers are visited by honeybees for pollen and nectar when other bee feed are scarce.

Tagetes minuta *L. /* Asteraceae

GEMMA-HASHISH, YAHIYASHITO (Amh); MISH-MISH, MUKA AJAYA (Or)

An erect annual herb with a strong aromatic smell, densely branched and woody at the base growing to 2 m high. Leaves yellow-green, deeply divided with linear-lanceolate, serrate leaflets. Flower heads small, whitish-yellow, arranged in erect clusters at the ends of the branches.

A common weed of cultivation, also growing in waste ground, along paths and roadsides and in *Acacia* woodland, at altitudes between 700 and 2400 m.

The roots are used in local medicine against constipation and the strong smell of the plant is said to irritate ants.

Flowering all year round, *honeybees collect pollen and nectar from the flowers.*

Tagetes patula *L. /* Asteraceae

STUDENTENBLUME (German)

An erect annual herb, branching above, growing to 90 cm high rooting at the lower nodes. Leaves usually alternate, deeply divided with toothed leaflets which are linear-elliptic. Flower heads deep orange to dark red, solitary and arranged on erect stalks.

An introduced garden ornamental, native to Central America, widely planted in public and private gardens. Nowadays it is found as an escape in fields and along riverbanks, at altitudes between 1600 and 2400 m.

Flowering all year round, *honeybees collect pollen and nectar from the flowers frequently.*

Tridax procumbens L. /
Asteraceae

A prostrate or ascending perennial herb up to 50 cm high. Leaves opposite below and alternate above, the lamina 3-lobed, ovate and toothed. Flower heads yellowish-white to greenish-white, solitary and borne on long stalks.

Found along roadside ditches and in dry deciduous woodland, at altitudes between 200 and 2000 m. The species is a native of Mexico, but nowadays it has become a pantropical weed and the most widespread species in the genus.

Flowering all year round, *bees forage for pollen and nectar.*

Vernonia auriculifera Hiern. /
Asteraceae

GUJO, REGI (Amh); DANGIRATO (Kef); REGI (Sid)

A shrub to 4 m high. Leaves oblong-lanceolate, 10-15 cm long. Flower heads pale mauve and very small, arranged in large spreading corymbs.

Widely distributed in the south western and southern parts of the country, it is found in humid lowland woodland, wooded grassland and scrub, in rocky slopes and along forest edges, at altitudes between 1600 and 2800 m.

Flowering from November to May, *honeybees forage on abundant pollen and nectar. Where the shrub is plentiful it can provide a honey flow and very good pollen supplies for strengthening colonies.*

Vernonia adoensis Sch.-Bip. ex Walp. / Asteraceae

YEFERES-ZENG, TIKWA (Amh)

An erect, branched pubescent shrub growing to 2 m tall. Leaves ovate with crenate margins. Flower heads white-violet, in dense terminal corymbs.

A common shrub growing in dry areas, roadsides and in rocky and disturbed areas, deciduous woodland and wooded grassland, at altitudes between 1300 and 2400 m.

Flowering from September to July, *honeybees collect pollen and nectar from the flowers frequently.*

Vernonia biafrae Oliv. & Hiern. /
Asteraceae

An erect, sometimes single-stemmed shrub growing to 2 m high. Leaves elliptic with minutely toothed margins. Flower heads blue or pale blue to violet, arranged in dense terminal corymbs.

Commonly found in the western parts of the country, along roadsides and forest edges, at altitudes between 1500 and 2500 m.

Flowering from January to March, *honeybees collect pollen and nectar from the flowers frequently.*

Vernonia ituriensis *Muschl.* var. ituriensis / Asteraceae

An erect shrub growing to 1.5 m high. Leaves alternate with toothed margins. Flower heads whitish-pink, borne at the end of branches.

Growing in evergreen woodland, disturbed ground, along roadsides and forest edges, at altitudes up to 2600 m.

Flowering from December up to March, *honeybees forage on abundant pollen and nectar from the flowers. When the plant grows in dense stands it can provide a good nectar flow and is very important for bee colony strengthening.*

Vernonia rueppellii *Sch.-Bip. ex Walp.* / Asteraceae

An erect shrub growing to 3 m high. Leaves alternate, elliptic-lanceolate and toothed at the margins. Flower heads pale pink and very small, borne singly in a large spreading corymb.

Growing in deciduous and evergreen woodland, along paths and roadsides and near homesteads, at altitudes between 1700 and 3000 m.

Flowering from September to March, *honeybees forage on abundant pollen and nectar from the flowers. In dense stands the bees produce a surplus of honey and its late flowering characteristic make this plant very important for strengthening colonies after harvesting times.*

Vernonia leopoldii *(Sch.-Bip. ex Walp.) Vatke* / Asteraceae

CHIBO (Amh); SUKUALE, MARRAT (Tya)

An erect annual herb, covered with soft hairs, growing to 1 m high. Leaves grey-green with crenate margins. Flower heads purple, in large terminal corymbs.

Growing in open bushland, along roadsides and on rocky hills, at altitudes between 2300 and 2900 m.

The leaves and flowers are used for dressing wounds. The roots are used against gastric disorders.

Flowering from October to January, *honeybees collect pollen and nectar from the flowers very frequently and in dense stands it can provide a good nectar flow.*

Vernonia schimperi *DC.* / Asteraceae

An annual herb, growing to 1 m high. Leaves alternate and simple. Flower heads white-pinkish, arranged in terminal corymbs.

Growing on black soils, in shade of trees, along forest edges and on degraded mountain slopes, at altitudes of 1600 to 3000 m.

Flowering after the big rains from September to November, *a very valuable pollen and nectar source for honeybees which work on the flowers all day round.*

Vernonia theophrastifolia

Schweinf. ex Oliv. & Hiern /
Asteraceae

An erect woody herb growing to 2 m. Leaves lanceolate. Flower heads pinkish, in terminal corymbs.

Growing along roadsides, among other bushes and beside streams, in wooded grassland and riverine forests, at altitudes between 1400 and 2500 m.

Flowering from October to March, *honeybees collect pollen and nectar from the flowers frequently. The prolonged flowering period of this species is important for strengthening bee colonies and maintenance of brood rearing.*

Vernonia thomsoniana *Oliv. &*

Hiern. / Asteraceae

SOYAMA (Or); SHEBBO (Kef)

An erect single-stemmed to much-branched shrub growing to 5 m high. Leaves alternate, elliptic to lanceolate with almost entire margins and acuminate tips. Flower heads white to pink, small, sweetly-scented and arranged in dense clusters at the end of branches.

Found along paths, roadsides, and waterways, in evergreen woodland and scrub and sometimes planted as a live fence around farmland and homesteads, at altitudes between 1400 and 2500 m.

In Wellega it is commonly used for house construction and bee basket making.

Flowering from January to March, *honeybees forage on abundant pollen and copious nectar. In dense stands the flowers can provide a significant surplus of honey.*

Vernonia urticifolia *A.Rich. /*
Asteraceae

A scabrid-pubescent, scrambling perennial or annual herb, up to 1.5 m tall. Leaves elliptic, with crenate margins. Flower heads white to pale purple in large terminal corymbs.

Found in dry evergreen woodland along paths and small waterways and in partial shade of trees at altitudes between 1600 and 2600 m.

Flowering from October up to March, *honeybees collect pollen and nectar from the flowers frequently. When growing in dense stand the bees can forage significant amounts of pollen and nectar to strengthen the colony and maintaining brood rearing.*

Xanthium spinosum *L. /*
Asteraceae

TORSERAWIT, KOSHESHLA, YESET-MILAS (Amh); KORE-BUSE (Or); SPINY COCKLEBUR (Eng)

A much-branched annual herb up to 75 cm high, with yellow stems. Leaves sessile, with prominent venation, dark green above and white to grey beneath, with one or two 3-branched yellow spines at the leaf axil. Flower heads creamy-green, solitary. Fruits are covered in hooked prickles.

A bad weed of heavy clay soils, irrigated fields and roadsides, at altitudes between 1700 and 2600 m. It is a cosmopolitan weed, found through all continents.

Flowering from November to May, *honeybees forage on pollen and nectar from the flowers. It provides good amounts of nectar and some surplus of honey may be stored. The honey is said to be dark and strongly flavoured.*

Impatiens glandulifera _Royle_ / Balsaminaceae

HIMALAYAN BALSAM (Eng); INDISCHES SPRINGKRAUT (German)

An erect annual herb growing to 1 m tall often with red stems. Leaves alternate, elliptic with serrate margins. Flowers pinkish-red, quite large and conspicuous, on long stalks.

First appearing in masses in Ethiopia in Northern Shewa in 1993 along waterways, in swampy grassland and some rocky areas up to 2800 m.

This species is native to the Himalayan region. It has spread rapidly and naturalized along waterways througout temperate Europe.

Flowering after the rains the _honeybees collect pollen and nectar from the flowers. In other countries, this plant has become widespread and an important bee plant._

Impatiens hochstetteri _Warb._ / Balsaminaceae

A pubescent herb with ascending stems, growing to 40 cm and rooting at the nodes. Leaves are ovate-elliptic. Flowers pale pink to lilac with spreading petals.

Commonly found in wet forests and along streamsides, in swampy places mainly of the Western and South-Western parts of the country at altitudes between 1300 and 2400 m.

Flowering from September to May, _honeybees collect some pollen and abundant nectar from the flowers frequently._

Impatiens rothii _Hook.f._ / Balsaminaceae

GURSHT (Amh)

An endemic annual herb, growing to 80 cm with much-branched stems. Leaves dark green and glossy with red toothed margins. Flowers deep orange, very irregular, with one sepal forming a long cylindrical nectar tube at the back of the hanging flower.

Growing beside roads, on stream banks, in damp but well-drained areas of the plateau at altitudes between 1400 and 3100 m.

Flowering from August to May, _honeybees collect pollen and nectar from the flowers._

Begonia wollastonii _Bak._ / Begoniaceae

A rhizomatous perennial herb growing to 120 cm high with fleshy creeping and ascending stems and small ovoid tubers. Leaf-blade asymmetric with red veins and petioles. Flowers pale pink, with bright yellow stamens.

A rather rare plant of wet highland forests, growing under sprays of waterfalls, on moist slopes and along paths at altitudes between 1500 and 2500 m.

Flowering from August to December, _honeybees were observed to collect pollen only._

Berberis holstii L. /
Berberidaceae

ZENQILA (Amh)

An evergreen shrub growing to 2.5 m tall. The branches bear numerous short shoots carrying densely crowded leaves and flowers. Leaves 3-foliate, leathery with spiny teeth on the margin. Flowers cream to yellow, arranged in clustered panicles.

Found in edges of forests, in clearings and evergreen bushland at altitudes between 2500 and 3200 m.

The plant is used to treat tropical ulcer. Dried stems are burnt as a fumigant during child birth.

Flowering from June to December, *honeybees are frequently visiting the flowers for pollen and nectar.*

Tecoma stans (L.) Jussieu /
Bignoniaceae

YELLOW TRUMPET TREE (Eng)

A bush or small tree growing to 5 m tall. Leaves opposite and pinnately compound, leaflets ovate-lanceolate, with toothed margins. Flowers bright yellow and funnel- to bell-shaped with 5 lobes, arranged in terminal clusters.

Introduced from tropical Central America and nowadays grown as an ornamental in many towns at altitudes from 500 up to 2400 m.

Flowering at all times of the year but profusely after rain. *This is a valuable and reliable nectar and pollen source for honeybees and is frequently visited throughout the year, especially when other sources of bee food are lacking.*

Tecomaria capensis (Thun.)
Spach. / Bignoniaceae

CAPE HONEY SUCKLE (Eng)

An evergreen multi-stemmed shrub, climber or small tree, growing to 4 m high. Leaves opposite, pinnately compound, leaflets dark glossy green and up to 15 cm long. Flowers vermilion red, funnel-shaped and arranged in showy panicles.

This shrub is native to South Africa and is now cultivated in most Ethiopian towns as an ornamental hedgeplant at altitudes between 1600 up to 2400 m.

Flowering is almost all year round, but especially after rains, *honeybees collect pollen and nectar from the flowers frequently.*

Borago officinalis L. /
Boraginaceae

BORAGE (Eng); GURKENKRAUT (German)

A robust annual herb, up to 60 cm high, covered with coarse hairs. Leaves oval and covered in rough hairs. Flowers bright blue, star-shaped and grouped in branching cymes.

Found in public and private gardens as an ornamental at altitudes from 1600 to 2400 m.

Native to the Mediterranean region, it is cultivated elsewhere for its leaves and flowers which are used in salads, for flavouring cold drinks, and in pharmacy. It also has some medicinal value.

Flowering the whole year round *honeybees collect nectar and pollen and the plant is a honey source only where it is grown in quite large quantities.*

Cynoglossum coeruleum

Steud. ex DC. / Boraginaceae

CH'UGOGET, FERISH-TENU (Amh);
KACHEBA (Had); MATANE-CHATI (Or)

A trailing, sometimes shrubby, scabrid perennial herb growing to 60 cm high. Leaves soft, grey-green, linear to lanceolate with the basal ones borne in rosettes. Flowers small, bright deep blue, in curled racemes. Fruits usually covered with short curved spines.

Growing along roadsides and in montane grassland and Afro-alpine meadows at altitudes between 1700 to 3500 m.

Flowering almost all year round, *honeybees collect pollen and nectar from the flowers very frequently.*

Echium plantagineum *L.* / Boraginaceae

PATERSON'S CURSE (Eng);
NATTERNKOPF (German)

An erect annual or biennial rough to tough herb growing to a height of 1 m. Basal leaves ovate and stalked, rough and harsh with conspicuous lateral veins; stem leaves oblong to lanceolate and sessile. Flowers blue, funnel-shaped, arranged in panicles.

This species is closely related to *E. vulgare* but here only 4 stamens protrude beyond the corolla while there are 2 in *E. plantagineum*.

Considered to be a garden escape from the Mediterranean, it is found on degraded soils, waste land, in dry overgrazed grassland and along roads at altitudes between 1800 and 2400 m.

Flowering from November to February, *honeybees are very frequently foraging for the abundant nectar and copious dark blue pollen.*

Heliotropium cinerascens *D.C.* / Boraginaceae

SHEKO (Amh); BAGANAPSI (Or); AHO-GADMA, AMANGEMEL (Tya)

A small shrub growing to 50 cm high, covered with fine white hairs. Leaves simple and alternate with entire margins. Flowers small, white, arranged along one side of the inflorescences which curl under at the ends.

Found in fallow land, along roadsides and occasionally as a weed in crops, growing at altitudes between 800 to 2000 m.

Flowering is from August to May, *honeybees collect pollen and nectar from the flowers.*

Trichodesma zeylanicum *(L.)*

R.Br. / Boraginaceae

KOSKUS (Amh); AREMU LAEZAB (Or); LATE WEED (Eng)

An annual herb growing to 1 m tall, with erect stem, covered with stiff hairs. Leaves lanceolate, opposite and simple. Flowers pale blue or white, bell-shaped and hanging down.

A common weed usually found at the end of the growing season on light soils in dry areas, on grassland and on water-logged soils at altitudes between 1500 and 2000 m.

Flowering throughout the year, *honeybees collect pollen and nectar from the flowers.*

Brassica carinata A.Braun /
Brassicaceae

YEGURAGHE-GOMMEN, MASHASHE (Amh); SACHAB (Kef); GOMENA-GURAGE, MIDAN-RAFU (Or); KAYA (Nuw); GRUMBA (Tya); ABYSSINIAN MUSTARD (Eng)

An annual cultivated plant with erect, much branched stems, very variable in size and shape, even forming a small bush. Leaves alternate, dark green and thick, sometimes with dark purple stems and ribs. Flowers light yellow in very long inflorescences.

Found very commonly cultivated in homegardens as one of the most important leafy vegetables in Ethiopian traditional cooking, at altitudes between 1350 and 2600 m.

It is grown for both its leaves and its seeds. The leaves are eaten cooked as vegetable while the seeds are used to oil the baking plate of INJERA stoves.

Flowering time is from November to April, *honeybees collect pollen and nectar very frequently.*

Brassica napus L. / Brassicaceae

RAPE, OILSEED RAPE (Eng); RAPS (German)

An annual crop plant, up to 100 cm high. Leaves dark green, with bluish-veins. Flowers light yellow in clustered at the top of long racemems.

A major oil crop of Arsi and Bale regions, cultivated at altitudes between 2100 and 2400 m.

Flowering from September to November, *honeybees collect nectar and pollen and the plant is an important honey source. Honeybees are the most important pollinators to increase seed set and oil yield.*

Brassica nigra (L.) Koch /
Brassicaceae

SENAFCH' (Amh & Tya); SANAVI, SENAFICCIA (Or); AMLI, GRUMBA (Tya); KAFO-DREGANTA (Wel); BLACK MUSTARD (Eng); SCHWARZER SENF (German)

An erect annual, loosely branched herb growing to 90 cm tall. Leaves alternate and pinnatifid with irregularly dentate margin. Flowers pale yellow, small and clustered at the top of racemes.

Cultivated and found as a weed in waste areas and along stream banks at altitudes between 2000 and 2600 m.

Commonly used as vegetable. The crushed seeds are used to prepare SILYO and AWAZE.

Flowering from September to April the *honeybees collect abundant pollen and copious nectar from the flowers.*

Crambe hispanica L. /
Brassicaceae

FUJUL (Or); ABYSSINIAN KALE (Eng)

An erect, much-branched, annual herb growing to 90 cm tall. Leaves alternate, pinnately lobed with entire to dentate leaf margins. Flowers small, pale-yellow to dirty-white on long erect racemes.

Occurs spontaneously in cultivated fields particularly in northern parts of the country. It grows well at altitudes of about 1900 to 2500 m.

Under the name *Crambe abyssinica* this species is becoming an important industrial oil crop.

Flowering time is from May to December, *honeybees are very frequently visiting the flowers for pollen and nectar.*

Erucastrum abyssinicum

(A.Rich.) Schulz / Brassicaceae

GOMANZA (Or); HIMFIDE AS (Som)

An erect annual herb growing to 80 cm high. Leaves with an uneven surface, deep green and somewhat shiny. Flowers small and yellow.

Endemic, found in disturbed areas, fallow ground and as a scattered plant in TEFF fields, along roadsides at altitudes between 1000 and 2600 m.

Leaves used as a vegetable and the seeds as a source of oil, but less often than the similar *E. arabicum.*

Flowering almost all year round, *honeybees collect pollen and nectar from the flowers.*

Lepidium sativum *L.* /

Brassicaceae

FETO (Amh & Or); SHIMP (Kef); CIRCUFA, FECIO, SHIMFI (Or); KOTTO, SHIMFA, SUMFA (Tya); KRESSE (German)

An erect glabrous annual, up to 80 cm high. Leaves pinnate, entire and alternate. Flowers white or pale-pink, small, widely spaced in terminal racemes.

Scattered into and grown with other crops, particularly TEFF, at altitudes between 750 to 2900 m.

Cultivated for its seeds because it is considered as one of the standard home medicine plants used to treat a variety of skin complaints as well as colds, stomach upsets and swollen glands. In many parts of Ethiopia a special dish, called FETO FITFIT is prepared from seeds.

Flowering during October and November the *honeybees collect pollen and nectar from the flowers frequently.*

Raphanus raphanistrum *L.* /

Brassicaceae

HEDERICH (German); WILD RADISH (Eng)

An erect annual herb growing to a height of 50 cm from a tough slender taproot. Leaves form a rosette and are deeply lobed. Flowers quite large, white or cream yellow or even light bluish, borne in conspicuous racemes at the end of the stems.

An uncommon weed, introduced from Europe, found in crop and fallow land, at altitudes between 1900 and 2800 m.

Flowering during and after the rains *it provides an abundance of nectar and pollen and is a valuable stimulant for bee colony development.*

Rorippa nasturtium-aquaticum *(L.) Hayele* /

Brassicaceae

WATERCRESS (Eng); BRUNNENKRESSE (German)

A perennial herb with prostrate to ascending juicy stems, often rooting at lower nodes with stems growing from 10 to 100 cm long. Leaves dissected with 2-9 pairs of leaflets which are elliptic to suborbicular, with uneven or wavy margins. Flowers small, bright white and numerous.

Common but never eaten in Ethopia. Found in and along small waterways, ditches, and in grassland which is overrun by water. Very common in open sewers of towns and bigger villages at altitudes between 2200 and 2600 m.

Flowering all year round, *honeybees forage very frequently for pollen and nectar and in some places where the plant is plentiful it will provide a significant surplus of honey.*

Sinapis alba *L.* / Brassicaceae

SENAFCH (Amh & Tre); MUSTARD (Eng); SENF (German)

A cultivated annual herb growing to 100 cm high, stem with or without spreading hairs. Leaves pinnately lobed or divided, rough and coarsely toothed. Flowers bright yellow and rather large.

Cultivated as an oil crop on the plateau at altitudes to 2600 m.

Elsewhere used as a fodder crop, and green manure. The seeds are ground to make table mustard.

Flowering profusely during October, *honeybees collect nectar and pollen very frequently and the plant is a honey source.*

Opuntia cylindrica *(Lam.) DC* / Cactaceae

A shrub or small tree growing to 3 m high. Stems erect, cylindrical, green with few branches, covered with groups of 2-6 pale yellow to whitish spines about 1 cm long mixed with fine hairs. Leaves mostly absent. Flowers red, up to 2.5 cm across and solitary arranged near tops of ascending stems.

Native to Peru, now planted as an efficient hedge plant and sometimes as an ornamental at altitudes between 1900 and 2800 m.

Some plants may be found with flowers cacti are found throughout the year but most profusely after the rains when it is *very frequently visited by honeybees for pollen and nectar.*

Campanula edulis *Forssk.* / Campanulaceae

YEREGNA-MSA (Amh)

An annual herb with some creeping stems growing to 40 cm tall. Leaves lanceolate with widely-spaced toothed margins. Flowers blue, bell-shaped and drooping.

Found on rocky slopes, in short grassland, in mountain scrub and evergreen forests at altitudes between 2000 and 3600 m.

Flowering almost all year round, *honeybees collect pollen and nectar.*

Canarina abyssinica *Engl.* / Campanulaceae

TUTU (Amh)

A glaucous annual climber with a large underground tuber and stems growing to 150 cm long. Leaves triangular-ovate with twining leaf-stalks. Flowers bright orange to orange-scarlet, bell-shaped and hanging.

Found in shrubby areas, deciduous woodland, on grassland and rocky slopes during the rainy season at altitudes between 1800 and 2400 m.

Flowering from June to September, *honeybees are foraging pollen and nectar.*

Gynandropsis gynandra *(L.)*
Briq. / Capparidaceae

ABETEYO (Amh); BOEKBEHA, GARGAMMA (Tya); SPIDER FLOWER (Eng)

A glandular or glabrescent weed with erect stem growing to 60 cm high. Leaves palmately compound with obovate to elliptic leaflets. Flowers sweetly scented, with 4 pink or white or purple petals, arranged in long racemes.

More common on irrigated land, this annual also occurs in cultivated areas and along paths at altitudes between 1200 to 2400 m.

In local medicine the leaves are used as perfume and against renal calculus. Leaves are edible and relished by goats and sheep.

Flowering all year round but particularly profusely after rains, *honeybees collect pollen and nectar from the flowers.*

Maerua angolensis *DC.* subsp. **angolensis** / Capparidaceae

SHISHIE (Som); MERE, KOROMO (Tya)

A shrub, sometimes small tree, usually less than 5 m high, occasionally more. Leaves variable in size and shape, usually elliptic or ovate-lanceolate. Flowers sweet scented with numerous long white stamens, arranged in leafy, corymbose racemes.

Found on rocky and stony ground, in semi-arid lowland woodland, in wooded grassland and evergreen bushland at altitudes from 500 m up to 1800 m.

Flowering from October to April, *honeybees are foraging frequently for pollen and nectar throughout the day.*

Ritchiea albersii *Gilg.* / Capparidaceae

DNGAY-SEBER (Amh)

Mostly a hedge-forming shrub, sometimes a tree growing to 20 m. Leaves petiolate, simple to 5-foliolate; leaflets elliptic or oblong-elliptic. Flowers white with very long petals arranged in terminal inflorescences on long leafy branches.

Found in upland grassland, wet montane forest and also in drier areas at altitudes between 1100 to 2400 m.

Flowering from October to June, *honeybees collect pollen and nectar from the flowers.*

Catha edulis *(Vahl) Forssk. ex Endl.* / Celastraceae

CHAT (Amh, Gur & Tya); CATA (Kem); CATI, GOFA JIMA' (Or); CATIYYA (Wel); KHAT, FLOWER OF PARADISE (Eng); KATHSTRAUCH (German)

A shrub or small tree to 15 m high. Leaves greyish-green, glossy, oblong to elliptic. Flowers white, on short cymes in the leaf axils.

An important local and export crop in many areas, particularly in Hararghe and S Shewa. It also grows naturally in evergreen submontane or medium altitude forest, usually near margins, or in woodland often on rocky slopes at altitudes from 1400 to 2400 m.

The leaves are chewed as a mild stimulant, staining the mouth red, and both the leaves and the roots are used to treat a number of illnesses.

Flowering after the rains, *honeybees collect pollen and nectar from the flowers only occasionally.*

Maytenus arbutifolia *(Hochst. ex A.Rich.) Wilczek* / Celastraceae

A shrub or tree growing to 0.3 to 6 m high with grey to brown branches with white breathing pores. Leaves alternately arranged, elliptic or oblong to oblanceolate, ovate or orbicular and toothed. Flowers sweetly-scented, white, small, solitary or axillary.

Found in forests, forest margins, degraded woodland, along riverbanks and in grassland at altitudes between 1200 and 3000 m.

Flowering from September to December, *honeybees are foraging pollen and nectar.*

Maytenus gracilipes subsp. arguta *(Loes.) Sebsebe* / Celastraceae

ATAT, KAMU, KURAVA, TELALO, TALO (Amh); KOMBOLCHA (Or); DUBOBEIS (Som) DEGMUT, HATCHAT (Tya)

A shrub or bushy tree up to 5 or 7 m high, sometimes to 10 m. Leaves simple and alternate, oblong, lanceolate or obovate. Flowers sweet-scented, creamy white to pink in panicles.

Found in humid mountainous woodland as an understorey tree at altitudes between 2200 and 3200 m.

Flowering shortly after the rains have stopped. *Honeybees collect pollen and nectar from the flowers.*

Combretum paniculatum *Vent.* / Combretaceae

GABAI, SHAGA, BEGE (Or)

A twining woody scrambler with a brown-grey bark and short stiff thorns. Leaves opposite, elliptic and alternate. Flowers flaming red, very showy, in numerous panicles on non-twining sprouts.

An impressive plant, growing in humid woodland, forest and forest edges, very often covering the tree it grows over at altitudes between 1400 and 2000 m.

In local medicine the flowers are used against eye diseases and the whole plant is used against leprosy.

Flowering from September to February, *countless bee colonies abscond from their hives during the flowering period in the western part of the country to reach C. paniculatum areas. The plant is an important honey source.*

Commelina benghalensis *L.* / Commelinaceae

YEWHA-ANQUR, WOFANQUR (Amh); AMBACEIO, LALUNTYE (Gur); SHATO (Kef); DILISHA, HOLEGEBIS, LABUNCHE (Or); MASCHILL (Tya)

A trailing annual or perennial herb with ascending or erect branches growing to 2 m long. Leaves broadly ovate clasping the stem. Flowers showy bright blue, emerging from a broadened, flattened, sessile spathe. Flower stay open for only one day.

Widespread in rocky places beside streams, in woodland and as a weed from 1200 to 2700 m.

Flowering from July to February, *honeybees collect pollen only from the flowers.*

Cyanotis barbata D.Don. / Commelinaceae

YEWOT'-QOLO, YEJB-DNCH (Amh); BURKO (Tya)

A frequent, often abundant perennial herb, with erect to ascending stems growing to 30 cm high. Leaves linear. Flowers blue-violet or blue-pink, with very hairy stamens, arranged in dense clusters at the top of the stems.

Found in masses in open areas, in creavices between rocks, on meadows and in fallow ground at altitudes between 1650 and 2800 m.

Flowering in masses towards the end and after the big rains up to October or November. *Honeybees collect abundant pollen and some nectar from the flowers very frequently.*

Ipomoea purpurea (L.) Roth. / Convolvulaceae

MORNING GLORY (Eng); WINDE (German)

An annual hairy trailer or twiner. Leaves entire or 3-lobed, glabrous or pubescent. Flowers purple, funnel-shaped, solitary or in few-flowered cymes.

Introduced from South America this plant is now naturalized. Commonly growing on waste ground and very often cultivated in hedges found at altitudes between 1300 and 2400 m.

Flowering almost all year round, *it is frequently visited by honeybees for pollen and nectar.*

Ipomoea tenuirostris Choisy / Convolvulaceae

YAIT'-AREG (Amh); MORNING GLORY (Eng)

A perennial herb with twining or prostrate stems, to 3 m long. Leaves ovate to oblong, with cordate bases. Flowers pink, also white or blue with a dark mauve centre.

Often abundant in cleared upland woodland, in deciduous woodland at altitudes from 1500 up to 2200 m.

Flowering from November to March, *honeybees collect pollen and nectar from the flowers frequently.*

Kalanchoe densiflora Rolfe / Crassulaceae

'NDAHULLA (Amh); ANDHO (Gur); ANCORURA (Or)

A common erect succulent herb growing to 120 cm tall. Leaves opposite, ovate with crenate margins. Flowers yellow to orange, arranged in dense terminal heads.

A common plant disliked by domestic animals found in disturbed habitats, at forest edges and along roadsides between 1000 and 2500 m.

The fleshy leaves are used in ENSET-growing areas for wrapping local bread KOCHO or BULLA and are used in making a dressing for sores.

Flowering from October to December, it is often visited by butterflies. *Honeybees collect pollen and nectar from the flowers.*

Kalanchoe lanceolata *(Forssk.)* Pers. / Crassulaceae

YEQQOLLA-'NDAHULLA (Amh); FURGUGE, QONTOMA (Or); BIBILE (Som); GEDIL (Tre)

An erect glandular-pubescent annual, stems often 4-angled at the base, growing to 1 m high. Leaves obovate to oblong, with toothed margins. Flowers usually yellow or orange, sometimes pinkish, in dense heads.

A widespread plant found along roadsides, in disturbed areas, open woodland, bushland or grassland on deep or rocky soils at altitudes between 1100 to 2400 m.

Flowering late in the dry season from November to February, *honeybees occasionally collect pollen and nectar from the flowers.*

Kalanchoe marmorata *Bak.* / Crassulaceae

'NDAHULLA (Amh); BOSOKE (Or); DEK'WA'TA (Tya)

A perennial succulent subshrub up to 1.2 m high with decumbent stems at the base. Leaves sessile or nearly so, grey-green and often with large purple spots on both sides and toothed margins. Flowers sweetly scented , pure white, rarely flushed very pale pink, arranged on up to 18 cm long inflorescences.

Found in open rocky sites, grassland or clearings in evergreen bushland and in hot dry habitats at altitudes between 1900 and 2500 m.

An important local medicinal plant with many uses. The leaves provide a cool dressing for wounds.

Flowering from October to January, *honeybees are occasionally foraging for nectar from the flowers.*

Kalanchoe petitiana *A. Rich.* / Crassulaceae

YEQUOLLA-'NDAHULLA (Amh); MUDA (Gam); AMDOHALE, ANDOHAHELE, BOSOQQE, HANCURA (Or)

A drought tolerant, perennial herb, forming dense stands of stems. Leaves succulent with crenate margins. Flowers sweet scented, deep pink to white, produced in heads on stems up to 1.7 m tall.

This plant is disliked by domestic animals and is found in forest margins and open evergreen bushland under trees, often in disturbed areas, at altitudes between 1300 and 3100 m.

The fleshy leaves are used in baking local bread, KOCHO or BULLA and are used in making a dressing for sores.

Flowering almost all year round it is often visited by butterflies and *occasionally by honeybees.*

Kalanchoe quartiniana *A. Rich.* / Crassulaceae

'NDAHULLA; SHNQAQ (Amh); MUDA (Gam); ANCURA (Had); BOSOQQE; LUGO; WITU (Or); GEDIL (Tre); TSA'DA-DEKWA'TA (Tya)

A perennial herb growing to 70 cm high. Leaves elliptic to ovate with an irregularly crenate margin. Flowers white to pale pink in heads. They are larger than *K. petitiana* with the tube 3-5 cm long.

Endemic, found in forest margins and open evergreen bushland under trees, often in disturbed areas and commonly along roadsides at altitudes between 2100 and 2600 m.

Flowering from October to February, it is occasionally *visited by honeybees.*

Sedum churchillianum *Robyns & Boutique* / Crassulaceae

A small subshrub with usually erect stems up to 24 cm high, apparently not rooting at the nodes. Leaves arranged in whorls, narrowly-oblong. Flowers lemon-yellow, arranged in cymes.

Found on cliffs or rock outcrops amongst *Erica* and *Philippia* at altitudes between 2900 and 4050 m.

Flowering from September to April the *honeybees are frequently foraging for nectar and pollen*

Sedum mooneyi *M.Gilbert* / Crassulaceae

A much-branched annual herb, usually prostrate and rooting at nodes, growing to 5 cm high. Stems very densely covered with papery scales when young. Leaves arranged in crowded whorls, fleshy with convex lower side, often flushed dark red. Flowers bright yellow, arranged in numerous few-flowered cymes.

Endemic, found on moss-covered rocks at forest margins and in Afro-alpine moorland, mostly in exposed habitats at altitudes between 3000 and 4100 m.

Flowering from October to February, *honeybees are frequently foraging pollen and nectar. This and similar Sedum species are probably important sources of bee food in Afro-alpine areas.*

Citrullus lanatus *(Thumb.) Mansf.* / Cucurbitaceae

WATERMELON (Eng)

An annual, slender, hairy and spreading herb with thin stems and tendrils. Leaves are subdivided into pairs of pinnate lobes with rounded outlines. Flowers pale yellow, solitary and born in leaf axils.

Grown on alluvial soil from flood retreats in the Rift Valley and elsewhere at altitudes from 500 up to 2000 m.

A recently important cash crop grown for its delicious fruits which have a sweet red flesh.

Bees are important pollinators and are foraging pollen and nectar from the flowers.

Coccinia abyssinica *(Lam.) Coyn.* / Cucurbitaceae

ANCHOTE (Or)

A biennial or perennial climbing or trailing herb growing to 3.5 m long. The tuberous rootstock is fleshy. Leaves heart-shaped to palmately lobed and slightly toothed. Flowers yellow, on long stalks, sometimes nodding.

Found wild in evergreen woodland or scrub and cultivated in backyards for its edible young shoots and tubers at altitudes between 1750 to 2400 m.

The tubers from both wild and cultivated plants are eaten. In the western part of the country the roots are boiled and prepared with local butter for the MESKEL holiday.

Flowering from July to November, *honeybees collect some pollen and abundant nectar from the flowers.*

Cucumis sativus L. /
Cucurbitaceae

KIYARE (Amh); CUCUMBER (Eng);
GURKE (German)

A prostrate annual herbaceous plant
with stems growing to 2 m long.
Leaves heart-shaped, shiny green,
born on long stalks, smooth on the
upper surface and covered with short
bristly hairs beneath. Flowers shiny
yellow, appearing in the leaf axils.

Only cultivated on loamy soil where
there is a good supply of water in
some areas between the altitudes of
1600 and 2400 m.

A cultivated crop plant grown as a
vegetable and for salad and usually
only sold in urban centres. Previously
only bought by expatriates, now
becoming more popular with
Ethiopians.

*Honeybees collect pollen and nectar
from the flowers occasionally.*

Cucurbita pepo L. /
Cucurbitaceae

DUBA (Amh); ARABE, FIRI DUBA (Or)

A vigorous usually trailing annual herb
with stems growing to 5 m long.
Leaves large, ovate or broadly
triangular, palmately 5-lobed, cordate,
rough and covered with short spiny
hairs. Flowers large and bright yellow.

Cultivated for its edible fruits it is found
at altitudes between 800 and 2500 m.

In traditional medicine the seeds are
used as a taenifuge. The flowers are
also edible.

Flowering from April to December,
*honeybees collect pollen and nectar
from the flowers frequently.*

Lagenaria abyssinica (Hook.f.)
C.Jeffrey / Cucurbitaceae

KUL (Amh)

A vigorous climbing or trailing
perennial herb with stems growing to 7
m long. Leaves ovate, weakly cordate
and usually palmately 5-lobed.
Flowers sweetly scented, white or
creamy-white with green veins, funnel-
shaped or cylindrical. Male flowers are
either solitary or in 2-5 flowered
racemes while female flowers are
always solitary.

Growing in forest and scrub and along
paths, roadsides and riverine
vegetation at altitudes between 1600
and 2750 m.

Flowering from October to December,
*honeybees are foraging pollen and
nectar.*

Luffa cylindrica (L.) M.J.Roem. /
Cucurbitaceae

DISHCLOTH GOURD (Eng)

A vigorous climber or trailer growing
to 15 m long with tendrils. Leaves dark
green, palmately lobed, the lobes are
triangular to narrowly oblong-
lanceolate, with the central largest.
Flowers large, deep yellow: male
arranged in racemes and the female
solitary.

Found along river banks and also
cultivated as a hedge plant and for
ornament at altitudes between 550 and
1500 m.

Young fruits can be eaten. Fibres of
old fruits provide the commerical
LUFFA.

It is flowering throughout the year
where adequate watering is given,
*honeybees are foraging abundant
nectar and pollen.*

Dipsacus pinnatifidus *Steud. ex A.Rich.* / Dipsacaceae

TEASEL (Eng)

A spiny, stiff and erect herb growing to 3 m high. Leaves ovate to lanceolate, with spiny toothed marginbs. Flower heads globose, white sometimes yellowish, on stiff erect stems.

Growing in damp grassland and moist areas, in upper forest and lower alpine zones, along waterways at altitudes between 1900 and 4000 m.

Flowering almost all year round, *honeybees collect pollen and nectar from the flowers frequently.*

Scabiosa columbaria *L.* / Dipsacaceae

THEIABI (Tya); GEMEINE SKABIOSE (German)

An erect perennial herb growing from a thick rootstock with a rosette of entire or divided leaves at ground level. Flowers pinkish-violet, in dense heads with hairless bristles between the flowers.

Found in grassy meadows, *Erica* shrub, along roadsides and in forest clearings at altitudes between 2000 and 3500 m.

In local medicine the plant is used against constipation.

Flowering at any time of the year, *honeybees collect pollen and nectar from the flowers.*

Pterocephalus frutescens *Hochst. ex A.Rich.* / Dipsacaceae

HENSERASE (Amh); BOCATTA, HILLO (Kef)

A small, erect herb, up to 80 cm tall. Leaves opposite, linear-lanceolate, entire, with toothed margins, crowded at the base of the stem. Flowers pale pink, in dense heads with hairy bristles in between.

Found in eroded grassland and disturbed areas and on rocky hillsides at altitudes between 1400 and 2500 m.

Leaves are used as a dressing for boils.

Flowering at any time of the year but more profusely after the rains, *honeybees collect pollen and nectar from the flowers.*

Euphorbia pulcherima *Willd. ex Klotzsch* / Euphorbiaceae

POINSETTIA (Eng); WEIHNACHTSSTERN (German)

A ornamental, little-branched shrub with a woody brown trunk. Leaves alternate, dark green, prominently veined, ovate, simple or lobed. Flowers held in a green cup surrounded by large red, pink or yellow bracts. All parts exude a milky juice when cut.

Introduced from Central America now widely planted as a decorative hedge-plant grown in many villages and towns at altitudes up to 2400 m.

Flowering all year round. *Bees are foraging mainly nectar which has a high sugar concentration.*

Euphorbia tirucalli L. /
Euphorbiaceae

QN'CHB (Amh); KINCHIBA (Kef); DANNO (Som)

A shrub or tree with a straight cylindrical bole and a dense bushy crown, growing to 18m high, but more often an untidy shrub up to 5 m high. Stems are dark green and leafless, except when young. Flowers creamy white, arranged in terminal clusters.

Mostly grown as a hedge plant but also often escaping or at least persisting in long-abandoned areas at altitudes between 1300 and 2000 m.

Flowering plants are found throughout the year. *Honeybees forage for pollen and nectar.*

Erodium moschatum (L.) Ait. /
Geraniaceae

An annual or short-lived perennial herb with musk-like smell. Several stems arise from the base and grow up to 50 cm long. Leaves opposite, pinnately compound with alternate to opposite leaflets which are sessile, ovate to elliptic. Flowers pink to purple or violet, arranged in 4-7-flowered umbels.

Found on grassy meadows, in moist disturbed habitats and fallow land, sometimes as a weed of cultivation at altitudes between 2100 and 3500 m.

Flowering from August to November, *honeybees collect pollen and nectar from the flowers frequently.*

Swertia abyssinica Hochst. /
Gentianaceae

A small much-branched annual herb with slender stems which are 4-angled, and up to 30 cm tall. Leaves arranged in 3-5 distant pairs, ovate to lanceolate and entire. Flowers white with pale-green veins and golden nectaries at the base, held up as a open cup, arranged in few-flowered panicles.

Found in short montane grassland, on wet, shallow and stony areas in higher altitudes between 2000 to 3000 m.

Sometimes this and closely related species form flowering carpets. Flowering from August to January, *honeybees collect pollen and nectar from the flowers.*

Geranium aculeolatum Oliv. /
Geraniaceae

A perennial herb with trailing stems which root at the nodes or scramble through other plants and grow to 1.5 m long. Most parts of the plant are glandular hairy when young and have scattered sharp reflexed prickles. Leaves opposite and divided into pinnatifid lobes. Flowers usually white, pale pink or pale mauve, arranged in 2-flowered inflorescences in the leaf axils.

Found at edges of montane forest, usually in moist habitats such as along river banks, in fallow land and occasionally as a weed of cultivation at altitudes between 1400 and 3000 m.

Flowering from September to December, *honeybees forage for pollen and nectar.*

Geranium arabicum *Forssk. /*
Geraniaceae

A hairy perennial herb with stems rooting at the nodes or sometimes scrambling through other plants and occasionally (at high altitudes) forming dense tufts growing to 60 cm high. Leaves orbicular, opposite and solitary. Flowers white with pink veins.

All parts give off a distinct geranium smell when crushed.

Growing in evergreen shrub, in grassland regions extending into the alpine belt at altitudes from 1300 to 4000 m.

This species is very variable and three subspecies have been recognized.

Flowering during and after the rains, *honeybees collect pollen and nectar from the flowers frequently.*

Geranium ocellatum *Cambess. /*
Geraniaceae

An ascending annual, diffusely branched herb with spreading hairs or glands. Stems are prostrate or ascending and growing to 2m long. Leaves orbicular and palmatisect. Flowers pink to dark purple, in pairs in the leaf axils.

All parts smell of geranium oil when crushed.

Found in meadows, along forest edges and in fields, growing at altitudes between 1500 and 2700 m.

Flowering during September and October, *honeybees collect pollen and nectar from the flowers frequently.*

Mansonia angustifolia *E.Mey. ex A.Rich. /* Geraniaceae

An annual herb with slightly succulent stems growing to 45 cm long. Small plants are erect, larger plants become decumbent and much branched. Leaves opposite, linear to narrowly elliptic or lanceolate and toothed. Flowers are pale mauve to blue with darker veins, less often white or pink, rarely yellow.

Growing in a variety of open habitats in grassland, bushland and open woodland and sometimes as a weed in crops and fallow land at altitudes between 1000 and 2800 m.

Flowering from September to December, *honeybees forage for pollen and nectar.*

Pelargonium multibracteatum
Hochst. in A.Rich. / Geraniaceae
DEBBESOM (Tya)

A perennial low-growing or scandent herb, well-branched with stens to 2 m long growing from a tuberous and fleshy rootstock. Stems smooth and somewhat succulent. Leaves simple and orbicular with 5 lobes. Flowers sweet-scented, usually white, rarely pale pink, 3-12 together, arranged in hanging clusters.

All parts of the plant smell strongly of geranium oil when crushed.

Widespread throughout the country in rocky places, particularly cliff edges and steep broken slopes, sometimes also in grassland or open savanna at altitudes from 1000 to 2700 m.

Flowering from May to December, *honeybees visit the plant for pollen and nectar.*

Hypericum peplidifolium

A.Rich / Guttiferae/Hypericaceae

ROSE OF SHARON (Eng)

A perennial herb, with prostrate to ascending stems up to 60 cm long. Leaves subsessile, in opposite pairs, ovate, elliptic or oblong to lanceolate with 7 main longitudinal veins. Flowers yellow, arranged in termin and lateral leafy branches.

Commonly found in damp grassland and meadows of the plateau and sub-Afroalpine regions, on disturbed ground and along stream sides at altitudes between 1600 and 3700 m.

Flowering almost all year round, *honeybees collect pollen from the flowers.*

Hypericum quartinianum

A.Rich. / Guttiferae / Hypericaceae

AMJA (Amh); GORGORO, HINNEH, MITO, GARAMBA, MUKOFONI (Or); AWETSCHA (Tya)

Mostly a much-branched shrub, sometimes a small tree. Leaves opposite, glossy green; sessile, oblong-elliptic with gland dots. Flowers golden yellow and large, up to 6 cm in diameter, arranged in few-flowered terminal clusters.

Widespread in the western parts of the country, in bushland, evergreen wooded grassland, wet evergreen woodland and forest margins at altitudes from 2000 to 3000 m.

Flowering all year round, but particularly from September to February, *honeybees collect abundant pollen from the flowers frequently. Because of its flowering time and its rich pollen supply this shrub is a valuable bee plant for strengthening bee colonies.*

Phacelia tanacetifolia *Benth.* / Hydrophyllaceae

PHACELIA (Eng); BÜSCHELSCHÖN (German)

An introduced cultivated annual, up to 70 cm high, with hairy stems, which are hollow and much-branched, so that the plant is often falls down if there are heavy rains. Flowers in conspicuous heads which are pink-purplish.

In temperate countries this is an important plant for green manure, but in Ethiopia this plant is only used as an ornamental in public and private gardens.

Flowering during and after rains. As a supplementary feed resource it is a valuable honeybee plant. *Honeybees collect pollen and some nectar very frequently.*

Achyrospermum schimperi

(Hochst.) Perkins. / Lamiaceae

BALANDALECHA (Or)

A stiff, woody, erect herb or subshrub growing to 2 m high. Leaves broad-elliptic or narrowly ovate. Flowers pink, pale purple or white, in dense terminal spikes.

Usually growing in partial shade, it is found in forests, at forest margins, in bushland, coffee plantations, and hedges at altitudes between 1200 and 2900 m.

Flowering from August to January, *honeybees collect pollen and nectar from the flowers frequently.*

Aeollanthus abyssinicus
Hochst. ex Benth. / Lamiaceae

An endemic, perennial herb with tuberous or woody roots and many stems, either erect or lying on the ground, up to 50 cm long. Leaves subsessile, lanceolate or linear with widely-spaced teeth on the margins. Flowers conspicuous pale lilac, in spikes on ascending flowering stalks.

Only found in Ethiopia, it grows on shallow soils over rocks, also in wooded grassland and on sloping ground where there is water seepage, between 1600 and 3100 m.

Flowering from May to September, *Honeybees visit the flowers for pollen and the abundant nectar. This plant plays an important role for strengthening bee colonies after the June honey harvest.*

Ajuga integrifolia *Ham.-Buch.*
(synonym *A. remota* Benth.) / Lamiaceae

MEDANIT, ARMAGUSA (Amh); BSSANA (Am & Tya); A'NGO-GUASOT (Tya); TALE (Wel)

A herb often lying on the ground and rooting at the nodes, covered with soft hairs, stems growing to 40 cm high. Leaves oblanceolate and coarsely toothed. Flowers small, pale blue, white or pale violet found in small clusters in the leaf axils.

A common herb of wetter areas in disturbed grassland, along roadsides and in ditches. It is found between 1500 to 3200 m.

Widely used in local medicine.

Flowering from late August to October, *honeybees are frequently visiting the flowers for pollen and nectar.*

Becium grandiflorum *(Lam.)*
Pichi-Sermolli / Lamiaceae

MATOSCH (Amh); ISKEE (Tre) TEBEB (Tya);

A small aromatic shrub or subshrub with light brown bark growing to 1.5 m tall. Leaves light green with a slightly toothed margin and a fairly strong acrid smell when crushed. Flowers large, pale pink with violet veins, arranged in terminal inflorescences.

Endemic to the Ethiopian highlands, growing on eroded soils, particularly rocky slopes, and sandy ground, in montane bushland and pastures, between 1600 to 3100 m.

In local medicine the herb is used against malaria.

Flowering throughout the year but more profusely after the short rains. *Honeybees visit the flowers for pollen and nectar. This plant is particularly important as a honey source in the northern parts of the country.*

Isodon schimperi *(Vatke) Morton*
(synonym *Plectranthus schimperi* Vatke) / Lamiaceae

YEFYEL-GOMEN (Amh)

A much-branched annual with slender fragile glabrous stems growing to 3 m high. Leaves ovate, acute, toothed and slightly hairy. Flowers white to pale-blue, in whorls in the axils of the upper leaves forming a terminal panicle.

Commonly found in hedges and in montane forest edges between 1000 and 2800 m.

Flowering from July to February but more profusely after the big rains up to December. *Honeybees frequently collect pollen and nectar from the flowers.*

Leonotis ocymifolia *(Burm. F.)* Iwarsson var. **raineriana**
(Visiani) Iwarsson (synonyms *L. mollisima* Guerke and *L. velutina* Fenzl.) / Lamiaceae

RAS KMR (Amh)

An erect and stiff woody herb or shrub up to 3 m tall. Leaves rough, heart-shaped, which have a strong smelling when crushed. Flowers large, hairy, orange, borne in dense whorls.

Growing around houses, along roadsides and abundant at forest edges and montane bushland between 1500 and 3400 m.

In local medicine the leaves are used against hook worms. Flowers and roots are used against gout, leishmaniasis and MISHIRO NEKERSA.

Its flowers attract sunbirds and are found from October to March and also in May. It has abundant nectar, *honeybees collect pollen and nectar from the flowers.*

Leucas abyssinica *(Benth) Briq.* / Lamiaceae

A shrub growing to 2.5 m tall. Leaves linear to obovate, up to 8 cm long and grey-green to white. Flowers white and arranged in many-flowered erect cymes.

Very variable with 4 subspecies recognized, one of which is endemic to northern Ethiopia.

Widespread in many disturbed habitats, particularly mountain bushland between 1300 and 2600 m.

In traditional medicine the roots are used against haemorrhoids.

Flowering from September to November, *honeybees collect pollen and nectar from the flowers.*

Leucas martinicensis *(Jacq.)* R.Br. / Lamiaceae

RAS KMR (Amh); JIMAERTU, BOCCU-FARDA (Or); KATATR (Tya); BOBBIN WEED (Eng)

An erect herb growing to 1 m tall. Leaves ovate to elliptic, with toothed margins. Flowers white with spiny calyces, in tight whorls borne in the axils of the upper leaves.

Growing in disturbed bushland and grassland and also as a weed between 800 and 2500 m.

Some plants can be found flowering at any time in the year. *Honeybees collect pollen and nectar from the flowers.*

Mentha spicata L. /Lamiaceae

ANANA (Amh & Or); COMMON GREEN MINT (Eng); GRÜNE ROßMINZE (German)

A perennial herb growing to 60 cm high, spreading by creeping rhizomes in moist soil. Leaves opposite, nearly sessile, up to 7 cm long with toothed margins. Flowers pink to violet, arranged in whorls on up to 10 cm long spikes.

Cultivated in homegardens at altitudes up to 2500 m.

Commonly used as a condiment in tea. In traditional medicine the whole herb is used against the common cold and headaches.

Flowering all year round, *honeybees are very frequently visiting the flowers for the nectar and some pollen.*

Nepeta azurea R.Br. ex Benth. / Lamiaceae

DAMAKA (Amh); ABBAAHRAH (Tya)

A woody and hairy herb growing to 2 m tall. Leaves lanceolate or sometimes ovate and usually greyish below with toothed margins. Flowers usually bright blue, sometimes purplish, sometimes whitish, found in whorls in unbranched erect inflorescences.

Growing in grassland and open bushland, usually where there is some water like river banks and seepage ground on hillsides between 2000 and 3400 m.

In local medicine the leaves are used against headache.

Flowering from August to December, *honeybees visit the flowers all day round*.

Ocimum basilicum L. / Lamiaceae

BESO-BLA, ADJUBAN, HULKOT, ZAKAKEWE (Amh); KASSE, KEFO, KENDAMA, URGO, ZAHAHENE (Or); SESEG (Tya); SWEET BASIL (Eng); BASILIKUM (German)

An erect, branching annual growing to 75 cm high. Leaves ovate to lanceolate and simple, light to purplish green with toothed margins. Flowers small, pale blue-mauve to purple, borne in racemes up to 30 cm long.

Cultivated throughout the country as a culinary herb in home gardens at altitudes between 1000 and 2600 m.

Leaves and inflorescences are widely used as a flavouring agent in preparing BRBERE and all kinds of WOT.

Flowering all year round, *honeybees collect pollen and the abundant nectar from the flowers throughout the day and it is a honey plant*.

Ocimum lamiifolium Hochst. ex Benth. / Lamiaceae

DAMA-KESIE (Amh); DARGU, MUCA MICHIANCHABI, DAMAKESEH (Or); DAMAKHER (Tya)

An erect, robust branching shrub or herb growing to 3 m tall. Leaves ovate and opposite. Flowers pinkish in racemes.

Growing beside roads and streams, in bushland and at forest edges and on grassland between 1200 to 2900 m.

Leaves are used against eye diseases and headachea.

Flowering from April to December, *honeybees collect pollen and nectar from the flowers frequently. The plant is a good honey source.*

Ocimum urticifolium Roth. / Lamiaceae

BESO BLA (Amh); DAMAKASE (Had); ANGIABI (Or)

A perennial herb or shrub, often densely and profusely branched, up to 3 m high. Leaves entire, petioled with prominent pinnate venetian. Flowers small, white, sweet-scented, found in whorls in spikes.

This plant is widely cultivated in home gardens and is common on shallow soils, evergreen bushland between 600 and 2200 m.

The leaves and flowers are used in local medicine against headaches and skin problems and the sap against eye disease and typhus.

Flowering all year round but most profusely after the rains, *honeybees collect pollen and nectar from the flowers frequently.*

Origanum majorana L. /
Lamiaceae

HASSAB (Amh); SWEET MARJORAM
(Eng); OREGANO (Italian); MAJORAN
(German)

A herb or small shrub, growing to 40
cm high. Leaves ovate to elliptic with a
strong pleasant smell when crushed.
Flowers pale pink to pale lilac,
arranged on erect elongated panicles.

Native to Cyprus and southern Turkey,
it is cultivated as a herb in home
gardens to 2600 m.

This is an important spice in Italian
cooking and provides an aromatic
volatile oil.

Flowering throughout the year,
*honeybees forage for the abundant
nectar and pollen throughout the day.*

Otostegia integrifolia Benth. /
Lamiaceae

MARARAJA, TENGYUT, T'NJUT (Amh &
Tya); TUNGIT (Or); CH'NDOG (Tya)

An erect perennial, spiny, much-
branched shrub growing to 3 m tall.
Leaves grey-green lanceolate. Flowers
hairy, yellow and white, borne in erect
racemes. The flowers fall quickly,
leaving the papery yellow calyx.

Widespread throughout the plateau,
found particularly on rocky slopes and
around houses between 1700 and
2500 m.

O. integrifolia is said to have
insecticidal properties and is often
used as a fumigant for pots and
houses. The roots are used for treating
lung diseases.

Flowering all year round, *honeybees
often collect pollen and nectar from
the flowers.*

Otostegia tomentosa subsp.
ambigiens *(Chiov.) Sebald* /
Lamiaceae

YEFERES-ZENG (Amh); ILILI ADDI (Or);
HORSE-WHIP (Eng)

A small to medium shrub growing to 4
m tall. Leaves sessile and lanceolate.
Flowers hairy, white, funnel-shaped on
spineless stems. The white, papery
calyx remains after flowers fall.

Found in mountain scrub, on stony
hillsides and along paths between
1500 and 2700 m.

In local medicine the roots are used
against bloat.

Flowering almost all year round but
more profusely after the big rains to
January, *honeybees collect both
pollen and nectar from the flowers.*

Plectranthus assurgens
(Beaker) Morton / Lamiaceae
AJOFTU (Or)

A perennial, aromatic, straggling to
scrambling herb, with stems up to 150
cm long. Leaves triangular lanceolate
to ovate. Flowers purple-blue, in
whorls in lax terminal panicles.

Commonly found in openings and
clearings in moist forests and
woodland between 1800 and 2800 m.

Flowering from September to March,
*bees forage for nectar and pollen
throughout the day.*

Plectranthus barbatus *Andr.*

(synonym *Coleus speciosus* Baker) / Lamiaceae

YEMARYAM-WEHA-QEJI, YE-FIYEL-DOKA (Amh)

An erect, softly hairy herb or small shrub, occasionally growing to 4 m tall. Leaves ovate or ovate-elliptic, strongly-scented and covered with short, soft hairs. Flowers blue, in whorls found in long terminal spikes.

Commonly cultivated in gardens, it grows wild on dry rocky slopes, in degraded and open bushland, along roadsides and in dry rocky woodland between 1000 to 2700 m.

Though not poisonous, it is not eaten by domestic stock.

Flowering from September to February, *honeybees frequently collect pollen and nectar from the flowers. The plant is a good honey source.*

Plectranthus garckeanus *Vatke*

/ Lamiaceae

A perennial herb with an unpleasant somewhat rotten smell growing to 3 m tall. Leaves large, lanceolate with toothed margins. Flowers brilliant blue, in whorls on long erect terminal panicles.

Endemic, growing and often forming a dense mass in montane forest, forest openings and thickets from 1800 to 2700 m.

Flowering from August to December, it is commonly visited by "carpenter bees", *honeybees for pollen and nectar.*

Plectranthus lanunginosus

(Benth.) Agnews / Lamiaceae

DAMACSE (Or); ZOMMER (Tya)

A hairy, trailing, somewhat fleshy herb, with stems growing to 30 cm long. Leaves orbicular, wide-elliptic to ovate. Flowers bright blue, in whorls found in terminal, ascending, simple racemes.

Found in dry upland grassland and on mountain slopes, in deciduous woodland and forest, also commonly growing along paths and roadsides between 400 and 3400 m.

In local medicine the sap is used against headaches.

Flowering throughout the year, but mostly during and after the rains, *bees forage for the abundant nectar and pollen.*

Plectranthus ornatus *Codd.* /

Lamiaceae

INDEFDELE (Tre)

A coarse, woody and hairy, semi-succulent herb up to 1 m tall. Leaves obovate, with toothed margins. They have an unpleasant smell when crushed. Flowers blue to purple-blue, in whorls arranged in dense terminal spikes.

Growing on rocky ground, in grassland and cultivated land between 1300 and 3500 m.

Flowering profusely after the rains but also throughout the year, *honeybees often collect pollen and nectar. This herb is an important honey source.*

114

Plectranthus punctatus L'Hérit.
/ Lamiaceae

A pubescent annual or perennial herb growing to 75 cm high. Leaves elliptic, broadly-ovate and finally toothed. Flowers blue to blue-violet in few-flowered whorls.

Growing on damp areas, along roadsides, in evergreen bushland and along forest edges between 1400 and 3200 m.

This is the wild subspecies of the cultivated plant described below.

Flowering throughout the year, but more profusely after rains, *honeybees frequently collect pollen and nectar from the flowers. This is a good honey source.*

Plectranthus punctatus subsp. edulis *(Vatke) Morton* (synonym *Coleus edulis* Vatke)

DNCH, YEWOLLAMO-DNCH, YEOROMO-DNCH (Amh); DONIKE, BARBARASH (Or)

Similar to the wild species but producing swollen underground tubers, larger leaves and stouter stems.

Cultivated for its edible root tubers in the west, southwest and southern parts of the country between 1300 and 2600 m.

The edible tubers have a fine starch grain and are good for invalids and people with asthma. The leaves are used for treating bloat.

Flowering from April to January, *bees forage all day for the abundant nectar and some pollen. In cultivation the plant is a good honey source.*

Pycnostachys abyssinica
Fresen. / Lamiaceae

TONTAN (Amh); BOBANKA (Had); OLOMO (Wel)

An erect woody, much-branched shrub growing to 3 m high. Leaves large, lanceolate to ovate. Flowers bluish to violet, in numerous terminal spikes.

Endemic, found growing in wet montane forest and scrub and also a very common hedge-forming plant found in the southwest between 1100 and 2700 m.

Flowering from the middle of the big rains from August to March, *honeybees frequently collect pollen and nectar from the flowers.*

Pycnostachys eminii *Gurke* / Lamiaceae

ASHOALA (Had)

An erect woody herb or shrub growing to 3 m tall. Leaves ovate and acute. Flowers blue or violet, in whorls arranged in dense terminal spikes.

The pulverised leaves are have a strong distinctive smell.

Growing on waste ground, among bushes and in undergrowth; commonly found as a roadside shrub, and sometimes as a hedge plant, in partial shade at forest edges and on moist grassland between 1500 and 2200 m.

Flowering from September to March, *the plant is important for strengthening bee colonies after the harvesting period in November. Honeybees are very frequently visiting the flowers for pollen and nectar.*

Pycnostachys reticulata *(E. Mey.) Benth.* / Lamiaceae

An erect, perennial herb growing to 2 m tall. Leaves opposite, dull greyish-green to yellowish green and narrow-lanceolate to narrow-elliptic. Flowers blue, in whorls arranged in dense terminal spikes.

The pulverized leaves have a strong smell.

Growing in marshy ground, grassland, beside paths, and in partial shade of trees; common in secondary growth of evergreen forests between 1400 and 2000 m.

Flowering from October to November, *honeybees forage for nectar and some pollen throughout the day.*

Rosmarinus officinalis *L.* / Lamiaceae

ROSMARINO, YE'TBS-QTEL (Amh); KORA (Or); ROSEMARY (Eng); ROSMARIN (German)

A shrub growing to 2 m high, with densely-leafy erect branches. Leaves persistent, linear, up to 2 cm long, dark olive green. Flowers white to pale blue, in small clusters in the leaf axils at the tops of stems.

A cultivated spice plant from the Mediterranean, now planted in many gardens between 1800 and 2400 m.

Flowering throughout the year but mainly after the big rains from September to February, *honeybees collect pollen and abundant nectar from the flowers throughout the year.*

Salvia leucantha *Cav.* / Lamiaceae

SAGE (Eng)

A small weak-stemmed shrub growing to 80 cm tall with stems and leaves densely covered with whitish hairs. Leaves lanceolate and often whitish beneath. Flowers hairy, white or violet, arranged in long one-sided hairy racemes.

Introduced from Mexico and cultivated in home gardens this plant has escaped into dry grassland and other man-made habitats up to 2600 m.

Flowering all year round the *flowers are frequently visited by honeybees for nectar only.*

Salvia merjamie *Forssk.* / Lamiaceae

ANTATEH-WOLLAKHA (Tya)

An erect perennial herb, very variable in shape and size, with stems up to 40 cm tall growing from a rosette of leaves. Leaves oblong, often lobed and somewhat rough to touch. Flowers white, pale yellowish or purple to bluish, in terminal racemes.

Very common in grassland, open woodland and scrub, on bare ground and often at roadsides or on hillsides between 2200 and 4200 m.

In local medicine the plant is used against throat inflammations.

Flowering all year round but more profusely after the rains from September to November, *honeybees collect pollen and nectar from the flowers very frequently.*

Salvia nilotica *Juss. ex Jacq.* / Lamiaceae

BASOBILA (Amh); SOKOKSA (Or); ANTATE WOLLAKHA, ENTATIE VALLAHA, FERESHEI (Tya)

A rhizomatous, perennial herb covered with stiff coarse hairs. Leaves usually lobed, ovate, often in basal rosettes. Flowers mostly blue-violet but sometimes white, violet or pink, arranged in cymes.

Very common in grassland, meadows and along roadsides between 1800 and 3800 m.

In local medicine it is used as a pain-killer, against sunburns and as medicine after vomiting.

Flowering profusely both during and after the rains, *honeybees collect pollen and nectar from the flowers frequently. This plant is an important honey source in higher altitudes.*

Salvia schimperi *Benth.* / Lamiaceae

ABBADERA (Tya)

A perennial strongly fragrant herb growing from a woody rootstock up to 80 cm high with a stout stem. Leaves ovate to almost elliptic with prominent veins. Flowers usually white flushed with blue or lilac, arranged in 1-3-flowered erect cymes.

Found on dry, open places, often on bare and sloping stony ground at altitudes between 1800 and 3200 m.

Flowering almost all year round, *honeybees forage for pollen and abundant nectar from the flowers. This plant is very important for beekeepers especially in dry and eroded habitats.*

Salvia officinalis *L.* / Lamiaceae

SALBEI (German); GARDEN SAGE (Eng)

An erect subshrub growing to 80 cm tall. The stems are erect from a woody rootstock. Leaves lanceolate and rough, very aromatic when crushed. Flowers pale violet, pink, blue or white and arranged in whorls.

Native to the Mediterranean, it is cultivated in home gardens up to 2600 m for ornament or as a spice.

Flowering throughout the year, *honeybees collect abundant nectar and some pollen throughout the day.*

Salvia splendens *Sello ex Roem. et Schult.* / Lamiaceae

A robust erect shrub or subshrub, usually with several erect branched stems which grow to 80 cm. Leaves elliptic to ovate with toothed margins. Flowers conspicuous red or violet, in long erect racemes.

Not known wild in Ethiopia; commonly cultivated as an ornamental and as a decorative hedge-forming plant in public and private gardens from 500 to 2400 m.

Flowering throughout the year, *honeybees collect pollen and nectar from the flowers.*

Satureja abyssinica *(Benth.)* *Briq.* / Lamiaceae

SASSAG WUCHARIA, BUTTANSA, BUTLANSA, JELOMISCET, MUTANSA (Amh); SESSEG-GOLLA (Tya)

An annual or perennial herb with ascending stems up to 80 cm high from a woody rootstock. Leaves broadly-ovate to elliptic. Flowers white to pale-purple, in loose terminal racemes.

Growing on stony slopes and grassland, in open woodland between 900 and 2700 m.

Flowering profusely after the big rains from September to December, *Honeybees frequently collect pollen and nectar from the flowers.*

Satureja paradoxa *(Vatke) Engler ex Seybold* / Lamiaceae

TOSGN, ZENADDAM, NADDO (Amh); TENADDAM (Or)

An endemic, erect, weak-stemmed, perennial herb with runners, 20 to 40 cm long. Leaves entire and elliptic. Flowers violet to pink, in head-like axillary clusters.

This aromatic herb is widely used as a condiment.

Growing in masses along streams banks and on moist soils in open and shady grassland, in forests, rarely a weed in tea-plantations. Its altitudinal range is from 1350 to 3200 m.

Flowering during and after the rains, *honeybees collect pollen and abundant nectar from the flowers very frequently and the plant is a honey source.*

Satureja punctata *(Benth.) Briq.* / Lamiaceae

TOSGN, YELOSKIT (Amh); DOK (Gur); TOSSINGO (Or)

A very variable woody herb or shrub from creeping shrublets with small lanceolate leaves to erect shrubs to 100 cm high with broad ovate leaves. Flowers mostly pale purple, sometimes red or violet, arranged in axillary clusters.

The stems are strongly lemon-scented when crushed.

Commonly growing on rocky slopes, and upland dry grassland in the Afro-alpine zone between 600 and 3800 m.

In local medicine leaves are used against fever and common cold.

Flowering all year round but more profusely after rains, *honeybees collect pollen and nectar from the flowers frequently and it is a honey source.*

Satureja simensis *(Benth.) Briq.* / Lamiaceae

SESSEG-WU'KARIA (Tya)

A low prostrate or small ascending, wiry shrub. Leaves ovate with cordate bases. Flowers small, generally pink, also white or rose or lilac, in dense clusters forming broken whorls in the leaf axils.

Found on rocky slopes and marshy ground, in forests and moist grassland to the Afro-alpine zone between 2600 and 4100 m.

Flowering all year round but profusely during and after the rains, *the plant is a rich nectar source and is particularly important for bees at high altitudes.*

Stachys aculeolata *Hook.f.* / Lamiaceae

A sometimes erect, but more often a scrambling or prostrate perennial with ascending flowering branches, up to 3 m long. Leaves heart-shaped, cordate and acuminate with stiff hairs on the upper surface. Flowers large, pink to red, appearing one at a time from the leaf axils.

Found in edges of wet montane forest, wet upland grassland, and very common in the undergrowth of *Erica* shrub between 1900 and 3900 m.

Flowering all year round, *bees work on the flowers all day round. They collect pollen and nectar from the flowers frequently.*

Thymus schimperi *Roninger* / Lamiaceae

TOSGN (Amh), THYME (Eng)

A low, much-branched spreading shrubby herb, up to 30 cm high. Leaves strong smelling, small and entire. Flowers purplish-pink in terminal heads.

The whole plant gives off the characteristic smell of thyme.

Found abundantly in Afro-alpine areas, also in *Erica arborea* scrub and montane grassland between 2300 and 3800 m.

An important spice in local food and herb in local medicine.

Forming dense carpets spreading up to 10 m in diameter, the scented flowers attract large numbers of bees during the main flowering period of March to June. Some plants are found flowering all year round. *Honeybees collect nectar and pollen and the plant is an important honey source.*

Aeschynomene abyssinica *(A. Rich.) Vatke* / Leguminosae (Fabaceae) - Papilionoideae

An erect herb or shrub growing to 4.5 m tall. Stems sometimes covered with sticky hairs. Leaves with asymmetric crowded linear to oblanceolate leaflets. Flowers yellow.

Growing in grassland, woodland or scrub, also beside roadsides, and other disturbed areas between 1300 and 2900 m.

Flowering from September to May, *honeybees collect pollen and nectar from the flowers very frequently. The long lasting flowering period makes this plant very useful for colony maintenance and stimulating brood rearing.*

Aeschynomene americana *L.* / Leguminosae (Fabaceae) - Papilionoideae

A sprawling herb to 60 cm high. Leaves with with 20-60 closely crowded leaflets and a few-flowered inflorescence. Flowers pale pink with yellowish central spot.

Naturalised in southwestern Ethiopia at altitudes of about 1000 m, it is found along roadsides, in forest clearings and even cultivated for fodder. A native of tropical and subtropical America.

Flowering after the big rains up to January, *honeybees frequent visit the flowers for pollen and nectar. Where this plant is plentiful it can provide a honey flow.*

Argyrolobium ramosissimum

Bak. / Leguminosae (Fabaceae) - Papilionoideae

GERENGERE (Amh)

A straggling slender-stemmed perennial growing to 70 cm tall with woody spreading stems. Leaves elliptic-obovate and hairy. Flowers yellow.

Growing in upland grassland and bushland, at forest margins at altitudes between 2000 and 3550 m.

Flowering from July to November when it sometimes forms dense carpets, *honeybees collect pollen and nectar from the flowers frequently.*

Astralagus atropilosulus

(Hochst.) Bunge Leguminosae (Fabaceae) - Papilionoideae

H'AMAT-KAKI'TO, T'ET'EM-AGAZEN (Tya)

A perennial herb or small shrub growing to 60 cm high. Leaves imparipinnate, up to 25 cm long with 11-51 leaflets which are oppositely or suboppositely arranged, narrowly elliptic or lanceolate. Flowers pale green with purplish markings, on erect many-flowered racemes.

This is a very variable species with several endemic subspecies recognised.

Found in upland grassland, on rocky places at altitudes between 1500 and 2400 m.

Flowering from August to February, *honeybees forage for pollen and nectar.*

Caesalpina decapetala *(Roth)*

Alston / Leguminosae (Fabaceae) Caesalpinioideae

YEFERENJ-KTKTTA, QONT'R (Amh); MYSORE THORN (Eng)

A scrambling or climbing woody shrub with stems up to 10 m long, armed with scattered, sharp recurved prickles on the branches and leaf rhachides. Flowers yellow or yellowish white, in attractive, long, terminal, racemes.

A native of tropical Asia, but now naturalised and spread over much of Ethiopia in grassland and evergreen bushland, and frequently established on dry hillsides and valley slopes at altitudes from 1700 to 2400 m.

It is often used as a hedge plant, forming an impenetrable fence. The seeds are used to make necklaces.

Flowering from October to January, *honeybees collect pollen and nectar from the flowers.*

Caesalpina spinosa *(Molina)*

Kuntze / Leguminosae (Fabaceae) Caesalpinioideae

QONT'R (Amh)

A tree or shrub growing to 5 m tall with short paired and scattered prickles. Leaves bipinnate, pinnae 2-8 pairs, leaflets 4-8 pairs per pinna, oblong-ovate. Flowers yellow and arranged in terminal racemes.

Cultivated in some parts of the country, mostly in Shewa and Sidamo regions, at altitudes up to 2200 m.

Grown for ornament, and in hedges, the pods are used for dyeing and tanning.

Flowering from October to January, *honeybees forage for nectar and pollen and the plant is helpful for colony maintenance.*

Chamaecytisus proliferus (L.f.)
Link / Leguminosae (Fabaceae) - Papilionoideae

TAGASASTE, TREE LUCERNE (Eng)

An attractive evergreen shrub or small tree with long drooping branches. Leaves trifoliate with pale green, lanceolate leaflets. Flowers white, in terminal panicles, at the end of small branchlets.

Cultivated throughout the country in research stations and agricultural development programmes at altitudes up to 3200 m. Extremely drought resistant once established.

Flowering profusely after the big rains from September to October and also from April to May. *Honeybees visit the flowers frequently mainly for nectar.*

Cicer arietinum L. / Leguminosae
(Fabaceae) - Papilionoideae

SUMBURA (Ade & Afar); SHMBRA (Amh, Tya & Tre); SHUMBURA (Gam, Gur, Had, Or & Wel); SANT, ZIFAL, A'TER (Ge'ez & Tya); SUMBURO (Kem); ATIR (Saho); A'TER-QEYYH (Tya); CHICK PEA (Eng); KICHERERBSE (German)

An annual cultivated herb covered with glandular hairs which produce a weak solution of acetic acid. Leaves pinnate with 3-8 pairs of leaflets which are oblong and serrate. Flowers bluish-pink to white.

Cultivated throughout the highlands for its edible seeds up to 2100 m.

In local medicine the fruits and roots are used against liver disease and KOFA.

Flowering profusely from October to February, *honeybees collect nectar and pollen and the plant is a honey source.*

Desmodium intortum (Mill.) Urb.
Leguminosae (Fabaceae) - Papilionoideae

GREEN LEAF DESMODIUM (Eng)

A scrambling perennial herb with ascending flowering stems growing several meters long. Stems densely covered with hooked hairs. Leaves trifoliate with narrowly ovate leaflets. Flowers pink to red in lax unbranched inflorescences.

Introduced to improve forage production, now cultivated in some areas and found as an escape along roadsides, in evergreen bushland and farmland at altitudes between 1700 and 2100 m.

The closely related *D. uncinatum* (Jacq.) DC. with which *D.intortum* is often combined has pale silvery markings along the midrib above and is also found as an escape.

Flowering from September to December, *honeybees forage for pollen and nectar.*

Desmodium repandum (Vahl)
DC. Leguminosae (Fabaceae) - Papilionoideae

A perennial herb or a slender shrub growing to 1 m tall. Leaves pinnately trifoliate, with rhombic leaflets. Flowers pink to brick red, arranged in terminal or axillary lax panicles.

Found at forest edges, in clearings and along streambanks and paths at altitudes between 1600 and 2700 m.

Flowering from December to May, *bees forage for pollen and nectar.*

Dichrostachys cinera (L.) Wight & Arn. Leguminosae (Fabaceae) - Mimosoideae

ADER, ARSHE-MERSHA (Amh); GARGARU, GERGERU (Gam & Wel); ADESSA, GIRMI, GRMA, HATTE, JEREMME (Or); CALENTA (Kon); DHAY-DHAY, DHIGDAR, GALOÖL-SUR (Som); ARSHAMARSHA, GWENEQW, KENEY (Tya)

A shrub or small tree, armed with spines and growing to 5 m tall. Leaves with 4-19 pairs of pinnae, each with 9-41 pairs of leaflets, linear to oblong. Flower heads hanging, upper part yellow, lower part mauve, pink or white.

Found in woodland and bushland at altitudes between 500 and 2000 m.

Flowering from February to May, *honeybees frequently forage for pollen and nectar.*

Glycine max (L.) Merr. / Leguminosae (Fabaceae) - Papilionoideae

AKWRI-ATER (Amh); SOYBEAN (Eng)

A bushy annual crop plant with all parts distinctly hairy. Leaves trifoliolate with leaflets up to 15 cm long. Flowers white to bluish borne in the leaf axils.

A native of China, now grown on some mechanised farms in Gojam and elsewhere around 1900 m. Used as a major ingredient in a locally-produced infant food, FAFA, and to produce a milk substitute.

Its value for honey production is variable and depends on the environment and on the use of insecticides. *Honeybees collect nectar and pollen and the plant can be a honey source.*

Glycine wightii (Wight & Arn.) Verdc. var longicauda (Schweinf.) Verdc. (synonym Neonotonia wightii (Wight & Arn.) Lackey) / Leguminosae (Fabaceae) - Papilionoideae

AKURI (Amh); GLYCINE (Eng)

A climbing perennial with slightly hairy to velvety stems to 2 m long. Leaflets ovate to elliptic. Flowers white.

There are two subspecies, one with white flowers 4.5 to 7.5 mm long and the other with blue or mauve flowers 8 to 11 mm long in many-flowered racemes.

The white-flowered subspecies is very common, growing in grassland, woodland and sometimes in fields at altitudes between 380 and 2600 m.

Flowering from September to November, *honeybees collect pollen and nectar from the flowers frequently and where this plant is plentiful it is a honey source.*

Glycine wightii (Wight. & Arn.) Verdc. subsp. petitiana (A.Rich.) Verdc. / Papilionoideae

DOLMUNCHA (Had)

A climbing perennial with slightly hairy to velvety stems to 3 m long. Flowers blue or mauve in erect many-flowered racemes.

This subspecies is also very common found in upland forest and bushland at altitudes between 2100 to 2800 m.

It is valued for its drought resistance and therefore a good animal food.

Flowering from September to November, *honeybees collect pollen and nectar from the flowers frequently and the plant is an important stimulus for bee colonies.*

Indigofera zavattarii *Chiov.*
Leguminosae (Fabaceae) -
Papilionoideae

A perennial herb growing to 50 cm
high and covered with silvery hairs.
Leaves with 5-7 opposite leaflets which
are cuneate-oblong or oblanceolate.
Flowers red, arranged in 1-4 flowered
axillary racemes.

Found on rocky hillsides, along
roadsides and on heavily grazed
slopes at altitudes between 1200 and
2300 m.

Flowering from September to
November, *honeybees forage for
pollen and nectar.*

Lablab purpureus *(L.) Sweet /*
Leguminosae (Fabaceae) -
Papilionoideae

YEÄMORA-GWAYA (Amh); GERENGA
(Bil); OKALA (Kon); HYACINTH BEAN,
LABLAB (Eng)

A climbing perennial herb with stems
growing to 2 m long. Leaves 3-foliate
with ovate-triangular leaflets. Flowers
large, white, purple or crimson,
arranged in axillary raceme-like
inflorescences.

Found in grassland, bushland and
gallery forests and also cultivated for
its edible seeds and as a hedging
plant at altitudes between 400 and
2350 m.

Flowering from October to April,
honeybees gather pollen and nectar.

Lathyrus sativus *L. /*
Leguminosae (Fabaceae) -
Papilionoideae

GWAYYA (Amh); GAYYA (Gur & Or);
GAYU (Or); SEBBERE (Tya & Saho);
GRASS PEA (Eng); SAATPLATTERBSE
(German)

A glabrous annual herb, 30-50 cm
high. Leaves with 2 leaflets, narrowly
elliptic-oblong. Flowers violet-blue or
white.

Cultivated for its edible seeds on
residual moisture in vertisols and for
fodder at medium altitudes up to 2300
m. In local medicine the plant is used
as a pain-killer for children. But, if
GRASS PEA exceeds 30 per cent of diet,
it can cause lathyrism.

Flowering from September to May,
*honeybees collect nectar and pollen
very frequently and the plant is a
honey source.*

Lotus discolor *E.Mey.*
Leguminosae (Fabaceae) -
Papilionoideae

A perennial often bushy herb growing
from a woody rootstock, with
spreading stems up to 30 cm long.
Leaflets very variable in size and
shape, cuneate-ovate to oblanceolate.
Flowers white with pink markings,
arranged in umbels.

Found in upland grassland, scrub or
forest edges at altitudes between 2000
and 4000 m.

Flowering throughout the year but
profusely after the main rains,
*honeybees forage frequently for the
abundant nectar and some pollen.
Where this plant is plentiful it is a very
important honey source. It seems also
that this species is the most important
bee plant of this genus*

Lupinus albus L. Leguminosae (Fabaceae) - Papilionoideae

GBTO (Amh & Tya); WHITE LUPIN, EGYPTIAN LUPIN (Eng); WEIßLUPINE (German)

A bushy annual herb growing to 120 cm tall covered with short hairs. Leaflets: lower obovate and upper ones obovate-cuneate. Flowers white to blue, in 5-10 cm long racemes.

Native to the Mediterranean region, in Ethiopia it is cultivated in for its seeds, particularly in province of Gojjam. It also grows wild at altitudes between 1800 and 3000 m.

The seeds are eaten after soaking for 2-3 days to remove the bitter taste and then boiling. They are also used to make high quality ARAKI.

Flowering from October to May, *honeybees forage both nectar and pollen.*

Lupinus angustifolius L. / Leguminosae (Fabaceae) - Papilionoideae

A somewhat bushy annual herb with stems to 100 cm high and digitately compound leaves. Flowers large, bright blue to white, in racemes.

This species is native to the Mediterranean region and is now introduced and partly naturalized in some parts of Ethiopia at altitudes between 1800 and 2400 m.

Pods are used for fodder and the plant can be used for silage.

Flowering after the big rains from September to December, *honeybees collect pollen and nectar from the flowers. Honeybees are important pollinators of lupins to increase the number and weight of seeds produced.*

Macroptilium atropurpureum (DC.) Urb. / Leguminosae (Fabaceae) - Papilionoideae

PURPLE BEAN (Eng)

A creeping perennial herb with stems to 3 m long. Leaflets broadly ovate to 5 cm long and wide. Flowers striking, crimson to dark purple, on long stalks from the leaf axils.

Introduced as a forage plant, now locally naturalised in warmer areas between 750 and 1500 m altitude, particularly on lighter soils and irrigated areas.

Flowering from December to January or all year round in cultivation, *honeybees collect pollen and nectar from the flowers.*

Medicago polymorpha L. / Leguminosae (Fabaceae) - Papilionoideae

WAJEMA, KURNCHT (Amh); ASHU (Gum); KUMUTO, HAMAQITA (Or); KWA'KITO (Tya)

A prostrate and spreading annual herb with stems to 20 cm long. Leaves 3-foliolate. Flowers small, yellow, born in leaf axils. Fruits spirally coiled pods covered in hard spines.

Growing throughout the highlands in disturbed open habitats, pastures and as a weed at altitudes between 1400 and 3000 m.

An important pasture plant during dry season, but not suitable for sheep because the fruits become entangled in the wool.

Flowering from June to December, *honeybees gather copious nectar and pollen during favourable seasons. The flowers provide a good stimulus for colony development and occasionally a surplus of honey may be stored.*

Medicago sativa L. /
Leguminosae (Fabaceae) - Papilionoideae

ALFALFA, (Tya); ALFALFA, LUCERN (Eng); LUCERNE (German)

A hardy, deep-rooted, perennial legume with erect stems growing to 1 m tall. Leaves with 3 lanceolate leaflets. Flowers purplish blue, produced in racemes of 5-40 flowers.

M. sativa is grown for forage in both the highlands (2500 m) and lowlands down to 450 m and does very well under irrigation.

Flowers after any rain from July to February in the highlands or all year round under irrigation. *Honeybees collect nectar and pollen and the plant is an important honey source.*

Melilotus alba L. / Leguminosae
(Fabaceae) - Papilionoideae

WHITE MELILOT (Eng); STEINKLEE (German)

An annual or longer-lived woody herb growing to 1 m tall. Leaves 3-foliolate with toothed margins. Flowers white, strongly scented, in many-flowered racemes. All parts of the plant smell strongly of coumarin.

Introduced and now found naturalised on waste land and along roadside and also in gardens at altitudes to 2600 m.

A drought resistant plant used to improve and protect soil.

Flowering from June to February, *honeybees collect nectar and pollen and the plant is a honey source where it is plentiful.*

Melilotus suaveolens Ledeb.
(synonym *Melilotus officinalis*) / Leguminosae (Fabaceae) - Papilionoideae

TITAKO (Or); ECHTER STEINKLEE (German)

An erect herb up to 1 m or more tall. Flowers yellow with short calyces, in spike-like racemes. All parts smell strongly of coumarin.

An introduced plant which is drought resistant now found growing as a weed or cultivated at altitudes up to 2400 m.

Good for improving soil it can also be used for erosion control.

Flowering from October to February, *the nectar is readily reached by honeybees and other insects with short tongues that visit the flowers. Honeybees collect nectar and pollen and the plant is a honey source.*

Mimosa invasa Mart. ex Colla /
Leguminosae (Fabaceae) - Mimosoideae

A shrub often scrambling with stems up to 4.5 m long, densely armed with recurved prickles. Leaves sensitive, and close up if touched or moved violently. Flowers pale pink or pink in globose heads, on stalks in pairs.

Very common in western parts of Ethiopia where it is grown as a living fence. Also found along river banks, lake-shores, swamps and roadsides, and in forest clearings at altitudes from 1400 to 2000 m.

Flowering from November to March, *honeybees forage for the abundant nectar and pollen and the plant is a honey source.*

Parochaetus communis *D.Don*

Leguminosae (Fabaceae) - Papilionoideae

YEMDR-KOSO (Amh)

A creeping herb, rooting at the nodes, stems growing to 15 cm high. Leaves 3-foliate with leaflets cuneate-obovate, entire to crenate or coarsely toothed. Flowers bright blue on axillary stalks.

Found in upland forest, bamboo forest, especially in damp places, in clearings and along roadsides, under shade of trees and along river banks at altitudes between 1800 and 3500 m.

Flowering from August to April, *honeybees frequently visit the flowers for copious nectar and abundant pollen. Where the plant is plentiful it contributes significantly to strengthening colonies and even in providing a surplus of honey.*

Phaseolus coccineus *L.*

Leguminosae (Fabaceae) - Papilionoideae

SCARLET RUNNER BEAN (Eng); FEUERBOHNE (German)

A climbing annual or perennial herb. Leaflets ovate-rhombic and sparsely hairy. Flowers scarlet, less often white, in many-flowered inflorescences.

Native to America, now widely cultivated in temperate countries and nowadays grown in higher regions of Ethiopia at altitudes between 2000 and 2400 m at least in the Southwest and in Addis Ababa.

Flowering from September to February, *honeybees visiting the flowers for pollen and nectar when other bee feed is scarce.*

Phaseolus lunatus *L. /*

Leguminosae (Fabaceae) - Papilionoideae

LIMA BEAN (Eng)

A perennial or biennial climber to 3 m long. Leaflets ovate to lanceolate. Flowers white, in few-many-flowered lax inflorescences.

This introduced plant is now widely cultivated in western and southwestern parts and perhaps locally naturalized. It is found at altitudes to 2200 m.

Flowering plants are found almost all year round and profusely after rains. *Honeybees collect pollen and nectar.*

Pisum sativum *L. /* Leguminosae (Fabaceae) - Papilionoideae

ATER (Amh); QISHEWE (Gur); ATERE (Gur & Gof); ATERO, GITEE (Had); GISHI-SHAATO (Kef); ATERA, ATERA-DONGOLO, DANGULLE (Or); A'YNI-A'TER (Tya); ATARA, ATERIYYA (Wel); FIELD PEA, GARDEN PEA (Eng); ERBSE (German)

An annual herb climbing with tendrils, stems to 2 m long. Leaflets entire. Flowers white to pink wings and dark blue to purple keel.

A widely cultivated crop grown in the highlands of all regions up to 3000 m.

Flowering from September to October, *it is both self-pollinated and self-fertile and visited by honeybees only when other bee feed is scarce.*

Pterolobium stellatum *(Forssk.)*
Brenan / Leguminosae (Fabaceae)
Caesalpinioideae

QENT'AFFA (Amh); QONT'R (Amh &
Gur); SNDUQO (Gam); CEKA-QEMELE,
GARU, HARANGAMA, KAJIMA, QEQEWWI
(Or); LIBAH-HALALALIS (Som);
QONT'EFT'EFE (Tya); GOMÖRYYA
(Wel)

A well-armed climbing or straggling
shrub with a thick, knotted stem.
Leaves also with recurved prickles;
leaflets narrowly oblong or elliptic-
oblong. Flowers sweetly-scented, pale
creamy yellow, in dense terminal
racemes.

Commonly forming thickets in upland
dry evergreen degraded bushland,
also on forest margins and clearings,
and *Acacia* woodland at altitudes from
1200 to 2500 m.

Flowering after the big rains from
October to May, *honeybees collect
pollen and nectar from the flowers
very frequently and the plant is an
important bee plant producing even a
surplus of honey.*

Scorpiurus muricatus *L.* /
Leguminosae (Fabaceae) -
Papilionoideae

YEBEG-LAT (Amh); KOTEBAY (Or);
ERWE (Tya)

A common herb with stems to 20 cm
tall. Leaves simple lanceolate. Flower
yellow arising from leaf axils.

Found mostly on vertisols throughout
the plateau at altitudes between 2000
and 2800 m.

It flowers from August to November,
*honeybees collect pollen and nectar
from the flowers.*

Trifolium acaule *Steud. ex A.
Rich.* / Leguminosae (Fabaceae) -
Papilionoideae

MAGET, WAGGMA (Amh); SEEDDEESA
(Kef); MESI (Tya)

A small, perennial herb with a deep tap
root and stems usually flat on the
ground. Leaflets obcordate to
oblanceolate. Flower heads of 1-5
mauve or blue-violet flowers.

It grows on bare soil, in short grass
and rock crevices, forming a very
short, dense carpet spreading over
areas 2-3 m in diameter at altitudes
from 2400 to 4150 m.

It is a useful plant against erosion at
high altitudes.

Flowering throughout the year but
especially from June to December, *the
sweet-scented flowers attract large
numbers of bees and butterflies.
Honeybees collect pollen and nectar
from the flowers very frequently.*

Trifolium burchellianum *Ser.*
subsp. **johnstonii** *(Oliv.) Cuf. ex
Gillet* Leguminosae (Fabaceae) -
Papilionoideae

ALMA (Amh); MAGOSHIMO (Kef)

A perennial herb with taproots. Stems
usually creeping and rooting at the
nodes. Leaflets are cuneate-obovate
to oblong. The purple flowers are
arranged on globose inflorescences
which are up to 30 mm across.

Found in upland grassland and
moorland, forest glades and edges at
altitudes between 2000 and 3900 m.

Flowering from August to April,
*honeybees forage for pollen and
nectar frequently.*

Trifolium calocephalum *Fresen.*
/ Leguminosae (Fabaceae) - Papilionoideae

MAGETT (Amh)

An endemic perennial herb with stems to 50 cm long. Leaflets oblanceolate to elliptic. Flowers dark purple, large to 20 mm long in 4-8-flowered heads.

Found in upland grassland, usually in wet places and along streams, growing at altitudes between 2400 and 3600 m.

Flowers most profusely at the end of the big rains from July to December but some flowers can be found open in most months in damp places. *Honeybees collect pollen and nectar from the flowers.*

Trifolium decorum *Chiov.* /
Leguminosae (Fabaceae) - Papilionoideae

MAGETT (Amh); MESI (Tya)

An annual or short-lived perennial herb with stems ascending to 50 cm. Leaflets ovate to suborbicular. The inflorescences are 6-15-flowered heads of purple, occasionally white flowers.

Found in upland grassland, especially in moist places at altitudes between 1800 and 3000 m.

Flowering is from September to October. *Honeybees collect nectar and pollen very frequently and the plant is a honey source.*

Trifolium polystachyum *Fresen.*
/ Leguminosae (Fabaceae) - Papilionoideae

SHAL (Amh)

An annual or short-lived perennial with ascending stems, up to 1 m tall, often rooting at the lower nodes. Leaflets elliptic or oblanceolate. Flower heads oblong and many-flowered up to 35 mm long and 15 mm wide. The flowers have a hairy calyx and purple corolla.

Grows along waterways and on swampy grassland at altitudes between 1750 and 3550 m.

In local medicine the leaves are used against headache.

Flowering profusely from September to December, but some plants can be found in flower throughout the year in moist places under shade of trees. *Honeybees collect pollen and nectar from the flowers very frequently.*

Trifolium quartinianum *A.Rich.*
Leguminosae (Fabaceae) - Papilionoideae

MAGET, YEBEG-LAT, WAZMA (Amh); NADDO (Kef); SIDDISA (Or); GWRDMAKWYO, MESI (Tya); ARZIMA (Wel)

An annual herb up to 60 cm tall. Leaflets narrowly oblong to 52 mm long. Flowers purplish red, rarely white, arranged on long-stalked globose inflorescences.

Found in upland grassland especially in damp places at altitudes between 1500 and 2600 m.

Flowering from September to October, *honeybees forage for the abundant nectar and some pollen.*

Trifolium rueppellianum

Fresen. / Leguminosae (Fabaceae) - Papilionoideae

MAGETT (Amh); SIDISSA (Gur); NADDO (Kef); KADDO (Or); MESI (Tya)

An annual herb with glabrous erect or sometimes prostrate stems to 50 cm long. Leaflets glabrous, oblong or obovate. Flower heads of many purple flowers.

A very common *Trifolium* found in fields, particularly fallows, throughout the wetter and cooler highlands. It is also an important pasture plant between 1700 and 3650 m.

In local medicine used to treat elephantiasis.

Flowering from June to December, *honeybees collect nectar and pollen and the plant is an important honey source* in the Ethiopian highlands.

Trifolium semipilosum *Fresen.*

/ Leguminosae (Fabaceae) - Papilionoideae

MAGET (Amh); KENYA WHITE CLOVER (Eng)

A perennial herb with creeping stems to 20 cm long, often rooting at the nodes. Leaflets dark green, obovate or oblong-elliptic with half the lower surface covered in hairs. Flowers white or pale pink, in small heads borne on short erect stalks.

Found abundantly in upland grassland and bushland and at forest edges at altitudes between 1800 to 3150 m.

Flowering plants are found throughout the year with the flowering peak from August to November. *It provides large amounts of nectar and also pollen is produced in moderate to large amounts. This plant is an important honey source.*

Trifolium schimperi *A. Rich.* / Leguminosae (Fabaceae) - Papilionoideae

MAGETT (Amh); MESI, GWSSA'MAI (Tya)

An erect annual herb, often very small, with stems from 3 or 4 cm to 35 cm long. Leaflets linear. Flowers large, bright orange-red in heads of 1 to 5 flowers.

Endemic, growing in damp or seasonally water-logged pasture, short grassland and along waterways at altitudes from 1400 to 3150 m.

Flowering from August to November, *honeybees collect pollen and nectar from the flowers.*

Trifolium simense *Fresen.* / Leguminosae (Fabaceae) - Papilionoideae

MAGET (Amh); SIDDISA (Or); MESI (Tya); ARZIMA (Wel)

Erect or creeping perennial herb with stems to 60 cm long. Leaflets linear-lanceolate. Flowers purplish or red-violet in many-flowered round or ovoid heads about 15 mm wide.

Found in upland grassland and bushland, between 1750 and 3800 m.

Flowering from August to November, *honeybees collect pollen and nectar from the flowers frequently.*

Trifolium steudneri *Schweinf.* /
Leguminosae (Fabaceae) -
Papilionoideae

MAGET, YEBEG-LAT, WAZMA (Amh);
NADDO (Kef); SIDDISA (Or);
GWRDMAKWYO, MESI (Tya); ARZIMA
(Wel)

An annual herb growing to 60 cm tall.
Leaflets narrowly elliptic, to 4 cm long.
Flowers purplish arranged in globose
heads, up to 20 mm across.

Growing in upland grassland and
bushland and especially in damp
places at altitudes between 1100 and
2800 m.

Flowering from August to October,
*honeybees forage for the copious
amounts of nectar and some pollen.*

Trigonella foenum-graecum *L.*
Leguminosae (Fabaceae) -
Papilionoideae

HLBET (Ade); ABI'KAYE (Afar); ABSH
(Amh); SHUQO (Gamo); SILAN
(Ge'ez); ABISHE (Gur); SHIQOTA
(Had); ABISH, GRARO (Kef); SHUÖ
(Kem); HULBATA, SINQO, ABISHI (Or);
ABAK'E (Tya); SHUQWA (Wel);
FENUGREEK (Eng); BOCKSHORNKLEE
(German)

An erect and aromatic annual herb
growing to 50 cm tall. Leaflets ovate
and toothed. Flowers pale yellow or
white, found in leaf axils.

Widely cultivated at altitudes between
1600 and 2300 m all over Ethiopia for
various uses but mainly for its edible
seeds.

It is also used to make unfermented
drinks, and as a spice or condiment in
baking.

Flowering from October to January,
*honeybees forage for nectar and
pollen.*

Tylosema fassoglensis
*(Kotschy ex Schweinf.) Torre &
Hillc.* / Leguminosae (Fabaceae) -
Caesalpinioideae

YEJB-ATER (Amh); FISH POISON BEAN
(Eng)

A shrubby herb to 4 m tall. Leaflets are
elliptic-oblong or elliptic-oblanceolate
and covered with soft hairs above.
Flowers white or purple; all other parts
covered with dark red-brown hairs.

Growing at forest margins, and in
waste ground at altitudes from 500 to
1950 m.

It is not native to Ethiopia, but has
been cultivated as a fish poison and is
now naturalized. The leaves contain
rotenone which is an important non-
residual insecticide.

Flowering throughout the year,
*honeybees collect pollen and nectar
from the flowers.*

Vicia dassycarpa *L.* /
Leguminosae (Fabaceae) -
Papilionoideae

VETCH (Eng); WICKE (German)

A straggling or ascending annual.
Leaflets linear to obovate in 6-16 pairs.
Flowers violet, arranged in elongated
racemes with up to 30 flowers.

Now escaped into meadows and
upland grassland, it was introduced
and cultivated for fodder at altitudes
up to 2600 m.

This is a drought-tolerant crop very
palatable to livestock.

Flowering from April to December,
*honeybees collect nectar and pollen
and the plant is a honey source.*

Vicia faba L. / Leguminosae (Fabaceae) - Papilionoideae

BAQIELA (Ade, Afar, Amh, Kem & Wel); QOMOLO (Gam); AWTIEBEDL, BEDL, FUL (Ge'ez); ATERE, BAIELA (Gur); BAQEL (HAD); BAQELA (Or); A'LQWAY, A'TER-BAHRI BALDENGWA (Tya); HORSE BEAN (Eng); SAUBOHNE (German)

An erect, annual herb up to 1 m high. Leaves glabrous, somewhat blue-green. Flowers sweet-scented, white to pale mauve with black markings.

A widely cultivated pulse crop found thoughout the Ethiopian highlands up to 3000 m. producing small dry beans used as food for people.

Flowering mainly in September and October. *The presence of extrafloral nectaries, which function throughout the vegetative period of the plant, attract insects away from the flowers which produce rather little nectar with a low sugar concentration. However, honeybees collect pollen and nectar and the plant is a honey source.*

Vicia sativa L. Leguminosae (Fabaceae) - Papilionoideae

SEBBERE-ANCH'WA, SEBBERE-GWASOT (Tya); ACKERWICKE (German)

A straggling or ascending annual herb growing to 80 cm long. Leaflets 6-16, linear to obovate. Flowers purplish, solitary or paired in leaf-axils.

Cultivated for forage and fodder throughout the highlands and also wild in upland grassland and scrub at altitudes between 1500 and 3300 m.

Flowering from June to March with a peak from June to September. *Honeybees forage for both pollen and nectar from the flowers.*

Fodder Legumes

Desmanthus virgatus (L.) Willd. / Leguminosae (Fabaceae) Mimosoideae

An erect or ascending woody herb or subshrub growing to 2 m high under favourable conditions. Leaves have 1-7 pairs of pinnae which are with 10-25 pairs of linear to linear-oblong leaflets. Flowers white arranged in axillary solitary heads.

A native of tropical America now cultivated as a valuable fodder plant in many Old World countries and naturalized in West Africa. Now being grown in research stations at altitudes around 1900 m.

Flowering after the big rains from September to December, *honeybees forage for abundant pollen and nectar very frequently.*

Trifolium repens L. / Leguminosae (Fabaceae) Papilionoideae

WHITE CLOVER (Eng); WEIßKLEE (German)

A perennial herb with long creeping stems rooting at the nodes. Leaflets obovate or elliptic and relatively large. Flower heads white or pale pink on long erect stalks.

Introduced for experimental cultivation in many research stations at altitudes up to 2400 m. It is widespread in Eurasia where it is extensively cultivated for fodder.

Flowering after the rains, *honeybees forage for the abundant nectar and pollen. White clover is the most important honeybee clover world-wide.*

Stylosanthes guianensis

(Aubl.) Sw. / Leguminosae
(Fabaceae) Papilionoideae

BRAZILIAN LUCERNE (Eng)

An erect herbaceous perennial herb
with branching ascending stems to 1
m tall which become woody with age.
Leaves pinnately trifoliate with elliptic
leaflets. Flowers yellow, crowded into
terminal heads.

Native to Brazil and now widespread in
the tropics and naturalized in many
countries. It is very similar to *S.
hamata (L.) Taub.* and *S. scabra Vog.*
which have also been introduced for
experimental cultivation.

Flowering is after the rains when
*honeybees forage for pollen and
nectar.*

Calliandra calothyrsus *Meissn.*

/ Leguminosae (Fabaceae)
Mimosoideae

RED CALLIANDRA (Eng)

A tree or shrub growing 5 to 10 m high
with spreading branches. Leaves are
bipinnate. Flowers sweetly-scented,
conspicuous, with numerous long red
stamens in large erect racemes.

A native to Central America and an
important tree for producing fuel,
fodder and mulch. It thrives on a wide
range of soils and requires about 1000
mm rainfall, It can withstand several
months of drought. It has been
introduced for experimental cultivation
at altitudes of around 1900 m.

Flowering lasts several months and
elsewhere the tree *is a very important
pollen and nectar source for
honeybees. It is recommended for
planting to increase honey
production.*

Allium cepa *L.* / Liliaceae (now
generally put in Alliaceae)

QEY-SHNKURT (Amh); SHIGURTI (Tya);
ONION (Eng); ZWIEBEL (German)

A biennial herb which produces a bulb
in the first season and then the flower
in the second. Leaves linear, smelling
of onion when crushed. Fowers white
with green veins in terminal umbels.

Onions are grown all over the country
at altitudes up to 2500 m.

A very important vegetable used in
making BERBERI and cooking all types
of WOT, particularly that made with
chicken. Onions were cultivated by the
earliest known civilization in Egypt and
China.

*Honeybees collect pollen and nectar
from the flowers and are important
pollinators to aid seed set.*

Asparagus africanus *Lam.* /
Liliaceae (now generally put in
Asparagaceae)

KESTENNICHA (Amh); SERREETTEE
(Or); KASTA ANSITEE (Tya)

A common perennial scrambler or
woody climber growing to 3 m or
more. The stems are covered with
strong, curved hooks. Leaves needle-
like grow up to 2.5 cm long. Flowers
small white and numerous.

Commonly found in scrub at altitudes
between 2000 to 3000 m.

The young shoots are edible either
raw or cooked and have a strong but
pleasant flavour.

Flowering appear after the rains, from
October to December, *honeybees
collect pollen and nectar from the
flowers.*

Gloriosa simplex *L.* / Liliaceae
(now generally put in Colchicaceae)

ARAMANDAWA (Or); SEKORRU (Kef); TSILAL-A'NOY-MARYAM (Tya & Tre); GLORY LILY (Eng)

An erect or climbing annual herb with tendrils growing from an irregularly-shaped, smooth-surfaced tuber. Leaves lanceolate. Flowers showy, hanging, orange to red, sometimes yellow.

Widespread from 500 to 2500 m, it grows in bushland and forest edges on well-drained soils.

All parts of this plant are extremely poisonous, especially the tuber.

Flowering during the rains it is occasionally visited by *honeybees for pollen only.*

Kniphofia foliosa *Hochst.* /
Liliaceae (now generally put in Asphodelaceae)

ASHENDA, SHEMET'MAT', ABELBILLA (Amh); LELDA (Or-Bale)

A robust herb to 1.2 m high. Leaves long, linear, continuing to grow after the flowers have died. Flowers yellow, red or orange in dense terminal spikes.

Endemic, it grows on mountain slopes and beside roads, often found in masses on hillsides and meadows at altitudes between 2050 and 4000 m in the Sub-Afroalpine zone.

In local medicine the plant is used in the treatment of abdominal cramp.

Flowering varies from April to May or from June to October or December to January. It is visited by *honeybees for pollen only.*

Kniphofia insignis *Rendle* /
Liliaceae (now generally put in Asphodelaceae)

A robust, herb growing to 40 cm high from a rhizome. Leaves all basal and long-lanceolate. Flowers white, hanging down in a fairly dense spike on long stalks.

It grows on damp and seasonally waterlogged areas at altitudes from 2400 to 2800 m.

Flowering during and after the rains it is *visited by honeybees for pollen only.*

Linum usitatissimum *L.* /
Linaceae

TALBA, TELBA (Amh); MUTTO (Kef); KONTER (Or); NT'AT'I (Tya); FLAX (Eng); FLACHS (German)

An erect annual herb growing to 80 cm high. Leaves alternate linear-lanceolate. Flowers bluish-white.

Cultivated throughout the highlands to 3000 m, this is the most drought resistant of the highland oil crops.

An old crop grown for over 5000 years for the fibre from the stems and oil from the seeds. In Egypt mummy cloth made from flax date back to at least 2300 B.C. The press cake is a valuable fodder for domestic animals.

Seeds are also used for wound dressing. Boiled uncrushed seeds are drunk to sooth stomach ache, particularly stomach ulcers in local medicine.

Flowering almost all year round but profusely in Octover and November, *honeybees collect nectar and pollen and the plant is an important honey source.*

153

Tapinanthus globiferus
(A.Rich.) Tiegh. / Loranthaceae
TEKATILLA (Amh); ERTU (Or); DIKWALA (Tya); MISTLETOE (Eng)

A semi-parasite shrub growing on trees to 2 m across. Leaves green, leathery, linear-lanceolate to oblong-ovate. Flowers reddish with green to yellow tips, up to 4.5 cm long and arranged in sessile umbels.

This parasite occurs on coffee and citrus as well as on other woody hosts especially on *Rhus* spp. at altitudes between 540 to 2350 m.

The green leaves produce their own sugar but other nutrients are taken from the host.

Flowering almost all year round, *honeybees forage for nectar and pollen.*

Caucanthus auriculatus
(Radlk.) Niedenzu / Malphigiaceae

A woody climber with stems up to 5 m in length. The young stems are covered with short, soft, white silk-like hairs. Leaves ovate-cordate with grey woolly hairs beneath. Flowers pale yellow, arranged in dense axillary and terminal corymbs, with a strong unpleasant smell.

Found in deciduous woodland, bushland and thickets, often in riverine forest or rocky places and also extending into dry upland evergreen forests and bushlands at altitudes between 750 and 1800 m.

Flowering is almost all year round, *honeybees forage for pollen and nectar.*

Rotala repens *(Hochst.) Kœhne /*
Lythraceae

An aquatic herb growing to 15 cm tall with anchored root-like stems. Leaves slender and thread-like, crowded on the upper parts of the stem. Flowers white to pink, numerous and arranged on ascending erect spikes.

This rarely collected species, found in Central and north Ethiopia, grows in medium altitudes of about 1700 m on stones in stagnant water and streams where it forms reddish-purple tufts on the surface.

Flowering from January to July, *it is very frequently visited by honeybees for pollen and nectar.*

Abutilon longicuspe *Hochst. ex*
A.Rich. / Malvaceae

A shrubby herb or even a shrub growing to 3 m high. Leaves cordate to broadly ovate and toothed. Flowers pink to violet, arranged in often large terminal and lateral panicles.

Found at forest edges, in clearings of upland forests, secondary forest and scrub, in coffee plantations and edges of riverine forests and rocky outcrops at altitudes between 1500 and 2800 m.

Flowering from September to November, *honeybees forage for pollen and nectar.*

Abutilon mauritianum *(Jacq.)*
Medic. / Malvaceae

A shrubby herb or shrub growing to 2 m tall. All parts of the plant are covered with long simple hairs and the stems have glands. Leaves cordate to broadly so. Flowers yellow to orange, arranged in short axillary heads.

Very common in along river banks and under partial shade of trees at altitudes between 1200 and 2200 m.

Flowering from August to November, *honeybees forage for pollen and nectar.*

Alcea rosea *L.* / Malvaceae

HOLLYHOCK (Eng); STOCKROSE (German)

A coarse annual herb growing to 3 m high. The stem is covered with small hairs. Leaves ovate, simple, soft and hairy. Flowers subsessile, white to pink or violet, arranged in axillary clusters merging into spike-like panicles.

In Ethiopia HOLLYHOCK is cultivated in both public and private gardens in many towns at altitudes between 1600 and 2400 m.

The origin of this plant is unknown but it is possibly a hybrid widely now cultivated in temperate areas throughout the world and often naturalized.

Flowering all year round, *honeybees forage for the abundant nectar and pollen from the flowers.*

Gossypium hirsutum *L.* / Malvaceae

T'IFT'IRRIE (Amh & Or); GIRBI (Or); T'UT' (Tya); COTTON (Eng); BAUMWOLLSTRAUCH (German)

This perennial shrub grows to 3 m high. Leaves more or less heart-shaped, unlobed or shallowly 3-5-lobed. Flowers white to yellowish which change to pink with age.

This native to America is now widely grown for its fine fibre (cotton) and seed oils at altitudes between 1200 and 2300 m. Sometimes found as an escape in deciduous and evergreen woodland.

G. barbadense L. is closely resembling *G. hirsutum* but the leaves are more 3-5-lobed.

Flowering from December to May, *honeybees are the most important pollinators of cotton. They collect nectar and pollen and the plant is an important honey source.*

Hibiscus calyphyllus *Cav.* / Malvaceae

HOMER (Tya)

A shrubby herb or shrub growing to 2 m high. Leaves ovate to cordate generally unlobed, rarely 3-lobed. Flowers yellow with a maroon centre and arranged in leaf axils.

Growing in lowland rainforest, groundwater forest, riverine forest and extending into upland bushland in altitudes between 450 and 2100 m.

Flowering from October to December, *honeybees forage for pollen and nectar from the flowers.*

Hibiscus cannabinus *L.* /
Malvaceae

A stiffly, erect coarse annual growing to 2.5 m high with sparsely to densely prickly stems. Leaves broadly ovate to cordate, unlobed near the base and deeply 3-7 lobed or almost divided near the apex. Flowers yellow borne in leaf axils or in well defined racemes.

Found in *Acacia* woodland and wooded grassland, in swamps, on grassland and along riverbanks and as a weed in cultivation at altitudes between 400 to 1900 m.

In Sudan, south tropical Africa and India it is grown as a fibre plant giving JUTE. In Ethiopia trials were carried out but it has not been taken up by farmers because of the difficulty in obtaining water to rett the stems and extract the fibres.

Flowering from June to December, *honeybees forage for pollen and nectar.*

Hibiscus crassinervius *Hochst. ex A.Rich.* / Malvaceae

A hairy shrubby herb or a shrub growing to 2 m high. Leaves ovate or elliptic to orbicular. Flowers small, bright red to scarlet.

Found in a wide variety of habitats: woodland, bushland and scrub on a just as wide a variety of soils at altitudes between 1300 and 2300 m.

Flowering from June to April, *honeybees forage for pollen and nectar.*

Hibiscus ludwigii *Eckl. & Zeyh.* /
Malvaceae

SUKOT (Tya)

An erect branched, soft-wooded shrub up to 3 m high. Leaves alternate, with palmate nerves. Flowers bright yellow. The stem is covered with a lot of spiny hairs, which are very painful to touch.

Found in upland woodland, evergreen forest margins and along roadsides and paths at altitudes between 1500 and 3300 m.

In local medicine the leaves are used against paralysis.

Flowering from September to December, *honeybees collect pollen and nectar from the flowers.*

Hibiscus trionum *L.* / Malvaceae

FLOWER IN AN HOUR (Eng)

An annual herb growing to 50 cm high with a tough stem. Leaves broadly ovate to broadly cordate, deeply 3-lobed to divided. Flowers pale yellow, with a purple centre and conspicuous purple veins, borne in leaf axils. Fruits enclosed by a papery capsule.

A common herb with striking flowers found in disturbed areas, fields and on degraded mountain slopes and in short grassland in altitudes from 1500 to 2500 m.

Plants can be found in flower almost all year round and *honeybees collect pollen and nectar from the flowers frequently.*

Malva verticillata L. / Malvaceae

ADGUAR (Amh); LITI (Or)

An erect to decumbent or ascending annual or biennial herb growing to 3 m high. Leaves cordate to kidney-shaped and shallowly lobed with toothed margins. Flowers pink to pale violet, arranged in dense axillary clusters merging into interrupted spike-like panicles.

Found along paths and roadsides and in clearings in upland forests, also common in upland grassland and cultivated areas, often near houses and villages at altitudes between 2000 and 3700 m.

In local medicine the leaves are used as a wound dressing and roots are used as a purgative. Both leaves and roots are used to expel worms.

Found flowering all year round, *honeybees collect pollen and abundant nectar from the flowers very frequently.*

Pavonia schimperiana Hochst. ex A.Rich. / Malvaceae

A shrubby herb or shrub growing to 3 m high under favourable conditions but also a small herb in heavily grazed areas. Leaves with crenate margins. Flowers conspicuous, white with a dark red or a dark purple centre, borne in leaf axils.

Growing in disturbed areas and grassland, in montane forests and at forest edges, along streambanks and in partial shade of trees at altitudes between 1300 and 2200 m.

Flowering from September to May, *honeybees forage for nectar and pollen throughout the day. When the plant is massed it is a honey source.*

Pavonia urens Cav. / Malvaceae

ABLALAT (Amh); INCHINI, KARCHABA, LITA (Or)

A shrubby herb or shrub growing to 3 m high with branchlets and stalks covered with large, easily detached, irritating hairs. Leaves with 5-7 triangular lobes. Flowers pinkish, arranged in racemes.

It grows along roadsides and in disturbed areas, edges of upland forest and in riverine communities, on waste ground and grassland at altitudes between 1700 and 2800 m.

In local medicine the leaves are used against ulcers.

Flowering from August to January, *honeybees collect pollen and abundant nectar from the flowers very frequently.*

Sida rhombifolia L. / Malvaceae

KALABA (Or); DEKE-DAHRO (Tya)

An erect, annual or short-lived perennial, shrubby herb growing to 1.3 m high. Leaves ovate-elliptic and simple. Flowers white to pale yellow, born in leaf axils.

Found in evergreen bushland, under shade of trees and along roadsides, at forest edges and in forest clearings and in fields at altitudes between 1000 and 2600 m.

Flowering from September to March, *honeybees collect pollen and nectar from the flowers frequently.*

Sida schimperiana *Hochst. ex Rich.* / Malvaceae

GORJEJIT (Amh); GUFTEH (Or); KIAFREG, TEF'RERIA (Tya)

A small spreading to prostrate dwarf bush, growing to a height of only 30 cm. Leaves small, dark green and hairless. Flowers pale yellow.

This small shrub is very common on the Plateau, growing in grassland and on overgrazed and degraded areas, on dry rocky outcrops, in fields and inside Eucalypt plantations at altitudes between 1500 and 2600 m.

The plant is used to make a hand brush to sweep the floor. It provides some grazing for goats and sheep.

Flowering from August to April, *honeybees collect pollen and nectar from the flowers.*

Sida tenuicarpa *Vollesen* / Malvaceae

A much-branched shrubby herb or shrub growing up to 1 m high. Leaves narrowly wedge-shaped, with a notched apex, sometimes with a single tooth each side. Flowers yellow to orange, sometimes with reddish veins, solitary or in up to 6-flowered heads at the end of branches.

Found in woodland, grassland, often on steep slopes and commonly on overgrazed and degraded areas, along roadsides and in old cultivations at altitudes between 1550 and 2300 m.

Flowering from July to February, *honeybees frequently forage for pollen and nectar.*

Dissotis canescens *(Graham) Hook.f.*s / Melastomataceae

A hairy perennial herb growing from a woody rootstock up to 1 m high. Leaves oblong-linear and sessile. Flowers bright purple, arranged on erect stalks.

Found on eroded soils, in grassland and along paths at altitudes from 700 to 2100 m.

Flowering after the rains from November to February it is pollinated by carpenter bees. Honeybees visit sometimes to collect pollen only.

Morus alba *L.* / Moraceae

YEFERENJI 'NJORIE, 'NJORIE (Amh); WHITE MULBERRY (Eng); MAULBEERBAUM (German)

A slow growing shrub or tree usually up to 5 m high but also attaining a height up to 20 m. Leaves very variable in shape even on the same branch: lanceolate, ovate or trilobed, sometimes lobed on one side only. Male and female flowers very small, borne in tightly-packed clusters (catkins) on the same tree.

Very common in towns and villages throughout the country, it is grown as a hedge and a shade plant around houses; also found naturalized in hedgerows and secondary bushland and thickets at altitudes from 1500 to 2400 m.

Flowering after the rains, *honeybees only forage for pollen,* because the flowers are not producing any nectar and are cross-pollinated by wind.

Maesa lanceolata Forssk. / Myrsinaceae

YEREGNA-QOLO, GECHA, HAMARARA, KALAWA (Amh); IMBIS (Gur); GESHI, ABAYE, GALABA (Or); SAORIA (Tya); GERGECO, KELAUA (Wel)

A shrub or tree growing to 10 m tall with greenish brown stems. Leaves elliptic with coarsely toothed margins. Flowers white to cream, arranged in dense, single or compound racemes.

Found throughout the highlands in degraded bushland, forest edges and scrub from 1500 to 3000 m.

The oil obtained from the seeds is used to grease the baking plate for INJERA. In local medicine the fruits are used as a vermifuge. The wood is used as firewood and an extract of it is used to tan leather red.

Flowering is almost all year round, but more abundantly from September to December. *Honeybees collect pollen and nectar.*

Commicarpus plumbagineus

(Cav.) Standley / Nyctaginaceae

H'AMLI-GILA (Tya)

A trailing or scandent annual herb with stems growing to 3 m long from a woody rootstock. Leaves ovate, entire or with wavey margins. Flowers white (very rarely pale pink) in umbels, usually aggregated into irregular panicles.

Found in drier regions, growing among hedge plants and in scrub, in woodlands, often with *Acacia*, mostly near waterways and often in disturbed habitats at altitudes between 500 and 2000 m.

Flowering is almost throughout the year, *honeybees collect pollen and nectar from the flowers.*

Nymphaea nouchali Burm.f. var. caerulea / Nymphaeaceae

GELE-ILA (Afar); BELBATE (Or)

A perennial aquatic herb with an long tuberous rhizome and long white roots anchored in wet mud. Leaves floating, round, simple, alternate, shiny green above and pale, often tinged dark purple beneath. Flowers blue, white or pinkish-blue and strongly scented, 4 to 16 cm in diameter.

Found in lakes, slow-flowing rivers and pools at altitudes between 500 to 2100 m.

The roots and seeds are edible. The root has also been used for making a dye and a cure for diabetes.

Flowers can be found almost all year round. *Honeybees collect abundant pollen and some nectar.*

Jasminum abyssinicum

Hochst. ex DC. / Oleaceae

MESSERIK, T'EMBELAL, TERERAK, WEMBELEL,, ZOHUN-KACHAMO (Amh); ELKEMME, TEO, TEMBELEL-BILU (Or); HABBI-SELIM, ABITEREK (Tya)

A climbing shrub with stems growing to 7 m long. Leaves dark green, shiny and trifoliate. Flowers with a strong sweet scent, white, in axillary clusters amd terminal panicles.

Growing in evergreen forests and montane bushland, especially beside streams, and also in fences round houses throughout the country at altitudes up to 3000 m.

The roots are used to dress wounds in animals.

Flowering profusely from December to February, but some plants can be found flowering at other times. *It is occasionally visited by honeybees.*

Jasminum stans *Pax* / Oleaceae

INTABUYE (Or)

A much-branched shrub growing to 3 m high. Leaves dark green with 5 entire and ovate leaflets. Flowers deep golden yellow.

Endemic, growing in montane bushland and scrub and sometimes found in gardens between 2500 and 3000 m.

Flowering mostly after the big rains up to December, *honeybees collect pollen and nectar from the flowers.*

Oenothera fruticosa *A.Gray.* / Onagraceae

An erect biennial herb growing to a height of 1 m. The stem arises from a rosette of sessile, lanceolate leaves, which have slightly toothed margins. Flowers large, yellow, in erect racemes.

Growing in disturbed areas, fallow ground, and along roadsides and tracks at altitudes between 2000 and 2400 m.

Originally from Canada this plant found its way to Ethiopia through Kenya.

Flowering is all year round but profusely during and after the rains. *Honeybees gather abundant pollen and small amounts of nectar.*

Epilobium hirsutum *L.* / Onagraceae

YELAM-CHEW (Amh); WILLOW-HERB, FIREWEED (Eng)

An erect rhizomatous herb with ascending branches. Leaves sessile, opposite, lanceolate to elliptic. Flowers showy, bright purple with creamy-white centres, arranged in irregular leafy racemes.

Growing at altitudes between 1200 and 3200 m, in swamps, along streams and damp areas and on disturbed land.

The plant is poisonous for human beings, but the leaves are licked for the salty deposit on the surface but not swallowed by shepherd-boys.

Flowering from August to January, *honeybees collect pollen and nectar from the flowers.*

Oxalis corniculata *L.* / Oxalidaceae

YEBERE-CHEW (Amh); SOGIDAREA (Or); YELLOW SORREL (Eng)

A creeping much-branched hairy herb growing to 15 cm high. Leaves trifoliate leaves with traingularly-shaped leaflets. Flowers pale yellow.

Commonly found in disturbed ground, in fields and grassland and at altitudes between 1400 and 2900 m.

In local medicine the leaves are used against snake bites. The leaves contain oxalic acid which can be dangerous for animals.

Flowering from July to January, *honeybees collect pollen and nectar from the flowers.*

Oxalis obliquifolia *A.Rich.* / Oxalidaceae

YEBERE-CHEW (Amh); OXALIS (Eng)

An erect perennial herb reaching a height of 15 cm. It is without a stem and the leaves and flowers arise from an underground bulb. Leaves trifoliate with dark green clover-like leaflets. Flowers pink, showy, trumpet-shaped, in many-flowered umbels.

Growing in disturbed ground, particularly gardens and fields, it can become a troublesome weed at altitudes between 1300 and 2900 m.

Flowering almost all year round, *honeybees collect pollen and nectar from the flowers.*

Argemone mexicana *L.* / Papaveraceae

MEDAFE (Amh); FIFO, MEDAFE-T'ILIAN (Tya); WHITE THISTLE; MEXICAN POPPY (Eng)

An erect prickly annual herb which grows to 80 cm tall. Leaves blue-green, sessile, with spiny margins and white veins which produce a white to yellow milky juice when broken. Flowers white or pale yellow.

Found on well-drained, particularly eroded soil in disturbed areas and fields from 400 up to 2500 m.

In local medicine the sap is used against eye disease and as a narcotic and the seeds as purgative.

Farmers do not consider this species as a serious weed, because it grows after crops are harvested. It grows in masses and flowers profusely during the dry season. *It is visited by honeybees for pollen only.*

Passiflora edulis *Sims.* / Passifloraceae

PASSION FRUIT (Eng); GRENADILLA (German)

A shrubby perennial climber with stems growing to 6 m long. Leaves shining, three-lobbed with toothed margins. Flowers large, mainly white to pale green with white and purple threads.

Widely grown as a hedge plant for its edible fruits from 500 up to 2500 m. Also found as an escape in forest margins and other disturbed sites at altitudes between 1700 and 1750 m.

Honeybees collect pollen and nectar from the flowers and are important pollinators along with carpenter bees.

Sesamum indicum *L.* / Pedaliaceae

MENCHA, SELIT' (Amh); ZEDI (Or); ANGADA (Tya); SESAM (German)

An annual, stout, erect, sometimes branched herb growing to 1.5 m tall. Leaves opposite and narrowly elliptic. Flowers white to pale yellow, born in small clusters in leaf axils.

Cultivated on heavier soils at altitudes between 600 to 1700 m.

Sesame is one of the oldest oilseeds known. In Ethiopia, sesame oil is added to sauces instead of butter. The oil is used for frying sweets and breads or mixed with other oilseeds to be roasted and eaten as snacks.

Flowering from February to November, *honeybees collect abundant pollen and nectar from the flowers and from extrafloral nectaries. The plant is an important honey source.*

Phytolacca dodecandra L'Her.
/ Phytolaccaceae

NDOD (Amh); ENDODI, HARANGA (Or); SHBT'I, (Tya); ENDOD (Eng)

A scrambling, much-branched shrub with stems up to 8 m long, growing from a woody base. Leaves dark green, alternate, simple and ovate. Flowers sweet-scented, white in axillary or terminal racemes.

ENDOD is commonly found in degraded vegetation along river banks, in thickets and hedges in and around villages at altitudes between 1500 and 3000 m.

Thus is the most widely used soapberry for washing clothes. A medicinal plant which is notoriously poisonous to humans and animals.

Flowering is after any rain, but profusely from October to April. *Honeybees collect nectar and pollen and the plant is a honey source if growing plentiful*

Pittosporum abyssinicum Del.
/ Pittosporaceae

WEYL, SOLA (Afar & Som); LOLA, DENGYA-SEBBER, ANGALLIT, AHOT (Amh); AMBL-BAY (Gur); SHOLO, AMSHIKA, ARA, BONCO, CEKA, RAHA, TOSSU (Or); CEQENTE, BESSO-ATAL, WEYELO (Tya); MITESHIYYE (Wel)

A shrub or tree growing to 8 m tall with leaves crowded at ends of branches. Flowers greenish to yellow, in short racemes or panicles.

Found in dry upland evergreen forests and upland evergreen bushland at altitudes between 1500 and 3600 m.

Flowering from November to April, *honeybees collect sufficient pollen and nectar from the flowers.*

Plantago lanceolata L. /
Plantaginaceae

GOETOEB (Amh & Tre); GAMBELA (Gamo); KORTOBI (Gur); KORISSA (Or); MANDELDO (Tya); RIBGRASS (Eng); WEGERICH (German)

A herb with flowering stems growing to 40 cm high from a rosette of leaves. Leaves lanceolate, mostly erect but sometimes also flat on the ground. Flower heads are cylindrical spikes with small green flowers and creamy white anthers and filaments.

This cosmopolitan weed grows along paths and roadsides, in pasture and cultivated fields at altitudes between 1200 and 3200 m.

In local medicine the leaves are used against trachoma.

It flowers throughout the year and profusely during rains and *is frequently visited by honeybees for pollen only.*

Andropogon abyssinicus
(Fresen.) R.Br. / Poaceae

CAJJA, BELEME (Amh); BALAMI (Or)

An an erect loosely tufted annual or short-lived perennial grass, up to 60 cm tall. Flowering stems simple or sparingly branched, with spike-like densely hairy racemes.

The whole plant is sweetly-scented, particularly in the morning. An important grazing grass all kind of animals. It is found in meadows and fallow areas at altitudes between 1800 and 2900 m.

Most probably the small aphids on this grass are responsible for the *honey-dew production, which is commonly reported by beekeepers of in northern Ethiopia. Honeybees also collect pollen.*

Eleusine floccifolia *(Forssk.)*
Spreng. / Poaceae

SERDO (Amh); AKERMA, AKRIMA (Or)

A perennial grass of variable size with flowering stems growing to 60 cm high. Leaf blades are narrow-lanceolate with small tufts of white hairs on the margins. Flowers in racemes up to 7 cm long and covered with greenish-yellow pollen.

It is a very widespread grass found in meadows and fallow ground at altitudes between 1700 and 3200 m.

The flowering stalks are collected during the rainy season, then dried and sometimes died for basketwork to make kitchen utensils and decorative baskets for the home.

Flowering from August to November, *it is frequently visited by honeybees for pollen only*

Pennisetum humile *Hochst. ex A.Rich.* / Poaceae

A low, densely tufted perennial grass growing from an underground rhizome. Leaves flat or rolled with finely acuminate tips. Flowering stems grow from an ascending base up to 20 cm high. Inflorescences are compact ovoid to oblong heads, 1 to 2 cm long.

Endemic, found in damp upland meadows and grassy glades in *Hypericum* and *Hagenia* woodland at altitudes between 2800 and 4000 m.

Flowering almost all year round, *honeybees are very frequently found foraging pollen.*

Saccharum officinarum *L.* / Poaceae

SHINKUR-AGEDA, T'NQSH (Amh); SHNKORA (Amh & Or); SUGAR CANE (Eng); ZUCKERROHR (German)

A tall perennial herb with stout, thick culms up to 5 m tall. Leaves large and broad, up to 2 m long. Inflorescences large, with numerous racemes which are covered with silvery-white hairs.

Sugar cane is cultivated in home gardens of towns and villages up to 2400 m and also in sugar plantations at altitudes up to 1900 m.

A native of New Guinea, sigar cane has been cultivated since ancient times. The Arabs brought this plant to Africa in the 7th century A.D. *Honeybees suck the sweet juice of broken or cut sugar plants.*

Sorghum bicolor *L.* / Poaceae

IHIY (Ade); DERO (Afar); MASHLA (Amh & Or); MISINGA (Kef, Or & Som); BESHINGA (Kem); RUAYNI (Nuw); SHANGO (Or); BACHANKA, BACHANGA (Sid); MAKOTA (Wel)

A cultivated annual herb growing to 4 m high, with light yellow flowers in open or closed heads.

Cultivated throughout the country at altitudes up to 2000 m.

This is the fourth most important world cereal after wheat, rice and maize. It is a staple food in the drier parts of tropical Africa, India and China. In Ethiopia it is used to make INJERA, unleavened bread, popped as a snack and as both the malt and body in brewing TALLA. Stems and leaves are used for animal fodder.

Flowering from October to December it is visited by *honeybees for pollen only.*

Zea mays *L.* / Poaceae

BAHR-MASHLA, YEBAHR-MASHLA (Amh); BARO (Kef); BAKALO (Or); MAIZE (Eng); MAIS (German)

An erect annual, up to 3 m high. The stem is hollow but stout with stilt roots and many nodes. Male flowers in large creamy-white panicles.

Grown throughout the country in fields and homegardens up to 2300 m.

This crop originated in Central and South America. It is now cultivated for food and fodder throughout the world and is one of the most important cereal crops with the highest yield potential.

Flowering mostly during the long rains, it is *visited by honeybees for pollen only. However, some beekeepers have reported honey harvests from maize due to honeydew produced by aphids on the leaves.*

Polygala persicariifolia *DC.* / Polygalaceae

BIKILTU (Or)

A softly hairy annual herb growing to 40 cm high. Leaves linear-elliptic. Flowers pinkish-violet to pale purple, in short racemes.

An uncommon plant of rocky hillsides and evergreen forest at altitudes between 1100 to 2400.

Flowering from August to November, *honeybees collect pollen and nectar from the flowers.*

Polygala abyssinica *R.Br. ex Fres.* / Polygalaceae

A glabrous or sparsely hairy annual, growing to 40 cm tall. Leaves linear, somewhat blue-green. Flowers white to pink-purple in one-sided loose 10 cm long racemes.

Found in meadows and scrub, montane forests and on rocky slopes in higher altitudes between 1500 and 2800 m.

Flowering from August to March, *honeybees collect pollen and nectar from the flowers.*

Polygala steudneri *Chordat* / Polygalaceae

An erect, annual herb growing to 40 cm tall. Leaves shiny green, narrowly linear to linear-oblong. Flowers pinkish-red in long racemes.

Growing under shade of trees, particularly in evergreen forests at altitudes between 1300 and 3500 m.

Flowering from October to March, *honeybees collect pollen and nectar from the flowers.*

Oxygonum sinuatum *Dammer /* Polygonaceae

KIRNCHIT, AKAKIMA (Amh); SOGDO (Or); CH'EW-MRA'KUT, DASHAN-MIREHAT, GAGUME (Tya); KOOMUTO (Gur); DOUBLE THORN (Eng)

A sprawling prostrate, much-branched annual herb growing to 30 cm tall. Leaves ovate and irregularly lobed. flowers pinkish-white, in 10 cm long spikes. Fruits are spiny.

Growing along roadsides and in fields on sandy soils, also in dry and eroded areas at altitudes from 600 to 2400 m.

In traditional medicine the whole plant is used against NEKERSA.

Flowering almost all year round, *honeybees collect pollen and nectar from the flowers frequently.*

Persicaria nepalense *(Meisen)* Miyabe (syn. *Polygonum nepalensis*) / Polygonaceae

YETJA-SGA (Amh)

A weak-stemmed straggling or erect annual herb growing to 30 cm high. Leaves alternate and simple. Flowers small, white or pink, in terminal heads.

A common weed in highland crops, sometimes dominant, also on fallow land at altitudes from 1350 to 3200 m.

Flowering all year round but more profusely during the rainy season up to December. *Honeybees collect nectar and pollen and the plant is a honey source.*

Persicaria labathifolium *(L.)* S.F. Gray (syn. *Polygonum labathifolium* / Polygonaceae

An erect, branched annual herb growing to 60 cm high. Leaves entire, lanceolate and alternate with petioles. Flowers dull dark yellow, borne in waxy-looking racemes at the end of branches.

Found growing in damp areas and along paths and waterways at altitudes from 1700 to 2400 m.

Flowering just after rains in September and October, *honeybees collect pollen and nectar from the flowers.*

Persicaria setosula *(A.Rich.) K.L.* Wilson (syn. *Polygonum setosulum*) / Polygonaceae

SATAWEE (Or); LEYEKWA RIBA (Tya); KNOTWEED (Eng)

A perennial herb with fleshy stems, growing to 100 cm high. Leaves lanceolate-ovate or elliptic. Flowers pink to red, in terminal racemes.

A common waterside plant, growing on damp places, creeping over wet mud, along waterways and waterlogged places at altitudes between 1200 and 2900 m.

Flowering throughout the year, *honeybees collect pollen and nectar from the flowers frequently.*

Rumex nepalensis *Spreng.* (syn. *Rumex bequartii* De Wild.) / Polygonaceae

QTELE-REJIM (Amh); BALDER, MUCHA-ARAB (Or)

A glabrous erect perennial herb growing to 90 cm tall. Leaves dark green, lanceolate or linear-oblong. Flowers green with red marking and large yellow stamens, in racemes.

Found in upland forest, along streamsides and in fields as a weed at higher altitudes between 1200 and 3900 m.

In local medicine the leaves are used to dress wounds, against rheumatism and stomach ache.

Flowering is throughout the dry season from September to May. *Honeybees collect pollen and nectar from the flowers.*

Rumex nervosus *Vahl* / Polygonaceae

IM'BWACH'O (Amh); DANGEGO (Or); H'EH'OT (Tya)

An erect, much branched and clump-forming shrub growing to 3 m high. Leaves bright-green, simple and lanceolate, leathery to succulent. Flowers small, pink to red, in erect terminal panicles.

Common in degraded or overgrazed areas on mountain slopes and rocky hillsides, often forming a hedge along roads and paths. It is widespread throughout the country at altitudes between 400 and 3300 m.

The young shoots, slightly sour, are stripped of their thin bark and eagerly eaten by children. The whole plant is also used against AJIL and SIRAY.

Flowering throughout the year, *honeybees forage for pollen only.*

Eichhornia crassipes *(Mart.)* *Solms in A.DC* / Pontederiaceae

WATER HYACINTH (Eng)

A floating plant, sometimes perennial. Leaves in basal clusters with swollen petioles which trap air. Flowers pale-blue or pale violet, arranged in spike-like inflorescences.

Now found in both the Baro and Awash river systems at altitudes up to 1900 m.

This plant spreads very rapidly from runners which develop from the leaf axils and a dangerous weed of waterways and lakes.

Flowering almost all year round, *honeybees forage for some pollen and nectar.*

Portulacca quadrifida *L.* / Portulacaceae

JIABARA, MELKHENA (Tya)

A prostrate annual or short-lived perennial herb with stems growing to 30 cm long. Leaves opposite, variable in size and shape, but often lanceolate to elliptic-oblong. Flowers yellow or orange, rarely pink or purplish, in the leaf axils.

Found on waste and fallow land, in seasonally burnt or cleared areas and in heavily overgrazed land at altitudes between 500 and 2300 m.

This is a cosmopolitan weed of tropical and temperate areas.

Flowering almost all year round with a peak in October and November, *honeybees forage for pollen and nectar. The long lasting flowering period makes this plant a valuable nectar and pollen source especially in heavily disturbed habitats.*

Anagallis arvensis L. /
Primulaceae

CHIGAQWA'HIT (Tya); PIMPERNIL
(Eng); ACKERGAUCHHEIL (German)

A weak-stemmed, erect, much-
branched herb growing to 20 cm high.
Leaves opposite, ovate to lanceolate.
Flowers solitary usually bright blue,
occasionally red.

Commonly found in disturbed and
open areas on fertile soils, in short
grassland and fields, and in shade of
trees at altitudes between 1400 and
2700 m.

In Libya it is grown as a medicinal
plant applied to wounds, ulcers and
snake bites. It also has insecticidal
properties.

Flowering from August to January,
*honeybees collect pollen and nectar
from the flowers.*

Punica granatum L. / Punicaceae
ROOMAN (Amh); RUMANA (Kef);
POMEGRANATE (Eng); GRANATAPFEL
(German)

A thorny ornamental shrub or tree
growing to 6 m tall. Leaves evergreen,
simple, and lanceolate. Flowers deep
red, emerge from the leaf axils.

Grown in many public and private
gardens at altitudes up to 2400 m.

Cultivated since ancient times as an
ornamental hedge plant and for its
edible fruits, this shrub is found wild
from India to Iran. It is salt and drought
tolerant and contains tannin.

In local medicine the leaves are used
against liver disorders and the fruits
against diarrhoea and for wound
dressing.

Flowering after the rains it is visited by
honeybees for pollen and nectar.

Clematis hirsuta Perr. & Guill. /
Ranunculaceae

AZO-HAREG, HASO (Amh); HIDDA (Or);
QEMIDA (Tya)

A vigorous annual climber, with stems
up to 5 m long. Leaves dark green,
smooth toothed. Flowers conspicuous
creamy-white, borne in leaf axils.

Growing on rich forest soils, at forest
edges and in remnants of montane
forests, often covering other bushes
and rocks at altitudes between 850
and 3200 m.

Flowering from October to January,
*honeybees collect pollen and nectar
from the flowers very frequently.*

Clematis simensis Fres. /
Ranunculaceae

ELAYDEEA, TILLO, HASO, ALAYA (Amh);
IDEFETI (Or); H'AREG (Tya)

A shrubby climber with stems growing
to 2 m long. Leaves dark shiny green,
with up to 5 leaflets. Flowers creamy-
white, borne in the leaf axils.

Commonly found in humid upland
forests, particularly at forest edges
and in bushland, often behaving as a
strong woody climber at altitudes
between 1500 and 3350 m.

In local medicine the leaves are used
for wound dressing, the sap for
febrifuge and bloat and seeds against
rheumatic pains. The very acid juice is
used for making tattoos, and possibly
also for engraving iron.

The very tough stems are used to tie
up the frame of CHIKKA houses.

Flowering from September to January,
*honeybees collect pollen and nectar
from the fowers frequently.*

Delphinium dasycaulon Fres. / Ranunculaceae

GEDEL-AMUQ (Amh); ILILI HURDY (Or); TSELLIM-DEBBESOM (Tre & Tya)

An erect perennial herb growing to 1 m tall from a woody elongated root. The stems are often solitary with a few divided leaves. Flowers vary from white, pale mauve and pink to dark blue.

Found in evergreen and deciduous forests, in partial shade of isolated trees, also on steep banks beside roads, paths and fields at altitudes between 1140 and 3350 m.

In local medicine the sap is used against coughs.

Flowering from September to April, *honeybees collect pollen and nectar from the flowers.*

Delphinium wellbyi Hemsl. / Ranunculaceae

GEDEL-AMUQ (Amh); TSELLIM-DEBBESOM (Tre & Tya)

A stout, rarely slender herb growing to 2 m tall from a fleshy rootstock. Leaves palmately divided into unequal segments. Flowers large and showy, sweetly scented, usually powder-blue with darker blue markings, sometimes mauve to pink, very rarely white.

Growing, often in masses, along waterways, on hillsides, along roads, in damp areas and in montane forests at altitudes from 1525 to 3800 m.

The flowers of both *D.dasycaulon* and *D.wellbyi* are used in preparing the blue-black dye with which some Ethiopian women tattoo the skin and gums.

Flowering from August to December, *honeybees collect pollen and nectar from the flowers.*

Nigella sativa L. / Ranunculaceae

T'KUR-AZMUD, AZMUD (Amh); AAF (Kef); HABASUDU, ABOSADA, NUGI GURACHA, GURATI (Or); AWOSETTA (Tya);

An erect annual, profusely branched herb growing to a height of 70 cm. Leaves pinnately dissected, with fine almost linear segments. Flowers star-shaped, usually pale blue, but sometimes blue-green.

Cultivated as a crop mostly in homegardens in higher altitudes between 1500 to 2500 m.

It is grown for its seeds which have a strong, pungent smell and flavour. They are used to flavour some kinds of bread and sauces, and in preparation of BERBERI. In local medicine the seeds are used against headaches and to induce abortions.

Flowering from August to October, *honeybees collect nectar and pollen very frequently.*

Ranunculus multifidus Forrsk. / Ranunculacea

HOGIO (Kef); MAKRUS (Tre); METMETI (Tya); BUTTERCUP (Eng)

A perennial herb, mostly erect but sometimes prostrate and rooting at some of the nodes, growing to 1 m tall. Leaves much divided into narrow lanceolate segments. Flowers numerous and shiny yellow.

Found in wet upland grassland, streamsides and swamps, near rivers and lakes, on wet slopes and in open montane forest at altitudes between 1200 and 3800 m.

Flowering all year round along waterways, *honeybees collect pollen and nectar from the flowers.*

Caylusea abyssinica *(Fresen.)*
Hilet & Mey. / Resedaceae

YERENCHI, TOLOLAT (Amh); RENDI,
JERENCHI, ARRANCHI (Or); MERRERET
(Tre)

An erect and ascending herb, mostly
annual or sometimes a short-lived
perennial. Leaves lanceolate. Flowers
small, white in racemes up to 20 cm
long.

Growing mostly in fallow ground and
fields, it is regarded as a harmless
weed of middle and higher altitudes
between 1600 and 2400 m.

The leaves are boiled and eaten as
greens in some places.

*Flowering from July to February,
honeybees collect pollen and nectar
from the flowers very frequently*

Gouania longispicata *Engl.* /
Rhamnaceae

A woody climber or scrambling shrub
with stems to 8 m long. Leaves
alternate, greyish with rusty brown
hairs on the conspicuous veins, and
toothed margins. Flowers small with
white to cream-coloured petals in
rusty-brown terminal panicles.

Growing in scrub, lowland and upland
forests and in riverine forests at
altitudes between 1000 to 2350 m.

*Flowering after the rains, honeybees
collect pollen and nectar from the
flowers.*

Helinus mystacinus *(Ait.) E. Mey.*
ex Steud. / Rhamnaceae

GALIMA (Amh)

A woody climber with pubescent
branches growing to 10 m long.
Leaves ovate or elliptic to almost
circular with some hairs. Flowers small
with white to yellowish-green petals.

Found throughout the country in forest
margins and clearings as well as
various types of open woodland and
bushland growing at altitudes from
1200 to 2200 m.

In local medicine fruits are used in
wound dressings.

*Flowering from September to October,
honeybees collect pollen and nectar.*

Fragaria x ananassa *Duchesne* /
Rosaceae
and also **F. vesca** *L.*

YEMDR-'NJORIE (Amh); STRAWBERRY
(Eng); ERDBEERE (German)

Low growing perennial herbs with
runners. In *F. x ananassa* the leaves
are blue-green and almost without
hairs while in *F. vesca* the leaves are
bright green and hairy on the upper
surface. Flowers with white petals and
many yellow stamens.

Grown in gardens and on a small
commercial scale around Addis Ababa
and Nasret. Yields can be very high
(20 t/ha or more), but the commercial
possibilities are limited due to the poor
keeping quality of the fruits.

*Honeybees are the chief pollinators of
strawberry flowers. The bees collect
small amounts of pollen and nectar
from the flowers.*

Rosa abyssinica *Lindley* / Rosaceae

MAWORDI (Ade); QEGA (Amh & Or); ARBEQ, MIRSENS, (Ge'ez); 'NGOCA (Gur); SEGO (Had); GORA, 'NCOTO, QAQAWWE, QEQEWWI (Or); DAYERO (Som); GAQA (Tya); SGIE-REDA-CISHA (Wel); ABYSSINIAN ROSE (Eng)

A prickly, climbing shrub, sometimes even forming a small tree, growing to 7 m high. Leaves evergreen and somewhat leathery; leaflets ovate to almost lanceolate with toothed margins. Flowers sweet-smelling with white or pale yellow petals and numerous yellow stamens.

Very common throughout the plateau, often forming thickets, sometimes standing alone as a small tree, at altitudes between 1900 and 3300 m.

Flowering throughout the year, *it is frequently visited by honeybees for pollen only.*

Rosa x richardii *Rehd.* / Rosaceae

TS'GIE-REDA (Amh); HBRE-MESRY, MESRY (Ge'ez); MUMMY-WREATH ROSE, SACRED ROSE (Eng)

A shrub growing to 4 m high, stems covered in prickles and stiff bristles. Leaflets broadly elliptic or ovate. Flowers pink, solitary or in heads.

This rose, very probably a hybrid of *R. gallica x phoenicia*, has been planted in churches and graveyards since ancient times. It has also escaped into dry forests and is found around villages and on roadsides at altitudes between 1000-2400 m.

Flowers are found all year round. *Honeybees collect pollen from the flowers frequently.*

Rubus apetalus *Poir.* / Rosaceae

'NJORIE (Amh); ARGI MELLITANO (Gam); JORE (Gur); HINJARO (Had); HAMAROO (Kem); GODA, GORCO, GUMERE, HALTUFA (Or); KOSHESHLLA (Tya); HENJORIYA (Wel)

A scrambling shrub growing to 2.5 m tall with scattered hooked spines on the stems. Leaves trifoliate; leaflets lanceolate to oblong-elliptic with toothed margins. Flowers with small pale pink petals or none, in panicles. The edible fruit is black when ripe.

Growing on forest edges, in secondary scrub, along streamsides at altitudes between 1500 to 3200 m.

In local medicine the leaves are used against diabetes mellitus.

Flowering is throughout the year with a peak from October to December. *Honeybees collect pollen and nectar from the flowers frequently.*

Rubus rosifolius *Sm.* / Rosaceae

'NJORIE (Amh)

A scrambling shrub with stems growing to 2.5 m long. The branches are covered with white hairs and straight spines. Leaflets in 3-5-pairs with a terminal leaflet. Flowers white or pink, arranged in few-flowered panicles. Fruits are pink, edible and acid.

This native of India and Sri Lanka has escaped from cultivation and is found in secondary growth in forests, bushland and wooded grassland and along roads and streams at altitudes of about 1950 m mainly in Keffa region.

Flowering from September to February, *honeybees frequently forage for the abundant pollen and nectar.*

Rubus steudneri *Schweinf.* / Rosaceae

'NJORIE (Amh); ARGI, MELLITANO (Gam); 'JORE (Gur); GORA, HINJARO (Had); HAMAROO (Kem); GODA, GORCO, GUMERE, HALTUFA (Or); KOSHESHLLA (Tya); HENJORIYA (Wel)

A scandent, very prickly shrub with deeply furrowed stems up to 4 m long. Leaves simple, with 3 or 5 leaflets which are obovate-elliptic and toothed. Flowers pink in large panicles and orange to dark red edible fruits.

Growing on forest edges and in secondary scrub and grassland at altitudes between 1600 and 3000 m.

Flowering from August to January, *honeybees collect pollen and nectar from the flowers frequently.*

Galineria saxifraga *(Hochst.)* Bridson / Rubiaceae

SOLIE, TOTAKOLLA (Amh); ADAMO, MITO, DIDU (Or)

A shrub up to 4 m or sometimes a small tree growing to 10 m high often with long, down-curved branches. Leaves opposite, glossy green above, pale green and often with reddish veins below, elliptic-oblong to lanceolate. Flowers waxy white, tinged pink, fragrant. The berries are red.

Found in evergreen montane grassland along forest edges and in evergreen scrub, often near streams at altitudes between 1500 to 2900 m.

In traditional medicine the fruits are used against GURMIT.

Flowering after the big rains the *honeybees collect pollen and nectar frequently.*

Pentanisia ouranogyne *S.Moore* / Rubiaceae

A perennial herb, much-branched or unbranched, growing to 30 cm high. The mostly hairy stems are arising from a somewhat woody branched rootstock. Leaves lanceolate to linear-lanceolate. Flowers bright blue arranged in many-flowered, sometimes branched umbels.

Found in *Acacia* woodland or bushland and wooded grassland at altitudes between 1400 and 1900 m.

Flowering almost all year round, *honeybees forage for pollen and nectar.*

Pentas schimperiana *(Rich.)* Vatke / Rubiaceae

WEYINAGIFT (Amh); KASSY (Or)

An erect woody herb with unbranched stems covered with soft hairs and growing to 1 m high. Leaves ovate. Flowers creamy-white to pink with 5-9 mm long tubes in a dense terminal corymb.

This plant is not very common. It is found in upland montane forests at altitudes up to 2600 m.

Leaves and flowers are used as an anthelmintic in local medicine.

Flowering is after the small rains from March to June. *Honeybees collect pollen and nectar from the flowers.*

Spermacoce sphaerostigma
(A.Rich.) Vatke / Rubiaceae

A small, often much-branched annual herb with erect quadrangular stems up to 40 cm long. Leaves elliptic-lanceolate to linear-lanceolate and entire. Flowers small, mauve, pale purple, lilac, or white with purple streaks; several to many, borne in axillary or terminal clusters.

Often found in disturbed areas, along roadsides and on waste places, occasionally in wooded grassland or montane scrub at altitudes between 520 and 2500 m.

Flowering during and after rains, *honeybees collect pollen and nectar from the flowers.*

Ruta chalepensis *L.* / Rutaceae

T'IENA-ADDAM (Amh); SALADO, SELOTIE (Gam); SENATAM (Ge'ez); TALATAM, CIRAKOTA (Or); CH'ENA-ADDAM (Tya); HERB OF GRACE, RUE (Eng); WEINRAUTE (German)

An erect, blue-green, perennial herb up to 1 m high. Leaves divided into many narrow segments. Flowers small, with dull yellow fringed petals. All parts of the plant have a distinctive spicy smell.

This spice plant is widely cultivated throughout the highlands above 1500 m as a culinary herb to flavour milk, cottage cheese, coffee and tea and a local beverage, called KUTI. It is also used in the preparation of BERBEFE.

Considered to be an important medicinal plant, the amharic name T'IENA-ADDAM means 'Health of Adam'.

It can be found in flower at most times in the year after the rains. *Honeybees frequently collect pollen and nectar from the flowers*.

Osyris quadripartita *Decn.* / Santalaceae

QUERET (Amh); QERES (Amh, Tre & Tya); KARO (Gur); REGA, WATO, ASASO (Or); QRUBITA-ARAZ (Saho); QERES (Tya)

A much-branched shrub growing to 7 m tall. Leaves elliptic to elliptic-oblong. Flowers yellow-green, either female and male flowers, born in leaf axils.

Found in gallery forest, degraded woodland and scrub at altitudes between 1600 to 2900 m.

The bark is used for tanning.

Flowering is almost all year round. *Honeybees collect both pollen and nectar.*

Sideroxylon oxyacantha *Baill.* / Sapotaceae

ATAT, TIFFE (Amh); BITTE (Or); SERREROT (Tya)

A shrub or tree growing to a height of 25 m with thorny stems. Leaves sessile, obovate and up to 6 cm long, arranged in clusters. Flowers white, born in axillary clusters with the leaves.

Found in upper highland forests, evergreen bushland and in hedges around compounds in altitudes between 2200 and 2500 m.

In local medicine the leaves are used against eye diseases.

Flowering from March to May, *honeybees collect pollen and nectar from the flowers.*

Alectra sessiliflora (Vahl) O. Kuntze var. senegalensis (Benth.) Hepper / Scrophulariaceae

A semi-parasitic, stoutly stemmed annual or perennial herb, branching or simple at the base, with purplish stems, growing to 50 cm high. Leaves dull green above and pale beneath, broadly lanceolate. Flowers yellow in branched terminal inflorescences.

Found as a parasite occasionally on *Guizotia abyssinica* and other Asteraceae at altitudes between 1400 and 2900 m.

Flowering from October to December, *honeybees forage for pollen and nectar.*

Celsia scrophulariaefolia Hochst. ex A.Rich. / Scrophulariaceae

An erect, often woody, hairless herb. Leaves ovate to lanceolate. Flowers lagrge, yellow with reddish markings, in simple terminal racemes.

Similar to *V. sinaiticum*, but only having 4 stamens.

Growing in drier scrub areas of the Plateau particularly on red soils and also along streams. This is the most widespread species of *Celsia* in Ethiopia at altitudes between 1300 and 3800 m.

Flowering almost all year round, *honeybees collect pollen and nectar from the flowers.*

Bellardia trixago (L.) All. / Scrophulariaceae

An erect, sometimes branched, annual herb growing to 40 cm high. Leaves linear-lanceolate and sparsely toothed. Flowers white, with pink to red spots.

Growing along waterways and in damp areas, along roadsides, in grassland and on disturbed areas at altitudes between 1900 and 3500 m.

Flowering from September to February, *honeybees collect pollen and nectar from the flowers.*

Craterostigma plantagineum Hochst. / Scrophulariaceae

BABUN (Amh); FOSI-ANQRBIT (Tya)

A small perennial plant to 10 cm tall. Leaves broadly ovate, slightly succulent, forming a tight rosette on the ground. Flowers whitish with blue to pink veins.

Found on bare ground in grassland and rocky slopes at altitudes between 950 and 2800 m.

In local medicine the herb is used against snake, insect and scorpion bites and the roots against headaches.

Flowering mainly at the beginning of any rainy season, *honeybees collect pollen and nectar.*

Hebenstretia dentata *L.* /
Scrophulariaceae

A shrubby herb with erect stems growing to 30 cm tall. Leaves narrow, needle-shaped. Flowers usually white with orange markings.

Found throughout the country on grassy mountain slopes, grassland, rocky slopes and along roadsides at altitudes between 2100 and 4200 m.

Flowering almost all year round in wetter places, *honeybees collect pollen and nectar from the flowers.*

Verbascum sinaiticum *Benth.* /
Scrophulariaceae

KETETINNA, YEAHYA-JERO, DABAKADET (Amh); GURRA-HARRE, AMBOKANA (Or); TIRNAHA (Tya)

An erect woolly herb growing to 2 m high. Leaves large, grey-green and covered with a dense felt of soft hairs, ovate to oblong or lanceolate, forming a basal rosette. Flowers large, yellow, in erect simple or branched terminal racemes.

Found in rocky places, on disturbed ground, beside roads and as a weed in fallow ground at altitudes between 900 and 3000 m.

The leaves are used in local medicine against coughs.

Flowering all year round, but more profusely from August to May, *honeybees collect pollen and nectar from the flowers frequently.*

Veronica abyssinica *Fresen.* /
Scrophulariaceae

A trailing pubescent herb with sometimes ascending stems. Leaves ovate and cordate with toothed margins. Flowers blue and quite large.

This plant is common in upland grassland, forest edges, in open pasture land at edges of cultivation and under partial shade of trees at altitudes between 1500 and 3200 m. Flowering almost all year round, *honeybees collect pollen and nectar from the flowers frequently.*

Veronica persica *Chiov.* /
Scrophulariaceae

An erect soft-stemmed annual weed, up to 40 cm high. Leaves ovate, subcordate, with crenate to toothed margins. Flowers pale blue, erect or sometimes hanging on stalks in leaf axiles.

This herb is a colonizer from the Middle East which is very common in fields and grassland at altitudes up to 2500 m.

Flowering almost all year round, *honeybees collect pollen and nectar from the flowers.*

Brucea antidysenterica

J.F.Miller / Simaroubaceae

KAKERO, WAGINOS (Amh); DADATU,
TOLLO, TAMIGGIA (Or); HADAWI (Som);
MELITA (Tya)

An evergreen, erect shrub or small
tree growing to 7 m high. Leaves with
ovate to oblong or elliptic leaflets,
usually crowded at the end of
branches. Flowers pale-yellow in erect
racemes from the leaf axils.

Found at altitudes from 1000 to 3700
m in bushland, at forest edges or in
regrowth of deforested areas.

In local medicine the dry powdered
bark is used against dysentery and
decoctions of fruits and leaves are
used against dysentery, diarrhoea and
fever.

It is flowering all year round and
*frequently visited by honeybees for
pollen and nectar.*

Capsicum annuum *L. /*

Solanaceae

BERBERE, SCHIRBA, MIT'MIT'A, QARYA
(Amh); BERBERE (Or); GREEN PEPPER
(Eng); PAPRIKA (German)

A cultivated annual or perennial
growing to 1.5 m high. Leaves ovate
and acuminate, very variable in size.
Flowers white, solitary or in pairs,
terminal or apparently axillary.

Probably native to Central America the
plant spread rapidly over the whole
world in the 16th century and is
cultivated as the most important spice
of the country at altitudes between
1000 to 3000 m.

*Honeybees collect pollen and nectar
from the flowers occasionally.*

Cyphomandra betacea *(Cav.)*

Sendtn. / Solanaceae

AMBARUT (Amh); TREE TOMATO (Eng)

A branched shrub growing to 5 m tall.
Leaves large, lanceolate to heart-
shaped, alternate and with irregularly
sharply toothed margins. Flowers
small, greenish-white and scented.

Cultivated for its fruits, which are eaten
raw or stewed, it has only been
introduced to Ethiopia at an
experimental level.

The fruits are red, egg-shaped, in
clusters and with a sweet-sour flavour.
Native to tropical America it is a quite
widely cultivated in East Africa.

*Honeybees collect pollen and nectar
from the flowers.*

Datura arborea *L.* / Solanaceae

A shrub growing to 4 m high. Leaves
large, soft, and hairy, up to about 40
cm long. Flowers white, trumpet-
shaped, 20 cm long and sweetly-
scented.

A common garden and hedge plant,
originally from Chile / Peru. It grows at
altitudes up to 2400 m. It is poisonous.

Flowering after the rains, *honeybees
collect pollen and nectar from the
flowers occasionally.*

Datura stramonium L. /
Solanaceae

AT'E-FARIS, ASTENAGER (Amh); KIMATARI, MANJI, ASANGIRRA (Or); MESERBA', THRIFRA (Tya); THORN APPLE, JIMSON WEED (Eng); WEIßER STECHAPFEL (German)

A strong smelling annual herb, up to 1.2 m tall. Leaves dark shiny green, large with irregular sharply toothed margins. Flowers large white and tubular.

Found abundantly on fertile soils in fields and beside roads and paths at altitudes between 1250 and 2400 m.

This introduced weed is poisonous to livestock. In local medicine leaves are used against headache and for wound dressing for animals. Boiled seeds are used against toothaches.

Flowering from August to February, *honeybees collect pollen and nectar from the flowers.*

Discopodium penninervium
Hochst. / Solanaceae

ALUMA, AMERARO (Amh); MARARO (Or); ALHEM (Tya)

A shrub or small tree growing to 12 m tall with slightly fleshy stems and brown-hairy branchlets. Leaves large, slightly fleshy, simple, elliptic to oblong-elliptic. Flowers yellow-green or yellowish-white, borne in the leaf axils.

Found in forest margins, along roadsides, fences and in scrub at altitudes between 2100 and 2600 m.

In local medicine it is used for its strong smell. The dried stem is burnt as a fumigant during child birth.

Flowering from September to April, *honeybees collect pollen and nectar from the flowers.*

Lycopersicon esculentum *Mill.*
/ Solanaceae

TIMATIM (Amh); TOMATO (Eng); TOMATE (German)

A variable herb growing to 2 m tall with solid hairy stems which are rooting at the nodes. Leaves spirally arranged, often divided into unevenly shaped pinnae which are usually oval and irregularly toothed. Flowers yellow, borne in cymes opposite to or even in between the leaves. Fruits fleshy, round and yellow to red when ripe.

Cultivated in home gardens and on a larger scale throughout the country at altitudes up to 2500 m.

Because the fruits are sensitive to sunburn the leaves are not pruned so the fruits get protection.

Honeybees are helpful pollinating agents and they collect pollen and nectar from the flowers.

Nicandra physalodes (L.)
Gaertn. / Solanaceae

AT'E-FARIS (Amh); CHECHEYE (Had); AZANGIRA (Or); GHERACCIA (Tya); APPLE OF PERU (Eng)

A much-branched, erect, annual herb growing to 1.2 m high. Leaves alternate with irregularly deeply-toothed margins. Flowers pale blue to purplish with white centres.

Frequently found in fertile areas, on disturbed ground, and very often as a weed of crops like maize at altitudes between 600 and 2400 m.

Flowering is almost all year round and *honeybees collect abundant pollen and some nectar from the flowers frequently.*

Nicotiana rustica L. / Solanaceae

TAMBO (Or)

An erect glandular-pubescent cultivated plant up to 70 cm tall. Leaves soft, yellow-green and entire. Flowers yellow in terminal cymose panicles with a bell-shaped calyx.

Grown on some farms in the Arba Minch area, ornamental varieties are found in public and private gardens up to 2400 m.

This is "the farmer's tobacco", probably cultivated first in USA and now throughout the tropics.

Flowering after the big rain *honeybees collect pollen and nectar from the flowers.*

Nicotiana tabacum L. / Solanaceae

TMBAHO (Amh); TIMBO, BALATIMBO (Or); SINKHEN (Tya); TOBACCO (Eng); TABAK (German)

An erect glandular-pubescent annual or biennial growing to 2.5 m high. Leaves ovate-elliptic. Flowers white to pinkish in terminal panicles.

A cultivated crop plant found in house gardens in some parts of the country, and sometimes escaped into waste ground and along streams at altitudes between 1700 and 2400 m.

Tobacco is considered an agent of the devil by the Ethiopian Orthodox Church.

In southern Ethiopia chewed leaves are put into the throats of sheep and oxen to kill internal parasites.

Honeybees collect nectar and pollen frequently and the plant is a honey source.

Physalis peruviana L. / Solanaceae

AWTT' (Amh); AUTI, BISI (Or); CAPE GOOSEBERRY (Eng)

A trailing to erect pubescent herbaceous annual or perennial herb to 80 cm high. Leaves ovate, entire and alternate. Flowers small and yellow and borne in leaf axils. Fruits are yellow berries enclosed in a papery calyx.

This introduced plant is abundant in waste areas and also found at forest edges and on bushland at altitudes between 2000 and 2600 m.

Fruits are commonly used against insect bites and used during time of food shortages for surviving.

Flowering almost all year round, *honeybees collect pollen and small amounts of nectar from the flowers.*

Solanum benderianum Dammer / Solanaceae

A densely hairy climbing shrub with stems growing to 10 m long. Leaves ovate-elliptic, dark green above and pale beneath. Flowers blue-purple or white to pale blue or lilac, arranged in lax pendent terminal corymbs.

Found in evergreen montane forests, along roadsides, in clearings of forests and at forest edges and sometimes grown as an ornamental at altitudes between 1500 and 3300 m.

Flowering all year round, *honeybees forage for good amounts of pollen and nectar very frequently.*

Solanum giganteum *Jacq.* /
Solanaceae

MBWAI (Amh)

A soft-wooded wide-branching erect shrub growing to 3.5 m tall with stems covered with short triangular prickles. Leaves oblanceolate, entire or with wavy margins, upper surface thinly downy and white-velvety beneath. Flowers white, arranged in dense subterminal corymbs.

Found in waste land and disturbed areas and along roadsides in altitudes between 1500 and 2400 m.

Flowering from September to February, *honeybees are occasionally visiting the flowers for pollen only.*

Solanum incanum *L.* /
Solanaceae

HIDDEE (Or); 'NGULE (Tya); SODOM APPLE (Eng)

An erect woody herb with prickles growing to 2.5 m. Leaves ovate to lanceolate and entire to sinuate. Flowers pale mauve to violet in racemes.

A widespread and troublesome weed and roadside shrub, found from 450 m to 2000 m and sometimes higher (2500 m).

The unripe fruits are poisonous. The ripe fruit of *S. incanum*, which is extremely hard, causes severe tooth-decay if eaten. Often the spiny stems with yellow fruits remain standing long after the plant has died.

Fruits are used for wound dressing.

Flowering throughout the year it is occasionally *visited by honeybees for pollen only*

Solanum indicum *L.* /
Solanaceae

IMBWAY, MKOKO (Amh); HANCUCU (Or)

A shrubby herb growing to 80 cm high with spines on stems, leaves and calyx. It is sometimes covered with hairs and sometimes hairless. Flowers are white, sometimes pale mauve.

The fruits are orange-red and poisonous, but used in local medicine against intestinal complaints.

It is a widespread herb of disturbed habitats at altitudes from 1400 to 2500 m.

Flowering all year round it is occasionally visited by *honeybees for pollen and nectar.*

Solanum melongena *L.* /
Solanaceae

DEBERJAN, BAZINJA (Amh); EGG PLANT, EGG-FRUIT, AUBERGINE (Eng)

A short-lived branched perennial herb or even a shrub, grown as an annual, and growing to 1.5 m high. Leaves simple, arranged singly or in pairs, ovate or sometimes lobed and leathery. Flowers purple or violet, either solitary or in 2-5-flowered cymes. Fruits large and ovoid, smooth and shiny, yellow, purple, black or white in colour.

This crop probably originated in India and is nowadays a grown by vegetables producers and in many backyards and home gardens at altitudes between 1700 and 2100 m.

Honeybees collect pollen and nectar from the flowers and are important pollinators.

Solanum nigrum L. / Solanaceae

T'KUR-AWTT' (Amh); ACHO (Kef); SAMAREYE (Or); BLACK NIGHT SHADE (Eng); SCHWARZER NACHTSCHATTEN (German)

A soft and erect, annual herb growing to 60 cm high, unarmed. Leaves elliptic, entire. Flowers small white, arranged in clusters.

Commonly found on cropland and in disturbed areas, along roadsides, at altitudes between 900 and 2900 m.

It is known as NECH AWTT' (Amh), when the fruits are unripe, and KEYEE AWTT' or T'KUR AWTT' (Amh), when the red or black berries are ripe and edible.

Flowering all year round, *honeybees collect occasional small amounts of pollen from the flowers.*

Solanum tuberosum L. / Solanaceae

DNCH (Amh); DOKO (Kef); DINICHA-SHEWA (Or); POTATOES (Eng); KARTOFFEL (German)

A short-lived perennial herb, grown as an annual with angular stems to 1 m tall. Leaves pinnate, with small leaflets. Flowers fairly large, white, yellow, blue or purple arranged in few-flowered erect cymes.

Cultivated at higher elevations throughout the country because of its edible swollen underground tubers at altitudes up to 2400 m.

The plant is propagated vegetatively, therefore the flowers are only important to plant breeders.

The potato flower secretes no nectar and only little pollen is available and insects visits are few. *Honeybees were observed to visit the flowers for pollen only.*

Grewia ferruginea Hochst. ex Rich. / Tiliaceae

LONGATA (Amh); BURURI, DOKONNU (Or); ZUNGUAH, SAUMAH (Tya)

A shrub or small tree growing to 4 m tall. Leaves obovate-elliptic with closely crenate margins and covered with short hairs beneath. Flowers large, white, sweet-scented, arranged in threes with the middle one opening first.

Found in semi-arid woodland, in shrub and evergreen bushland and along river banks at altitudes from 1000 to 2100 m.

In local medicine the roots are used as anthelmintic. Locally the leaves are used to wash wooden utensils, such as TELA containers.

Flowering almost all year round, *honeybees collect pollen and nectar from the flowers frequently.*

Sparmannia ricinocarpa (Eckl. & Zeyh.) Kuntze / Tiliaceae

CHIMKI, WULKEFA (Amh); ANCIN (Or)

A hairy, much-branched, erect or scandent shrub, reaching a height of 3 m. Leaves deeply 3-5-lobed, cordate to ovate and soft to touch. Flowers white to pink.

Widespread between 2300 and 3300 m, at forest edges, in forest clearings and in scrub and bushes along stream-beds and persisting in hedges.

The fruit, red-brown when ripe, catches on to clothing and animal coats with its long spines.

Flowering from August to February, *honeybees collect pollen and nectar from the flowers frequently.*

Triumfetta pilosa *Roth.* /
Tiliaceae

SCIAMHEGIT (Amh); GETCHAE, GHECCIE (Tya)

An erect pubescent perennial herb or undershrub growing to 3 m high. Leaves narrowly elliptic or narrowly to broadly ovate, unlobed (rarely indistinctly 3-lobed). Flowers small and yellow.

Growing in upland grassland, along roadsides and paths, in upland forests and in riverine thicket, in old cultivation and as a weed in altitudes between 1000 and 2200 m.

Flowering from July to November, *the honeybees work on the flowers all day round and they collect pollen and nectar from the flowers very frequently.*

Triumfetta rhomboidea *Jacq.* /
Tiliaceae

WEEO (Anu); KATHI (Mur); DAARO, MEDER, DUBBA (Tya)

An erect woody herb or shrub growing to 1 m high with longitudinally grooved stems. Leaves simple and alternate, broadly elliptic or obovate and deeply lobed. Flowers yellow, borne in short, condensed axillary cymes.

Growing as a weed in fields, along roadsides, in clearings and along paths in forests and scrub, along riverbanks and degraded bushland at altitudes between 500 and 2000 m.

Flowering from September to December, *honeybees forage for pollen and nectar very frequently.*

Tropaeolum majus *L.* /
Tropaeolaceae

INDIAN CROSS, GARDEN NASTURTIUM (Eng); KAPUZINERKRESSE (German)

A prostrate, soft-stemmed annual or sometimes perennial, more or less succulent herb, with stems up to 2 m long. Leaves simple orbicular or somewhat kidney-shaped. Flowers sweet-scented, large, yellow, red, scarlet, maroon or creamy-white or even mixed in colour.

Commonly cultivated in gardens and naturalised in hedgerows at altitudes between 1300 and 2400 m.

This native to South America is a popular garden plant, the common garden nasturtium, with edible leaves and flowers which have a mild mustard flavour.

Flowering all year round it provides *honeybees with pollen and nectar.*

Girardinia bullosa *(Steudel)*
Wedd. / Urticaceae

DOBI (Or); DEGUSTA (Tya)

An erect annual herb growing to 3 m high. Leaves ovate to cordate, with braod lobes. Flowers yellowish, male flowers are in 20 cm long spikes, those of female flowers are smaller and with fewer flowers. The whole plant is covered with long stinging hairs.

Found at forest edges and in clearings, along roads and often near houses at altitudes from 1750 to 3000 m.

A fibre for making string can be extracted from the stems.

Flowering after the rains, *honeybees collect pollen from the male flowers.*

Urtica simensis *Steudel* /
Urticaceae

SAMMA (Amh & Tya); DOBI (Or)

An erect, unbranched, perennial herb up to 1 m high. Leaves oval and coarsely toothed. Flowers greenish-white, produced on stems up to 5 cm long from the leaf axils. The whole plant is covered with stinging hairs containing formic, acetic and other organic acids.

Endemic, often found in disturbed areas particularly around houses as it thrives best where there are high concentrations of nitrogenous compounds, such as in Addis Ababa and other towns in Ethiopia, at altitudes between 1500 and 3400 m.

The leaves of *Urtica simensis* are boiled and eaten as a leafy vegetable in some parts of the country.

Flowering all year round it is *frequently visited by honeybees for pollen only.*

Clerodendron cordifolium
A.Rich. / Verbenaceae

MISSIRICH (Amh)

A weakly erect perennial herb growing from a stout rootstock up to 1.2 m tall. Leaves ovate and acuminate. Flowers have white petals with bright to deep red central markings.

Growing on red soils, in grassland, deciduous open woodland, along roadsides and in wooded savanna at altitudes between 1300 and 2100 m.

Flowering is all year round, in drier parts the plant *is a very important nectar and pollen supply for bees which are frequently visiting the flowers all day round.*

Clerodendron myricoides
(Hochst.) R.Br. ex Vatke /
Verbenaceae

SULTHE, ABEKA, MISSIRICH, BUSHA-DUBSIS (Amh); AGHIO (Kef); MUSERICH, SOYYOMA HARMAL ADI, TIRRO (Or); MEDISSA (Sid); SURBATRI (Tya)

A slender shrub growing to 3 m high, with some branches scrambling through other plants. Leaves simple, elliptic or oblanceolate and toothed. Flowers sweetly scented, purple-blue to pale-lilac.

Commonly found at forest edges and in mountain scrub, on degraded woodland and along roadsides throughout the country from 900 to 2500 m.

The leaves and stem have a distinctive smell when crushed. It has many uses in local medicine.

Flowering at any time of the year, *honeybees collect pollen and nectar from the flowers.*

Duranta erecta *L.* / Verbenaceae

An evergreen shrub or tree up to 6 m tall with drooping and sometimes prickly branches. Leaves opposite, simple and oval. Flowers small, pale mauve, trumpet-shaped, in terminal clusters.

Grown as an ornamental as well as a hedge plant and commonly found in degraded savanna woodland, at forest edges and riverine forests at altitudes between 1500 and 2400 m.

The young stems are used as a toothbrush.

Flowering from all year round, *honeybees collect pollen and nectar frequently.*

Lantana camera L. / Verbenaceae

YEWOF-QOLO (Amh); SHIMBERO, KATEKATE (Or); LANTANA (Eng)

A large shrub growing to a height of 3 m and even forming thick hedges with its rough branches having short recurved prickles. Leaves dark green, lanceolate and cordate. Flower heads circular, composed of small, sessile tubular flowers, which are yellow, orange and later on deep red.

Introduced from South America it is cultivated as an ornamental hedge plant in altitudes between 1300 to 2700 m.

It is toxic to livestock and becoming a noxious weed in grazing areas.

Flowering all year round, *bees only visit it when there is a dearth of more beneficial flowers.*

Lantana trifolia L. / Verbenaceae

YEREGNA-QOLO, KESSIE (Amh); MIDANI-BERA, SUKE (Or)

A low shrub growing to 3 m high with slender branches. Leaves simple, dark greyish green above and arranged in a whorls or clusters of 3. Flowers lilac or pink to red sessile on long stalks.

Found in forest regrowth, on dry scrubland and in evergreen forests, on wooded grassland and along paths at altitudes between 1300 and 2500 m.

It is used as a condiment in milk and in local medicine against colds, ringworm and udder inflammation. The roots are used against wet eczema and BARLE. The fruits are edible.

Flowering from February to November, *it is occasionally visited by honeybees if there is no other food source available.*

Lippia adoensis Hochst. ex Walp. / Verbenaceae

KOSERET, KESSIE (Amh); QUERERET (Gur); KASEY (Or); KUSAY (Tya)

An erect shrubby herb, growing to 3 m tall from a woody rootstock. Leaves aromatic, covered with soft hairs. Flowers small, pink to purple, sometimes yellowish in long spikes.

Growing on rocky hillsides, at margins of secondary forests, along paths and in dry evergreen woodland, sometimes cultivated in gardens at altitudes between 1700 to 2800 m.

The crushed leaves are used as a termite repellent and are commonly used to clean milk pots and also for flavouring butter.

Flowering from May to February, *honeybees collect pollen and nectar from the flowers.*

Premna schimperi Engl. / Verbenaceae

CHECHO (Amh); TOTOKE, URGESA (Or)

A much-branched spreading shrub, growing to 4m high, or more rarely a small spreading tree, up to 8m tall. Leaves yellowish-green, simple and broadly ovate with a strong spicy smell when crushed. Flowers sweetly scented, white or greenish-white, numerous and arranged in terminal corymbs.

Found along riverbanks, in open and dry *Acacia* bushland, along forest edges and margins of secondary growth, on stony hillsides and on degraded woodland at altitudes between 1300 and 2400 m.

Flowering all year round but more profusely after rains, *honeybees collect pollen and nectar frequently.*

Verbena officinalis *L.* / Verbenaceae

AKKORAGAG, ATTUCH (Amh); SERRUFIT (Tya); EISENKRAUT (German)

An erect, very branching, pubescent annual, growing to 1 m tall. Leaves subsessile pinnately or ternately lobed. Flowers pale mauve in thin spikes.

Found on dry grassland and along roadsides, in fallow land, dry hillsides and as a weed in cultivation at altitudes between 1500 and 3100 m.

It has many uses in local medicine: against dysentery, throat inflammations, burns, vermifuge and respiratory complaints.

Flowering after the rains from August to November and from February to June, *honeybees collect pollen and nectar from the flowers very frequently.*

Cyphostemma adenocaule

(Steud.ex A.Rich) Desc. ex Wild & Dr. / Vitaceae

ASSERKUSH (Amh); H'AREG-TEMEN, QWRHO (Tya)

A herbaceous climber or scrambler with stems growing to 6 m long. Leaves 5-11-foliate; leaflets elliptic or ovate, with crenate or toothed margins. Flowers pale yellow in large panicles.

Found on wooded grassland, in riverine forest and clearings of forests at altitudes between 850 to 2650 m.

The tuberous roots are edible and are used in local medicine to treat suppurating wounds.

Flowering from April to June, *honeybees are very frequently foraging for pollen and nectar.*

Vitis vinifera *L.* / Vitaceae

AYNEB (Ade); WEYN (Amh); 'NKUTI (Ge'ez); WEYNI (Gur & Tya); 'NABA (Or); WEYNIYYA (Wel); GRAPE (Eng); WEINSTOCK (German)

A woody perennial climber or trailer with stems up to 20 m long. Leaves usually deeply lobed with a wide heart-shaped lamina. Flowers small yellowish-white, produced in dense many-flowered panicles. The fruits are green, yellowish to purplish violet.

The grapevine has been cultivated for many centuries by priests throughout most of the Ethiopian highlands to make communion wine.

Honeybees are valuable for this plant as their visits increase both yield and quality of fruit. *Honeybees collect pollen and small amounts of nectar from the flowers and the juice from fruits which have burst open.*

Tribulus terrestris *L.* / Zygophyllaceae

AQAQMA (Amh); KURUMSHIT (Or); KAKITE-HARMATH, KWA'KITO, KUREMEHIT, QOTTBET (Tya)

A tap-rooted prostrate, annual herb with much-branched stems growing to 1 m long, covered with silky hairs. Leaves pinnately compound in opposite pairs; leaflets oblong to elliptic. Flowers yellow, borne on single stalks from the leaf axils.

This herb is found in fields and pastures at altitudes between 600 to 2400 m.

It flowers throughout the year and the *quantity and quality of pollen and nectar has great value for the development and maintenance of bee colonies at lower altitudes.*

100 TREES

FOR BEES

Introduction

In the past, contributions to knowledge on trees made by various national botanical institutions, ICRAF, and others, were publications concentrating on the indigenous trees and shrubs of countries such as Kenya, Uganda, Tanzania, Sudan and Ethiopia. These publications were developed primarily to serve as identification guides for trees, and contained their botanical descriptions, often with hand-drawn pictures and later photographs, their agro-ecological or geographical distribution, and their established uses and value as timber and fuelwood species. In all these, a specific initiative to list their minor forest product values as medicinal herbs, spices, etc., and particularly with regard to apiculture, has been lacking.

In the 1930s annual reports produced by the colonial forestry authorities of East Africa, particularly from the southern provinces of the Sudan, recorded the significant financial export value that ivory, honey, and beeswax made to the local economy.

In Ethiopia, the production of TEJ as a local festive drink and the use of beeswax for candle making, has a long tradition and is an integral part of the cultural heritage within the many ethnic and religious groups.

In the past, apiculture had always been a component of the extension work within the Ministry of Agriculture and the Relief and Rehabilitation Commission (RRC). In 1991, the Transitional Government of Ethiopia began anew the task to develop, as part of its total approach to natural resource management and development, a policy to encourage, at the grassroots level, private tree planting and tree farming initiatives by and for the farmers (both men and women) on their own holdings.

Within regional and national forest priority areas, farmers are being encouraged to put out private domestic bee colonies, particularly along the edges of forests where bees can profit from both flowering trees as well as the accompanying herbs and shrubs. Private farmers have taken up this challenge and peasant apiculture is again coming alive. Benefit-sharing from wild bee colonies found within these forests is also permitted.

The revitalized planting of indigenous trees and shrubs for multipurpose and/or agro-forestry usage is pressing forward. Local-level land use planning by the farming community is becoming a reality again. This encompases all elements of natural resource management, utilization, including benefit-sharing and the combining of trees, shrubs, medicinal plants, including beekeeping traditions and their complicated and delicate ecological interlinkage.

Private farmers are being motivated to plant multipurpose tree and shrub species as windbreaks across their fields, living fences around their property, for woodfuel energy and polewood woodlots. Wherever possible, honey, pollen and nectar producing trees and shrubs are to be included within all of these silvicultural alternatives. At the same time, private farming groups, schools, church groups, and private commercial agriculturalists are being encouraged to go into tree farming by planting shelter belts and larger plots for woodfuel. Pollen and nectar tree and shrub species are to be interwoven into these programmes.

This publication is meant to meet the needs of the both individual farmers and farmer groups, by pointing out the tree and shrub species best suited for them to provide pollen and nectar for their bee colonies. It will hopefully also provide the Ministry of Natural Resources Development and Environmental Protection and the Ministry of Agriculture at both the Central and Regional levels, as well as bilateral and multilateral agencies, NGO development agents and extension service personnel with a vital source of pictorial and factual data regarding honey, nectar and pollen-producing trees and shrubs. With this information, they can then professionally approach and encourage farmers better to diversify their farming techniques, thereby motivating both men and women to produce more per unit of land.

Providing the farmer with the alternative to plant nectar and pollen-producing honeybee friendly tree and shrub species, should contribute significantly to the farmer's annual cash crop possibilities, supplement dietary needs, and enhance the total health and welfare of the family.

The GTZ Forestry Project in Ethiopia, PN 87.2059.1-01.100, has encouraged the initiatives undertake by the Ministry of Agriculture of the Transitional Government of Ethiopia, the National Herbarium of Addis Ababa University, and the German Development Service (DED) to prepare and produce this book. It is hoped that the book will find a place not only in the libraries of teaching institutions, but also, and preferably, in the villages and homes of the rural extension workers and farmers of Ethiopia.

George Conn (Dr)
GTZ Project Co-ordinator
PN 87.2059.1-01.158
Addis Ababa
1994-03-07

215

Dracaena steudneri *Engl.*

CHOWYEH, TABATOS (Amh); YUƆO (Kef); LANKUSO, MERKO, SHOWYE (Or)

Family: Agavaceae

Description: Shrub or small tree, up to 15 m, with an unbranched stem or stem branched at the base only. <u>Bark</u>: grey-brown to reddish with horizontal markings from detached leaves. The trunk is swollen at the base. <u>Leaves</u>: crowded, dark shiny green, arranged in large terminal rosettes; lanceolate to linear-lanceolate, up to 1 m long. <u>Flowers</u>: white or pale yellow-green and fragrant; arranged in tight terminal clusters on green stems forming a massive flowering head, about 1 m long. <u>Fruits</u>: black when ripe and about 1 cm long, juicy and eaten by birds.

Flowering in January and February.

Distribution: Growing in Afromontane forests, particularly in clearings and at forest edges from 1300 to 2500 m around Lake Tana and in forest of western, southwest and southeastern Ethiopia. Also commonly planted as a live fence around compounds and in gardens in many parts of the country where there is enough rainfall. Its rainfall range is from 1000 to 2200 mm per year.

In similar habitats throughout East, Central and Southern Africa including Angola.

Practical notes: Fast-growing from cuttings.

Uses: A very common hedge plant of wetter parts of the country. It is also used as a boundary marker and as a windbreak. Leaves are used for wrapping food, particularly KOCHO, BULLA and butter. It is also often used as an ornamental in gardens and a pot plant in hotels, public buildings and houses.

Apicultural value: *Honeybees collect pollen and nectar from the flowers throughout the day. Because of the late flowering period the tree is valuable for strengthening bee colonies after harvests in December.*

217

Mangifera indica L.

MANGO (Amh, Or & Tya); MANGO (Eng)

Family: Anacardiaceae

Description: An evergreen tree with a large, dense, widely spreading crown. Bark: brown and smooth when young and almost black and fissured when old, exuding a resinous latex when damaged. Leaves: dark green, simple, alternate and lanceolate, up to 30 cm long, smelling of turpentine when crushed; young leaves often copper-coloured. Flowers: cream-coloured to pinkish in large terminal panicles up to 20 cm long; abundant, very small with 200 to 6000 flowers in each panicle; either male or bisexual in the same inflorescence. Fruit: large and heavy, almost round to irregularly ovoid, hanging on long stalks.

Flowering from December to March.

Distribution: A cultivated crop plant. It grows best between 500 (Gambella) and 1800 m. Originally from the Indo-Burmese monsoon region, the mango was brought from Arabia to Africa in the first millenium AD. However, it is a recent introduction to Ethiopia. Nowadays grown in warmer areas throughout the country, particularly along the edges of rivers or where irrigation is available.

It is now widely grown throughout tropical and subtropical America, Asia and Africa.

Practical notes: The tree is often a favoured habitat for mosquitos.

Uses: The tree is very suitable as a windbreak and for soil conservation measures and for shade.

It is a very important fruit tree rich in vitamins, but it plays a minor role in local trade because it needs very careful handling due to the sensitivity of the fruit to bruising. It is also very heavy to transport because of the large stone.

It is suitable for planting on terraces in soil erosion prevention. It also makes a decorative roadside tree and an useful firebreak.

The wood can be used for firewood.

Apicultural value: *Honeybees forage for the abundant nectar and pollen from the flowers all day round. Nectar secretion is reduced by drought. Juice from damaged fruit may be collected by bees and flavour the honey which is reddish amber. Bees are the most important pollinators to increase fruit production, and colony density should be high.*

Rhus glutinosa subsp. **neoglutinosa** *(M. Gilbert) M. Gilbert*

'MBS, QMMO (Amh); SAMO, WERKELLO (Gam); ADESSA, MUGAN, TATESSA (Or); HAMS, MECECO, SHEMUT, SHEMUT-EFRUS (Tre); MENGI, TETA'LO (Tya)

Family: Anacardiaceae

Description: Small endemic tree, up to 10 m high, with shiny sticky reddish-brown stems, usually glabrous; sweetly aromatic when cut; the trunk is up to 25 cm in diameter. <u>Leaves</u>: alternate and trifoliate; leaflets oblong-elliptic to lanceolate, always acuminate, with a reddish midrib. <u>Flowers</u>: small, yellowish-white to greenish and grouped in terminal or axillary clusters. <u>Fruits</u>: drupes slightly compressed with maximum dimension of 3.5 to 5 mm.

Flowering from October to January.

Distribution: Only found in Ethiopia from 2000 to 3300 m in montane forest, especially along margins, in dry evergreen woodland or bushland and sometimes left as a remnant tree on farmland. Its rainfall range is from 750 to 1250 mm per year.

Uses: Used for firewood and for making handles for farm tools.

Similar species:

Rhus glutinosa subsp. **abyssinica** *(Oliv.) M.Gilbert*

Usually smaller with stems densely covered in yellow hairs, not shiny, and leaves without red mid-ribs. Found from 1950 to 2600 m, it occurs in evergreen bushland. It is also found in Sudan and Egypt.

Rhus glutinosa subsp. **glutinosa** *Gilbert*

Leaves usually shiny and entire, stems dull brown. An endemic subspecies found in evergreen bushland and forest margins between 1800 and 3300 m.

Rhus vulgaris *Meikle.*

Small tree with brownish twigs sometimes forming blunt spines and middle leaflet obovate. Found in dry montane forest, very common at margins, also in evergreen bushland, woodland and wooded grassland in altitudes between 1500 and 2800 m.

Also in Cameroun, Zaire, Rwanda, Sudan, Uganda, Kenya, Tanzania, Zambia and Malawi.

> **Apicultural value**: *All Rhus species are valuable for honeybees as they provide nectar and good amounts of pollen for colony strengthening and maintainance.*

Schinus molle L.

T'QUR-BERBERIE (Amh); BERBERE-TSELLIM, T'QUR-BERBERE (Tya); PEPPER TREE (Eng)

Family: Anacardiaceae

Description: Small evergreen tree, with characteristic hanging or 'weeping' light-green foliage. Trunk short soon branching to give a spreading rounded crown. <u>Bark</u>: brown, rather scaly and fissured, often marked with drops of the strong-smelling gummy substance. <u>Leaves</u>: strongly smelling of black pepper, shiny green, pinnate with sessile leaflets. <u>Flowers</u>: small, creamy white, borne in conspicuous hanging clusters which are either male of female. There are separate male and female trees. <u>Fruits</u>: deep pink to reddish almost spherical berries in conspicuous clusters; smelling and tasting of peppercorns.

Flowering all year round and profusely after rains.

Distribution: Planted throughout the country from Afar lowlands to 2400 m. It is very drought resistant and can survive in an annual rainfall of of 300 to 600 mm per year. It is now naturalised in some places. It can also withstand a fair amount of frost, except when young, and can also grow where rainfall exceeds 1000 mm per year.

Native to Peru this heat and drought-resistant tree is widely planted in all but the coldest and wettest areas of the tropics and sub-tropics throughout the world.

Practical notes: It is fast growing from seed, but seedlings are often attacked by termites. However, the wood of mature trees is termite resistant.

Uses: Cultivated for shade and amenity its wood is termite resistant and generally suitable for firewood and charcoal.

Leaves are used as insect repellant and the fruits as a spice.

It is recommended as a windbreak, particularly in semi-arid areas.

Apicultural value: *The flowers provide some amount of nectar and heavy yields of pollen, especially during mornings. Honeybees collect nectar and pollen frequently and the tree is indirectly very important for honey production by strengthening colonies and stimulating strong brood rearing.*

Recommended for planting to increase honey production

Adenium obesum *Auct. non (Forssk.) R. & S.*

ORKETA (Gam); OMBI (Som); DESERT ROSE (Eng)

Family: Apocynaceae

Description: Thickset succulent shrub or tree, attaining a height of 6 m with much-swollen stems. All parts contain copious watery sap. <u>Bark</u>: grey-green, smooth. <u>Leaves</u>: thick, fleshy, bluish-green and narrowly elliptic, crowded at the ends of branches. <u>Flowers</u>: funnel-shaped, about 5 cm across, bright pink to deep rose. <u>Fruits</u>: long thin pink-green capsules, drying brown later and splitting to release the seeds.

Flowering time almost all year round with flowering peaks after rains.

Distribution: Fairly common in lowland areas of southern Ethiopia at altitudes between 500 and 1400 m in the Ogaden and the Rift Valley down to Lake Chew Bahir and the Omo valley. It requires an annual rainfall of at least 400 mm.

It is widespread in semi-arid areas of eastern Africa.

Practical notes: Propagation is done from seeds and cuttings. The seeds are said to be very poisonous.

Uses: Grown as an useful ornamental even on poor soils.

Apicultural value: Bees forage for nectar and pollen in the very early morning.

This plant is useful in the semi-arid areas to ensure the survival of honeybees.

Cussonia holstii *Engl.*

GEDETAMO, CAQMOSH, YEZNJERO-GOMMEN, GOMBOCERIE, DUDUNA (Amh); HARFATU, GETEMI, ANDEROCCI, ARFATTU (Or); AHARAGU (Som); GADAM, GEDDEM (Tya)

Family: Araliaceae

Description: Tree up to 20 m tall with a straight bole. Bark: thick, rough and fissured. Leaves: palmately compound, young ones palmately lobed, with 3 to 7 leaflets, elliptic to ovate and sometimes toothed. Flowers: sessile and creamy-white, arranged in many spikes, up to 15 cm long.

Flowering from September to November.

Distribution: Found between 1500 and 2600 m in Afromontane forest, evergreen and semi-evergreen bushland and also in secondary montane evergreen bushland, derived *Acacia* woodland and wooded grassland where rainfall ranges between 500 and 1000 mm a year.

Also in Zaire, Rwanda, Sudan, Eritrea, Somalia, Uganda, Kenya and Tanzania.

Uses: It is used for fuel.

In traditional medicine the roots are used against "elephantiasis". The bark is used against vomiting and diarrhoea in animals.

Similar species:

Cussonia arborea *A.Rich.*

A tree up to 10 m tall with numerous flowering spikes up to 60 cm long. This species occurs in woodland, tree and shrub savanna, often in rocky places in altitudes up to 2300 m.

Apicultural value: *Honeybees forage very vigorously for nectar and pollen from the flowers. The tree, often found in single stands, contributes to the strengthening of colonies and can even yield a surplus of honey.*

Recommended for planting to increase honey production.

Polyscias fulva *(Hiern.) Harms*

YEZNJERO-WENBER (Amh); KARACO (Kef); ABERRA, ANDALO, ANDOJE, ANKISSA, ANTALLO, GUDUBA, HUDA, KARASHO KORIBA, TALAÖ (Or); KERBONI (Sid)

Family: Araliaceae

Description: Tall, evergreen forest tree with a long, straight, slender, cylindrical trunk which can have a breast-height diameter of 80 cm. The umbrella-shaped crown is composed of a whorl of limbs, each of which bears whorls of branches ending in whorls of leaves. Bark: grey and smooth. Leaves: compound, pinnate and very large, up to 1 m long; the leaflets are paired and with a terminal leaflet, ovate to oblong, up to 20 cm long; they are dark green above and somewhat leathery. Flowers: sessile, greenish-yellow, tightly covering the stems, borne in axillary-arranged racemes up to 60 cm long.

Flowering from November to April.

Distribution: Commonly found from 1500 to 2500 m in upland and lowland rainforest, often in clearings and forest regrowth. It is also frequently left standing when forest is cleared for cultivation. It is restricted to the central and southern part of the highlands where rainfall ranges from 1500 to 2000 mm per year.

Also in Guinea Republic, Sierra Leone, Ghana, Togo, Nigeria, Cameroun, Central African Republic, Zaire, Rwanda, Burundi, Sudan, Uganda, Kenya, Tanzania, Angola, Zambia, Malawi, Zimbabwe and Mozambique.

Practical notes: It is fast growing and potentially useful in agroforestry for shade.

Uses: The wood is soft, very light, white and odourless and useful for making food containers and inner layers of plywood.

The regular and wide branching makes it very suitable for storing items such as sorghum head and also for holding beehives.

Apicultural value: *Honeybees collect pollen and nectar from the flowers very frequently. The abundance of nectar and pollen makes the tree very attractive to bee swarms and beekeepers very often hang their bee baskets in it.*

Schefflera abyssinica *(Hochst. ex A. Rich.) Harms*

KETEME, QUSTYA (Amh); GABTZE (Gam); GETEM (Had & Sid); WTTO (Kef); ARFATTU, GATAMA, HARFATU, MARFATU (Or); ORONCE (Sid); BOBOLUHU (Som); get'em (Tya)

Family: Araliaceae

Description: Tall tree, up to 30 m high, with a spreading crown, sometimes found growing as an epiphyte. Bark: grey-black and corky. Leaves: simple and palmately lobed, clustered at the ends of the branches; leaflets ovate or elliptic, rarely obovate; papery or somewhat leathery usually toothed margins. Flowers: creamy-yellowish or creamy-white in small umbels which are grouped into 30 to 40 cm long racemes. Fruits: red, 0.5 to 1 cm long.

Flowering from March to May.

Distribution: Found between 1500 and 3500 m in wet montane forest, often along streams and in riverine forests. It is sometimes left as an isolated tree in farmland after forest clearing. Its rainfall range is from 1000 to 2200 mm per year.

Also in Cameroon, Zaire, Burundi, Sudan, Uganda, Kenya, Tanzania and Malawi.

Practical notes: It grows easily from cuttings planted at the end of the rainy season.

Uses: The soft and light wood provides valuable timber for furniture and boxes as well as for farm tools. It is also quite often used for a living fence.

In traditional medicine the roots are used against elephantiasis.

Similar species:

Schefflera volkensii *(Engl.) Harms*

A tall tree up to 30 m high or a scandent shrub, sometimes epiphytic. Leaves with 4 to 6 leaflets which are obovate, oblanceolate or elliptic and up to 15 cm long. It grows in upland forest between 1600 to 3250 m.

Apicultural value: Schefflera abyssinica *is one of the most important honey trees of the country. It has abundant pollen and nectar which honeybees collect from the flowers throughout the day.*

It yields large quantities of a light and pure white honey which fetches the best prices. The granulation of honey is very fine.

Recommended for planting to increase honey production

Phoenix reclinata *Jacq.*

ZMBABA, SELIEN, HOSANA (Amh); METTI (Or); WILD DATE PALM (Eng)

Family: Arecaceae

Description: Tree, up to 15 m high, with a wide cylindrical stem, encircled by leaf-scars. Crown of many leaves spread out and turned down. <u>Leaves</u>: very strong, up to 3 m long; leaflets narrow, linear-lanceolate, stiff and sharply pointed, up to 35 cm long. <u>Flowers</u>: creamy white, arranged in a close panicle of wavy spikes. Male and female flowers are on different trees. <u>Fruits</u>: edible, yellow-brown, oblong-ellipsoid and about 2.5 cm long, resembling small dry dates. and the fruits are edible.

Flowering from October to December.

Distribution: It is found from 100 to 2500 m throughout the highlands and lowlands where sufficient ground water is available. Common along forest edges and waterways, it also grows in dense clumps near streams, pools and swamps and in riverine forest. It's rainfall range is from 150 to 2200 mm per year.

It is found in almost all Sub-Saharan African countries.

Practical notes: ZIMBABA is slow growing but provides many useful items. It is grown from seedlings and suckers.

Uses: An important multi-purpose plant. The leaves are used for making basket and mats and the roots for dye. It gives a valuable timber commonly used for local doors, roofing and windows. It's grown as an ornamental and for soil conservation. The sap is very sweet and can be used for making palm wine in other countries.

In traditional medicine the fruits and roots are used against haemorrhoids.

Apicultural value: *Honeybees collect much pollen and nectar from the flowers. When the tree is found in dense stands it contributes significant food for strengthening bee colonies.*

<u>Similar species:</u>

Borassus aethiopum *Mart.* / Arecaceae

This is the tallest indigenous palm, up to 25 m high with large fan-shaped, blue-green, deeply divided leaves. It produces large bunches of orange-brown edible fruits.

It is found throughout the moister areas of tropical Africa. The seeds are distributed by elephants. This palm is commonly cultivated by the Nilotic tribes in western Ethiopia along the Baro river and is found along other water-courses and on flood-plains between 300 and 1000 m. It is used by some Nilotic peoples to make palm wine.

Apicultural value: *It is known as a good source of nectar and pollen and the juice of damaged fruits is also sucked by bees.*

Vernonia amygdalina *Del. in Caill.*

GRAWA (Amh); EBICHA (Or); HEBA (Kem); GARA (Wel); BITTER LEAF (Eng)

Family: Asteraceae

Description: Small tree or shrub, growing up to 10 m tall. <u>Bark</u>: rusty to dark-brown, slightly fissured and sometimes much branched; the young branches are with numerous white breathing pores (lenticels). <u>Leaves</u>: somewhat coarse and rough, alternate, simple, green above and pale below, ovate-lanceolate, up to 20 cm long with regularly toothed margins. <u>Flowers</u>: white, tinged purple or pink and sweetly scented particularly in the evening; arranged in numerous heads at the ends of the branches.

Flowering trees can be found from December to May but the main flowering period is from January to February.

Distribution: Found in wide range of bushland, woodland and forest habitats between 500 and 2800 m, it is also often found around houses. Its rainfall range is from 750 to 2000 mm per year.

Found in almost all of sub-Saharan African countries, also in Yemen.

Practical notes: Fast growing from seeds and flowering in the second or third year after planting.

Uses: GRAWA is widely used as a hedge-forming shrub/tree and as a boundary marker. The wood is used for fuel and is also termite resistant. The leaves are used to scour pots used for making TELA, the local beer, and TEJ, honey wine.

The leaves and bark are bitter and in local medicine they are used against menstruation pain, as a purgative and vermifuge, in wound dressing and against urinary inflammations. Together with roots they are used against malaria. Leaves can also be browsed and the stems used as toothbrushes.

Apicultural value: GRAWA *is a very valuable honey source in the country. Especially in warmer areas the nectar secretion is abundant and bees produce a significant surplus of a dark aromatic honey. Honeybees generally collect the nectar and whitish pollen throughout the day.*

During flowering time honeybees develop very rapidly with a tendency to swarm easily. In some areas honey is generally harvested after the flowering season of GRAWA.

Recommended for planting to increase honey production

Balanites aegyptiaca (L.) Del.

QUSSA, QUTTA (Agew); BEDDENNO, KUDKUDDA, JEMO, GUZA, QACONA (Amh); TOW (Anu); SELIBATIQO (Bil); DOMAY, DOMAYE (Gam); JULI (Kun); BADDANNO, DOMOHO (Or); BEDDENNA (Or & Wel); GOT, GUT (Som); QAQ, QOG (Tre); MEQI, GWEZA (Tya); BADENA (Wel); DESERT DATE (Eng)

Family: Balanitaceae

Description: Small evergreen tree usually 5 to 7 m tall but occasionally reaching a height of about 10 m, with a dense rounded crown which is a tangled mass of thorny twigs from which leafless stems drop down or stick out. Young branches are green, smooth and armed with straight, green, forward-directed spines up to 8 cm long. Bark: smooth, greenish first, later grey to dark brown with ragged scales and long vertical fissures. Leaves: grey-green with distinctive pairs of ovate leaflets up to 5 cm long. Flowers: fragrant, yellow-green, up to 1 cm across, arranged in loose or tight cymose fascicles on spineless stems. Fruits: up to 5 cm long, oblong, surrounded by a yellow-brown bitter-sweet flesh.

Flowering from January to March.

Distribution: Found in dry savannah, woodland, and bushland between sea-level and 1700 m with an annual rainfall from 200 to 800 mm.

Widespread throughout the arid to subhumid tropical savannas of Africa, particularly throughout the Sahel from the Atlantic coast to the Red Sea.

Practical notes: It can be grown from seedlings, direct sowing and root suckers.

Uses: This is an important multi-purpose tree with many uses and highly recommended in reafforestation and agroforestry programmes. The termite-resistant wood is used for furniture, utensils and tool handles as well as for poles and timber. It is also very suitable for firewood and charcoal making. Cut branches make good fences.

The fruits are edible and very refreshing to suck. Fruits and shoots are also used as animal fodder and the trees are heavily browsed.

The kernels yield 40% of valuable oil. An emulsion made from the fruits is lethal to freshwater snails including the intermediate hosts for bilharzia. It is also lethal to the water-flea which carries Guinea-worm disease. However, the fruits are non-toxic to men and domestic animals. Therefore, wells and other water supplies can be treated with safety. Very strong emulsions of the fruits are used for poisoning fish.

In traditional medicine the bark and roots are used against worms, yellow fever and as a laxative. The leaves are used for wound dressing and the bark against Elephantiasis.

Apicultural value: *The flowers are visited by honeybees for nectar only. As the pulp contains 40% sugar, it can be ground into a flour and dissolved in water as a very valuable supplementary bee feed in times when other feed resources are scarce.*

236

Jacaranda mimosifolia *D.Don*

YETEBMENJA-ZAF (Amh); JACARANDA (Eng)

Family: Bignoniaceae

Description: Ornamental deciduous tree, up to 25 m tall, all parts giving off a sweet smell particularly after rain. Bark: pale grey to brown and smooth. Leaves: fern-like, feathery with very small leaflets. Flowers: mauve-blue, bell-shaped, in terminal clusters; often appearing before the leaves so that the tree is spectacular in full flower. The fallen flowers form a conspicuous bluish carpet on the ground. Fruits: flattened, round, woody capsules with a wavy edge; up to 7 cm in diameter.

Some trees are found in flower throughout the year but the main flowering time is from November to March.

Distribution: JACARANDA is grown in streets and gardens in almost all towns of the country from sea-level to 2500 m and is even becoming naturalised in some places. It needs an annual rainfall of between 650 and 1800 mm per year.

This tree is native to Brazil. It was introduced to Ethiopia early in this century. Now widely grown in tropical and subtropical America, Asia and Africa.

Practical notes: This is a fast growing tree which is easily raised from seeds. It is commonly found in nurseries.

Uses: Although mainly grown as an ornamental, JACARANDA produces a dark-purple wood which is termite resistant. It is suitable for cabinet work, carving and tool handles. It is also used as poles and for firewood. Living trees provide pleasant broken shade and windbreaks.

Apicultural value: *Honeybees collect both pollen and nectar from the flowers. Because of its late flowering season,* JACARANDA *contributes a lot for the survival of bee colonies in drier areas.*

Beekeepers in northern parts of Ethiopia have repeatedly reported about the good nectar production of the flowers which are even foraged after dropping down on the ground. However, in other areas it seems that no nectar is produced.

Stereospermum kunthianum *Cham.*

WASHNT, ZANA (Amh); UTORO, BODORO (Or); GUNK'I, ADI-ZANA (Tya); PINK JACARANDA (Eng)

Family: Bignoniaceae

Description: Small tree up to 8 m high with a usually bent or spirally twisted trunk. Bark: grey, flaking to expose contrasting light patches. Leaves: pinnately compound with 5 to 9 leaflets per leaf which are oblong-elliptic and usually 5 to 10 cm long; margins entire on adult trees, but toothed on saplings. Flowers: bell-shaped, pale pink or lilac, rarely almost white, fragrant and borne in large drooping bunches. Fruits: long, cylindrical, spirally twisted and dark brown with seeds which are winged at each side and edible.

Flowering most profusely after the small rains in April and May, some trees can be found with flowers any time from September up to May.

Distribution: Found from 700 to 2000 m in areas with an annual rainfall range between 700 and 1800 mm per year in dry deciduous woodland, and semi-arid lowland savanna, particularly where the area is regularly burnt to remove grass and other herbs. *Stereospermum* also stands out as remnant trees on farmland.

It is widespread in savanna regions of Africa, from Senegal to Zaire, and in East Africa.

Practical notes: Seeds are difficult to obtain but germinate immediately. Propagation is also possible by root suckering. Young shoots are very sensitive to bush fires. It does not make good charcoal, because it disintegrates directly to ashes.

Uses: This *Stereospermum* is a very decorative tree which could be planted more often in towns and villages at lower altitudes. The leaves can be browsed. The wood is hard and heavy, pale brown, tinged with yellow and pink coloration. Mortars are made from bole sections. It is often used for firewood, but not charcoal.

It has some medicinal applications: bark, roots, leaves and pods for coughs, venereal and respiratory diseases, for asthma, leprosy and skin eruptions. The bark is useful for controlling flatulence in horses. The roots are used in traditional medicine against AJIL.

Apicultural value: *There is plenty of pollen and abundant nectar which honeybees frequently collect from the flowers.*

In dense stands a surplus of honey can be harvested. The long flowering period makes this tree very valuable for beekeeping.

Recommended for planting to increase honey production

241

Adansonia digitata L.

BAMBA (Amh); HERMER BANBA, KOMMER, MOMRET (Tya); BAOBAB (Eng); AFFENBROTBAUM (German)

Family: Bombacaceae

Description: Deciduous tree up to 25 m tall. The trunk is very massive (diameter up to 8 m and girth up to 20 m) and bottle-shaped and the stiff branches are bare of leaves for as much as 9 months of the year, resembling large roots so that the tree is sometimes called Africa's "Upside-down-tree". Bark: up to 10 cm thick, grey and smooth, fibrous and often pock-marked and heavily folded. Leaves: dark green, palmate with 5 obovate to oblanceolate leaflets. Flowers: white, large, up to 20 cm across, solitary on long hanging stalks; 5 waxy white petals surround a ball of fine stamens. Very short-lived and unpleasantly scented. the flowers open at night, and are pollinated by fruit bats and flies. Fruits: large, up to 22 cm long, hanging on long stalks and remaining on the tree after ripening.

Flowering from May to July.

Distribution: Found in semi-arid lowland-steppe, dry deciduous woodland, riverine forests, and other areas with a high water table in the western parts of Ethiopia up to 1700 m where annual rainfall range is from 250 to 1500 mm. Common in the Tekeze Valley, its occurrence in Wellega and Sidamo remains unconfirmed.

Widespread throughout semi-arid to subhumid tropical Africa south of the Sahara.

Practical notes: This is one of the longest living trees and can reach an age of up to 3000 years. It is very fire and drought resistant.

Uses: A very important tree both culturally and ecologically with many uses for all its parts. For example: dry fruit cases are used for fuel; the wood makes utensils and carvings;. young shoots, leaves and seeds are edible; a vitamin-rich drink can be made from the fruit pulp; leaves, shoots and fruits are eaten by cattle, sheep and goats. The fibre from the bark can be woven or used to make ropes. Tannin is obtained from the bark and a red dye from the roots. Hollow trunks can store large quantities of water and the leaves provide a good mulch.

Baobab is a shade tree and an outstanding landmark. In many places outside Ethiopia it is a preferred place for markets, meetings and other social events. It is sometimes called the "Mother of the Sahel".

In local medicine all parts of the tree are used especially as a remedy against fever, intestinal diseases, dysentery, diarrhoea and infections.

Apicultural value: *Honeybees gather the abundant nectar from the flowers and work on them until late evening. The baobab plays an important role in strengthening bee colonies in dry habitats where other bee feeds are scarce.*

Ceiba pentandra *(L.) Gaertn.*

YE'TIT'-ZAF, YEKBRITT-N'CHET (Amh); DUM-DUM (Som); KAPOK, SILK-COTTON TREE (Eng)

Family: Bombacaceae

Description: Tall deciduous tree with very shallow roots; the trunk is covered with sharp conical spines when young which become large, blunt buttresses with age; the branches are horizontal or ascending, more or less whorled. <u>Bark</u>: grey and smooth, young branches are green. <u>Leaves</u>: palmately compound, with 5 to 11 leaflets which are sessile, lanceolate to oblanceolate, each drooping; main stalk up to 20 cm long. <u>Flowers</u>: white to pink, large and showy, arranged in clusters; they appear either when the whole tree is bare or on individual leafless branches. <u>Fruit</u>: large woody capsules, pale-brownish, ellipsoid, up to 25 cm long, with masses of silky hairs surrounding the seeds.

Some trees can be found in flower at any time of the year.

Distribution: KAPOK is found in lowland evergreen and groundwater forests. It has become naturalised in Illubabor between 500 and 1200 m and is grown in lowland areas of Hararghe, Tigray, Arsi and Wellega regions. It is semi-naturalized up to 2250 m where planted.

It is a native of tropical America, and the Amazon region. In tropical Africa now widely grown at lower altitudes, and also in subtropical N and S America, Asia and Africa.

Practical notes: The tree is easily damaged by high winds.

Uses: Leaves and shoots are used as fodder. Fibre is obtained from fruit capsules to make mattresses. It is commonly planted for shade and amenity. The fibre is water repellent and lighter than cotton. The unripe fruit and seed oil are edible and important crops elsewhere.

Before the development of synthetic fibres, KAPOK was used to stuff mattress, pillows and other items.

Apicultural value: *Bees forage very frequently for the abundant nectar and heavy loads of orange pollen. The nectar secretion is copious and tends to run out from the corolla. The sugar concentration is medium. The honey is said to have a characteristic aroma and light amber colour.*

Recommended for planting to increase honey production

246

Cordia africana *Lam.*

WANZA (Amh); WADESSA, MOKOTO (Or); WADICHO (Sid); AWHII (Tya)

Family: Boraginaceae

Description: Tree growing up to 30 m, with a rounded crown and often a rather crooked trunk. The stems of trees that grow in open land branches at a height of 1 to 2 m from the ground. The bole of old trees reaches 1 m in diameter. <u>Bark</u>: dark-brown or even blackish and finely fissured; the slash is white. <u>Leaves</u>: leathery, simple, alternate, broadly ovate to egg-shaped, rough to feel, dull dark green above and paler beneath often with soft, light brown hairs. <u>Flowers</u>: funnel-shaped, pure white, sweetly scented, produced in quite large bunches. All the flowers on one tree open at the same time giving a very decorative effect. <u>Fruit</u>: circular, up to 1 cm in diameter, yellow when mature and single-seeded. The sweet sticky flesh is edible.

Some trees can be found in flower at any time in the year but the main flowering period is from October to March.

Distribution: Widespread in moist evergreen highland and riverine forest of the NW and SW highlands and very common in western Ethiopia between 550 and 2600 m where the rainfall range is 700 to 2000 mm per year. WANZA is an early colonizer in forest re-growth and is often found along forest margins and in clearings. It is also orchard-like, particularly in western Ethiopia, as it is often retained as a remnant when forest is cleared for farmland.

Most countries in sub-Saharan Africa and also in Yemen.

Practical notes: Under good conditions WANZA is a fast-growing tree. Seeds germinate easily but the young seedlings need shade and regular watering to help them get established.

Uses: WANZA is an excellent shade tree for coffee, a most attractive ornamental, and also for conserving soil. It provides excellent timber. The wood is very suitable for making many types of furniture, mortars, windows and house doors. In the western part of the country log-hives for bees and TEJ (honey-beer) barrels are made from hollowed out stems.

In local medicine the fruits and the roots are used against ascariasis. Fried leaves are used, together with butter, to treat all kinds of wounds and wood-ash mixed with butter is used against skin diseases.

Apicultural value: WANZA *supplies abundant pollen and copious nectar for bees which forage all day. This is one of the major honey sources of Ethiopia mainly in the western parts. It also often contributes to mixed honeys in which its flavour predominates. The honey is very aromatic with a slow granulation and light brown in colour. Crushed seeds, dissolved in water, can be used for feeding bees during dry periods.*

Recommended for planting to increase honey production

Ehretia cymosa *Thonn.*

GAME, HULAGA, MUKERBA, GARMI (Amh); WAGAMO (Kef); BORBORIS (Konso); WAGI, WURUGU, URAGA (Or); KARUAK (Tya)

Family: Boraginaceae

Description: Much-branched tree or shrub very variable in size from a few metres in dry areas to a tree over 10 m tall in wetter places. Bark: light to dark grey and rather rough; young branchlets are covered in dense white hairs. Leaves: ovate to broadly elliptic, entire, glabrous to thinly hairy, mostly on the lower surface, glossy green above Flowers: sweetly-scented, white, small, sessile and arranged in crowded terminal heads, often covering the tree in white bloom. Fruits: small, round, orange-red berries, edible but acid.

Flowering almost all year round with a peak from February to May.

Distribution: A very common shrub or tree from 500 in the wetter western lowlands to 2700 m in Afromontane rain forest and drier Afromontane forest. It also occurs often in secondary medium-altitude evergreen bushland and as a remnant tree around dwellings and on farmland. It grows in a rainfall of between 500 to 2000 mm per year.

Also in Sierra Leone, Cote d'Ivoire, Ghana, Togo, Nigeria, Cameroun, Gabon, Congo, Zaire, Rwanda, Sudan, Uganda, Kenya, Tanzania, Malawi and Zimbabwe. It is also found in Madagascar, on the Comoro Islands and in Yemen.

Practical notes: This is a relatively fast growing tree easily raised from seeds. Roots and leaves are poisonous to people.

Uses: It is often used as a boundary marker. The wood is used for firewood and provides valuable timber for furniture as well as for farm tools. Leaves are useful for browse.

In traditional medicine the bark and flowers are used against "conjunctivitis". The juice from the leaves and roots is astringent and is used for healing wounds.

Apicultural value: *Honeybees collect pollen and abundant nectar from the flowers frequently throughout the day. It is a very valuable bee tree with a prolonged flowering period. It contributes to mixed honeys. In some areas the tree is even planted for beekeeping around dwellings.*

Recommended for planting to increase honey production

Buddleja polystachya *Fresen.*

AMFAR, ANFAR, ATKUAR (Amh); ADADO, CHIAI (Or); MATARI, MADEREH, MATTERI (Tya)

Family: Buddlejaceae (also often put in the Loganiaceae, as in the Flora of Ethiopia)

Description: Small tree or tall shrub with a rounded crown and spreading and arching branches, sometimes with a very well developed trunk up to 1.5 m in diameter. Bark: reddish brown on the trunk but the branches and the twigs are pale because they are covered with dense, pale brown hairs. Leaves: ovate or elliptic, up to 18 cm long, dark green above, light greyish-green below. Flowers: fragrant, orange and small, arranged on up to 20 cm long flowering spikes. Fruits: small dry capsules.

Flowering almost all the year round but most abundantly in the dry season from November to May.

Distribution: Found from 1000 to 3300 m in Afromontane forest, particularly along margins and in clearings. It is also common in secondary montane evergreen and riverine bushland. Often found as an isolated tree or shrub in montane grassland, around houses and retained as a remnant from the former forest on farmland. It grows where rainfall ranges between 750 to 1500 mm per year.

Also in Sudan, Eritrea, Somalia, Uganda, Kenya, Tanzania and also in Yemen and Saudi Arabia.

Practical notes: It is easily propagated by cuttings and seedlings are easily raised from seeds.

Uses: It is planted around houses were it makes a living fence. The leafy branches are commonly used to wash cooking and brewing pots as they are rough and can make water froth. The leaves also provide fodder.

Dried twigs and branches can be used for starting fires by friction and it is a popular fuel.

In traditional medicine all parts of the tree are used as anthelmintic, purgative, against skin diseases and as a wound dressing for animals.

Apicultural value: *Honeybees collect pollen and nectar from the flowers frequently. This tree is also visited by numerous butterflies, but not as much as the purple-flowered introduced ornamentals.*

Nuxia congesta *Fresen.*

CHOCHO (Amh); ANFARE, IRBA (Or); ATCHARO (Tya)

Family: Buddlejaceae (also often put in the Loganiaceae, as in the Flora of Ethiopia)

Description: Small to medium-sized tree, sometimes only a shrub, growing up to 20 m high. The bole is often short, twisted and the low branches droop down; young branchlets are clearly 3 to 6-sided. <u>Bark</u>: rough, blackish and corrugated. <u>Leaves</u>: entire, elliptic to oblanceolate, dull green and rather leathery; usually in threes at the end of branches. <u>Flowers</u>: heavily scented, numerous, white-mauve and arranged in dense terminal panicles or cymes.

Flowering from October to May.

Distribution: Found between 1500 and 3100 m in Afromontane forest, especially at the upper limit and at forest margins. At high-altitudes it is found in the Erica belt and is often left as an isolated tree in high-altitude montane grassland and on farmland. Its rainfall range is from 500 to 2000 mm per year.

Also in Guinea Republic, Sierra Leone, Cote d'Ivoire, Ghana, Nigeria, Zaire, Rwanda, Burundi, Sudan, Eritrea, Somalia, Uganda, Kenya, Tanzania, Angola, Zambia, Malawi, Zimbabwe, Mozambique, Botswana, Namibia, Swaziland, South Africa and Yemen.

Practical notes: Propagation is done by seedlings.

Uses: It is a popular wood for firewood and charcoal. Trees can be found in living fences. It is believed that the tree will repel evil spirits.

Apicultural value: *Honeybees in general collect the abundant nectar and pollen throughout the day.*

"Nuxia" is a very valuable honey source at high altitudes. Under favourable conditions the nectar secretion is abundant and bees produce a significant surplus of honey. During flowering time honeybee colonies develop very rapidly with a tendency to swarm.

Recommended for planting to increase honey production

Boswellia papyrifera *(Del.) Hochst.*

LIBANAT (Ade & Or); FATUQA (Agew); WALWAL (Bil); QERERRIE, YETAN-ZAF (Amh); GALGALAM, KAFAL (Or); WALBA, MEQER (Tya); BITTER FRANKINCENSE (Eng); WEIHRAUCHBAUM (German)

Family: Burseraceae

Description: Deciduous tree growing to 12 m tall, with a rounded crown and a straight, regular bole. Bark: whitish to pale brown, peeling off in large papery pieces; slash red-brown and exuding a fragrant resin. Leaves: large, compound, arranged on long stalks with 11 to 29 leaflets which are narrowly ovate to oblong, waved or toothed along the margin. Flowers: sweetly scented, white to pink, arranged on long red flowers stalks, in loose panicles at the end of branches. Fruits: red capsules about 2 cm long.

Flowering from October to February.

Distribution: Found between 950 to 1800 m in dry woodland and wooded grassland, often the dominant on steep rocky slopes and also on lava flows.

It is also found in Nigeria, Cameroun, Central African Republic, Chad, Sudan and Uganda.

Practical notes: This *Boswellia* can be grown from seedlings and cuttings. The cuttings should be taken shortly before the trees loose their leaves.

Uses: This tree is very suitable for the productive reafforestation of dry savannas and dry rocky slopes. The resin, which is the raw material of the Ethiopian frankincense, is widely collected in North Ethiopia but is considered of poorer quality than the product obtained from Arabian and Somalian *B. sacra*.

In traditional medicine the resin is used as a febrifuge, and the leaves and roots are used against Lymphadenopathy.

Similar species:

Boswellia pirottae *Chiov.*

A rare endemic species, only found from the Tekeze, Abay and Gibe river systems. It differs from *B. papyrifera* by having a rough or grooved bark and smaller flowers on more contracted inflorescences.

Apicultural value: *The flowers are frequently visited by honeybees for pollen and nectar. It might be true that* Boswellia *spp. provide a significant surplus of stored nectar and contribute to mixed honeys together with* Combretum *spp. and* Piliostigma *spp.*
It is an important tree for beekeepers in dry woodlands and the long lasting flowering periods are very helpful for bee colony maintainance.

Recommended for planting to increase honey production

Opuntia ficus-indica *(L.) Miller*

QULQWAL (Amh); TINI, GURA (Or); PRICKLY PEAR, INDIAN FIG (Eng)

Family: Cactaceae

Description: Succulent, usually small tree or dense bush, attaining a height of 5 m. The stem and branches are formed of large, elliptic to obovate flattened ear-like joints which are up to 40 cm long. They are covered with tufts of spiny brittle hairs. Normal leaves are only produced at the tops of very young shoots and soon fall off. Flowers: yellow to orange, up to 8 cm in diameter, born in rows on the upper edges of young joints. Fruits: fleshy, pear-shaped, with sweet edible flesh after the spiny skin is removed.

Some plants with flowers can be found almost all year. But the peak is usually after some rain and, on the eastern escarpment there is an important fruiting peak in the main rainy season.

Distribution: Now grown widely throughout the country in arid, semi-arid to humid zones up to 2400 m.

Opuntia was introduced to Eritrea and Ethiopia by the Italians, particularly to stabilize hillsides when they were building roads and railways. This plant has now been spread to many of the drier parts of the country.

Now widespread in all arid and semi-arid parts of the world.

Practical notes: It is easily propagated by cuttings during the rains.

Uses: A common hedge plant round compounds. The fruits are important market items and eaten in many places as they come during the rainy season when other food stuffs are in short supply.

After the spines are removed it is a very useful browse plant for livestock.

It is a very suitable shrub for erosion control measures and afforesting programmes, because it protects other naturally regenerating plants from browsing animals.

In traditional medicine the leaves are used against bloat and the sap against shin fungus.

Apicultural value: *The honeybees are frequently foraging the abundant pollen and nectar of the flowers. They also suck the juice of ripe fruits.*
The honey potential is high, especially during partial drought and guarantee the bee's surviving. This plant is an important honey source in the northern part of the country. The honey is aromatic and white with a slow, fine and creamy granulation.

Recommended for planting to increase honey production

Crateva adansonii *DC.*

DINKIA-SEBBER (Amh)

Family: Capparidaceae

Description: Tree or shrub growing up to 7 m, occasionally to 15 m high. <u>Bark</u>: pale brown. <u>Leaves</u>: large, trifoliate, pale green, on long petioles; leaflets ovate to lanceolate up to 10 cm long. <u>Flowers</u>: sweetly-scented, arranged in many-flowered corymbs at or near the ends of the twigs; petals white to yellow-white with lilac tips grouped on one side of the flowers. <u>Fruit</u>: yellow to pale brown, 4 to 6 cm across.

Flowering from November to March.

Distribution: Found in wooded grassland, deciduous woodland and *Acacia* woodland from 560 m up to 1700 m.

It is found throughout east tropical Africa from Zambia and Tanzania north to Ethiopia and west to Senegal.

Practical notes: The wood has a peculiar distinctive odour which is noticeable when even a twig is broken.

Uses: The wood is used for firewood and charcoal as well as for making utensils and farm tools.

Fruits are edible and the leaves can be used as animal fodder.

Elsewhere it is sometimes grown as an ornamental for its sweet-scented flowers.

Apicultural value: *Honeybees forage for both pollen and nectar.*

259

Carica papaya L.

PAPAYA (Amh); TREE MELON (Eng)

Family: Caricaceae

Description: Erect, short-lived, unbranched dioecious tree growing to 6 m tall with a tuft of leaves at the top. <u>Bark</u>: greenish with conspicuous triangular markings from detached leaves. <u>Leaves</u>: palmately lobed, very large and with long stalks. <u>Flowers</u>: very fragrant, the white, bell-shaped female flowers are borne in small groups in the leaf axils; the male flowers are in long inflorescences. <u>Fruits</u>: the melon-shaped, tasty and easily digestible fruits turn yellow to orange-red when mature.

Flowering all year round.

Distribution: Cultivated throughout the country up to 1900 m where ever there is some water for irrigation.

It is a native of Central and South America where it has been cultivated since ancient times. Now widely distributed throughout the tropics of Africa, Asia, South America and the Pacific islands.

Practical notes: Easily grown from seed once the outer gelatinous coat has been removed.

Trees of some varieties are either male or female, so several are planted together and then when flowering starts all the males except a few are taken out.

Uses: It is cultivated for its fruit. All residues, and also the leaves, can be used as animal fodder.

All parts of the plant contain large quantities of a milky juice which is the commercial source of the protein digesting enzyme papain.

Apicultural value: *Honeybees collect nectar and pollen from bisexual flowers, nectar from female flowers, and pollen from male flowers throughout the day. Juice from damaged fruits are collected by the bees. The pollen value is significant to stimulate brood rearing.*

262

Maytenus obscura *(A.Rich.) Cuf.*

HACAT (Agew); ATAT (Amh & Gur); ANGITO (Kef); KOMBOLCA (Or); ATAT, SL'LO (Tya); TUTWA (Wel)

Family: Celastraceae

Description: Shrub or tree, 2 to 10 m tall, with spines up to 4 cm long. Bark: grey; branches black or dark brown. Leaves: elliptic or oblong to ovate or lanceolate with toothed margins. Flowers: bisexual or unisexual; very small, greenish-white or creamy-white in clusters in the leaf axils. Fruits: greenish when young and red to red-brown when mature.

Flowering from October to December.

Distribution: Found between 1700 and 3100 m in open woodland, grassland, forest margins and sometimes along streams. It can be retained on farmland as a remnant from the former forest. Widely distributed in the NW Highlands with a rainfall range from 750 to 2000 mm per year.

It also occurs in Uganda, Kenya and Tanzania.

Uses: Commonly used for firewood and the timber for local house construction and farm tool making. It is sometimes used as boundary marker as well as for a live fence.

Apicultural value: *Honeybees collect both pollen and nectar from the flowers.*

Maytenus senegalensis *(Lam.) Exell*

NEC-ATAT, GULO-KOKKOBA, QOQQOBA (Amh); JIMA'-HARRE, KOMBOLCA (Or); ARGTI, HRGTE (Tre); QEBQEB, ARGWDI (Tya)

Family: Celastraceae

Description: Shrub or tree, usually growing up to 8 m, occasionally up to 13 m high, unarmed or with spines up to 5 cm long. <u>Bark</u>: grey; the young stems are wine red to grey and smooth with whitish breathing pores. <u>Leaves</u>: alternate or in clusters, ash coloured to mottled green, elliptic or oblong to obovate or oblanceolate, with wavy leaf margins. <u>Flowers</u>: white to yellow, solitary or a few together in leaf axils. <u>Fruit</u>: globose, pink to red when mature.

Flowering from October to May.

Distribution: Found in deciduous woodland, open dry scrub, dry mountain slopes and along river banks from sea-level up to 2400 m.

Very widespread, westwards to Senegal and southwards to South Africa. Also in North Africa, southern Spain and the Canary Islands, eastwards to the Arabian peninsula, Afghanistan, Iran, Pakistan, India and Madagascar.

Uses: Commonly used for firewood and to make charcoal.

In traditional medicine the leaves are used against cataract, haemorrhoids and SHINT MAT.

Apicultural value: *Honeybees gather both pollen and nectar from the flowers.*

This species is a valuable bee plant because of its wide altitudinal range.

265

266

Combretum molle *(R.Br. ex Don.) Engl. & Diels*

AGALO, AVALO (Amh); BIKA, DADAMSA, ANANSA, DIDESSA (Or); OBAH (Som); ANFARFARO, HAZIBA, WEIBA (Tya)

Family: Combretaceae

Description: Small deciduous tree growing up to 15 m high with an often crooked trunk, commonly branching near the base. <u>Bark</u>: dark brown to black and deeply grooved in squares. <u>Leaves</u>: oppositely arranged, elliptic to lanceolate, large, covered with soft hairs, rounded at the base. <u>Flowers</u>: sweetly scented, many crowded into greenish-yellowish spikes; the flowers generally appear before the leaves. <u>Fruits</u>: yellowish, four-sided with wings.

Flowering from January to April.

Distribution: Widespread between 500 and 2200 m in dry woodland, wooded grassland and bushland. This plant and others in this genus give their name to one of the most widespread vegetation types, combretaceous woodland, of the country.

Widespread throughout tropical Africa, southwards to South Africa and also in Yemen.

Practical notes: Propagated by root suckers and seedlings.

Uses: The wood is very suitable for firewood and charcoal and also for making poles, posts, timber and tool handles.

In traditional medicine the bark is used against liver diseases.

Apicultural value: *Honeybees forage for the abundant nectar and pollen from the flowers all day round. Beekeepers in the "Didessa" valley have often reported the quantity of honey harvested from this nectar source.*

Recommended for planting to increase honey production

Diospyros mespeliformis *A. DC.*

BTREMUSEH (Amh); AYEH (Amh & Tya); ADIU (Anu); AFRICAN EBONY (Eng)

Family: Ebenaceae

Description: Tree or small shrub, usually 5 to 15 m high, occasionally reaching 25 m with a rounded or spreading crown. <u>Bark</u>: grey-black, rough with small regular scales. <u>Leaves</u>: shiny dark green, oblong to elliptic, up to 15 cm long and alternately arranged. <u>Flowers</u>: creamy-white, fragrant; male flowers in clusters and female flowers solitary. <u>Fruit</u>: rounded, red and becoming black, about 1.5 cm in diameter with a soft and sweet pulp.

Flowering from February to April.

Distribution: Growing between 500 and 2000 m mainly in riverine forest, but also found in deciduous woodland, often associated with rocky outcrops where annual rainfall ranges between 500 and 1000 mm.

Also in Senegal, Gambia, Mali, Sierra Leone, Cote d'Ivoire, Burkina Faso, Ghana, Togo, Benin, Niger, Chad, Nigeria, Cameroun, Central African Republic, Zaire, Sudan, Eritrea, Kenya, Uganda, Tanzania, Zambia, Malawi, Zimbabwe, Mozambique, Botswana, Namibia, South Africa and also Yemen.

Practical notes: This species is very slow growing, hence the heavy strong wood. It can be grown from seedlings as well as cuttings.

Uses: The wood is very strong, fairly resistant to fungi, and almost termite proof. It provides a valuable timber which is can be used for construction work and furniture. Some trees yield a very dark-coloured wood which develops through seasoning to true ebony and is much prized for carving. Straight branches are used to make strong durable walking sticks. The tree also makes good firewood.

The fruits are edible and can be used to make fermented drinks.

Apicultural value: *This tree is a very valuable "bee tree" as it provides plenty of nectar. Bees are attracted to gathering pollen and nectar from the flowers. It seems to be a heavy nectar yielder and honeybees are able to produce a significant surplus of a light amber honey.*

Recommended for planting to increase honey production.

269

Erica arborea L.

ASTA, (Amh); SA-TO (Or); SHAKTO, ZAKDI, UDSHENA, UTSHENA, WUCHIU (Tya); TREE-HEATH (Eng)

Family: Ericaceae

Description: Evergreen shrub or tree, densely-branched, usually 3 to 7 m high, sometimes up to 10 m tall. Bark: dark brown to black, fissured. Leaves: scale- or needle-like, often less than 1 cm long only up to 1 mm wide. Flowers: white to pale-pink, bell-shaped and pendulous; held at the ends of branchlets, often so abundant as to appear in dense racemes; seeds are minute.

Flowering almost all the year round with flowering peaks after rains.

Distribution: Found above 1900 m to 4000 m usually as a distinct vegetation belt above Afromontane forests, but also in clearings within forest. Above 3500 m it is only found as a small bush. Where it is regularly cut and/or burnt it forms a dense low-ground cover in Afroalpine grassland. Its rainfall range is between 500 to 2000 mm per year.

Also in the Mediterranean region, Madeira, Canary Islands, Zaire, Rwanda, Sudan, Eritrea, Somalia, Uganda, Kenya, Tanzania and Yemen.

Practical notes: Propagation can be done by seedlings and probably also cuttings although it is mostly allowed to regenerate naturally. It regrows readily after being cut back and/or burnt over.

Uses: This plant burns very easily even when wet and is cut to make to make the large flaming torches during the festival of New Year (11 September) and Meskel (19 September).

The branches and wood are popular as firewood and it can be made into charcoal. Cut branches are used as fencing and bushes may be left to give living fences. Horses and mules browse the small branches with the leaves.

Elsewhere the wood from old roots is used for making briar pipes and dice.

In traditional medicine the smoked parts of branches are used to fumigate houses against contagious diseases.

Apicultural value: *Honeybees collect the copious pink pollen and abundant nectar from the flowers very frequently and the plant is one of the most important honey sources of higher altitudes of the country. The honey is golden-red with an intense and characteristic aroma.*

Higher monetary returns per hectare can be obtained by honey production than by clearing these Erica forests for agricultural purposes.

Recommended for planting to increase honey production

Croton macrostachys *Hochst. ex Del.*

BSANNA (Amh); WAGO (Kef); MASSAGANTA (Konso); BEKANISA, BAKANICHA, MOKONISSA, BAKANISSA (Or); TAMBUCH (Tre); AMBUCH (Tya)

Family: Euphorbiaceae

Description: Deciduous, medium-sized tree, growing up to 25 m high, with spreading branches. <u>Bark</u>: grey, fairly smooth, fissured with age; slash has a strong spicy odour, as of pepper, and abundant clear sap. <u>Leaves</u>: soft, green, simple and heart-shaped, margins wavy, crowded at the end of branches. <u>Flowers</u>: conspicuous yellow-white or creamy-white, sweet scented, in mostly hanging but sometimes erect spikes up to 25 cm long. <u>Fruits</u>: greyish woody capsules, 3-lobed and 1 cm in diameter with 3 flattened seeds.

Flowering profusely from April to July.

Distribution: This is a forest pioneer found from 1300 to 2700 m in both montane forest and evergreen bushland. It is also common in secondary forest, at forest edges, in and around compounds, and as a coffee shade tree. Its rainfall range is from 750 to 2000 mm per year.

It is found throughout sub-Saharan and southern Africa.

Practical notes: Easily grown from seeds, this is usually a fast growing tree under good conditions.

Uses: The wood is cream-coloured and very soft. It is suitable for indoor carpentry, ordinary furniture, veneers, boxes and crates, and tool handles. The tree is recommended for planting in soil conservation measures.

The fruits and the roots are used as a medicine against venereal diseases, while the pulverized bark together with the dried flowers of *Hagenia abyssinica* KOSSO are a very effective purgative. The juice from the leaves can be used to treat fungal skin diseases like ring-worm.

Warning: The wood is not suitable for firewood because of a bad smell and smoke given off when burnt. But it is commonly used.

Apicultural value: *This tree is an important source of honey. Honeybees collect both pollen and nectar from the flowers.*

An aromatic brownish honey is harvested from this tree mainly in the western humid parts. Granulation is very fast with a coarse cristallization.

Recommended for planting to increase honey production

272

273

Euphorbia abyssinica *Gmel.*

KOLQUAL (Amh); HADAMI, TULU (Or)

Family: Euphorbiaceae

Description: Succulent leafless tree up to 10 m high with branches held almost parallel and forming an almost flat top. The thick trunk becomes woody with age. The green branches are succulent and have taken over the function of leaves. They are spiny, leafless, dark green, 3 to 8-angled and irregularly constricted with wing-like angles. The spines are in pairs and up to 1 cm long. <u>Leaves</u>: only found on seedlings and soon falling off. <u>Flowers</u>: crowded cymes at the tops of branchlets, bright yellow. <u>Fruits</u>: capsules, first green later on deep crimson; up to 2 cm across;
Flowering from September to November.

Distribution: Found growing between 1400 and 2400 m in drier evergreen montane forest, woodland and scrub savannah. Locally abundant on steep hillsides, sometimes forming pure stands, often around churches. It is used for live-fencing at higher altitudes.
Also in Eritrea, Somalia and Sudan.

Practical notes: Propagation is done by cuttings.

Uses: The timber is light and porous and is used as support to make roofing from stones and soil. It is also used to make tables and wooden saddles.
In traditional medicine the sap is used as a disinfectant, against rabies, skin diseases and as a febrifuge. The latex can be used to kill ticks on cattle.

Apicultural value: *Bees forage for the abundant nectar and some pollen from the flowers. The tree is very helpful for strengthening colonies and maintaining brood rearing in the dry season.*
Warning: The yellow honey made from this plant is said to be poisonous.

Euphorbium candelabrum *Trem. ex Kotschy*

KALKWOL, QOLQWAL, QULQWAL, QN'CHB (Amh & Tya); ADAMI, HADAMI, AKIRSA (Or)

Family: Euphorbiaceae

Description: Scucculent tree that grows up to 12 m high with a short, thick trunk and a characteristic crown of massive ascending branches. The stem often produces numerous lateral branches but the lowermost branches fall off quickly as new ones are produced. Bark: green with grey lines. Branches: succulent, leafless and dark green, 3 to 5 winged, with each wing bearing paired spines; branches are slightly constricted at irregular intervals. Flowers: yellowish-cream, terminal, clustered on top of the branches. Fruits: reddish brown, pea-sized capsules, produced on tips of the branches. All parts of the tree produce a milky latex.

Flowering from September to January.

Distribution: Found between 1200 and 1900 m in dry deciduous or evergreen woodland or bushland where is can form dense stands and in evergreen montane woodland. In drier areas, it is frequently found growing on termite mounds. Rainfall range is from 800 to 2000 mm per year.

This speicies is widely distributed in tropical Africa, from Eritrea to South Africa and west to Cameroun.

Practical notes: It is easily grown from cuttings taken and planted during May and June when the soil is dry. The latex is extremely poisonous and a single drop in the eye may cause blindness.

Uses: Wood yellow, soft and very light, is suitable for making boxes and matches.

In the northern parts of the country where houses are built of stone, stems of this *Euphorbia* are the preferred material for holding other plants, earth and stones to make the roof.

The latex of the tree is spread over the outside of milk pots to seal them and make them last longer.

This is a commonly-used plant for a living fence.

Apicultural value: *Honeybees are foraging pollen and nectar from the flowers and the tree is a honey source. The abundant nectar of the flowers is attracting bees, but the honey is disliked because of fade smell and causing strange feelings. It is also said to irritate and burn the mouth.*
For bees the tree plays an important role to strengthen the colony and brood development mostly in drier parts of the country.

Recommended for planting to increase honey production

Ricinus communis L.

GULO, HABLALIT, CH'IAQMAL (Amh); KELLA (Tre); GUL'I (Tya); CASTOR OIL TREE (Eng); WUNDERBAUM (German)

Family: Euphorbiaceae

Description: Short-lived small tree or shrub with soft wood and hollow stems which can grow to 5 m or more. <u>Bark</u>: greenish to reddish brown, smooth. <u>Leaves</u>: palmately and deeply lobed with serrate leaf margins; long-stalked, alternate, dark green or even reddish. <u>Flowers</u>: crowded on upright spikes up to 40 cm long; both sexes occur on the same plant; the upper female flowers appear before the lower male ones. <u>Fruits</u>; round, deep red, prickly capsules, in dense clusters; containing three tick-like, brown or reddish-brown marbled, very poisonous seeds with a high oil content.

Flowering trees can be found throughout the year but very often after rains.

Distribution: GULO is a very common plant of compounds in rural and urban areas and also common along seasonally dry rivers in altitudes between 400 and 2500 m. Ethiopia is a possible centre of origin for this plant and contains a wide diversity of germplasm.

First cultivated for castor oil in ancient Egypt and now widely grown as a cash crop in the tropics, especially in India.

It is widespread in all African countries.

Practical notes: It is very fast growing. The leaves and residue from pressed seeds are poisonous to stock.

Uses: Crushed castor seeds are used to grease the METAD before INJERA is baked and the extracted oil is used as lamp oil for lighting and for tanning leather.

The oil is a lubricant used in many industrial situations elsewhere.

The extracted oil has been used for many centuries as a purgative. In traditional medicine the leaves and seeds are used as a laxative, for wound dressing, against rheumatism and mental illness.

Apicultural value: *The extra-floral nectaries on leaves below produce much nectar and large amount of pollen is obtained from male flowers. But bees do not have value as pollinators because castor is largely wind-pollinated.*

Sapium ellipticum *(Hochst.) Pax*

ARBOCHE (Amh); BAL (Gim); SHEDO (Kef); BOSAKA, WOSANGA (Or); GANCHO (Sid); BERBERE-ASLAMAY (Tya)

Family: Euphorbiaceae

Description: Usually a large deciduous tree, sometimes only a shrub, up to 25 m high with a trunk breast-height diameter up to 1 m and a large crown. Bark: brown and rough. Leaves: simple, elliptic to oblong-elliptic, up to 13 cm long, dark above and paler below, turning dark red before falling. Flowers: yellow, arranged in axillary or terminal spikes up to 14 cm long; with female flowers at the base of the spikes and numerous male flowers above them to the top of the spikes. Fruit: red capsules, 1 cm across.

Flowering from October to February.

Distribution: Growing between 1250 and 2450 m in Afromontane forest, particularly found in clearings and riverine forest, and also in secondary montane evergreen bushland where annual rainfall ranges between 1200 and 2000 mm.

Also in Guinea Republic, Sierra Leone, Cote d'Ivoire, Ghana, Togo, Benin, Nigeria, Cameroun, Gabon, Congo, Central African Republic, Rwanda, Sudan, Uganda, Kenya, Tanzania, Angola, Zambia, Malawi, Zimbabwe, Mozambique and South Africa.

Practical notes: Can be grown from seedlings raised in a nursery and carefully dug-up wild seedlings.

Uses: The wood is fairly tough and strong, but not durable in the ground and liable to borer attacks. It is used for making farm tools and tool handles and suitable for indoor carpentry. It is used for firewood but not charcoal.

Apicultural value: *Honeybees gather both pollen and nectar from the flowers. The tree seems to be very attractive to bee colonies and they can produce a surplus of honey from this tree under favourable conditions.*

Dovyalis caffra *(Hook.f. & Harv.) Hook.f.*

KOSHM (Amh); ANKAKUTEH (Or); KAI APPLE (Eng).

Family: Flacourtiaceae

Description: Evergreen shrub, armed with robust spines up to 7 cm long. <u>Leaves</u>: leathery, shiny dark to bright green, simple, elliptic or obovate, with venetian raised on upper surface. <u>Flowers</u>: small, creamy yellow, differentiated into male and female. The male flowers are arranged in 8 to 10-flowered clusters while female flowers are solitary. <u>Fruits</u>: fleshy, round, yellow-orange, up to 3 to 4 cm across, on short stalks. The flesh has a pleasant sharp refreshing flavour.

Flowers can be found all year round but the main flowering period is from February to June.

Distribution: KAI APPLE is a highly effective hedge plant and is now found planted around compounds in many towns and villages between 1500 and 2600 m.

A native of South Africa, Zimbabwe and Mozambique, nowadays introduced and cultivated in many countries throughout the tropics.

Practical notes: KAI APPLE is fairly fast growing when there is sufficient water, but it will also tolerate dry dusty conditions. It is easily grown from seed, and seedlings are often available in nurseries.

Uses: This plant has now become an important cultivated shrub in Ethiopia commonly used for fencing. Female plants can produce a lot of fruit which is eaten by children and also collected for sale or processing into jam or jelly.

Dovyalis abyssinica *(A. Rich.) Warb.*

KOSHM (Amh); AYHADA (Tya); ANKAKUTEH (Or).

Description: Similar to KAI APPLE, but an indigenous spiny evergreen shrub or small tree up to 8 m tall. <u>Leaves</u>: with a few small teeth on the margin. <u>Flowers</u>: either male (with petals and many stamens) or female (without petals and stamens). Fruit similar to KAI APPLE.

Distribution: Found between 1800 and 2500 m where rainfall is between 500 and 1500 mm per year in both drier and more humid montane forests, as well as riverine forest and evergreen bushland.

Practical notes: This is quite a fast growing small tree which can grown from seed. In local medicine, parts of the whole plant are used against NEKERSA, and the fruits are used against swelling of the throat.

Apicultural value: *Honeybees forage for the abundant pollen and nectar throughout the day. Bees are also important pollinators for setting fruit. In arid climates there are reports that bees suck the juice of damaged fruits. Where there are dense stands of* KAI APPLE *the bees store a significant surplus of honey and the tree is therefore an important honey source.*

Recommended for planting to increase honey production

Hypericum revolutum *Vahl* subsp. **revolutum**

AMJA (Amh); HENDI, EDERA, GARAMBA, GORGORO (Or); GARARABICHU (Sid); AVETIA (Tya); TREE ST. JOHN'S WORT (Eng)

Family: Guttiferae (also known as Clusiaceae with Hypericaceae sometimes given as a separate family)

Description: Slender tree or a shrub, attaining a height of 12 m and a trunk diameter of 25 cm. The crown of the tree is open with an irregular outline and the branchlets are often drooping. <u>Bark</u>: scaly and often roughly longitudinally fissured, dark brown and corky. <u>Leaves</u>: opposite, pale green, narrowly elliptic to lance-shaped up to 3 cm long; produced in dense clusters on short shoots; <u>Flowers</u>: terminal and solitary, large and about 6 cm in diameter. <u>Fruits</u>: woody capsules, containing very many minute black seeds.

Flowering all year round with individual trees being covered in blossoms at different times.

Distribution: A characteristic tree of upper Afromontane rain forests, and evergreen bushland, found from 2300 to 4000 m, especially along the upper tree limit and often associated with *Hagenia-Schefflera* forest and *Erica arborea*. It used to be very common in the Simien Mountains and still forms forests on the Bale Plateau. It is rarely found in the western parts of the highlands. It grows where rainfall ranges between 1000 and 1800 mm per year.

Also in Cameroun, Zaire, Rwanda, Burundi, Sudan, Uganda, Kenya, Tanzania, Zambia, Malawi, Mozambique, Swaziland, South Africa and also in Yemen, south western Saudi Arabia, on the Comoro Islands and in restricted areas of Madagascar.

Practical notes: Not an easy tree to grow. Propagation can be done from root suckers and cuttings, but seed germination seems to be very poor.

Uses: The wood is dark red-brown, fairly hard but flexible. It is quite popular for makning poles in house construction. The wood is also commonly used to make the yoke, QUENBER, of the local ox-plough.

Hypericum quartinianum and *H. peplidifolium* are described in the section on Herbs and Shrubs.

Apicultural value: *Honeybees collect copious pollen and abundant nectar from the flowers very frequently and this tree is an important honey source in high altitudes. Beekeepers in Bale region are repeatedly reporting about good quality honey harvested by bees from this tree. Because of its prolonged flowering time this tree is important for bee colony development and the rich pollen and nectar supply is a brood rearing stimulus even if only single trees are left.*

Recommended for planting to increase honey production

Apodytes dimidiata var. acutifolia *(A. Rich.) Boutique*

DONGA, CELEQLEQQA (Amh); BERDELE (Dor); DANNISA, MEI, ODA, ODA-BADA, ODA-KIYET, ODA-SEDA, QUMBALA, ULIFONI, WENDEBYO (Or); DONKIKO (Sid); WHITE PEAR (Eng)

Family: Icacinaceae

Description: Tall evergreen tree, up to 25 m high, with a rounded crown. <u>Bark</u>: smooth and pale grey-brown; young branches glabrous to sparsely pubescent. <u>Leaves</u>: dark glossy-green, turning black when drying, alternate with variable shape, but usually oval with regularly wavy margins or even sometimes slightly toothed. <u>Flowers</u>: fragrant, small, white and star-like, in terminal sprays; the flowering stems persist after the blossom has fallen from the tree. <u>Fruits</u>: small and flat, black when ripe, not edible.

Flowering from December to March.

Distribution: Growing in montane forest between 1200 to 3500 m, it often remains as a solitary tree in farmland after forest has been cleared. Its rainfall range is 500 to 2000 mm per year.

In most countries in East and Central Africa southwards to Mozambique, Swaziland and South Africa. It is also found in Madagascar, the Comoros and Mascarene Islands, India, tropical Asia as far as southwestern China and the Moluccas.

Practical notes: *Apodytes* is slow-growing but seedlings are easily raised from seeds.

Uses: The wood is tough and strong, easy to saw, plane and polish. It is suitable for indoor carpentry, tool handles, construction work, doors and veneers. The wood is also sometimes used as fuel and for making charcoal. This is a very ornamental tree.

Apicultural value: *Honeybees forage vigorously for the abundant nectar and pollen from the flowers. The pollen has a good value for stimulating brood rearing and is, therefore, important for strengthening honeybee colonies.*

When many trees in dense stands are flowering together a good yield of honey is produced.

Recommended for planting to increase honey production

Persea americana *Mill.*

AVOCADO (Amh & Eng)

Family: Lauraceae

Description: Evergreen tree which can grow up to 10 m tall with a dark dense crown. <u>Bark</u>: grey to dark brown, rough and fissured with age. <u>Leaves</u>: large and alternate, elliptic-lanceolate; glossy dark-green above, leathery with prominent midrib. <u>Flowers</u>: yellowish-green and small, abundant in long, dense panicles. <u>Fruits</u>: green and pear-shaped with a smooth peel; containing a soft yellowish-creamy flesh with a large woody seed;

Flowering after the big rains from October to December.

Distribution: Cultivated in many parts of the country between 1500 and 2400 m where rainfall is over 1000 mm a year and general humidity is high.

It is a native of Mexico and is said to have been cultivated by the Aztecs 8000 years ago.

Practical notes: Bark, leaves and seeds are all toxic to browsing stock. Propagation is done by seedlings.

Uses: It is cultivated for its nutritious fruits which are rich in fat, protein and vitamins. It is, therefore, one of the most valuable fruit types. It is also grown for shade.

A high quality oil can be extracted from the seeds which is used in preparing cosmetics.

Recently AVOCADO has gained much popularity as a drink and also for treating some minor skin and hair problems.

Apicultural value: *Honeybees collect pollen and nectar from the flowers frequently. The nectar secretion is abundant under favourable conditions like high humidity. However, it is much affected by climate and soil moisture. The pollen production is moderate.*
The honey has a strong aroma and is dark whereas the granulation is slow. Honeybees are the most important pollinators for setting satisfactory fruit.

Acacia abyssinica *Hochst. ex Benth.*

QSLTO (Afar); BAZRA-GRAR (Amh); ODARA (Kem); AMBO, DADECCA, DAGNISA, DEDECCA, GARBI, LAFTO, SONDI (Or); ALLA, CHE'A (Tya); ODORO, ODORWA (Wel)

Family: Fabaceae (Leguminosae) subfamily Mimosoideae

Description: Large tree with branches ascending to form a very flat crown which can be up to 30 m wide. <u>Bark</u>: brown to almost black, rough and fissured; branchlets longitudinally ridged; spines, straight, in pairs, variable in length, up to 4 cm long. <u>Leaves</u>: bipinnate, pinnae in up to 30 pairs; leaflets up to 40 pairs in a pinna. <u>Flowers</u>: sweet-scented, white, tinged red, in round heads. <u>Pods</u>: somewhat thick and woody, grey-brown or purplish-brown, straight or slightly curved; up to 12 cm long and splitting on the tree or on the ground to release elliptic, compressed seeds.

Flowering from January to May.

Distribution: Found from 1500 to 2900 m in Afromontane rainforest and montane forest, especially along clearings and forest edges where they can form pure stands. It also occurs in wooded grassland, sometimes forming a dense stand, and in secondary bushland. It will grow where rainfall ranges from 1000 to 2000 mm, but is not found in the Hararghe region.

Also in Zaire, Rwanda, Burundi, Sudan, Eritrea, Uganda, Kenya, Tanzania, Malawi, Zimbabwe, Mozambique and Yemen.

Practical notes: It is fairly fast growing from seed, but the seeds need pre-treatment either in boiling water or through chipping the seed coat so they will germinate.

Uses: It is one of the most prefered trees for fuelwood and for making charcoal. The wood is also suitable for poles, posts and tool handles. The timber is used for house construction. +Branches and twigs are commonly used to put round fields of growing crops, particularly tef and wheat, to protect them from grazing animals.

It is an excellent shade tree and leaves, young shoots and pods are very valuable for browsing. It is a very valuable tree for soil conservation measures. As with other Acacia species, crops grown near these trees benefit from the nitrogen fixation of the roots.

Apicultural value: *Honeybees are foraging abundant nectar and pollen and A.abyssinica is an important honey source. Bees start working on the flowers before the sunrise at 4 o'clock in the morning very frequently throughout the day. In dense stands the bees will produce even a significant surplus of honey and the tree contributes to mixed honeys in the highlands in which its flavour will sometimes predominate. In most cases the pollen and nectar of single trees will strengthen the colonies and stimulate brood rearing significantly.*

Recommended for planting to increase honey production

Acacia albida *Del.*

GERBI (Amh & Gur); QERETOR (Gam); DEROT, GARBI (Or); MAMAN (Saho); AQBA (Tre); MOMONA, GARSHA (Tya); APPLE-RING ACACIA (Eng)

Family: Fabaceae (Leguminosae) subfamily Mimosoideae

Description: One of the tallest of the acacias growing to 30 m high, with a spreading or rounded crown and trunk reaching up to 1 m in diameter. <u>Bark</u>: rough, dark brown or dull grey, fissured and scaling; branchlets often hanging and with pale brown to white bark; spines in pairs, straight, often pointing down. <u>Leaves</u>: bipinnate with 3 to 10 pairs of pinnae. <u>Flowers</u>: sweetly-scented, yellowish-white, sessile, in slender spikes, 3.5 to 17 cm long. <u>Pods</u>: bright orange, curled round or sickle-shaped, resembling dried apple-rings.

Flowering from July to December.

Distribution: Found from 500 to 2600 m in woodland and grassland, often along rivers and on seasonally waterlogged ground. It is particularly tolerant of heavier clay soil. It requires a rainfall range between 300 and 1800 mm per year.

It is found all over tropical and subtropical Africa and even in W Asia. It occurs from South Algeria to Transvaal, from Senegal to Somalia, preferring the semi-arid zones.

Practical notes: This species is fast growing, even in poor soils. Seeds need boiling for 5 minutes or chipping to make them germinate.

This tree retains its leaves during the dry season thus giving shade, but sheds them during rainy periods allowing light to penetrate to plants growing under it. This makes this tree highly compatible with annual crop plants.

Uses: The wood is used for manufacturing various tools and kitchen utensils. Previously in Ethiopia, planks for making large secure doors were made from *A.albida*. However, the wood is not suitable for making charcoal and is not so good as fuelwood. The branches are widely used for making fences.

This species is widely used and now promoted in agroforestry systems as it is a very good shade tree, termite resistant and soil stabilizing because of its deep taproot system.

This tree is nitrogen-fixing and the most important forage tree of much of dryland Africa. It is occasionally even called the "miracle tree" of the Sahel. In some Sahel regions the tree plays a significant role in tribal customs and traditional law.

In traditional medicine the bark, fruits and leaves are used against headaches, colds and stomach-aches.

Apicultural value: *Honeybees are foraging nectar and pollen from the flowers. The tree seems to be rather attractive for bees and beekeepers hang their beehives in the branches.*

Recommended for planting to increase honey production

294

Acacia dolichocephala *Harms*

LAFTO (Or); GUGANTA (Wel)

Family: Fabaceae (Leguminosae) subfamily Mimosoideae

Description: Tree which grows from 3 m up to 13 m tall, with glabrous branchlets which are often longitudinally ridged. <u>Bark</u>: dark brown to black and rough; spines at base of leaves, short and straight. <u>Leaves</u>: bipinnate, with pinnae 4 to 21 pairs and leaflets in up to 35 pairs, dark green above, paler beneath. <u>Flowers</u>: very sweetly scented; bright yellow in large heads on long peduncles. <u>Pods</u>: first greenish and then turning purplish brown when ripe; straight or slightly curved.

Flowering from February to November.

Distribution: Found from 1100 to 2130 m, commonly found in woodland and grassland, often at lake margins and on river banks. Also occuring in deciduous bushland which is regularly burnt through.

Also in Uganda, Sudan, Kenya and Tanzania.

Uses: Wood is fairly hard and commonly used for fuel and making charcoal. The branches and twigs are used for fences.

It can be found left on farmland after other woody plants have been cleared.

This attractive *Acacia* is sometimes found in public gardens and could be more widely grown as an ornamental.

Apicultural value: *Honeybees collect pollen and nectar from the flowers frequently.*

Acacia lahai *Steud. & Hochst. ex Benth.*

WTTIE, TKUR GRAR (Amh); QERETOR (Gam); BURQUQQE, DEROT, SONDI, GARBI, LAFTO (Or); LAHAY (Tya); GUGANTA (Wel)

Family: Fabaceae (Leguminosae), subfamily Mimosoideae

Description: Conspicuously flat-topped tree or shrub up to 15 m tall. <u>Bark</u>: grey to dark brown, rough and fissured, with brownish purple pubescent branchlets. The stipular spines are in pairs and up to 7 cm long, slender and straight. <u>Leaves</u>: compound with pinnae in 6 to 15 pairs and numerous small leaflets in 10 to 28 pairs. <u>Flowers</u>: white, cream or pale yellow in up to 9 cm long spikes. <u>Pods</u>: straight or curved like a sickle; shiny brown and splitting on the tree to release many flat, oval seeds.

A. lahai often forms thickets in Ethiopia when it flowers and fruits as a low shrub, often only 0.5 to 1 m high.

Flowering from April to October.

Distribution: Found in upland woodland and scrub, in secondary montane evergreen bushland and in wooded grassland from 1700 to 2600 m.

Elsewhere found in Kenya, Uganda and Tanzania.

Practical notes: LAHAY is easily grown from seeds which do not require any special treatment. Young seedlings need protecting from goats and other browsing animals.

Uses: The wood is very hard, heavy and durable. It is suitable for fence posts, bridge timber and heavy construction work. It also makes very good fuelwood and charcoal.

Apicultural value: *This* Acacia *species produces moderate amounts of pollen and nectar which are useful for bees at higher altitudes. Honeybees are often seen collecting pollen and nectar from the flowers.*

Acacia negrii *Pic.-Serm.*

TEDDECCA (Or)

Family: Fabaceae (Leguminosae) subfamily Mimosoideae

Description: Small tree, sometimes a shrub, growing up to 6 m high, under favourable conditions up to 10 m with an umbrella-shaped crown which can touch the ground around the tree. The trunk is often rather short soon forming widely diverging branches. Bark: pale with somewhat powdery flakes; young branches purplish-brown to black with white breathing pores. The stipulate spines are straight, up to 8.5 cm long. Leaves: 6 to 10 pinnae pairs with 13 to 31 pairs of leaflets, dark above, paler beneath. Flowers: sweetly scented, cream and arranged in fairly large heads. Pods: somewhat woody, straight or slightly curved and longitudinal veined.

Flowering from August to October and individual trees can be completely covered in blossoms.

Distribution: Endemic found between 2000 and 3100 m on the central highlands in upland wooded grassland and sometimes as a remnant tree on farmland, particularly on heavy clay soils. This is one of the trees often found in farmers' compounds.

Not known elsewhere.

Practical notes: Grows easily from seed as long as they are pre-treated either by chipping or putting into boiling water and allowing to cool.

Uses: The wood is fairly hard and is used for making firewood and charcoal.

It is a popular shade tree and boundary marker on farmland.

Apicultural value: *Honeybees are frequently visiting the flowers for pollen and nectar.*

Acacia persiciflora *Pax*

BATE (Or)

Family: Fabaceae (Leguminosae) subfamily Mimosoideae

Description: Tree with a spreading flat-topped crown, commonly growing to a height of 9 m, occasionally up to 15 m. <u>Bark</u>: brown and scaling in vertical strips; the young branches are covered with soft fine hairs. Prickles are in pairs recurved and up to 3 mm long but often absent from young stems. <u>Leaves</u>: pinnae 4 to 8 pairs with leaflets in 11 to 17 pairs, usually appearing after the tree has flowered. <u>Flowers</u>: very fragrant, overall impression from a distance is often pink, arranged in spikes 1.5 to 3 cm long. The calyx is red or purplish and the filaments of the stamens are white. The flowers usually appear before the leaves or are accompanied by very young leaves. <u>Pods</u>: straight or slightly curved, up to 15 cm long, brown and with transverse veins, persistent on the tree.

Flowering is from February to May.

Distribution: This *Acacia* is commonly found in woodland and wooded grassland between 1700 and 2100 m.

It is also found in Sudan, Uganda, Kenya and Zaire.

Practical notes: Seed treatment is required as for other species of *Acacia*.

Uses: The wood is very hard and strong and is commonly used for charcoal production and as a fuel. The tree remains very often as a boundary marker in fields.

Apicultural value: *Honeybees show exceptional interest in this tree. They forage from early morning up to evening taking pollen and nectar from the flowers very frequently even when the climate is hot and dry. Like a swarm plenty of bees can be seen on the tree, working on the flowers.*
Beekeepers have repeatedly reported about the quantity of honey harvested from this acacia. This species seems to be one of the most important acacias for honeybees of the country.

Recommended for planting to increase honey production

302

Acacia pilispina *Pic.-Serm.*

ACQ-GRAR (Amh); LAFTO (Or); CHE'A (Tya)

Family: Fabaceae (Leguminosae) subfamily Mimosoideae

Description: Small tree or shrub usually growing to around 5 m tall, sometimes up to 15 m high with an irregular somewhat flat crown. The trunk is usually short and sloping to one side and forming branches from near the base. <u>Bark</u>: light brown flaking with a powdery layer underneathy; young branchlets are brownish and densely clothed with long grey to yellowish spreading hairs; stipular spines are up to 5 cm long and straight. <u>Leaves</u>: pinnae 8 to 16 pairs and leaflets 8 to 28 pairs. <u>Flowers</u>: sweetly scented, cream, in heads. <u>Pods</u>: slightly woody, straight or slightly curved and longitudinally veined.

Flowering over a long period from July to December. In the dry season, trees can be found completely covered in blossoms.

Distribution: Found between 1700 and 3100 m in cultivated land, wooded grassland and upland bushlands, sometimes also in woodland of the highlands. Particularly found on black heavier soils.

Also in Tanzania, Zaire, Zambia, Malawi and Mozambique.

Practical notes: It is very similar to *A. negrii*. Seed treatment is required.

This acacia readily form suckers and can infest farmers fields if the roots are not cleared when the trees are cut.

The flowers are very sensitive to rain and will fall off very quickly following a shower.

Uses: Very commonly cut to make both temporary and more permanent fencing.

The wood is fairly hard and used for firewood and charcoal.

Apicultural value: *Honeybees forage for the adequate nectar and pollen from the flowers. It seems the tree yields enough nectar to contribute to mixed honeys.*

Acacia polyacantha *Willd.* subsp.. **campylacantha** *(Hochst. ex A.Rich.)* *Brenan*

GMARDA (Amh); GWMERO (Tya)

Family: Fabaceae (Leguminosae) subfamily Mimosoideae

Description: Tree up to 25 m high with feathery foliage and a spreading crown. The young branches are dark purplish covered with soft hairs and the twigs have paired, axillary prickles. <u>Bark</u>: ash-grey to yellowish, with brown scales and black scars in the place of former leaves and thorns. <u>Leaves</u>: delicate with many (up to 60) pinnae pairs and numerous (68 pairs) small leaflets. <u>Flowers</u>: fragrant, yellowish-white, sessile, in up to 13 cm long spikes, in pairs or in 3 together. <u>Pods</u>: straight, flat, dark brown and up to 12 cm long, containing 5 to 9 seeds.

Flowering from April to June.

Distribution: Found from 500 to 1800 m in wooded grassland, deciduous woodland and bushland. In some cases it is found as a solitary tree on farmland. It is also common in riverine and ground water forest.

It is found all over tropical Africa, generally as solitary trees in the Sahel.

Practical notes: Seeds have a good germination and it has a quick juvenile growth.

Uses: The ash of this species is used as a salt substitute. The gum is edible and used in confectionary and adhesives. The gum is also suitable for the treatment of new textile fibres. Bark and pods contain tannin.

The wood is hard and durable, difficult to saw but very good for making agricultural implements, poles and tool handles. It is also preferred for fuel and charcoal making.

The leaves are browsed by camels and goats.

The roots have some value to cure venereal diseases and to prepare an antidote for snakebites. A bark decoction is useful for dysentry and gastro-intestinal disorders.

Apicultural value: *Honeybees collect pollen and nectar from the flowers frequently. The nectar and pollen production is moderate.*

305

Acacia senegal *(L.) Willd.*

SBANSA-GRAR, QONTR (Amh); ADAD, AKKRSA (Gam); MAHARA (Kun); IDADO, SABANSA-DIMA, SAPESSA (Or); ADAD-MERU (Som); CH'FRI-DMU, QENTB, QENTBI, QENTIBA (Tya); BETUBA (Wel)

Family: Fabaceae (Leguminosae) subfamily Mimosoideae

Description: Tree with a flat crown and branching from near the base of the trunk, often forming thickets. Bark: dark brown to red-brown; prickles in threes, the central one hooked downwards, the two lateral are curved upwards or solitary. Leaves: bipinnate, pinnae 3 to 8 pairs; leaflets in 7 to 25 pairs, pubescent. Flowers: sweet smelling, cream or white, in up to 12 cm long spikes; usually appearing before the leaves. Pods: straight, yellowish brown to brown, flat with prominent veins, containing few light-brown round seeds.

Flowering trees may be found throughout the year with a flowering peak from April to May.

Distribution: Found between 600 and 1700 m in dry wooded grassland, deciduous bushland and dry scrub where rainfall ranges between 100 to 800 mm per year.

It is a typical tree of the Sahel and widespread from Senegal to the Red Sea where it can be an indicator of ground water.

Practical notes: It is very drought resistant. For germination pretreatment as with all acacias is necessary.

The curved spines readily catch and hold on to clothing.

Uses: This species is the source of *"Gum Arabic"* of international trade. It also has many uses as given for the genus and is an important tree for agroforestry systems in arid and semi-arid areas of Sudan and western Ethiopia.

The wood is very suitable for fuel and charcoal, as well as for poles and timber in general. Agricultural tools are made from the branches.

It is a very valuable browse plant. Because of its widely extended lateral root system it is a very valuable tree for erosion control and soil stabilization.

In traditional medicine the tree is commonly used as a panacea for many ailments.

Apicultural value: *Honeybees collect the abundant pollen and nectar from the flowers frequently and the tree is an important honey source. The aroma of the amber honey is mild and the granulation is fast.*

Recommended for planting to increase honey production

Acacia seyal *Del.*

MAKANI, ADIQENTO (Afar); CGINDA (Gam); WACU, WAJJI, WAKKO-DIMO, WASIYA (Or); AFLO (Saho); FULAÄY, JIIQ (Som); CHE'A (Tre & Tya); QEYYH-CHE'A, SA'DA-CHE'A (Tya)

Family: Fabaceae (Leguminosae) subfamily Mimosoideae

Description: Small to medium-sized tree with a characteristically umbrella-shaped crown. <u>Bark</u>: on trunk powdery, white to greenish yellow or even orange red; spines up to 8 cm long, straight, sometimes fused into "ant-galls". <u>Leaves</u>: dark green, bipinnate with 3 to 10 pairs of leaflets. <u>Flowers</u>: fragrant, in shining yellow globose heads, usually appearing before the leaves. <u>Pods</u>: slightly curved, constricted between the seeds, light brown, splitting on the tree; containing elliptic, flat seeds.

Flowering from August to February.

Distribution: Found from 500 to 2300 m it is widespread in woodland, wooded grassland and also found as a shade tree on farmland where rainfall ranges from 250 to 1000 mm per year.

It is a typical tree of the Sahel growing in semi-arid zones from Senegal to Egypt and Ethiopia.

Practical notes: Natural regeneration is usually good and deliberate planting is not widely practiced. It regrows very easily after cutting.

Uses: Leaves, young shoots and pods are a very valuable browse for livestock.

The wood is very suitable for fuel and charcoal as well as for making tools. Branches are used for fencing.

This *Acacia* is a recommended tree to improve silvo-pastoral systems in drylands because of the high nutritive value of its browse.

The bark and gum have medicinal uses and a red dye can also be extracted from the bark. An edible medium-quality gum is produced which, in Sudan, shares ten percent of the annually exported gum arabic.

Apicultural value: *Honeybees collect pollen and abundant nectar from the flowers frequently and under favourable conditions this tree is an honey source. The aroma of the honey is said to be mild.*

Recommended for planting to increase honey production

309

Acacia sieberiana DC. var. **sieberiana**

DEWENI-BUNNA (Gur); LAFTO, LAFTO-ADI, FULLSA, LALATO, BURQUQQE (Or); CERIN, JERIN (Som); GRMO, CHE'A, TSA'DA-CHE'A (Tya); GARA, ODORWA, PULLIESA (Wel)

Family: Fabaceae (Leguminosae) subfamily Mimosoideae

Description: Tree growing from 3 m to 18 m high with a wide bole and a spreading crown. <u>Bark</u>: grey-brown and rough; the paired stipular spines can be up to 9 cm long and straight. <u>Leaves</u>: pinnae 8 to 35 pairs, leaflets tiny and in 13 to 45 pairs. <u>Flowers</u>: fragrant, creamy-white in round heads, about 1 cm across. <u>Pods</u>: large and thick, woody in texture, up to 21 cm long.

Flowering from April to May after the small rains.

Distribution: Growing between 500 and 2200 m in drier deciduous woodland and riverine forests, sometimes found as a remnant tree on farmland. It needs an annual rainfall of between 400 and 800 mm per year.

It is also found from Senegal to Sudan, and southwards to Malawi and Mozambique.

Practical notes: Seed treatment as described for other acacias is required.

Uses: The wood is reported to be termite resistant. It is also suitable for tool handles. It is used for firewood, and making charcoal.

The branches are used for fences. The leaves, flowers and pods are used for feeding livestock.

In traditional medicine the bark and roots are used as a remedy against worms, rheumatism and bilharzia.

Apicultural value: *Honeybees forage very frequently for the abundant pollen and nectar from the flowers. Where there are dense stands of this tree, the bees will produce even a surplus of honey and the tree contributes to mixed honeys.*

Recommended for planting to increase honey production

Acacia tortilis *(Forssk.) Hayne* subsp. **spirocarpa** *(Hochst. ex A.Rich.) Brenan*

BEHBEY (Afar); SHERA (Gam); LOTTOBA, TEDDECCA (Or); TIMAD, ABAK, AKAB, ORA, GURHA-DARUYE, HARAH (Som); AQBA, TSA'DA-AQBA (Tre); ANQIEBA, A'LLA (Tya); UMBRELLA THORN (Eng)

Family: Fabaceae (Leguminosae) subfamily Mimosoideae

Description: Spreading tree with a wide, flat or umbrella-shaped crown. The branching is not dense and the shade is light. <u>Bark</u>: grey to black, rough and fissured; branches armed with a mixture of spines, paired stipular spines are hooked and up to 5 mm long, others are straight and slender up to 10 cm long. <u>Leaves</u>: pinnae in 2 to 10 pairs; leaflets in 6 to 22 pairs. <u>Flowers</u>: very fragrant, dirty-white in small round heads. <u>Pods</u>: spirally twisted, pale brown with numerous dark red glands, containing small compressed seeds.

Flowering from January to May.

Distribution: Found from 600 to 1900 m in dry bushland, ofteh the dominant tree *Acacia*-woodland and wooded grassland, also in dry scrub. This was the commonest tree of the Rift Valley Lakes region. It is very drought resistant and can grow in a rainfall range from 50 to 1000 mm per year.

It is found in the arid and semi-arid regions south and north of the Sahara, from Senegal to East Africa, Somalia and southwards to southern tropical Africa.

Practical notes: This is a particularly drought-resistant tree which very often indicates the tree limit on the edge of the desert. It can be grown easily from seed provided they are treated as described for other acacias.

Uses: This tree is recommended for afforestation programmes because of its wide ecological range.

The hard wood is very suitable for fuel and charcoal. Its thorny branches and twigs are preferred for fences.

The leaves, young shoots and especially the pods, when shed or shaken down, are a very valuable forage for livestock.

It is a good shade tree and a windbreak and recommended for stabilizing sandy soils. The seeds are said to be edible and used as a famine food.

Apicultural value: *Honeybees collect pollen and nectar from the flowers very frequently but the honey production is limited due to the generally dry climate. Where there is higher rainfall the tree is an important honey source. The honey has a very characteristic aroma. Granulation is relatively slow with a coarse cristallization.*

Recommended for planting to increase honey production

Albizia gummifera *(J.F.Gmel.) C.A.Sm.* var. **gummifera**

SESA (Amh); SASA (Amh & Or); CATTO (Kef & Or); AMBABESSA, CAWICCO, EMELA, GORBE, KARCOFFE, MUKKA-ARBA, SANKILE, SHIMORO, SISA, YUNGO (Or)

Family: Fabaceae (Leguminosae) subfamily Mimosoideae

Description: Large tree, growing up to 30 m tall, with a markedly flat or umbrella-shaped crown of dark green, shiny foliage. <u>Bark</u>: grey, smooth, often tinged with red; large quantities of glutinous latex bleed when the tree is cut. <u>Leaves</u>: bipinnate, leaflets in 9 to 16 pairs; dark green and shiny. <u>Flowers</u>: white and numerous, arranged in clusters. <u>Pods</u>: oblong, flat, papery, pale brown to purplish.

Flowering from January to April.

Distribution: Found between 1550 and 2150 m growing in Afromontane forest commonly along the forest edges and in clearings. Also occasionally found in riverine forests and secondary montane evergreen bushland, restricted to the western and southwestern parts of the NW Highlands where annual rainfall ranges between 1500 and 2000 mm.

Also in Nigeria, Cameroun, Zaire, Rwanda, Burundi, Sudan, Uganda, Kenya, Tanzania, Malawi, Zimbabwe, Mozambique and Madagascar.

Practical notes: It will grow from seed if the seeds are scratched or chipped before planting. Propagation is done by seedlings and wildlings.

Uses: This species is often kept as the natural shade-tree in the "coffee-forests" of Sidamo, Keffa and Illubabor regions.

The wood is medium strong and used for timber which is easy to work but not very durable and liable to be attacked by termites. It is also used for firewood.

The leaves provide animal fodder.

This *Albizia* is a recommended tree for soil conservation measures and agroforestry.

Apicultural value: *This tree is a prolific producer of pollen and nectar and honeybees produce a surplus of honey under favourable conditions. It is very attractive to bees and baskets are placed in the branches to attract wild swarms.*

Recommended for planting to increase honey production.

Albizia lebbek *(L.) Benth.*

LEBBEK (Amh); YOKE (Gim); SHASHO (Wel); EAST INDIAN WALNUT (Eng)

Family: Fabaceae (Leguminosae) subfamily Mimosoideae

Description: Deciduous tree, usually attaining a height of 15 m, occasionally up to 25 m tall with a short trunk and a low and spreading crown. Bark: grey and rough. Leaves: compound, 2 to 4 pairs pinnae each with 3 to 11 pairs of leaflets which are oblong or elliptic-oblong and rounded at the apex. Flowers: greenish-yellow and fragrant. Pods: shiny yellow-brown in clusters.

Flowering from January to May.

Distribution: Found planted, and naturalized in some places, from 400 m up to 1900 m in the both dry and moist lowlands where annual rainfall ranges between 500 and 2500 mm.

A native to tropical Asia and widely planted throughout the tropics.

Practical notes: Propagation is done from seedlings, direct sowing and cuttings. The tree is easily blown over by strong winds.

Uses: The hard and heavy wood provides poles, posts and valuable timber which is used for furniture, tool handles and utensils. The wood also makes good fuel and charcoal.

The pods and leaves are a good animal fodder. This is an attractive tree with dense foliage which is planted for shade on farmland and also beside roads and in gardens.

This tree is a highly recommended for soil conservation programmes and for erosion control.

Similar species:

Albizia malacophylla *(A.Rich.) Walp.*

Medium-sized tree with two subspecies: the endemic variety *malacophylla* occurs between 1400 and 1900 m and the other variety, *ugandensis* Bak.f., occurs between 550 to 2200 m.

Apicultural value: *Honeybees forage very frequently for pollen and nectar. These trees are important suppliers of nectar and pollen in lower altitudes, especially in drier parts of the country. They guarantee the survival of bee colonies and may even contribute to mixed honeys.*

Recommended for planting to increase honey production

317

318

Albizia schimperiana *Oliv.*

SESA (Amh); SASA (Amh & Or); AMBABESSA, CATTO, CAWICCO, EMELA, GORBE, KARCOFFE, MUKKA-ARBA, SANKILE, SHIMORO, SISA, YUNGO (Or)

Family: Fabaceae (Leguminosae) subfamily Mimosoideae

Description: Tree with umbrella-shaped crown. Bark: smooth, grey to brownish; the branchlets are velvety covered with brown hairs. Leaves: bipinnate, pinnae in 2 to 7 pairs; leaflets in up to 23 pairs, obliquely oblong. Flowers: white or creamy-white or pale yellow; borne in loose conspicuous heads; flower stalks hairy. Pods: oblong, dull brown, containing many large seeds.

Flowering from January to May.

Distribution: Found from 1550 to 2800 m in Afromontane rainforests, in riverine forests and evergreen bushland. It is often left as a single tree in farmland, and is used for hanging beehives. It is occurs where rainfall range is from 1200 to 2000 mm per year.

Also in Zaire, Sudan, Uganda, Kenya, Tanzania, Zambia, Malawi, Zimbabwe and Mozambique.

Practical notes: Seedlings are easily raised from seeds and germination is quick. In afforestation programmes a mixture with *Cordia* and *Milletia* is advisable because of attack of moth larvae. The tree is fast growing.

Uses: The wood is yellowish-brown and moderately hard. It is fairly durable and commonly used for making tools and suitable for plywood.

It is sometimes used for fuel, charcoal making and timber production.

It is a useful tree for shade in coffee plantations and for soil conservation measures.

Apicultural value: *Honeybees collect the abundant nectar and pollen very frequently throughout the day. In dense stands the bees will produce even a surplus of honey and the tree contributes to mixed honeys in the western parts in which its flavour will not predominate.*

Recommended for planting to increase honey production

Calpurnia aurea *(Ait.) Benth.*
subsp. **aurea**

WCQA **(Agew)**; DGTTA **(Amh & Gur)**; CEQSA **(Gam)**; SHIT **(Ge'ez)**; QONDE **(Had)**; ANCABI, CEKA, CEKATA, SOLITU **(Or)**; STRA **(Tre)**; HTSAWTS **(Tya)**

Family: Fabaceae (Leguminosae), subfamily Papilionoideae

Description: Shrub or small tree commonly growing up to 5 m in bushland and occasionally up to 10 m in forests. <u>Bark</u>: pale brown and darker with age; young branches and inflorescences densely covered with soft hairs. <u>Leaves</u>: pinnately compound; the leaflets are light-yellowish green to slightly grey-green, elliptic to oblong and rounded at the apex. <u>Flowers</u>: attractive, bright golden-yellow, in hanging clusters up to 20 cm long. <u>Pods</u>: pale to dark green, flat and straight up to 12 cm long when mature; the unopened pods remain attached to the tree for a long time.

Trees can be found in flower all year round but most profusely after the small rains in May.

Distribution: Widespread throughout the highlands from 1400 to 2500 m where rainfall is from 1000 to 2000 mm per year, this is both a pioneer plant and a remnant tree of montane evergreen forests; in forests it is especially found in clearings and at margins and along rivers.

Found in all eastern African countries, as well as in Sudan, Zaire, Angola, Swaziland and South Africa.

Practical notes: *Calpurnia* is easily propagated both from cuttings and seeds.

Uses: This species makes a good live fence. It is a useful plant for boundary markers and branches are used for fuel and torch-lights.

The seeds may be used as a fish-poison and are used in traditional medicine as a cure for dysentery. The fruits and roots are also used against headache and stomach disorders.

Apicultural value: *This species provides a significant amount of nectar and pollen with honeybees visiting the flowers frequently all day round.*

Some beekeepers have reported that they get substantial honey from this tree. But this is has not been confirmed by our observations or in the literature. Even in some areas, where there are preferred nectar sources, bees do not visit this plant so frequently.

Erythrina abyssinica Lam. ex DC.

QWARA (Agew, Amh, Bil & Tya); 'GOFT, QORC (Amh); AMBILLSH (Gum); WERA (Had);
BERU, KOLANCU, KALANICA (Kef); WELECCO (Kem); AFRARTU, ARFETU, BARTU, BORTO,
DUS, MELAKO, WAZO, WELENA, WELENSU (Or); 'NQWI-HBEY, 'NQWI-ZBI, ZWAW' (Tya);
BORTWA (Wel); RED HOT POKER TREE (Eng)

Family: Fabaceae (Leguminosae) subfamily Papilionoideae

Description: Deciduous tree with spreading, somewhat twisted branches and an open crown. The trunk is short and stout. <u>Bark</u>: yellow-brown, thick and corky, deeply fissured with woody spines; branchlets with black prickles, later turning woody. <u>Leaves</u>: trifoliate, petioles with or without prickles; leaflets broadly ovate with terminal leaflet larger than the lateral ones; usually with prickles on the midrib. <u>Flowers</u>: spectacular, red to orange-red in dense, erect, cone-like inflorescences, up to 15 cm long. <u>Pods</u>: up to 10 cm long, woody and strongly constricted between the seeds, which are red and shiny with a black hilum.

Flowering over a long period from September to April.

Distribution: Occurring between 1000 to 2800 m in grassland, woodland, preferably at forest edges and very frequent in secondary scrub, particularly on rocky areas. Often it appears orchard-like as it is retained as a remnant from the former forest on farmland. It grows where rainfall ranges between 800 and 1500 mm per year.

This is very wide-spread tree found throughout eastern tropical Africa south to Zimbabwe and in Angola.

Practical notes: Grows very easily from cuttings. Seedlings are also easily raised from seeds. The seeds are poisonous and contain minute amounts of a curare-like poison.

Uses: This *Erythrina* is widely used to form live fences around homesteads. The wood is light and soft and commonly used for making mortars and traditional beehives as well as for tools handles and local house construction.

A brown dye can be extracted from the bark.

The leaves are palatable for sheep and goats.

The tree is recommended for soil conservation programmes and erosion control measures.

Apicultural value: *The tree is worth cultivating for its flowers, because the bees forage for nectar and pollen during the end of the dry season. Therefore the tree is important for strengthening bee colonies.*

Recommended for planting to increase honey production

Erythrina brucei *Schweinf.*

QWARA (Agew & Amh); QORCH (Amh); BURTO (Dor); BORTO (Gam); BORTWA (Gof & Wel); WERA (Had); BERO, KOLANCU, KOLANICA (Kef); WELECO (Kem); AFRARTU, ARFETU, BARTU, MELAKO, WAZO, WELENSU (Or)

Family: Fabaceae (Leguminosae) subfamily Papilionoideae

Description: Endemic deciduous tree, up to 30 m tall, with a thick trunk up to 1.2 m in diameter. <u>Bark</u>: dark brown, fissured; the branches, leaf stalks and also young stems are armed with stout prickles. <u>Leaves</u>: trifoliate; leaflets lanceolate to broadly ovate, sometimes with a few prickles on the midrib. <u>Flowers</u>: orange-red, occasionally light yellow, produced on long erect stalks, usually appearing when the tree is leafless. <u>Fruits</u>: linear-oblong pods, up to 15 cm long; when mature they split open and expose a papery lining, and bright-red seeds which are smooth and shining.

Flowering from November to February.

Distribution: Found from 1550 to 2800 m throughout the plateau at forest edges and along streams, in woodland and open places of upland forests. It is often planted to make a live fence and sometimes as an ornamental, particularly in Addis Ababa. Its rainfall range is from 1000 to 2000 mm per year.

As an endemic it is only found in Ethiopia, occurring as far as north as north of Lake Tana, as far east as around Hararghe and very common in Shewa, Sidamo, Wellega, Illubabor and Keffa provinces.

Practical notes: Fresh seeds germinate easily, but it can also be grown from cuttings. Young trees need protecting from heavy frost.

Uses: KORCH is a good boundary marker and is commonly used to make live fences. The wood is very soft and hollowed-out branches are used for making traditional beehives. It is used for firewood, carving and the leaves provide valuable fodder. Children use the bright red seeds for making necklaces.

In traditional medicine the roots and bark are used in the treatment of elephantiasis.

<u>Similar species:</u>

Erythrina burana *Chiov.* is also an **endemic** tree so far known only from Hararghe and Shewa in woodlands and bushlands at altitudes between 1350 and 2150 m. It is distinguished from *E. brucei* by its smaller stature and leaflets which are truncate at the apex. The flowers are dull orange.

Apicultural value: *Although pollinated by birds, the abundant pollen and nectar attract honeybees which collect nectar from the flowers frequently. The flowering period of these trees is helpful for strengthening bee colonies after harvesting time in November and crushed seeds, dissolved in water, can be used for bee feeding.*

Recommended for planting to increase honey production

326

Leucaena leucocephala *(Lam.) De Wit.*

LUKINA (Amh, Or & Tya); LEAD TREE (Eng).

Family: Fabaceae (Leguminosae), subfamily Mimosoideae

Description: Evergreen shrub or tree up to 5 m tall. <u>Leaves</u>: large and feathery, alternate on the stem, compound with pinnae in pairs, each with 7 to 17 pairs of leaflets which are obliquely oblong-lanceolate; leaflets and complete leaves fold up in response to moisture stress, cool temperatures and darkness. <u>Flowers</u>: white, in globose heads up to 2 cm in diameter, emerging from leaf axils at the end of the branches, singly or in pairs. The dark brown <u>pods</u> are wide and flat, up to 15 cm long. They open to shed the seeds and can remain for sometime on the branches after the seeds have been shed.

Flowers most profusely after the big rains, but also throughout the year particularly if irrigated.

Distribution: Found from 400 m up to 2000 m with a rainfall range of 600 to 1200 mm per year. Introduced and cultivated in many parts of the country from the semi-arid to humid zones and now becoming naturalized. LUKINA was introduced from Central America to African countries in the 1950s.

Practical notes: LUKINA is very fast growing and can become an aggressive coloniser. It coppices (can be cut to regrow) well. Seedlings can easily be obtained by direct sowing.

Uses: *L. leucocephala* is a multi-purpose tree used for binding earth bunds, terrace walls, and contour strips for soil and water conservation, as well as in alley farming with food crops, and hedges and shelter belts. Because it is a legume with root nodules that can fix atmospheric nitrogen, it aids neighbouring plants by providing nitrogen. The deep rooting system acts as a nutrient pump pulling important minerals for plants back to the top soil. It is, therefore, recommended for reclaiming degraded soils.

LUKINA is the now the world's major fodder tree. It is also recommended for backyard browse or for cutting and feeding to tethered cattle and goats. However, widespread acceptance is hampered because the farmers remain reluctant to use the leaves for forage due to some cases of mimosine-poisoning of livestock.

The wood can be used for firewood and charcoal, as well as for making poles and handles for farm tools. The leaves and young green pods can be eaten as a vegetable and the seeds can be roasted and used as a coffee substitute.

Apicultural value: *The nectar and pollen production of LUKINA is more or less moderate. Especially in arid and semi-arid climates the shrub is a very useful bee plant because of its long flowering period. Planting LUKINA will strengthen bee colonies and guarantee their survival, especially in periods when other feed sources are not available.*

Lonchocarpus laxiflorus *Guill. & Perr.*

ALWARO, CILWIEDE, ULWIETO (Anu); RARAWAYE (Mes); AMERA, QANQALSHA (Or); CENGWEREFIA, SENGWEREFYA (Tya)

Family: Fabaceae (Leguminosae) subfamily Papilionoideae

Description: Deciduous tree growing 3 to 12 m tall. Bark: rough, dark grey. Leaves: compound, very long up to 45 cm long; with 5 to 7 leaflets which are opposite, grey-green, and narrowly oblong-elliptic. Flowers: pinkish-mauve to deep lilac; arranged in many-flowered panicles up to 60 cm long, which are erect at first and then hanging. Flowering trees are very striking because the flowers appear with or before the leaves. Pods: narrowly elliptic-oblong to linear-oblong, up to 10 cm long and slightly sinuate between the seeds and 1-3-seeded.

Flowering from January to March.

Distribution: Very common in wooded grassland and semi-arid lowland savanna between 450 and 2150 m with an annual rainfall up to 1500 mm a year.

It occurs in savanna regions across the Sahel from Senegal to Uganda and Ethiopia.

Practical notes: It is resistant to bushfires.

Uses: It is an important browse plant for domestic stock.

The hard wood is good for timber, fuelwood, and for making charcoal.

Apicultural value: *Honeybees work vigorously to collect the abundant pollen and nectar from the flowers and the tree is one of the most important lowland honey sources.*

Recommended for planting to increase honey production.

329

Milletia ferruginea *(Hochst.)* Bak.

BRBRRA (Amh, Gur & Tya); ZADYA, ZAGIE (Gof & Wel); BILEWU-HAQA (Had); BIBERO (Kef); YAGO (Kef & Or); RENGAZENA (Kem); SOTELLI; YAGOY (Mes); GDICCO, AKSIRA, ASRA, DEDATU, KARCECCE, KOTELLU, SARI, SOTALLO (Or); ZIYAG, ZIYAGU (Sha); 'NGEDICCO (Sid)

Family: Fabaceae (Leguminosae) subfamily Papilionoideae

Description: An **endemic** tree with a mainly straight trunk. <u>Bark</u>: smooth and greyish. <u>Leaves</u>: up to 40 cm long; leaflets up to 9 cm long, oblong-acuminate, hairy on both sides; usually the upper surface is green and the lower one ashy-green. <u>Flowers</u>: violet or lilac, produced in groups on stalks up to 30 cm long. <u>Pods</u>: flat, thick, brownish-hairy or almost without hairs and up to 27 cm long and 3 cm wide. The pods burst on the trees and the dark brown flat seeds are so scattered.

Flowering is November to April.

Distribution: BRBRRA is a very common tree in the streets and gardens of Addis Ababa. Commonly found in both moist and dry montane forest, especially along streams and forest edges, it is also found in montane evergreen bushland and in upland grassland. It grows between 1000 and 2800 m and needs a rainfall range from 1000 to 2000 mm per year.

Found in Ethiopia only.

Practical notes: BRBRRA is extremely fast growing and is easily propagated from seeds.

Uses: This is an important shade tree for coffee. The wood is used to make tool handles and other small household utensils. It is a valuable source of fuelwood and also used for timber. The seeds contain a narcotic and the flour from them is used to stun fish.

In traditional medicine the roots are used against elephantiasis and wet eczema.

Apicultural value: *Although the flowers are frequently visited and pollinated by carpenter bees, honeybees also collect pollen and nectar from the flowers and continue to forage for nectar, even when the flowers have fallen to the ground.*

This tree is very useful for strengthening bee colonies during the dearth periods.

Parkinsonia aculeata *L.*

JERUSALEM THORN (Eng)

Family: Fabaceae (Leguminosae) subfamily Caesalpinioideae

Description: Evergreen tree or large shrub growing to 10 m with slender, often hanging branches. Bark: smooth and green, even when old, with thin papery flakes on the trunk. Leaves: alternate, pinnate, leaf rhachis very short, extended into a straight well-developed spine; leaflets small, many and sessile, opposite to alternate, oblong-elliptic to obovate. Flowers: lightly scented, light yellow, born in axillary 15 to 20 cm long racemes. Pods: leathery and contricted into segments around the seeds; seeds are oblong-ellipsoid, in cylindrical, glabrous up to 18 cm long pods.

Flowering mainly from January to June, but some trees can be found in flower at all times of the year, particularly where there is some irrigation.

Distribution: Found from 450 m up to 2000 m both growing naturally and cultivated in Ethiopia in many of the semi-arid areas, particularly the Awash valley and Afar lowlands. It is very drounght tolerant and salt tolerant growing in a rainfall range from 200 to 1000 mm per year.

This is a native of tropical and subtropical America, now found in all semi-arid tropical countries.

Practical notes: It is an aggressive coloniser.

Uses: Often planted as a windbreak, for shade and ornamental purposes, it also forms impenetrable hedges and is, therefore, often used for living fences. In agroforestry systems it is planted also as boundary marker and for erosion control and terraces.

Its branches provide fodder for sheep and goats and the pods can be ground up and added to animal feed as a concentrate.

The wood is hard but only makes low-grade charcoal and fuel.

The fruit pulp is sweet and edible. Elsewhere the pods are used in the production of fibre pulp paper.

It is also used in local medicine internally and externally as a tea-like infusion for fever.

Apicultural value: *Honeybees collect pollen and plenty of nectar from the flowers.*
This tree is important for beekeepers in drier parts of the country as it is a constant food supply for bees. In hot climates the nectar secretion is limited.

334

Piliostigma thonningii *(Schumach.) Milne-Redh.*

FRQA (Agew); ALAMATI, ALAMATIE, DABDI YEQOLLA-WANZA (Amh); AMBARDA (Gur); LILU, KORA (Or); AMAM-GEMEL (Tya); QALQALLA, QALQALLO (Wel); CAMEL'S FOOT LEAF TREE (Eng)

Family: Fabaceae (Leguminosae) subfamily Caesalpinioideae

Description: Small deciduous tree, rare a shrub up to 5 m tall. <u>Bark</u>: fissured, rough, dark brown to black. <u>Leaves</u>: bilobed, shaped like the foot of a camel, strongly folded along the midrib, cordate at the base and rusty pubescent beneath. <u>Flowers</u>: fragrant, large, white to pink; drooping at the ends of branches. <u>Fruits</u>: long hanging woody pods containing dark brown flattened seeds.

Flowering during the dry season from January to May, particularly after there has been a fire.

Distribution: Found between 500 to 2000 m in semi-arid lowland savanna, deciduous woodland and wooded grassland, often in the large river valleys of the western escarpment. This a fire-resistant tree which survives the traditional burn-through of dry grass in lowland and river valley savanna.

P. thonningii is also common in typical Sudanian woodland of the Sahel region and is widespread eslwhere in tropical Africa.

Uses: The tree provides poles and timber for local house construction. The wood is used for firewood and charcoal making and is also suitable for carpentry.

The bark provides fibres for making ropes and cloth and is also used for tanning. Leaves can be browsed.

In traditional medicine the roots are used against leprosy and wet eczema.

Apicultural value: *Honeybees forage for the abundant pollen and nectar from the flowers all day round. The tree is an important honey source in the undifferentiated woodlands and drier parts of the country.*

Recommended for planting to increase honey production

Pithecellobium dulce *(Roxb.) Benth.*

N'CHET (Amh); MANILLA TAMARIND (Eng)

Family: Fabaceae (Leguminosae) subfamily Mimosoideae

Description: Tree which is green nearly all year round growing to 12 m tall. <u>Bark</u>: smoot, dark grey to brown, branches with small paired stipular spines. <u>Leaves</u>: with 1 pair of pinnae; leaflets 1 pair, elliptic to obovate-elliptic. <u>Flowers</u>: faintly scented, cream or yellow, in heads arranged in racemes or panicles. <u>Pods</u>: curved or spirally twisted; seeds black and edible.

Flowering from December to March.

Distribution: Planted between 500 and 1500 m in the lowlands of the Awash valley and Afar on the East and the Gambella area on the west. Probably now more widely planted than records show. It requires an annual rainfall between 450 and 1650 mm per year.

This is native western America from southern California to Colombia. It is now widespread in arid and semi-arid areas of Africa, India, Oceania, Caribbean and Asia.

Practical notes: Seeds germinate rapidly. Although drought tolerant, it is also waterlogging and salt tolerant.

Uses: Planted mainly for shade and as a live fence. The wood is hard and has similar qualities to those of acacias and can be used to make parts of the traditional ox-plough. It is also used for timber, fuelwood and making charcoal.

Leaves, twigs and pods provide good browse for livestock.

Apicultural value: *Honeybees visit the flowers frequently for the abundant nectar and pollen. The pollen value is very high and nectar secretion is good. The tree contributes to mixed honeys.*

Recommended for planting to increase honey production

338

Tamarindus indica L.

HUMER (Amh); ROQA (Amh, Or & Som); HUMER (Som & Tya); UBEL (Tre); TAMARIND (Eng); TAMARINDENBAUM (German)

Family: Fabaceae (Leguminosae) subfamily Caesalpinioideae.

Description: Growing into a large evergreen tree, usually about 20 m tall but getting up to 30 m tall. The bole is stout and the crown densely foliaged and rounded. <u>Bark</u>: rough, grey to dark grey-brown, fissured. <u>Leaves</u>: pinnately compound, with 10 to 18 pairs of leaflets which are narrowly oblong, up to 3 cm long. <u>Flowers</u>: fragrant, golden yellow with red veins, about 3 cm across, arranged in lax, slender terminal racemes. <u>Pods</u>: pale brown, up to 14 cm long, with an edible, sticky, dark brown, acid pulp around the seeds.

Flowering mainly from March to July but some trees can be found in flower at any time throughout the year.

Distribution: Found from sea-level up to 1500 m along water courses, in riverine and groundwater forests and also sometimes in woodland and wooded grassland where annual rainfall ranges from 400 to 1500 mm.

Occurring in almost all sub-Saharan African countries and also cultivated throughout the tropics and sub-tropics.

Practical notes: Can be grown from both seeds and cuttings. The tree is not very compatible with other plants.

Uses: The very hard and durable wood is highly suitable for poles, timber and general construction work. It also makes good firewood and charcoal. The acid pulpy part of the fruits is used in cooking and for making a cooling, mildly laxative drink. The seeds are also edible and valuable for human consumption and are commonly sold on local markets in countries other than Ethiopia. Leaves and fruits provide good animal fodder.

This tree is recommended for soil conservation measures and for use in agroforestry systems. It can also be planted as an ornamental and for shade and is very suitable as a wind break and as firebreak.

In traditional medicine the fruits are used as a remedy against fever, intestinal diseases and diarrhoea. The pulp is used against malaria and on wounds and haemorrhoids. Powdered seeds are used against dysentery.

Apicultural value: *The flowers are frequently visited by honeybees for the heavy yields of pollen and nectar. In dense stands the tamarind provides good yields of a dark honey which has a thin viscosity and a sour but pleasant flavour.*

Recommended for planting to increase honey production

Azadirachta indica *A.Juss.*

BYE-BYE (Anu); NIM (Tya, Tre & Saho); NEEM TREE (Eng)

Family: Meliaceae

Description: Hardy, fast growing tree up to 15 m tall but usually smaller, deciduous in drier areas, with a rounded crown which is fairly open. Bark: pale grey-brown, rough with wide longitudinal fissures. Leaves: up to 35 cm long, pinnately compound with 4 to 7 pairs of leaflets, which are lanceolate, and asymmetric at the base; margins coarsely serrate. Flowers: sweet smelling particularly in the evenings, white and small, hanging in long axillary panicles. Fruits: globose, yellowish-orange and up to 2 cm long.

Flowering from October to March.

Distribution: Growing well in a wide range of climates from semi-arid to semi-humid between 400 and 2000 m with a rainfall range from 130 to 1150 mm per year. Now widely planted in towns and villages in most parts of the country.

This species is native to India and Burma, and is now widely naturalized in some parts of Africa. It grows in Southeast Asia, East and Sub-sahelian Africa, Fiji, Mauritius and parts of Central America.

Practical notes: Seedlings are easily raised from seeds and the species is fast growing forming a deep tap root.

Uses: This is a multi-purpose tree with many uses in India. Although mostly planted in Ethiopia as a useful shade tree, the wood makes reasonable timber and can be used for fuel, charcoal making and poles.

It grows easily on on exhausted soils and is very suitable for rehabilitation and afforestation programmes.

The fruits have medicinal properties and are used for treating skin diseases such as leprosy elsewhere. The oil can be used as a paraffin substitute or to make soap, and the residue (neem cake) is a good cattle feed and fertiliser.

The leaves contain azadirachtin, which is a powerful insecticide. Dried leaves placed amongst clothes will protect them from moths, and in stored grain will prevent insect attack without leaving any smell or aftertaste. The smoke of burnt leaves drives off mosquitos and sand-flies. A solution from the leaves sprayed on crops will protect them from locust attack, and attempts are being made to develop a commercial pesticide.

Tests of a drug from the leaf extract to treat chloroquin-resistant strains of malaria are already at an advanced stage.

> **Apicultural value**: *Honeybees collect pollen and nectar from the flowers frequently and the tree is a important honey source. The honey is aromatic and red-brownish to light golden in colour with a slightly bitter flavour.*
>
> **Recommended for planting to increase honey production**

Ekebergia capensis *Sparrm.*

LOL (Amh); SEMBO (Amh & Or); DUDUNA, SOMBO (Or); QWET (Tya); CAPE ASH (Eng)

Family: Meliaceae

Description: Large tree with a cone-like outline growing to 30 m tall, sometimes deciduous, with a typical rounded crown reaching well down trunk. The stem reaches a breast height diameter of up to 1 m. Bark: grey and smooth, becoming rougher and furrowed with age; branchlets dotted with pale breathing pores. Leaves: compound, crowded at the end of branches; leaflets large, glossy green, elliptic to ovate-lanceolate. Flowers: heavily scented; white tinged with pink; arranged on up to 25 cm long stalks; male and female flowers are on different trees. Fruits: rounded, thin-skinned berries; up to 1.8 cm long, hanging on long stalks in heavy bunches, yellow to red when ripe.

Flowering from November to May.

Distribution: Found between 1550 and 2700 m where rainfall is over 750 mm per year in Afromontane forest, and often along edges. It is frequently found as a single tree in secondary montane evergreen bushland and as a relic tree on farmland.

Also in Senegal, Gambia, Mali, Guinea Bissau, Guinea Republic, Cote d'Ivoire, Ghana, Togo, Benin, Nigeria, Cameroun, Central African Republic, Zaire, Rwanda, Burundi, Sudan, Eritrea, Uganda, Kenya, Tanzania, Angola, Zambia, Malawi, Zimbabwe, Swaziland and South Africa.

Practical notes: Seedlings are easily raised from fresh seeds and the species is fairly fast-growing.

Uses: The wood is tough and strong but not very durable. It is useful for household carpentry, grain stores and household utensils and furniture. The wood is traditionally used for making milk pots LARJ. It is also used for firewood and poles.

It is also an excellent ornamental shade tree which could be more widely planted.

In traditional medicine the bark is used against elephantiasis, NEKERSA and wet eczema.

Apicultural value: *Honeybees visit the flowers frequently for pollen and nectar. The sweetly scented flowers attract many bees, so that beehives are very often placed among the branches. The bark is commonly used for smoking traditional hives to attract bee swarms.*

Recommended for planting to increase honey production

Melia azedarach L.

PERSIAN LILAC (Eng).

Family: Meliaceae

Description: Medium-sized deciduous tree growing to about 10 m tall with bushy foliage and a spreading crown. It readily sheds its lower branches. <u>Bark</u>: dark grey, smooth and slightly furrowed. <u>Leaves</u>: bright green at first, later dark green, hanging in terminal bunches; bipinnate with toothed, ovate, pointed leaflets. <u>Flowers</u>: fragrant, pale mauve to lilac, in profuse, rounded clusters. <u>Fruits</u>: yellow fleshy berries, containing a hard nut which often remains on the tree after the leaves are shed.

Flowering trees can be found throughout the year and each tree has its own peak flowering period.

Distribution: In Ethiopia known to be found from 450 m to 2400 m (in Addis Ababa), mostly below 1950 m and more widely cultivated in towns and gardens than records suggest.

It is a native of the Indian Himalayas and is now one of the most widely distributed trees in the world.

Practical notes: It grows fast from seed, but the tree is relatively short-lived.

The berries are extremely poisonous and human deaths as well as losses amongst livestock and poultry from eating fallen fruit have been recorded.

Uses: It is cultivated for ornamental purposes and for shade. Elsewhere it is used for reafforestation programmes. It is generally suitable as a source of fuel and charcoal, for making utensils and tools and very suitable for building poles because of its reputedly termite-resistant timber.

The seeds are said to possess insecticidal properties and are used together with dried leaves to protect cloth, books and leather.

Apicultural value: *Bees are attracted to this plant for its valuable nectar and pollen as a stimulus for colony development. The late flowering period of this species makes the tree important for beekeeping.*

345

Trichilia dregeana *Sond.*

BONGA (Amh); DESH (Gim); LUIYA (Kef); KONU, LUYA, SHEGO (Or)

Family: Meliaceae

Description: Large evergreen tree up to 30 m tall with a straight trunk and rounded crown. <u>Bark</u>: fairly thin, smooth brown with paler breathing pores. <u>Leaves</u>: compound, with 2 to 5 pairs of leaflets which are obovate to oblanceolate or oblanceolate-elliptic. <u>Flowers</u>: large, creamy-white, arranged in branched sprays up to 6 cm long, with hairy petals up to 2.5 cm long. <u>Fruit</u>: rounded pink to dull yellow-brown capsules, up to 3 cm across.
Flowering from November to March.

Distribution: Found from 1300 to 2000 m where the annual rainfall is over 1500 mm per year. Particularly found in the Afromontane rain forest and transitional rain forest of the southwestern parts and on mountains in the southern part of the Rift valley.

Also in Guinea Republic, Cote d'Ivoire, Cameroun, Zaire, Uganda, Kenya, Tanzania, Angola, Zambia, Malawi, Zimbabwe, Mozambique and South Africa.

Practical notes: Propagation is done by seedlings and wildlings.

Uses: The valuable timber is used for construction work and furniture. The wood can also be used for fuel and making charcoal.

This tree can be found left on farmland for shade and holding bee baskets. Traditional bee baskets are often placed in upper branches.

Apicultural value: *Honeybees forage for nectar and pollen very frequently. The tree seems to be very attractive to bees with beekeepers hanging baskets in the branches to attract wild swarms.*

Bersama abyssinica *Fresen* subsp. **abyssinica**

AFFAJESHN, AZAMR (Amh); ZAGIE (Gam) BATALLA (Gur); DOLKIISA, EBERRAKO, ETIBIRO, FORAKA, GESSA, HORAQQA, JUMEFOK, KIBIRU, KORAKA, LOLCISA, QARACCA, BOQO, SESA, TEBERQO, TIBIRA (Or); TEBERAKO (Sid); BRSMA, A'SHA-OM (Tya); WELESSIENU (Wel)

Family: Melianthaceae

Description: Small or medium-sized tree or shrub, up to 15 m tall with a straight trunk. <u>Bark</u>: grey-brown; smooth to rather rough and mottled. <u>Leaves</u>: up to 65 cm long and alternate; divided into many leaflets which are oppositely arranged, lanceolate to oblong or ovate-oblong with coarsely toothed margins. <u>Flowers</u>: creamy-white and pink-tinged; sweetly scented, arranged in drooping racemes up to 40 cm long. <u>Fruits</u>: reddish pink capsules with thick-walls, about 3 cm in diameter containing bright red to orange-red seeds.

Flowering from December to May.

Distribution: Found in essentially *Juniperus-Podocarpus* forest and in degraded remnants of it from 1250 to 2800 m. It is also found among clumps of bushes in grassland and at forest margins and in montane scrub. Its rainfall range is from 750 to 2200 mm per year.

Also in Eritrea, Guinea Bissau,, Guinea Republic, Sierra Leone, Liberia, Côte d'Ivoire, Ghana, Togo, Nigeria, Cameroun, Gabon, Central African Republic, Zaire, Rwanda, Burundi, Sudan, Uganda, Kenya, Tanzania, Zambia, Malawi, Zimbabwe and Mozambique.

Practical notes: *Bersama* is a forest pioneer which can tolerate marginal conditions. Propagation is done by seedlings, cuttings and root suckers.

Uses: Considered an important plant in traditional medicine, the roots are used against ascariasis and rabies.

Apicultural value: *Honeybees collect pollen and nectar from the flowers frequently.*

Beekeepers have a high regard for Bersama *as a valuable nectar and pollen source for their bee colonies.*

349

Ficus sur *Forssk.*

SHOLA (Amh); ETSA (Dor); KARRO (Kef); BOBBA (Gam); ODABEDDA, MEDALLE, HABRU, HARBU (Or); KODO, SHAFA (Tya)

Family: Moraceae

Description: A large tree growing to 30 m tall with a trunk up to 1 m or more in diameter, very handsome with a rounded crown and large buttresses. Bark: brown to grey, smooth; young branches are densely pubescent. Leaves: alternate, large, ovate to elliptic or oblong to lanceolate, up to 20 cm long with prominent veins; leaf margins entire or serrate. Fruits: figs are orange-grey when ripe, obovoid, 3 to 4 cm in diameter; hanging in heavy clusters from thick branches on the main stem.

Flowering time has not been recorded because bees visit the fruits and are neither visiting fig flowers nor involved in pollinating services.

Distribution: Found between 1250 to 2800 m in transitional rain forest, montane grassland and secondary scrub and sometimes as an isolated tree in secondary montane evergreen bushland. It also occurs in riverine forest and semi-deciduous lowland forest where rainfall range is from 1000 to 2000 mm a year.

It is widespread in tropical Africa, west to Senegal and Cape Verde Islands, south to the Cape Province of South Africa and east to Ethiopia and even occurring in Yemen.

Practical notes: The bark and the ripe figs are edible but without much flavour and often full of insects.

Uses: This tree is important in the ceremonies of several ethnic groups and is widely used as a meeting or resting place along traditional routes.

The wood is used for making mortars and is suitable for plywood cores. The leaves are rough and can be used like sandpaper.

In traditional medicine fruit and bark are used against LIB DIKAM and elephantiasis.

> **Apicultural value**: *Honeybees suck the juice of the ripe fruits and in dry seasons a solution of crushed fruits and water are a valuable bee feed.*

Ficus vasta *Forssk.*

WARKA (Amh); DARGUNA (Bil); TENAKA, TERBIENTO, WELKA (Ge'ez); DA'RO (Ge'ez, Tre & Tya); OLOLA (Had); MIELO (Kef); DEMBI, QILTU (Or); 'NDARO (Saho); BERDE (Som); WELA (Gam); WOLA (Wel)

Family: Moraceae

Description: One of the largest trees in the country growing to over 20 m tall with a crown spreading to 30 m or more in diameter. The trunk is often buttressed and that of old trees breaks open to form multiple trunks which are often hollow. <u>Bark</u>: smooth grey; young branches have a brownish bark, with soft hairs. <u>Leaves</u>: broadly-ovate, elliptic and papery, somewhat rough to feel. <u>Fruits</u>: globose figs up to 2 cm in diameter hanging in large clusters from the branches, visible from a considerable distance from the tree.

Flowering time is not recorded because bees are not visiting fig flowers and are not involved in pollination.

Distribution: Found from 1000 to 2400 m where it is the most often left large tree on farmland, beside tracks and in village market places where it is the site for meetings and other cultural activities. It is also commonly found on rocky land, in forest clearings and riverine forests, and lake shores. It also occurs in open woodland.

Also in Sudan, Somalia, Eritrea, Kenya, Tanzania and Yemen.

Uses: This is an excellent shade tree. The wood is soft but used for carving. The leaves provide a good mulch and the tree is very useful for soil improvement.

<u>Similar species:</u>

Ficus sycomorus *L.*

Similar to *F. vasta* but never growing so wide. A large buttressed spreading tree, with a short trunk up to 3.5 m in diameter and up to 30 m tall.

Found from 500 to 2000 m where ever rainfall is 500 mm per year or more. It grows in a wide range of habitats from dry rocky slopes up to wet Afromontane coffee forest. Like *F. vasta* it is often left as a single tree in farmland and beside raods. It also occurs beside rivers and lakes and in clearings. This is a more drought resistant tree than *F. vasta*.

Cultivated since ancient time and this species is the Biblical sycamore of Egypt and the Middle East. It is also one of the longest living trees of Africa.

Apicultural value: *Honeybees suck the juice of the ripe fruits and in dry seasons a solution of crushed fruits and water are a valuable bee feed.*

354

Eucalyptus camaldulensis *Dehnh.*

BARZAF (Ader); QEY-BARZAF (Amh); AKAKILTI, BARZAFI-DIMA (Or); RED RIVER GUM (Eng)

Family: Myrtaceae

Description: Evergreen, fast-growing, medium-sized tree up to 25 m tall, much branched with the foliage branches hanging. Bark: smooth, whitish to ash-coloured and thin, frequently peeling off in long strips, producing a ruby red gum which was the origin of the name Gum Tree. Leaves: alternate, lanceolate, with both surfaces the same greyish-blue colour, giving off a strong scent when crushed. Flowers: in small axillary clusters, bearing numerous white globose flowers.

Flowering trees can be found throughout the year.

Distribution: Adapted for semi-arid conditions, this tree is grown between 900 and 2400 m where annual rainfall is between 500 and 1250 mm.

Introduced from Eastern Australia at the end of the 19th century, *Eucalyptus camaldulensis* is the most commonly cultivated species after *E. globulus* both world-wide and in Ethiopia.

Practical notes: The cultivation in gardens or in combination with agricultural crops cannot be recommended because of competition for water. Other plant will not grow around this species because its strong use of minerals. It is, therefore, not suitable as a pioneer for rehabilitating degraded land.

Seeds germinate after 3 weeks and seedlings are ready for transplantation after 5 months. Germination percentage and survival after planting out are low.

Uses: It is primarily planted for fuelwood and charcoal production. The dense red wood is valuable and termite resistant. The timber is used as fence posts and poles for house construction. It withstands long dry periods and the tree coppices well. Other uses are medicinal, for paper-pulp, and to extract rayon and tannin from the bark.

Apicultural value: *This is one of the heaviest nectar yielders of all eucalypts. It is a major source of pollen and produces abundant nectar which gives heavy yields of honey. Honeybees collect both nectar and pollen.*

The sugar concentration is high and the pollen value is good. The colour of the honey is clear golden and the granulation is medium with fine-grained crystals. The flavour is mild and the aroma characteristic.

Recommended for planting to increase honey production

Callistemon citrinus *(Curt) Skeels*

BOTTLE BRUSH (Eng)

Family: Myrtaceae

Description: Attractive ornamental upright shrub or small tree with drooping branches. <u>Bark</u>: grey, first smooth and then getting rough with age. <u>Leaves</u>: young are reddish and silky, but darken with age; mature leaves are alternate, greyish-green, stiff and lanceolate; lemon scented when crushed. <u>Flowers</u>: in showy cylindrical spikes up to 10 cm long. <u>Fruits</u>: sessile woody capsules, which persist for many months in dense clusters around the stem.

Flowering mostly during the dry season, some trees but may be found with flowers any time of the year under good conditions.

Distribution: Native to Australia it is now widely grown in gardens and streets throughout the country up to 2500 m.

Practical notes: BOTTLE BRUSH is easily grown from seeds and is widely available from nurseries.

Uses: Cultivated for ornamental purposes it is to some extent salt tolerant and can grow on very poor dry soils.

Apicultural value: BOTTLE BRUSH *provides sufficient quantities of nectar and pollen for honeybees. Therefore, it assists indirectly with honey production by stimulating brood rearing and strengthening bee colonies, particularly when other plants are not flowering.*

Recommended for planting to increase honey production

Musa x paradisiaca L.

MUZ (Amh; Or); BANANA (Eng); BANANE (German).

Family: Musaceae

Description: Large perennial herb growing up to 5 m with a pseudostem formed by the bases of the leaves. The trunk is swollen at the base and the stem has horizontal markings where leaves have broken off. Leaves: very large, spirally arranged, with a thick midrib, smooth margin and numerous parallel nerves. Flowers: produced in a complex inflorescence with the male and female flowers borne in clusters. Fruits: edible, fleshy without seeds.

Flowering trees can be found throughout the year.

Distribution: Cultivated wherever there is sufficient moisture from 450 m to 2000 m. Internationally recognized commercial varieties are grown under irrigation on large farms in most of the major river valleys. More easily damaged varieties are common plants of home gardens; they can also be found planted beside streams away from home compounds.

BANANA was introduced to Africa more than 2000 years ago by Indo-Malayans or Arabs. Nowadays, they are cultivated in all tropical countries and in many subtropical regions. Globally, there has been an over-production of bananas for many years.

Uses: In some parts of the country leaves are used for animal fodder and for covering food. The fruits are an important source of income being sold in local markets as well as being exported.

Apicultural value: *Honeybees forage for the copious nectar and abundant pollen from the flowers all day round.*
The fruits and pulp develop from female flowers without pollination.
Nevertheless the plant contributes to some honey production.

Ensete ventricosum *(Welw.) G.E. Cheesm.*

ENSET or FALSE BANANA looks similar to BANANA but can grow up to 10 m high. When mature, the basal part of the stem is round and swollen. The leaves are simple, up to 7 m long and 1 m wide. The single massive stalk of flowers has a head up to 3 m long. It is monocarpic, flowering after the seventh year of planting.

Cultivated throughout south central and southwestern Ethiopia, it also grows naturally in upland rain and montane forests. It especially grows along streams from 1000 to 2200 m, but through cultivation it can be found up to 3000 m. It's rainfall range is from 1000 to 2200 mm per year.

Apicultural value: *Honeybees collect abundant pale violet pollen and nectar from the flowers. If Aphids contribute with honey dew is up to now not investigated, but is reported by rural beekeepers.*

Eucalyptus citriodora *Hook.*

SHITO-BARZAF (Amh); LEMON-SCENTED GUM (Eng)

Family: Myrtaceae

Description: Slender evergreen tree, usually growing to 30 or 40 m tall and with a straight trunk 40 to 60 cm in diameter. The crown is thin lightly branched with the leafy branches hanging down. <u>Bark</u>: smooth, white, with a powdery surface, which extends over the trunk and branches. It is shed in thin, irregular and jagged pieces. <u>Leaves</u>: alternate, lanceolate, up to 16 cm long; smooth, mid-green and smelling strongly of lemon when crushed. <u>Flowers</u>: white, in dense clusters on stalks. <u>Fruits</u>: ovoid, on short stalks.

Flowering irregularly but most profusely after the rains.

Distribution: Growing in a wide range of climates between 1300 and 2400 m where rainfall is more than 900 mm a year.

It is a native of Queensland, Australia, and nowadays widely planted in subtropical and tropical Africa, Asia, S America, Oceania and temperate southern Europe.

Practical notes: Grown from seedlings which are susceptible to termite attacks.

Uses: It is cultivated for firewood and charcoal. The timber is hard, strong and heavy and is used for poles.

This tree is recommended for planting as a most attractive ornamental, especially to provide light shade and as a windbreak.

Elsewhere it is grown for its essential citronellal oils.

Apicultural value: *Honeybees forage for some of the pollen but mostly for the abundant nectar from the flowers. When this tree is available, the bees produce a significant surplus of honey which is light amber and with a firm granulation.*

Recommended for planting to increase honey production.

362

Psidium guajava L.

ZEYITON (Ade); ZEYTUN, ZEYITUNA (Amh, Or & Afar); GUAVA (Eng)

Family: Myrtaceae

Description: Small evergreen tree up to 8 m tall with a rather irregular warted stem. Bark: smooth and light to greenish-brown; peeling and flaking. Leaves: opposite, broadly elliptic to elliptic-lanceolate, up to 15 cm long. Flowers: white with numerous stamens, axillary and 2.5 cm in diameter, growing singly or 2 to 3 together. Fruits: greenish-yellow, heavy, egg-shaped or spherical with a smooth peel; flesh is pink, white or yellowish, with a sweet-sour flavour and scented.

Flowering throughout the year, but profusely after rains.

Distribution: Grown throughout the country between 1200 and 2400 m, GUAVA is an extraordinarily tough and undemanding small tree.

It was introduced to Africa from Central America, and can now be found to have naturalized in some parts of the country.

It is grown in tropical America, Caribbean, Africa, Asia and Oceania.

Practical notes: Flowers already in the second year of planting.

Uses: The termite resistant wood is used for tool handles and making other utensils. The wood is suitable in some cases for making charcoal and can be used as firewood.

GUAVA is cultivated for it's vitamin C-rich fruits in home gardens and backyards and provides a useful source of cash-income for farm families, particularly women.

Apicultural value: *The nectar secretion is abundant all day round and this is one of the best pollen-producing species of Myrtaceae.*

Honeybees forage intensely for pollen and nectar from early morning up to late afternoon. The juice from damaged fruits is also said to be collected by bees. Cross-pollination by insects gives higher yields.

Eucalyptus globulus *Labill.*

BAHR-ZAF (Amh & Tya); AKACHITTA, AKAKILI (Or); BLUE GUM (Eng)

Family: Myrtaceae

Description: Evergreen tree, up to 55 m tall, trunk attaining a breast height diameter of almost 2 m. <u>Bark</u>: smooth, bluish-grey and peeling off in long strips. <u>Leaves</u>: waxy, juvenile, greyish-blue-green, opposite, sessile, heart-shaped at the base, ovate to broadly lanceolate; mature leaves are alternate, petiolate and dark glossy blue-green, lanceolate or curved sickle-shaped. <u>Flowers</u>: white, solitary and sessile, or in small clusters on very short stalks. <u>Fruits</u>: 1.5 cm long and 2 cm wide, globular and warty, with a depressed cap and covered with greyish-white wax.

All parts, but especially the leaves, smell strongly of eucalyptus oil.

The main flowering is from May to June but some trees are found with flowers at any time in the year.

Distribution: BLUE GUM is the most widespread eucalypt in Ethiopia, now grown in plantations between 1800 and 3200 m throughout the country where rainfall ranges 800 to 1500 mm per year. This tree was introduced from Australia to Ethiopia at the end of the 19th century.

Cultivated throughout tropical Africa, Asia, Mediterranean Europe, South and North America and temperate Parts islands in the pacific ocean.

Practical notes: An extremely fast growing tree which can well tolerate frost. Seedlings can be found in nurseries throughout the country. It is not suitable for growing near food crops.

Uses: BLUE GUM is very suitable for fuel, especially the leaves are used to bake INJERA, and mature wood for charcoal making. The wood is pale grey to cream, hard and durable, and is used for building poles and telegraph masts. Young branches are commonly used for house construction. The wood is to some extent termite resistant.

In local medicine the steam from boiled leaves is inhaled to relieve the common cold and other bronchial problems.

Apicultural value: *This species is the most important source of eucalypt honey in the country. It produces abundant nectar and pollen every year with a flowering peak every 4 to 5 years. The sugar concentration of the nectar is medium and the protein-rich pollen is pale yellow to creamy white.*
Honeybees work all day round on the flowers. Colonies near this eucalypt develop very fast with a tendency to frequent swarming.
The honey has a distinctive flavour and is light amber in colour. The granulation is medium to slow and fine.

Recommended for planting to increase honey production

365

366

Eucalyptus ficifolia *F.Muell.*

SCARLET GUM, RED-FLOWERING GUM (Eng)

Family: Myrtaceae

Description: Small ornamental tree, generally 6 to 12 m in height, with the crown more or less rounded. <u>Bark</u>: short-fibred, dark and fissured. <u>Leaves</u>: somewhat leathery, dark green and thick; mature leaves are alternate, broadly lanceolate; venetian is fine, regular and parallel. <u>Flowers</u>: large, in terminal clusters of 3- to 7-flowered groups on slender stalks; colour varying from deep crimson or pale pink to orange or white. <u>Fruits</u>: ovoid, bell-shaped, thick and woody.

Flowering over a long period, from November to May.

Distribution: Grown in Ethiopia as an ornamental roadside plant and in home gardens at altitudes up to 2400 m with an annual rainfall above 750 mm.

Native to a small area of the southern coast of Western Australia, this tree is now cultivated throughout the world for its striking flowers. It is now one of the best known ornamental eucalypts.

Practical notes: *E. ficifolia* is fairly slow growing and seedlings are difficult as yet to obtain in Ethiopia.

Uses: This attractive small tree is used for decorative purposes. The pale-coloured timber has no commercial value.

Apicultural value: *The honeybees gather the abundant nectar and pollen throughout the day. The nectar secretion is heavy and nectar drips in long threads from the flowers whereas the pollen supply is moderate. The honey shows a slow granulation and the flavour is pleasant.*

Recommended for planting to increase honey production.

Syzygium guineense subsp. afromontanum *F.White*

DOKMA, DGTA (Amh); KURRUNFULI, BADESSA, AACHA, OCHA (Or); WORARIKO, DUANDO (Sid); LA'HAM, ROHAZ (Tya); WATERBERRY (Eng)

Family: Myrtaceae

Description: Tree, attaining a height of up to 25 m and a breast height diameter of the trunk up to 1.5 m. The trunk is sometimes irregular and the crown large and dense. Branches are sometimes drooping. <u>Bark</u>: grey to dark brown and fairly smooth, slightly fissured longitudinally and scaling in rectangular flakes. <u>Leaves</u>: opposite and lanceolate to ovate-elliptic, smooth and waxy grey-green. <u>Flowers</u>: small, white, fragrant, sessile and usually borne in terminal bunches in such great profusion that the tree is a mass of bloom. <u>Fruits</u>: edible; ovoid, 1 to 2.5 cm long, 5 to 8 celled; red-violet to blue when ripe.

Flowering from December to May.

Distribution: Found in montane forest and also secondary forest growth. Occasionally seen as an isolated tree left in farmland which has been recently cleared from forest. It is restricted to the southern and the southwestern Highlands from 1500 to 2600 m where the rainfall range is from 1500 to 2000 mm per year.

Also in Zaire, Rwanda, Burundi, Sudan, Uganda, Kenya, Tanzania, Angola, Zambia, Malawi and Zimbabwe.

Practical notes: The seeds germinate rapidly and easily to give hardy seedlings which are easily transplanted.

Uses: The wood is used for making household utensils, tool handles and carvings. It is also commonly used for firewood, making charcoal. Logs can be used as poles.

The edible fruits can be used to make vinegar.

The fruits are also used to treat dysentery. The bark is a tonic and laxative, and also used as an ingredient in black dye. In traditional medicine the roots are used against intestinal diseases and against RAS ANKAR.

Apicultural value: *Bees forage vigorously for the abundant nectar and pollen from the flowers and this tree is an important honey source for the country.*
The honey is yellowish brown and mild by aroma. Granulation is slow and fine.

Recommended for planting to increase honey production

369

370

Olea capensis subsp. **hochstetteri** *(Bak.) Fries & P.S.Green*

DAMAT-WOIRA (Amh); AGERGURI (Or); SITAMO (Sid); AF-SCHOLLER (Tya)

Family: Oleaceae

Description: Tall, valuable, evergreen, timber tree growing to 25 m tall with a dense crown and steeply ascending branches. <u>Bark</u>: smooth, grey-white. <u>Leaves</u>: olive-green above, paler below; opposite and elliptic to elliptic-lanceolate in shape. <u>Flowers</u>: small and white; in branched terminal panicles up to 10 cm long. <u>Fruits</u>: oval, about 2 cm long.

Flowering from January to April.

Distribution: Found between 1400 and 3200 m where rainfall ranges between 1000 and 1500 mm per year. An important and common tree in wetter Afromontane forest and persisting in gallery forests in river valleys.

Also in Guinea Republic, Sierra Leone, Cote d'Ivoire, Cameroun, Zaire, Rwanda, Burundi, Sudan, Uganda, Kenya and Tanzania.

Practical notes: This is a fairly slow growing species but with valuable timber.

Uses: The wood is very fine in texture, and hard and heavy. It is easy to saw and plane, finishing to a very smooth surface. It is very suitable for high quality flooring, cabinet work and turnery and has proved to be excellent for veneering as well as for making tool handles.

It is good for fuel and charcoal making and provides strong poles.

The tree is also valuable in agroforestry systems for stabilizing terraces.

<u>Similar species:</u>

Olea capensis subsp. **welwitschii** *(Knobl.) Fries & P.S. Green*

Similar to subspecies *hochstetteri* but growing in wetter habitats at lower altitudes. Also a large tree attaining a height of 30 m with a straight trunk and a breast height diameter up to 1 m.

Found between 1550 to 2200 m only in the Afromontane rain forests of the southwestern part of the country.

Outside Ethiopia it is common through to Cameroun in the west and southward to Zimbabwe.

Apicultural value: *Honeybees collect pollen and nectar from the flowers frequently.*
The bark of all Olea species is used to smoke traditional bee baskets to attract swarms.

Ximenia americana *L.*

TUTUQA (Agew); 'NKOY, KOL (Amh); OLEÄMO (Anu); HAZTE (Gam); RAQAKA, SOBIEQAKA (Ge'ez); HUDA, HUDI, MAGALA (Or); AWRE-MUDUBE, MANDURAT, MONDRUK, MORHOD (Som); MLHTTA (Tre); ML'O (Tya); ASTIE (Wel); MONKEY PLUM, TALLOW NUT (Eng)

Family: Olacaceae

Description: Tree or shrub, growing up to 7, occasionally 10 m tall. <u>Bark</u>: dark grey to blackish, with small rectangular scales on old trunks; spines straight and sharp, up to 1.5 cm long. <u>Leaves</u>: leathery, ovate to elliptic, tending to fold up along the midrib. <u>Flowers</u>: white to cream and very fragrant with petals densely bearded inside, arranged in small axillary cymes. <u>Fruits</u>: edible, ellipsoid, yellow to orange, slightly acid and refreshing.

Flowering from December up to April.

Distribution: Found between 500 and 2100 m in *Acacia* woodland, wooded grassland, often together with *Balanites aegyptiaca*

A pantropical tree very widespread in Africa.

Practical notes: This useful tree will appear naturally if the natural vegetation is protected and allowed to regenerate. It makes a good live fence.

Uses: The scented wood is hard and heavy and used for local simple utensils. It is also very suitable for firewood and charcoal making. The fruits are edible and have a very refreshing taste.

This drought resistant tree is recommended for making shade and windbreaks, as a boundary marker and in reafforestation programmes as well as for living fences. In times when feed resources are scarce it is also browsed by livestock. Otherwise it is not usually browsed

The seeds contain a non-drying oil which is suitable for use as a lubricant and for making soap as well as body and hair oil and for softening leather.

In traditional medicine the fruits are used as a vermifuge, and the flowers and the roots are used against gastric disorders and for expelling a retained placenta after childbirth.

Apicultural value: *Honeybees forage for the pollen and nectar and the tree is a reliable supplier of proteins and carbohydrates for bee colonies in dry habitats.*

373

374

Syzygium guineense *(Willd.) DC.* subsp. **guineense**

DOKMA (Amh); LA'HAM (Tya)

Family: Myrtaceae

Description: Medium-sized tree growing up to 20 m tall with a sometimes irregular bole and a large and dense crown. Bark: grey to dark brown. Leaves: ovate to elliptic, up to 12 cm long; waxy grey-green; fragrant with a pleasant smell when crushed. Flowers: yellowish-white, arranged in terminal and axillary panicles. Fruit: ovoid, 2 to 4 cm long and red-violet to blue and fleshy when ripe.

Flowering from January to March.

Distribution: Growing in riverine forest, woodland and lake shores between 1200 and 2500 m. Occasionally also found in humid secondary evergreen bushland and woodland with a rainfall range between 750 and 1800 mm per year.

Also in Senegal, Gambia, Mali, Guinea Republic, Sierra Leone, Cote d'Ivoire, Ghana, Togo, Nigeria, Chad, Cameroun, Gabon, Congo, Central African Republic, Zaire, Rwanda, Burundi, Sudan, Eritrea, Somalia, Uganda, Kenya, Tanzania, Angola, Zambia, Malawi, Zimbabwe, Mozambique, Namibia and South Africa.

Uses: DOKMA is used for firewood and charcoal. The wood is hard and strong, used for poles and timber which is very suitable for construction work.

Similar species:

Syzygium guineense subsp. **macrocarpa** *(Engl.) F.White*

A tree growing up to 7 m high and often multi-stemmed with ovate-elliptic leaves and yellowish-white flowers in terminal and axillary panicles. This species is found in woodlands between 1600 and 2000 m.

Apicultural value: *The nectar secretion is abundant and also large quantities of pollen are produced. Honeybees forage on the flowers very frequently and the trees are an important honey source.*

Recommended for planting to increase honey production

Olea europaea subsp. **cuspidata** (Wall. ex DC.) Cifferri

WEYRA (Amh); EJERSA (Or); MEKICHU (Sid); WIGHIR (Som); AULI', WOGRET (Tya)

Family: Oleaceae

Description: Evergreen tree growing up to 18 m tall, with a much-branched rounded crown and a crooked bole which is fluted with characteristic pockets. The branches are grey. Bark: rough, dark-brown. Leaves: opposite, elliptic-lanceolate, lower surface almost silvery-white, grey-green above. Flowers: slightly scented, small, white and numerous in axillary panicles. Fruits: oval and fleshy, about 1 cm long and yellow to dark purple when ripe; they are edible and sweet, single seeded.

Flowering after the short rains from April to June.

Distribution: Commonly found between 1250 and 3100 m in Afromontane forests, particularly drier highland forests where juniper is common. Very common in secondary scrub and also in riverine forest. It is found as a relic tree on farmland and in church compounds where it is protected. It grows where rainfall ranges from 500 to 1500 mm a year.

It is widespread in tropical Africa: on the mountains of the Sahara, west to Senegal, south to the Cape Province of South Africa and east to Somalia and north to Egypt. The species is also found in the Mediterranean. It is also common in Yemen, Saudi Arabia, Oman, Pakistan, North India and southwestern China.

Practical notes: It is fairly slow growing, but reaches a great age. Seedlings are now more and more available in nurseries.

Uses: The pale to golden-brown wood is very hard and very heavy, strong and durable. It is recommended for fancy furniture, cabinet work and veneering. The wood is commonly used for making *"yoke"*, ploughshare, plough-handle, shaft and other parts of the Ethiopian ox-plough.

The wood is used for firewood, charcoal, poles and timber.

Smoking wood is used to sterilize pots and this gives a special flavour to milk. The twigs are popular as tooth brushes. Straight branches make good walking sticks.

Leaves are also used as condiment in drinks.

In traditional medicine the roots are used against "Haemorrhoids" and intestinal complaints as well as a purgative.

Apicultural value: *Honeybees collect pollen and nectar from the flowers frequently. The nectar secretion is moderate to high and pollen production is valuable. The tree is a valuable bee plant for strengthening colonies and stimulating brood rearing.*

Grevillea robusta *A.Cunn. ex R.Br.*

SILK OAK, GREVILLEA (Eng)

Family: Proteaceae

Description: A semi-deciduous tree up to 20 m tall, with a straight trunk and angular branches. <u>Bark</u>: greyish, rough, vertically furrowed. <u>Leaves</u>: leathery, fern-like, much divided, up to 30 cm long, olive-green above, silky silvery-grey below. <u>Flowers</u>: showy golden-orange, in dense terminal one-sided racemes; honey-scented. <u>Fruits</u>: dark capsules, boat-shaped, splitting to release two winged seeds.

Some trees are found flowering at any time of the year but most flower profusely after the rains from October to December and April to May.

Distribution: Commonly found between 1700 and 2700 m in both dry and wet climates, it can tolerate as little as 400 mm and as much as 2500 mm. However, the optimum rainfall range is between 700 and 1500 mm. A tree native to Australian rain forests, now often introduced and naturalized in a variety of climates.

Grown in tropical Asia, Africa, C America, subtropical Parts islands in the pacific ocean and N America.

Practical notes: Grown easily from seed, GREVILLEA is fast-growing and seedlings are available in many nurseries.

Uses: A multi-purpose tree, GREVILLEA is grown for fuel, timber and as a windbreak. It is often planted as a shade tree in coffee plantations and is a valuable tree for reafforestation. The wood is pale yellow-brown, tough and durable, and is used for making high quality furniture and light construction. It can also be used for making charcoal.

Apicultural value: GREVILLEA *is a very valuable pollen and nectar source for honeybees. The nectar secretion is abundant with a high sugar concentration and the pollen yield is heavy. The bees forage all day round and, when flowering is profuse, they produce a surplus of honey from dense stands of trees.*
The honey has a pronounced flavour and is almost reddish black with a rapid granulation.

Recommended for planting to increase honey production

Securidaca longepedunculata *Fresen.*

URAO (Anu); VIOLET TREE (Eng)

Family: Polygalaceae

Description: Tree or shrub, growing up to 5 m high, occasionally up to 10 m high. The branches are slender, erect or drooping, and hairy. <u>Bark</u>: pale brown to grey brown, rough with very small dark-coloured scales. <u>Leaves</u>: alternately arranged, simple and entire, oblong to oblong-lanceolate and up to 6 cm long. <u>Flowers</u>: very fragrant with the scent of violets, reddish purple to pink, borne in loose racemes. <u>Fruit</u>: winged, yellow green to red.

Flowering almost all year round.

Distribution: Found between 500 and 1700 m in semi-arid lowland savannah, and deciduous lowland woodland.

Uses: It is used for making poles which are reputed to be resistant to rot and termites. It is also used for firewood. The young stems yield a very strong fibre.

Apicultural value: *Honeybees are found very frequently visiting the flowers for pollen and nectar. This tree is one of the most valuable lowland honey sources and may yield very satisfactory surpluses of honey.*

Recommended for planting to increase honey production.

381

382

Olinia rochetiana *A.Jussieu*

TFIE, BEYE (Amh); GUNA, NOLLE, SOLLE, DALECHO, (Or)

Family: Oliniaceae

Description: Shrub or tree growing up to 15 m tall, occasionally up to 25 m high with a rounded crown. Bark: grey, smooth or finally grooved, with thin yellow flakes on old trunks; the young stems are 4-angled. Leaves: opposite, reddish and sweet-scented when young; elliptic-oblong to oblanceolate with a conspicuous network of veins on the lower surface and a pale pink midrib. Flowers: white to pink, often white at first and later on red, arranged in dense rounded heads up to 5 cm across. Fruits: arranged in heavy bunches, red-brown when ripe.

Flowering from January to May.

Distribution: Found between 1300 and 3500 m in many types of forests: montane, evergreen, riverine and frequently along forest edges. It also grows in evergreen bushland and is sometimes left as a single tree in grassland and farmland derived from forest. Its rainfall range is between 750 and 1500 mm per year.

Zaire, Rwanda, Kenya, Uganda, Tanzania, Angola, Zambia, Malawi, Zimbabwe and South Africa.

Practical notes: It can be grown from seed or by carefully transplanting naturally-grown small seedlings.

Uses: It is commonly used for firewood and as timber for local house construction, yokes, farm tools and walking sticks. Fences are made from cut branches and leaves are eaten by goats and oxen.

Apicultural value: *Honeybees forage for both nectar and pollen. Local beekeepers have repeatedly reported the value of this tree for strengthening bee colonies.*

Rhamnus prinoides L'Herit.

GEGHO (Agew); GIESHO (Amh, Ade, Gam, Had, Or & Tya); SIEWA (Ge'ez); GISHE (Gur); GESHA (Kem & Saho); RAHA, TADO (Or); GIESO (Tya); TANDO, GESWA (Wel); DOGWOOD (Eng); KREUZDORN (German)

Family: Rhamnaceae

Description: Small tree or shrub, much-branched, growing up to 8 m high with slender stems and drooping branches. <u>Bark</u>: smooth, grey-brown, getting darker with age; it is clearly dotted with white breathing pores. <u>Leaves</u>: alternate and pinnately veined, ovate to elliptic or lanceolate, up to 12 cm long; shiny dark green above with a finely toothed margin. <u>Flowers</u>: yellowish green and small, solitary or in axillary clusters. <u>Fruit</u>: small berries, 8 mm across, turning from green through red to blackish purple.

Flowering throughout the year.

Distribution: Found between 1400 and 3200 m growing in Afromontane rain forest, especially in clearings and along edges and also in secondary montane evergreen bushland and small clumps of trees and bushes in montane grassland where rainfall ranges between 750 to 2000 mm a year.

Also in Cameroun, Zaire, Rwanda,, Sudan, Eritrea, Uganda, Kenya, Tanzania, Angola, Zambia, Malawi, Zimbabwe, Mozambique, Swaziland, Lesotho and South Africa.

Practical notes: Seedlings are easily obtained by direct sowing.

Uses: GESHO is widely cultivated in backyards and gardens. The leaves, which are sold in markets, are used to flavour the local beer TELA and the honeywine TEJ and have a function like hops for beer.

In local medicine the roots are used to purify the blood. The plant is also used as a laxative, as a diuretic and as a preventive for syphilis. When the uvula of children are remove (a common practice to prevent diseases in general) leaves are put in the mouth to relieve pain. Crushed leaves are also rubbed onto the skin to cure mild fungal infections.

Apicultural value: *Honeybees are foraging pollen and nectar from the flowers, but this species is not very valuable for pollen and nectar production. In cultivation, with it's prolonged flowering periods it is a useful bee plant for colony maintainance during dearth periods.*

Eriobotrya japonica *(Thumb) Lindl*

WESHMELLA (Amh); LOQUAT (Eng)

Family: Rosaceae

Description: Evergreen tree growing to 6 m tall with a with dense rounded crown. Bark: sometimes powdery and greenish black; young branches covered in white woolly hairs. Leaves: large, alternate, dark green and shiny above, paler beneath; lanceolate-oblong to obovate; with prominent veins. Flowers: strongly scented, with a rather heavy perfume, white to creamy white, on up to 17 cm long panicles in woolly terminal clusters. Fruits: obovate to ellipsoi, usually 4 cm long, up to 10 cm in some cultivars; yellow to orange with a strong, juicy, sweet-and-sour flesh.

Flowering almost all year round but profusely after rains.

Distribution: Cultivated in many towns for its edible fruits in altitudes from 1800 to 2400 m with an annual rainfall range from 900 to 1200 mm. Also found growing in open areas, possible from discarded fruits.

It is a native of China and Japan and nowadays widely cultivated in higher altitudes of the tropics and subtropics.

Practical notes: Seedlings are available in nurseries and the tree is drought tolerant after it has become establishing. Seeds are poisonous and must be removed before eating the fruit.

Uses: It is cultivated in gardens and as a shade tree and for its edible fruit.

Apicultural value: *Honeybees collect pollen and nectar from the flowers very frequently. The nectar secretion is moderate to good but reduced during dry periods. The sugar concentration of the nectar is very high, up to 65 % and the pollen supply is very rich.*
Because of the long lasting flowering period, the tree is important for bees to strengthen colonies and maintain brood rearing.

Hagenia abyssinica *(Bruce) J.F.Gmelin*

GORA-GORA (Agew); KOSO (Amh); SOBERT, SOSEN (Ge'ez); WENQOQO (Gam);
KEBSE, TCHEMA (Gur); SUTO (Had); TIEMA (Kem); DUCCA, ETO, FICO, HETO (Or);
HETOT (Sid); H'ABBI, SONO (Tya); JOLIYA-MITA, KOSUWA, TALIYA (Wel); KOSSO,
HAGENIA (Eng)

Family: Rosaceae

Description: Forest tree growing to 25 m tall with a rounded or even umbrella-shaped crown. The short trunk or stem is sometimes very thick, up to 1 m in diameter, but rarely straight. <u>Bark</u>: reddish-brown, flaking irregularly; the young branchlets are covered with golden hairs; ringed by the scars of the sheathing leaf-bases. <u>Leaves</u>: compound, up to 40 cm long; divided into 11 to 13 pale to bright green leaflets which are arranged in a opposite manner on the stalk; the margins of leaflets are toothed like a saw; the surfaces are often silvery on the underside. <u>Flowers</u>: small and numerous in large, attractive hanging bunches up to 60 cm in length; the female flowers are bulkier and more reddish than the more feathery, orange-white male heads. <u>Fruits</u>: small and asymmetric.

Flowering after the big rains from October to February.

Distribution: Found between 1850 and 3700 m in both wetter and drier Afromontane forest, especially along the upper tree limit. In lower altitudes it is often found at forest edges. It is sometimes deliberately left as an isolated tree in high mountain farmland or derived grassland. *Hagenia abyssinica* was one of the dominant trees in the upper part of the montane forest belt in Ethiopia, as it still is in East Africa, but now only scattered trees remain in most areas. Its rainfall range is from 1000 to 1500 mm a year.

Also in Zaire, Rwanda, Burundi, Sudan, Kenya, Uganda, Tanzania, Zambia and Malawi.

Practical notes: Propagation is done by seedlings and naturally grown seedlings (wildlings).

Uses: The wood is dark red, hard but not very durable and subject to borer attack. It is very suitable for furniture, cabinet work, floors and especially veneers. In rural areas farmers use the wood for making the shovels called "LADA".

In Ethiopia the 'kosso' is considered as a panacea and the tree is one of the most useful medicinal plants of the country. The female flowers of "kosso" are used as a remedy for tapeworm infestation and it is often used together with other plants, which also have anthelmintic properties, against many diseases.

Apicultural value: *Honeybees collect the abundant pollen from the male flowers and sufficient nectar from the female ones. Therefore the tree plays an important role for strengthening bee colonies at higher altitudes and is even a honey source.*

Recommended for planting to increase honey production.

Prunus africana *(Hook.f.) Kalkm.*

AQOMA, TQUR-'NCET (Amh); ARARA (Had); GARBI, GURAYU, HOMI, SOSHE, SUQQE, MIESSA, MIKICCO, MUKKA-DIMA, MUKKA-RAJA (Or); BERU (Sha); MICIKKO (Sid); GARBE, ONSA (Wel); RED STINKWOOD (Eng)

Family: Rosaceae

Description: A tall evergreen forest tree with a cylindrical slim, very straight and clean bole. <u>Bark</u>: dark brown, scaling irregularly; the branchlets are dotted with prominent breathing pores. <u>Leaves</u>: glabrous, glossy green, elliptic to oblong and 5 to 15 cm long with toothed margins. The crushed leaves have a slight but distinct smell of bitter almonds. <u>Flowers</u>: very small, creamy white, and fragrant, arranged in simple racemes in clusters in the leaf axils. <u>Fruits</u>: round, up to 1 cm in diameter, dark red when ripe, with a single seed. They are extremely bitter and probably poisonous.

Flowering in October and November.

Distribution: TQUR-'NCET is an important component of Afromontane forest from 1550 to 3100 m and requires a rainfall of 1000 to 2000 mm per year. It often persists in remnant patches and along rivers. Occasionally it is the dominant tree in dry Afromontane forest and is very often left as an isolated tree in grassland and farmland.

Cameroon, Zaire, Rwanda, Sudan, Malawi, Uganda, Kenya, Tanzania, Angola, Zambia, Zimbabwe, Mozambique, Swaziland and South Africa.

Practical notes: Although easily germinated from seed, it is fairly slow growing.

Uses: TQUR-'NCET means BLACK WOOD and the heart wood is dark, hard and heavy. It is used for heavy construction work, poles and is also very suitable for strong furniture and veneers. Mortars and other utensils are made from the very durable wood. It also makes excellent firewood. Isolated trees are also used as boundary markers.

In traditional medicine the stem bark provides a popular medicine against urinary disorders.

Apicultural value: TQUR-'NCET *is a valuable pollen and nectar source in some parts of the country with honeybees foraging for nectar and pollen from the flowers. It is even reported as a source of honey and it might be true that it contributes to mixed honeys in which its flavour will not predominate.*

Prunus x domestica *L.*

PRUN (Amh); PLUM (Eng); PFLAUME (German)

Family: Rosaceae

Description: Small, deciduous tree, growing to 12 m tall but mostly much smaller, unarmed or with small spines. The twigs are hairy when young. <u>Leaves</u>: elliptic to oblong, pubescent when young, up to 10 cm long. <u>Flowers</u>: white and borne in clusters. <u>Fruits</u>: fleshy, hanging, ovoid to subglobose, mostly red to violet, sometimes yellow or green, with light green, yellow or red flesh, sweet and very delicious; the stone is rough to smooth.

Flowering from October to December.

Distribution: Cultivated in and around Addis Ababa with a good potential for other highland areas over 1900 m.

Cultivated since ancient times in Europe and Asia.

Practical notes: Propagated by seedlings and by grafting.

Bees are essential for this tree to set fruit.

Uses: PLUM trees are grown for their fruits and are now a very valuable crop in and around Addis Ababa and other major towns. The fruiting season is around January.

Apicultural value: *Honeybees collect pollen and nectar from the flowers frequently and are the primary pollinators.*

393

Prunus persica *(L.) Batsch*

KOK (Amh, Gur, Ge'ez & Tya); HOH, SEQUINON, SKINON, SQINON (Ge'ez); KOKI (Or); KOH' (TYA); PEACH (Eng); PFIRSICH (German)

Family: Rosaceae

Description: Small fruit tree with glabrous, reddish twigs. Bark: grey brown and splitting. Leaves: oblong-lanceolate with finely toothed margins. Flowers: pale to deep pink, subsessile and mostly solitary. Fruits: fleshy, round, 40 to 80 mm in diameter; skin greenish and velvety, seed in a hard pitted stone.

Flowering after the big rains from September up to November.

Distribution: Widely cultivated in the highlands in home gardens between 1800 and 2400 m.

Originally a native of SW Asia, now extensively cultivated for its fruit in the warm temperate parts of Europe, Asia and N America.

Practical notes: PEACHES are not self-fertile so that at least two, better three or four, cross-fertile cultivars must be planted together to ensure good fruit setting. The pollination is carried out by insects, especially bees, which also improve the pollination of the self-fertile cultivars.

Uses: Although severely affected with peach curl, PEACHES in Ethiopia produce large quantities of small, rather hard fruits which are eaten fresh and are very popular. The wood is durable and also used as firewood.

Apicultural value: *Honeybees collect the abundant pollen and copious nectar from the flowers through frequent visits. In dense stands the species contributes to strengthening colonies and improving honey production.*

Coffea arabica *L.*

BUNA (Amh; Tya; Or; Afar; Sid & Gur); BUN (TYA); ARABICA COFFEE (Eng); KAFFEEBAUM (German)

Family: Rubiaceae

Description: Evergreen shrub or small tree, that grows up to 5 m high when unpruned. <u>Leaves</u>: glabrous, shiny, simple, broadly oval, opposite and dark green when mature. <u>Flowers</u>: 2 to 20 fragrant white flowers are borne in leaf axils and last only a few days. <u>Fruits</u>: fleshy cherries, red when ripe, about 1.5 cm long. The green coffee bean is the seed.

Flowering profusely after rains, some coffee trees are found with flowers at any time of the year.

Distribution: An under storey tree in moist to humid Afromontane forests of between 1700 and 2100 m with a rainfall range of about 2000 mm per year.

Formerly an endemic of the southwestern forests of Ethiopia is spread through trade first into southern Arabia and from there it was taken to the East Indies by Dutch traders late in the 17th century.

Planted throughout the tropics, but particularly in East and West Africa and Central and South America and the West Indies.

Uses: ARABICA COFFEE is a grown for its beans (the seeds), which are washed, dried, roasted and ground to make coffee for drinking. In production, Ethiopia stands seventh world-wide. The residues from coffee processing are used as fertilizer and mulch elsewhere. The leaves can also be used as fuel and animal fodder.

In Ethiopia drinks are prepared from dried leaves and dried and roasted whole berries as well as the green beans. A tea is made from the leaves elsewhere.

Apicultural value: ARABICA COFFEE *is a very important nectar source and provides moderate amounts of pollen. The nectar flow is very intensive and only reduced by drought. The sugar concentration is medium and the pollen is heavy and sticky.*

Bees are found foraging all day round. It seems that bees can play some role in increasing yields and it is suggested that growers in Ethiopia should keep honeybee colonies in their plantations and grow nectar-producing plants as shade trees and other areas to strengthen colonies during periods when the coffee itself is not flowering.

The honey has a characteristic flavour and it's colour varies from brownish to black. In the western parts of the country it also usually contributes to mixed honeys in which its flavour predominates.

Coffea arabica is a major honey source of the western and southwestern parts of Ethiopia.

398

Casimiroa edulis *LaLava*

ABOKAR, KAZAMORA (Amh); KAZMIER (Tya); WHITE SAPOTE (Eng)

Family: Rutaceae

Description: Medium-sized, evergreen, much-branched tree with a short trunk often hidden by the hanging branches and foliage of older trees. <u>Bark</u>: smooth and pale brown. <u>Leaves</u>: alternate, palmately with 3 to 5 leaflets which are lanceolate, and dark glossy green. <u>Flowers</u>: small, greenish-white, borne in panicles. <u>Fruits</u>: resembling an green tomato, greenish-yellowish, with a soft peel and sweet whitish flesh.

Flowering almost all year round, profusely after rains.

Distribution: Cultivated in home gardens and backyards in towns between 1700 and 2400 m. Previously only known from a few larger towns, it is now spreading to many parts of the country.

This is a native of Central America which is now widespread throughout the tropics.

Practical notes: Seedlings are easily raised from seeds. The tree is slow growing but drought-resistant. It does not produce fruit until it is 10 or more years old.

Bee colonies are required to increase fruit setting by pollination.

Uses: It is cultivated for its edible fruits which are sold locally only as they are easily damaged when transported.

Apicultural value: *Bees forage all day round for pollen and nectar.*

The tree can be important for colony strengthening.

Citrus aurantifolia *(Christm.) Swingle*

LOMI (Amh & Or); TUTTO (Or); LEMUN (Tre); LEMIN (Tya); LIME (Eng)

Family: Rutaceae

Description: Evergreen tree, sometimes only a shrub, up to 5 m tall, with axillary spines. <u>Bark</u>: grey-brown to black; smooth to rather rough. <u>Leaves</u>: leathery, glossy green, rather small, narrow and elliptic. <u>Flowers</u>: conspicuous, with usually 5 but sometimes 4 to 8 white petals, pinkish outside; giving off a strong sweet perfume. <u>Fruits</u>: ovoid or subglobose, up to 5 cm long, green to greenish-yellow. The peel is difficult to remove and the pulp is green and rather acid.

Some trees can be found in flowering at any time in the year.

Distribution: LIME is the most widely available citrus fruit in Ethiopia. It is mostly cultivated in home gardens up to 2500 m. Sometimes it appears apparently naturalized as a riverine tree or shrub in altitudes at around 1000 m.

A native of south east Asia, it is now widely cultivated throughout the tropics, particularly the Caribbean and Middle America.

Practical notes: It can be grown from seed and also grafted onto the rootstock of another species of Citrus, usually SOUR ORANGE.

Uses: LIME is very important in the Ethiopian diet and culture as it is recognized as a general cleanser. Ripe fruits are sucked to help control colds and some mild forms of stomach disorders. Chicken is washed thoroughly and soaked in lime water before it is cooked. The peel and pulp are used to clean the hands after preparing and/or eating strong-flavoured food. Mixed with other herbs, particularly CRESS SEED (Eng) FEITO (Amh), the fruits and leaves are used to treat mild skin problems. Fresh fruits are used for flavouring and the juice is used in drinks. Elsewhere lime oil is made from the peel and citric acid is produced from the fruit.

<u>Similar species:</u>

Citrus aurantium *L.* SOUR ORANGE,

Small tree growing up to 3 m tall. It is cultivated at higher altitudes up to 2500 m in gardens and many towns and sometimes appears naturalised, e.g. in dense forests.

Further *Citrus* spp. commonly cultivated and important for beekeeping because of their nectar and pollen supply are *C. limetta* Risso, *C. limon* (L.) Burm.f., *C. medica* L., *C. paradisi* Macfad., *C. reticulata* Blanco and the valuable *C. sinensis* (L.) Osb (SWEET ORANGE).

Apicultural value: *Honeybees collect both nectar and pollen from all citrus and can be found foraging all day round.*
These trees contribute good nectar supplies which help in strengthening bee colonies because of their long flowering period. Bees find the flowers very attractive especially in times of scarcity of nectar.

402

Clausena anisata *(Willd.) Benth.*

LMMCH (Amh); GAMCLE, GAEJA (Gam); SNFKO (Gur); 'MBRITTO (Kef); ULUMAY, URMAYA, ADESSA, WALAYA (Or); BURO (Som); CIKOTE, DASHLOME (Wel)

Family: Rutaceae

Description: Deciduous tree or shrub growing up to 8 m high, sometimes to 10 m. All parts have a strong unpleasant smell when they are bruised. <u>Bark</u>: grey and smooth; twigs purplish to brown. <u>Leaves</u>: with 11 to 25 leaflets ovate to lanceolate to elliptic and strongly aromatic. <u>Flowers</u>: fragrant, more pleasant smelling than the leaves and wood, cream to white, arranged in axillary panicles which appear with young leaves. <u>Fruits</u>: globose berries, red-purple to blue-black.

Flowering from November to May.

Distribution: Growing between 1500 and 2300 m where rainfall is over 750 mm per year in Afromontane rain forests, and in dry single-dominant upland forest, particularly along forest margins and in clearings. It is also found in secondary montane evergreen bushland and is a typical forest pioneer. It is also sometimes found in gardens and in living fences.

It is also found in Guinea Republic, Sierra leone, Cote d'Ivoire, Benin, Nigeria, Cameroun, Gabon, Congo, Central African Republic, Zaire, Rwanda, Burundi, Sudan, Uganda, Kenya, Tanzania, Zambia, Malawi, Zimbabwe, Mozambique, Swaziland, South Africa and also in tropical Asia.

Practical notes: Can be grown from cuttings or seeds.

Uses: It is used for firewood. The twigs are commonly used for cleaning teeth.

It is grown in house compounds to ward off evil spirits.

In traditional medicine the plant is used as a disinfectant and the roots against ascariasis.

Apicultural value: *Honeybees forage frequently for the abundant nectar and pollen from the flowers.*

Salix subserrata *Willd.*

AHAYA, HAYA, RIGA (Amh); DUCYA, LANSO (Gam); ATA (Ge'ez); KWI'HA (Ge'ez & Tya); ELESELOSEK (Gum); ALALETI, ALANCA, ALELTU, BORODO (Or); BURO (Som)

Family: Salicaceae

Description: Much-branched shrub or tree growing to 10 m tall with a rounded crown and sometimes with branches hanging to the ground. Bark: dark grey and fissured; young twigs often covered with hairs at first and then becoming hairless and reddish-brown with age. Leaves: grass green and shiny, very variable in size and shape; they are simple, oblong-elliptic or narrowly ovate or lanceolate; leaf margins are toothed. Flowers: male and female flowers are separate in slender yellow spikes, 4 to 5 cm long; male flowers drop as soon as they finish flowering while the ovaries of the spike-like female flowers are on very short stalks. Fruits: capsule opening to release minute plumed seeds.

Flowering throughout the year but profusely after the rains from October to January.

Distribution: It is commonly found from 1000 to 3000 m where rainfall is over 500 mm per year. Usually beside permanent streams and rivers, sometimes forming a hedge along waterways. Also grown in some public and private gardens.

Also in Egypt, Senegal, Gambia, Guinea Republic, Niger, Nigeria, Cameroun, Zaire, Sudan, Eritrea, Uganda, Kenya, Tanzania, Angola, Zambia, Malawi, Zimbabwe, Botswana, Namibia, Lesotho, South Africa and also in tropical Arabia.

Practical notes: Easily propagated from cuttings.

Uses: This tree is very useful stabilizing river-banks and helping protect soil and other plants from torrents during the rainy season.

The wood is also used for firewood and the twigs as tooth brushes.

In traditional medicine the roots are used against rabies.

Apicultural value: *Honeybees collect pollen and nectar from the flowers very frequently and this species plays an important role for strengthening colonies after harvesting. Nectar is foraged from both male and female flowers and abundant pollen from male flowers only.*

405

Allophyllus abyssinicus *(Hochst.) Radlk.* (079)

'MBS (Amh); TESTES (Gum); SHEÖ (Kef); ABAR, ABERRA, ARAJE, DRUBA, HIRKAMO, HIRKUM, KEKAYI,SARAGI, SARARA, SEÖ (Or); QAMSHI, SWARYA (Tre & Tya); WRAFUTO (Wel)

Family: Sapindaceae

Description: Small tree, mostly reaching a height of 5 to 15 m, but occasionally up to 25 m. The trunk can reach a breast height diameter of up to 1 m and is sometimes irregular and fluted. <u>Bark</u>: grey and smooth. <u>Leaves</u>: alternate, compound with three quite large leaflets which have toothed margins. <u>Flowers</u>: very sweetly scented, the white to yellow-white flowers are arranged in much-branched panicles up to 22 cm long. <u>Fruits</u>: subglobose drupes, up to 6 mm in diameter, with 5 to 6 mm long seeds.

Flowering from May to November.

Distribution: Found from 1550 to 3300 m where the rainfall range is over 1000 mm per year in Afromontane rainforest and upland woodland, often in clearings, along forest edges and persisting in steep-sided valleys. It is also found in montane evergreen bushland and riverine forests.

Also in Rwanda, Burundi, Sudan, Eritrea, Uganda, Kenya, Tanzania, Malawi and Zimbabwe.

Uses: The wood is pale brown and not very durable, but it is easy to work and takes a good polish. It is also used for firewood, farm tools and to make the yokes of the traditional ox-plough.

In traditional medicine the leaves and fruits are used as an anthelmintic and against veneral diseases.

This is the most widely distributed species, but there are four other species which look very similar and probably have similar uses. They all occur in drier habitats. *A. africanus* occurs in drier woodland of the south and west, and *A. macrobotrys* and *A. rubifolius* occur in combretaceous woodland.

Apicultural value: *Honeybees collect pollen and nectar from the flowers frequently and the tree is a valuable bee plant.*

Dodonaea angustifolia *L.f.*

KERARA (Agew); KTKTTA (Amh, Gur, Kem & Saho); TASES (Bil); MANDARA (Bur); TITO (Gam); TERMIEN (Ge'ez); MACCA (Kef); MAREYTA (Kon); ETTECCA, ITTICCA, TEDDECCA, TLEM (Or); SASAT ADAHALAT, ADALKAT (Saho); INTANCA (Sid); HAYRAMAT, DEN (Som); TAHSES (Tre & Tya); GERGETWA, SENKARA (Wel)

Family: Sapindaceae

Description: Erect bushy shrub or thin-stemmed tree up to 8 m high with a light crown and thin reddish-brown bark. <u>Leaves</u>: simple, alternate and entire, elliptic to oblanceolate, glossy green on the upper surface. <u>Flowers</u>: small, yellowish-green, stalked, without petals, and arranged in short axillary clusters. <u>Fruits</u>: yellowish-green capsules with wide reddish tinged seeds.

Flowering after the big rains from September to January.

Distribution: Found from 800 to 2650 m on edges of upland forest, upland bushland and grassland, secondary forest and scrub, invading areas recently cleared of forest and invading overgrazed *Acacia-Commiphora* bushland, also in cultivated areas. It also occurs in abandoned cultivations in forest areas and sometimes also in deciduous woodland. Its rainfall range is from 500 to 1500 mm a year.

This is a pantropical woody plant, found in Senegal, Gambia, Guinea Republic, Sierra Leone, Liberia, Cote d'Ivoire, Ghana, Togo, Nigeria, Cameroun, Zaire, Sudan, Rwanda, Eritrea, Djibouti, Somalia, Uganda, Kenya, Tanzania, Angola, Zambia, Malawi, Zimbabwe, Mozambique and South Africa.

Practical notes: It regenerates rapidly after bush fires and is propagated by direct sowing.

Uses: It is commonly cut for firewood and charcoal making. It also provides poles and tool handles. It is a useful tree for soil conservation measures, for wind breaks and living fences. The leaves are eaten by cattle.

In traditional medicine the leaves and roots are used against AKOSHITA and haemorrhoids. The leaves are also used as febrifuge, for wound dressing and sore throats.

Apicultural value: KTKTTA *produces good supplies of pollen and some quantity of nectar. It is an important bee plant in drier parts of the country as it stimulates brood rearing and strengthening of bee colonies.*

410

Aningeria altissima *(A.Chev.) Aubrev. & Pellegr.*

QERERO (Amh); KARARO, KURO, GUDUBA (Or); AUERA, GUDUBO (Sid)

Family: Sapotaceae

Description: A tall tree of high forest growing up to 40 m and to 50 m elsewhere, with a straight trunk up to 30 m tall and a breast-height diameter of up to 2 m. It is slightly buttressed at the base. Bark: grey and smooth, white latex drips slowly when cut. Leaves: large, simple, entire, elliptic to oval. Flowers: small, creamy-yellow and clustered in the leaf-axils. Fruits: 2 cm across, red, covered with very short fine hairs.

Flowering from November to February.

Distribution: Found between 1000 and 1500 m broadleaved montane rain forests, restricted in Ethiopia to the SW escarpment and the southwestern part of the NW Highlands where the rainfall range is between 1500 and 2000 mm a year.

Also in Guinea Republic, Sierra Leone, Cote d'Ivoire, Ghana, Nigeria, Cameroun, Gabon, Central African Republic, Zaire, Rwanda, Burundi, Sudan, Uganda, Kenya and Tanzania.

Practical notes: Seeds lose their viability very quickly and need to be sown fresh. Seedlings need to have good shade until they are at least two years old.

Uses: It is widely found as a shade tree in coffee plantations. The pale pink heartwood is easy to saw and very suitable for timber, furniture and veneer, but not very suitable for outdoor constructions. The wood is also used as a source for fuel. Traditionally, people cut doors from the buttresses.

Similar species:

Aningeria adolfi-friederici *(Engl.) Robyns & Gilbert* subsp. **adolfi-friederici**

This tree is known as "male" KARARO as it is very similar to *A. altissima* which is called the "female" KARARO in the provinces of Sidamo and Arussi.

This tree is taller, up to 50 m high, with a breast-height diameter up to 4 m. The wood is very hard to saw.

Common in Afromontane rain forest between 1350 to 2450 m where rainfall range is between 1500 and 2200 mm a year.

Apicultural value: *Honeybees forage frequently for nectar and pollen and the tree is the source of the famous "kararo" honey from western Illubabor. The tree is a heavy yielder of nectar and colonies are harvested after the flowers have gone.*

Recommended for planting to increase honey production.

Dombeya torrida *(J.F.Gmel.) P.Bamps*

LENQUATA, WULQEFA, (Amh); DANISSA (Or); SONKUAH (Tya)

Family: Sterculiaceae

Description: Forest tree which can reach a height of 25 m. The crown is dense and the trunk can attain a breast-height diameter of 50 cm. <u>Bark</u>: grey and smooth. <u>Leaves</u>: alternate, up to 20 cm long, heart-shaped with palmate veins and toothed margins. <u>Flowers</u>: arranged in dense clusters, white or creamy-white or pinkish when newly opened, becoming yellow-brown later on. <u>Fruits</u>: globose to ovoid capsules, 4 to 10 mm long with reddish-brown to dark brown seeds.

Flowering from October to December.

Distribution: Found between 1800 and 3300 m in Afromontane forest, often growing along forest edges. It also persists in forest patches and gallery forests and often seen as a single tree in montane grassland and farmland. Its rainfall range is from 1000 to 2000 mm per year.

Also in Zaire, Rwanda, Burundi, Sudan, Eritrea, Djibouti, Uganda, Kenya, Tanzania and Malawi.

Practical notes: Propagation is done through seedlings.

Uses: The wood is hard and heavy, easy to work and therefore suitable for turnery and local house construction. It is also suitable for making poles and farm tools. Elsewhere, the fibre of the bark is used for making cloth and string.

Fallen leaves produce a rich mulch and can be used for soil improvement. The leaves are browsed by cattle.

In local medicine the root bark is used for wound dressing.

<u>Similar species:</u>

Dombeya aethiopica *Gilli* is an endemic understorey tree or shrub, growing up to 8 m high. It grows always in the understorey, along forest edges, in evergreen montane bushland or in clumps of trees in woodlands from 1700 to 2000 m. It is restricted to the southern part of the NW Highlands and the southwestern part of the SE Highlands.

> **Apicultural value**: *Honeybees collect abundant pollen and nectar from the flowers frequently all day round.*
> *In dense stands the trees will provide a surplus of honey.*
>
> **Recommended for planting to increase honey production**

413

Grewia velutina *(Forssk.) Vahl*

MAJITE, SEFA (Amh); ARORESSA, ARORIS (Or); HAWAUTI (Tya); DEBBI (Som)

Family: Tiliaceae

Description: Much-branched tree or spreading shrub growing to 8 m tall. <u>Bark</u>: black and rough, deeply fissured; branches ending in twigs which are flattened, purple to grey and with numerous breathing pores, often drying purplish. <u>Leaves</u>: pale green above and white tomentose beneath, elliptic, obovoid to rhomboidial, pubescent to tomentose on both surfaces; margin finely toothed. <u>Flowers</u>: fragrant, bright yellow; borne in small, axillary clusters. <u>Fruits</u>: globose, sparsely hairy, black when ripe.

Flowering from September to October.

Distribution: Found from 500 to 1900 m in deciduous lowland woodland and dry grassland, open *Acacia* woodland where rainfall range is from 500 to 700 mm a year.

It also occurs in Somalia, Kenya, Uganda, Tanzania and Yemen.

Uses: The under-bark (bast) yields a useful fibre used for making local rope and tying split wood together when building a house.

The leaves are browsed by cattle and sheep. The fruits are edible and the ash provides a vegetable salt.

The bark and the leaves are used for dressing wounds and treating snakebites.

The wood is suitable for making tool handles.

Apicultural value: *This species is a valuable source of honey for bees and they collect pollen and nectar from the flowers frequently.*

HONEYDEW

In Africa south of the Sahara more bee colonies exist than in the remaining part of the original area of *Apis mellifera* in Europe and Asia.

This figure is not only related to the big diversity of flowering plants, shrubs and trees of tropical and subtropical Africa but is most probably also related to the abundant occurrence of insects in the sub-order *Homoptera*.

Many of these insects, such as aphids, soft scales, and mealybugs, feed on plant sap and excrete large quantities of sap which they can not use. This is known as "honeydew". Often honeydew is excreted so abundantly that leaves, twigs, branches and even the ground below are fully covered with it in a glistening layer.

In many cases the honeydew is sweet enough to attract honeybees who gather the sweet drops either from the contaminated leaves and branches or even directly from the insects. They process the honeydew like nectar into honeydew honey or feed their brood with it. In addition to bees, there are huge numbers of ants which are also attracted to this sweet foodstuff. Ant-queues or ant-lines on shrubs and trees give a hint that there are some insects producing honeydew on that plant.

Ethiopian beekeepers have repeatedly mentioned that maize and sorghum are important crops for honey production - bit they do not produce nectar. The farmers have described a sticky sweet glue on grasses and legumes which is related to the presence of sap-sucking insects. This would indicate that the proportion of honeydew in many honeys must be quite high.

In addition, strong foraging behaviour on such plants has been observed by the beekeepers during times when flowering species are very scarce. These observations from experienced beekeepers explain why their bee colonies are able to survive during long dry periods when flowers are almost absent.

There are many families and species of the sub-order *Homoptera* found throughout the country and some are already known elsewhere as prolific honeydew producers.

The SOFT BROWN SCALE *Coccus hesperidum* L. / *Coccidae* feeds on CITRUS, MANGO, GUAVA, PAPAYA, FIG, TEA, OLEANDER, ACACIA, COTTON, SISAL, *Carissa edulis* and *Ceiba pentandra*. It is widely distributed at medium and lower altitudes throughout the country and is mainly found on CITRUS spp.

Another prolific honeydew producing insect is the COTTONY CUSHION SCALE *Icerya purchasi* MASKAL / *Margarodidae* which feeds on CITRUS, PIGEON PEA, YAM, FENNEL, RUE, ROSES, OLEANDER, ACACIAS, SESBANIA, *Albizia* and *Cassia* spp. It is mainly found on CITRUS and heavy populations are found particularly during the dry season. It is also widely distributed throughout the country.

To what extend the numerous different psyllids, aphids, mealybugs and scale insects, confirmed to be present in Ethiopia, contribute to mixed honeys is not studied yet.

A thick colony of COTTONY CUSHION SCALE *Icerya purchasi* on *Sesbania sesban*.

Drinking vessels for TEJ: a horn cup on the left and a glass BIRRILLE on the right full of yellow TEJ.

TEJ

TEJ or honeybeer is one of the popular beverages of Ethiopia which has been prepared since ancient times for many cultural and religious ceremonies. It plays a major role in maintaining social ties in rural areas. The quality and amount of TEJ which is served during traditional gatherings is directly linked with the reputation, social respect and wealth of the host.

During feudal times TEJ was not a public or mass beverage. It was a common tribute to the nobility and social elites and only brewed in the houses of the ruling class.

The honey for TEJ-making was contributed by the tenants to the churches or to the houses of the landlords as tax in kind since there were no coins in Ethiopia.

TEJ preparation

A wooden barrel, usually made from WANZA (*Cordia africana*), is thoroughly washed with water and scoured inside with the green leaves of GRAWA *Vernonia amygdalina.*

The barrel is filled to about three-quarters with clean water and honey is then added. The ratio of the mixture is 1 bucket of honey stirred in 5 buckets of water.

The barrel is covered with a clean cloth and the mixture allowed to settle for several days. During heavy fermentation the wax, wax particles and impurities float on the surface and are removed every day.

Meanwhile 5 to 7 kilogrammes of dried GESHO (*Rhamnus prinoides*) is finely cut and boiled to enhance better fermentation.

The honey-water mixture in the barrel is now in an advanced process of fermentation, but still very sweet. This fermentation stage, called BIRZ, is low in alcohol content but rich in yeast, and is mostly liked by children and women.

The boiled cut GESHO is now stirred into the honey water. Impurities are again daily removed and after some days the TEJ becomes "dry". Now half a bucket of honey is added to sweeten the brew and after careful stirring the beer will be served in special glass cups called BIRRILLE (Amh) in local beer houses or to guests during ceremonies.

The whole process takes about 15 days of brewing. Generally, the art of honeybeer brewing is done by women.

Variations to the basic recipe

In south Sidamo region the use of *gesho* for brewing is not known. Instead of *gesho*, hard and solid bile-stones (BOCA Amh) are added to the BIRZ.

This BOCA is often found in the bile of slaughtered oxen or cows of south Sidamo area.

The BOCA is first crushed and then wrapped in a piece of clothe or fibre, and inserted into the BIRZ container. It is, therefore, a catalytic agent to boost the fermentation. After half an hour the honeybeer has reached its full flavour, but is relatively sour.

"Half-Tej"

"HALF-TEJ" is a mixture of honey and traditional beer TELA.

A cleanly prepared barrel is filled about one-third full of clean water. About two kilograms of ground grain malt (made of barley, finger millet, or other grains) and about two kilograms of finely-cut GESHO are added. This mixture will ferment within two days. On the third day, about one to two kilograms of roasted ground grain are added. This flour is usually made into a paste and is baked for a short time on the METAD and then crushed into small pieces and stirred into the barrel. Additionally finely-cut GESHO leaves and twigs are added. The barrel is covered with a clean cloth and the mixture allowed to settle for eight hours. Quite an amount of crude honey is added in the ratio of 1 bucket honey to 7 buckets of fermented beer. The barrel is filled up with water and sealed. This is allowed to ferment from three to seven days for the best quality beer.

Many places in the highlands are renowned for the quality of the TELA brewed by the local ladies. Each region has its own variations in ingredients and procedures.

Acanthaceae

Members of this family are herbs or less often shrubs or sometimes climbers and rarely trees. The family is well represented in the dry as well as moist climates of eastern Africa. The *Acanthaceae* can be identified by the simple opposite leaves and the characteristic fruit possessing seed stalks or jaculators. The flowers have their petals fused to form a two-lipped or one-lipped corolla. The fruit is rather woody and splits lengthwise to reveal a relatively small number of large seeds borne on rather conspicuous woody stalks (jaculators).

This family is composed of about 250 genera and 2500 species which are widespread in the tropics and subtropics with only a few species in temperate regions.

Many species are very attractive to honeybees and some are known world-wide as important honey sources, like the Indian *Carvia callosa,* the African *Isoglossa deliculata* and *Petalidium linifolium*, the Asian *Justicia (Adhatoda) vasica, Mackenziea integrifolia*, *Phlebophyllum kunthianum* and *Thelepaepale ixiocephala* and the Australian *Monecha australe.*

In Ethiopia many of the *Acanthaceae* are very important bee plants because of their long lasting flowering periods and their wide altitudinal range. Their pollen production is moderate, whereas their nectar yield is substantial under favourable environmental conditions. The nectar and pollen from the flowers of this family provide a good stimulus for brood-rearing after the harvesting times. Some species of the *Acanthaceae* are very important honey plants, for example, *Hypoestes forskaolii, Asystasia gangetica, Justitia schimperiana* and *Hygrophila auriculata.*

Agavaceae

The family is composed of herbs, shrubs or trees. Members of the family are usually stout, simple or sparingly branched, often arborescent shrubs or even trees. They have alternate and simple leaves which are crowded at the base of stem (as in *Agave sisalana*) or near the top (as in *Dracaena*) with parallel venation. The leaves are in general very large with very strong fibres.

The *Agavaceae* is a small plant family with 18 genera and 600 species, widespread throughout the warm, mostly arid regions of New and Old Worlds. A few are found in distinctly temperate climates.

This family is the source of important fibres, like SISAL from *Agave sisalana*, named after a town in Mexico, and cultivated at Awasa in Ethiopia. This and other species of the genus *Agave*, which gives its name to the family *Agavaceae* are used as hedging plants in the Rift Valley and as ornamentals.

In Ethiopia the family is represented by the indigenous genera *Dracaena* and *Sanseviera* and the introduced genera *Agave* and *Yucca*. The *Agave spp.* are valuable bee plants because of their long lasting flowering periods. Where the plants are plentiful they are even honey sources.

The honey from *Agave spp.* is said to have a strong flavour and a poor taste and is glue-like.

Aloeaceae

The family is composed of stout, simple or sparingly branched shrubs or branching stout trees or herbs. The *Aloeaceae* have tough, succulent leaves, which are plain, striped or spotted and the majority of them are with toothed margins. When cut, they give out a sticky, yellow, bitter-smelling juice, believed to have medicinal qualities.

The *Aloeaceae* is a relatively small family with 5 genera and 700 species which are widespread in Africa, Madagascar, Arabia and neighbouring islands, and especially in South Africa. In Ethiopia only one genus, *Aloe*, is reported. It is likely that this genus is actively evolving in Ethiopia at the moment. In former times the Plateau was forested and *Aloes* were confined to cliffs and rocky outcrops, but deforestation, cultivation and subsequent erosion have created large areas where they can grow, and an entire hillsides can now be seen covered with them.

Many species are now very widely grown as ornamentals in drier and frost-free parts of the world.

Several African *Aloe* spp. are reported to be important bee plants, like *Aloe davyana*, *A. dichotoma* and *A. mutans*.

Amaranthaceae

The family is mostly composed of herbs, but seldom shrubs or climbers or even rarely small trees. Members of the *Amaranthaceae* have simple leaves and entire leaves. The flowers are small, crowded on the inflorescences and often surrounded by narrow, dry, sometimes shiny bracts and are commonly lacking petals. The stamens are opposite the sepals and the stalks of the stamens are partly united into a short tube.

The *Amaranthaceae* is a medium small family with 900 species in 65 genera which are spread throughout the tropical and subtropical regions, and especially in western North America. The family is represented in Ethiopia by 23 genera which often behave as weeds.

Several species are cultivated as ornamentals or as "pseudocereals", like *Amaranthus caudatus*, *A. cruentus* and *A. Hypochondriacus* in India, China and Central America.

In Ethiopia *Achyranthes aspera* is a very common weed and it represents the *Amaranthaceae* as an important honey plant. It is common in almost all altitudes and flowering plants are found throughout the year. *Celosia argentea* is in some parts cultivated for religious and cultural purposes and also provides good amounts of pollen and nectar.

Amaryllidaceae

Members of the *Amaryllidaceae* can easily be identified by their underground tubers or bulbs and by their alternate, simple and entire parallel-veined leaves which are usually basal or from the top of the bulb. The flowers are very showy and borne together at the top of leafless stalks, usually several together, enclosed at first in one or more thin bracts.

The *Amaryllidaceae* is a family with about 68 genera and 800 species. The family is widespread in warm temperate and tropical areas around the world.

It is a family of great horticultural and ornamental importance. Some species of this family are valuable for bee-keepers in Middle Europe, like *Galanthus nivalis* and *Leucojum vernum*. Honeys from these plants do not play a role but they are very helpful for early development of bee colonies in spring, due to some nectar and good yields of pollen. In Ethiopia many members of the *Amaryllidaceae* are not pollinated by bees but visited for pollen and nectar.

Anacardiaceae

The family is composed of trees and shrubs, or woody vines which can recognized by their resinous bark and fruit and their often compound leaves with prominent parallel secondary veins. The flowers are unisexual, small and borne in large densely-branched inflorescences, usually with a distinct swollen disc between the stamens and ovary

The *Anacardiaceae* is a small family with 60 to 80 genera and 600 species which are distributed throughout the tropics with some species also occurring in temperate areas. The family is represented by 10 genera in Ethiopia.

The widely cultivated CASHEW NUT *(Anacardium occidentale)* and the PISTACHIO NUT *(Pistacia vera)* belong to this family as well as the MANGO *(Mangifera indica)*.

Several species of this family are known world-wide as important honey sources, like the Brazilian *Anacardium occidentale* and *Schinus terebinthifolius,* the Asian *Holigarna grahamii* and *Rhus taitensis,* the North American *Rhus glabra* and *R. typhina* and the African *Sclerocarya caffra.*

The indigenous species *of Rhus* are very common in many climatic zones of Ethiopia and are like *Schinus molle* important pollen suppliers and less important in nectar production, whereas *Mangifera indica* with rich nectaries and also with the juicy fruits is one of the most important representatives of this family in terms of honey production.

Apiaceae

Members of this family are aromatic, often poisonous, herbs and rarely shrubs or small trees. They have usually alternate or rarely opposite, often very large, pinnately or ternately (less often palmately) compound or dissected or rarely simple leaves. The flowers are always small, often borne in compound umbels or in heads or simple umbels. They are bisexual or seldom unisexual and regular. The petals are commonly white or yellow, less often purple or of other colours. The stamens alternate with the petals and are borne above the nectary-disk.

The *Apiaceae* is a very uniform and natural family with a large number of species. The family is composed of 300 genera with about 3000 species and are distributed throughout the world and even found in most extreme climatic conditions.

One of the remarkable features of many species of this family is the production of ethereal oils. Many species are therefore used as medicinal plants, as spices and condiments and as poisonous plants. Many have the inherent predisposition to set taproots, to set tubercles or to have swollen stems which are used as food for humans.

The nectaries of all *Apiaceae* are exposed and are therefore acceptable for all bees and flies. The *Apiaceae* provide, in general, a good nectar production and are also valuable pollen sources. Pure *Apiaceae* honey is produced in Middle Europe from *Anthriscus and Heracleum.* The honey is a little bit tangy. *Foeniculum* honey is produced in Mediterranean countries.

In Ethiopia huge areas are covered with *Anethum foeniculum* at medium elevations and *Ferula communis* at higher altitudes, and these plants provide a good honey source for the beekeepers in the surroundings. In addition in some parts of the country cultivated *Trachispermum ammi* provides some surplus of honey.

Apocynaceae

Members of the family are shrubs or small trees often with succulent stems, or climbers which produce a lot of white sap if cut. The leaves are simple and entire and oppositely arranged. The flowers are showy with the petals fused to form a tube and the stamens are usually hidden. The fruits are variable, sometimes a single fleshy, egg-shaped fruit with one or two hard seeds inside or often in two distinctly separate parts, each producing many hairy seeds.

The *Apocynaceae* is a large family with 200 genera and 2000 species, which are widespread in tropical and subtropical regions, with relatively few genera and species in temperate climates. In Ethiopia the family is represented by 14 genera.

Several species of this family are important for latex production like *Couma macrocarpa* of the Amazon region and *Dyera costulata* in Malaysia as sources for chewing gum. Several others are cultivated for medicinal

purposes like the *Rauvolfia spp*, *Catharanthus roseus* and *Vinca minor.*

Thevetia peruviana is reported in South America as an important honey plant.

Araceae

Herbs, climbers or epiphytes or scrambling slender shrubs. Members of the family *Araceae* can be identified by their large leaves that clasp the stem at their base and the inflorescence enclosed at first in a single large bract and borne on an unbranched stalk. The inflorescence of the *Araceae* may be mistaken for a single large petal or sepal or a perianth tube. The small unisexual flowers are borne on a fleshy spike-like axis.

In addition, the *Araceae* are never woody and the flowers often have a disagreeable odour which attracts flies.

The *Araceae* is a large family with 1800 species distributed in 110 genera. They are widespread mostly in tropical and subtropical regions.

Philodendron and *Dieffenbachia* are widely grown as ornamental house plants but are very poisonous. Children or household pets eating the leaves of these plants are at the risk of death.

The *Araceae* are common in moist forests but can be found in other habitats during wet seasons and after long rains.

Araliaceae

The *Araliaceae* are represented by trees or shrubs or climbers (in the cultivated and introduced *Hedera helix)* or sometimes perennial herbs. Members of the family have alternate (rarely opposite) leaves which are palmately or pinnately compound or simple and often the leaf-stalk is clasping the stem at its base. The flowers are bisexual or sometimes unisexual, regular, and often arranged in umbels or condensed into heads or spikes. Each flower has 5 small sepals situated above the ovary or completely united to form a rim or it has no sepals. The petals are 5 (sometimes 3 to 8), and they are free or fused and coming off as a cap. The stamens are as many as the petals and alternating with them.

The *Araliaceae* is a medium small family with 70 genera and 800 species which are widespread in tropical and subtropical regions, and with some in temperate regions.

The *Araliaceae* are very attractive to honeybees due to their abundant pollen and nectar supplies. Several species are known world-wide as important honey sources like *Gilbertia arborea* and *Schefflera wallichiana*.

In Ethiopia *Sceffleria abyssinica* is one of the most important and valuable honey sources. White honey is harvested and highly priced. In Addis Ababa the cultivated *Hedera helix* is helpful for urban beekeepers in colony maintenance, and bee hives are often placed in the upper branches of the nectar yielding *Polyscias fulva* which occurs in the humid western and south western parts the country.

Arecaceae

A family composed of trees, shrubs, or sometimes climbers. Members of the family *Arecaceae* usually have a single unbranched stem or trunk. The family is very distinctive and recognized by its often tree-like habit and stem that usually does not grow in thickness and the usually large palmately or pinnately divided evergreen leaves are crowded at top of the stem. The generally large inflorescences are most commonly axillary or sometimes terminally arranged. The numerous flowers are usually individually small, sometimes large and showy, bisexual or unisexual. The tepals are leathery and fleshy, variously white, green, yellow, orange or red.

The *Arecaceae* or *Palmae* is a large family with 3000 species distributed in 200 genera, widespread in tropical and warm temperate regions.

Members of this family are often planted as ornamental trees as well as being the source of dates (*Phoenix dactylifera*), palm oil (*Elais guineensis*) and coconut milk and COPRA (*Cocos nucifera*). *Cocos nucifera* is also a very important source of honey, as *is Serenoa repens* in USA.

In Ethiopia several palm species are cultivated and the indigenous *Phoenix reclinata* is also a valuable source for pollen and honey.

Asclepiadaceae

The family is represented with herbs, shrubs, climbers or rarely small trees. Members of the family *Asclepiadaceae* have usually a white sap and are sometimes leafless succulents resembling euphorbs or cacts. The possession of white sap, their opposite leaves and the union of anthers and stigma distinguish this family from all others.

The *Asclepiadaceae* is a large family with 250 genera and 2000 species which are widespread in tropical and subtropical regions, especially in Africa and with relatively few species in temperate regions. In Ethiopia they are represented by 47 genera.

The American *Asclepias syriaca* has been cultivated as a food plant for bees and is also an important honey source.

In Ethiopia the climbing members of this family are mainly valuable nectar and pollen sources for honeybees. *Calotropis procera* is said to produce poisonous honey if harvested.

Asteraceae

The family is composed of herbs or shrubs, rarely climbers or trees. Members of the *Asteraceae* have alternate or sometimes opposite leaves which can also be in basal rosettes. The leaves are simple or lobed and apparently compound. The flowers are usually crowded to form a head *(capitulum)* which resembles and may be mistaken for a single flower.

The *Asteraceae* is the largest family of flowering plants with about 1100 genera and 20000 species. It is a cosmopolitan family, spread throughout the world especially in temperate and subtropical regions but is not the most common family in Ethiopia where most of the species are found in the highlands.

Many of the *Asteraceae* are excellent pollen and nectar suppliers for honeybees and some of them are known throughout the world as important honey sources, for example SUNFLOWER *(Helianthus)*, DANDELION *(Taraxacum)* and thistles *(Cirsium)*.

In Ethiopia plants belonging to *Echinops*, *Bidens*, *Guizotia* and *Vernonia* are important bee plants because of their abundant occurrence as well as their wide altitudinal range.

Heavy yields of pure honey are obtained from the different *Bidens spp.* (the MESKAL-FLOWERS) of the Ethiopian highlands. The province of Gojjam is famous for its dark-yellow, not very sweet *Guizotia abyssinica* honey and a dark brownish honey from the tree *Vernonia amygdalina* is harvested in the lowlands of Gambela. The *Echinops* thistles as well as the *Carduus* thistles are very important nectar and pollen suppliers and contribute a lot to the country's honey yields at all altitudes.

Balanitaceae

The family is composed of trees or shrubs. Members of the *Balanitaceae* have often simple or forked green spines arising from the axils of leaves. They are easily recognised by their woody habit, alternate 2-foliate leaves and flowers with free sepals and petals.

The *Balanitaceae* is a small family with 9 species 2 of which are distributed in India and Burma, and 7 in Africa. In Ethiopia this family is represented by 4 species which are common in drier *Acacia* woodlands and thornbush savannas.

Balanites aegyptiaca is cultivated since ancient times in Egypt and reports date back 4000 years ago.

B. aegyptiaca provides small amount of nectar for the honeybees, however, it is a valuable bee plant in dry habitats. A surplus of honey will never be stored but the late flowering period contributes for the survival of bees.

Balsaminaceae

The family *Balsaminaceae* consists of herbs with usually succulent stems and growing in wet places. The flowers are very irregular, with one sepal forming a long cylindrical nectar tube (spur) at the back of the hanging flower. The fruit capsules have 5 lengthwise ridges. When ripe they burst explosively if knocked or even gently squeezed.

The *Balsaminaceae* are a medium-sized family with 450 species belonging to 2 genera and are represented in Ethiopia with one genus, *Impatiens*.

The *Impatiens spp.* supply the honeybees mainly with nectar and only small amounts of pollen. Their nectaries are found in the long cylindrical nectar tube. Very often the nectar fills up the whole tube and the wide opening enables the bees to forage. In addition the *Impatiens spp.* have extrafloral nectaries at the leaf petioles.

It might be true that the newly introduced *Impatiens glandulifera*, native to Himalayan region, will contribute in the near future to honey production like what it has already done in Europe.

Begoniaceae

Members of this family are herbs or shrubs which usually have succulent stems with simple and alternate leaves, seldom compound, with an unequal blade, palmately veined and often palmately lobed. The flowers are unisexual, commonly in axillary inflorescences arranged with 4 to many stamens and the fruits are usually a 3-winged capsule.

The *Begoniaceae* is a family with up to 1020 species in 3-5 genera, found in the tropics, especially northern South America, but absent from Australia and Polynesia. In Ethiopia the family is represented by a single indigenous species and many cultivated.

Berberidaceae

The family *Berberidaceae* is composed of shrubs, or outside Africa of herbs which can be identified by their simple or compound and alternate leaves which are often clustered. The commonly small flowers are arranged in panicles or racemes or solitary with relatively small sepals and nectarless and nectariferous petals. The stamens 4-18 in number, most often 6, generally of the same number as the nectariferous petals and opposite them. Fruits are berries or capsules.

Berberidaceae is a small family with up to 650 species distributed in 15 genera which are widespread in temperate Northern Hemisphere, with few species occurring on tropical mountains.

B. holstii is the only species of this family found in tropical Africa.

Many species of *Berberidaceae* are very attractive to honeybees and *Mahonia trifoliata* in Central America is known world-wide as an important honey source and *Berberis vulgaris* in temperate Europe. Unfortunately, *B. vulgaris* is the alternate host of the stem rust of wheat.

Bignoniaceae

The family is composed of trees, shrubs or sometimes climbers. Members of the *Bignoniaceae* always have compound and oppositely arranged leaves. The showy flowers are large and colourful, with the petals fused to form a tube that is slightly curved. The fruits are large and woody, in most species splitting lengthwise to reveal the often-winged seeds which are attached to a dividing wall running the length of the fruit.

The *Bignoniaceae* is a medium-small family with 800 species distributed in 100 genera. Members of the family are widespread mainly in tropical regions especially in tropical America. In Ethiopia there are seven genera, most of them introduced.

Some species, like the African *Rhigozum trichotomum* are important honey sources. Some *Bignoniaceae* are cultivated as ornamentals and frequently visited by honeybees mainly for nectar like the American *Tecoma stans* and the South African *Tecomaria capensis*. In some areas *Spathoda campanulata* is reported to be visited for nectar only.

In Ethiopia *Stereospermum kunthianum* is one of the most important bee trees and yields abundant honey where the tree is plentiful.

Bombacaceae

The *Bombacaceae* are trees with thick trunks, often with a smooth bark and sometimes with thick spines. They are easily recognized by their alternate palmately compound deciduous leaves, large flowers with 5 distinct sepals and petals and 5 to many stamens united near the base and their woody fruits. Pollination is often carried out by bats.

The *Bombacaceae* is a small tropical family with in 20 to 30 genera and 200 species which are found especially in Central and South America and also in Africa and Asia. In Ethiopia they are represented by *Adansonia digitata* and *Ceiba pentandra*.

Several species have some economic importance, for example, the tropical American *Ochroma pyramidale*, the source of balsa-wood. Others are cultivated for various reasons, mostly in Asia.

Bombax ceiba is recommended for planting to increase honey production in tropical Asia and also *Durio zibethinus* is known as a valuable bee tree there.

In Ethiopia both indigenous species are valuable bee plants. *Ceiba pentandra* occurs in the very humid areas of Illubabor region and is nowadays widely cultivated whereas *Adansonia digitata* is restricted to the dry lowland woodlands of the Takkaze river systems.

The flowers of both species have unpleasant smell but are very attractive to bees due to the abundance of nectar they supply.

Boraginaceae

The family is composed of herbs, shrubs or trees. Members of the family *Boraginaceae* have usually alternate, simple and mostly entire leaves. Their flowers are bisexual, regular or sometimes irregular and are often arranged in cymes/scorpioid cymes. They have 5 free or united sepals which are 5-lobed. The united petals form a variously shaped corolla.

The *Boraginaceae* is a large family with 100 genera and 2000 species. The family is cosmopolitan and its members are distributed especially in western North America and Mediterranean region and to the east in Asia. In Ethiopia they are represented by 18 genera.

Several species of *Boraginaceae* are cultivated as ornamentals, whereas others are cultivated as condiments or for bee feed. Many species of this family are known world-wide as major honey sources, like *Borago spp., Echium spp., Myosotis spp., Cynoglossum spp.* and *Solenanthus spp.* In tropical Central America the famous trees for honey production are *Cordia alba, C. alliodora* and *C. gerascanthus.* In Asia *Ehretia acuminata* is recommended for planting to increase honey production.

In Ethiopia *Cordia africana* and *Ehretia cymosa* are the most important honey sources in this family and *C. africana* is considered as one of the most important honey sources of the country.

Brassicaceae

The family is composed of herbs or rarely small shrubs. Members of the *Brassicaceae* are recognized by their herbaceous habit, alternate leaves and flowers which have 4 sepals and petals and 6 stamens and by their unusual fruit.

The *Brassicaceae* is a large family with 3500 species in 370 genera which are widespread in the cool temperate or warm temperate Northern and Southern Hemisphere with the greatest diversity in the Mediterranean region, in West and Central Asia and parts of north America. In Ethiopia they are represented by 29 genera.

Many members of *Brassicaceae* are cultivated throughout the world as ornamentals, for lettuce, vegetable and for edible and technical oils.

In general, the *Brassicaceae* are substantial nectar and pollen suppliers. Because of their widespread occurrence as weeds and cultivated varieties, and their large areas under cultivation (for rape, mustard and others) they are with special importance for beekeeping.

Several species of this family are known throughout the world as important honey sources, like *Brassica spp., Sinapis spp., Rhaphanus spp.* and *Eruca spp.*

In Ethiopia several species are cultivated as important oil and vegetable crops *(Brassica, Crambe, Lepidium)* and known as important for beekeepers, like *Brassica napus, B. nigra, B. carinata, Lepidium sativa, Rorippa nasturtium-aquaticum* and *Sinapis alba.*

Buddlejaceae

Members of family *Buddlejaceae* include trees, shrubs and seldom herbs. They are recognised by their simple leaves which have opposite, whorled or rarely alternate arrangement, and which are entire to more often toothed or lobed. The small flowers have 4 or 5 petals and are borne in various sorts of dense inflorescences in the species most frequently met with. The number of stamens equals the number of petals, as indicated by the lobes of the tube.

The *Buddlejaceae* is a small family with 150 species distributed in 10 genera which are found mainly in tropical and subtropical regions. In Ethiopia the family is represented by two genera *Buddleja* and *Nuxia.*

Several species of the butterfly-bush *Buddleja*, most them from India, are cultivated even in temperate regions because of their attractive and scented flowers which are mauve, purple, crimson and white. They are commonly visited by butterflies. The Ethiopian species *Buddleia polystachya* is also visited by honeybees.

An important honey plant of this family is *Nuxia congesta* which is growing in a wide range of habitats and altitudes.

Burseraceae

Members of *Burseraceae* are trees or shrubs with aromatic oil or resin in the bark. They are recognized by the alternate compound leaves and the resinous bark which frequently peels off in thin flakes. The flowers are borne in panicles or racemes with 4-5 sepals and distinct petals.

The *Burseraceae* is a medium-small family with up to 600 species in 17 genera spread throughout the tropics, especially in tropical America and northeast Africa where these usually crooked little trees are a characteristic part of the vegetation of dry areas. In the Ethiopian flora there are 58 species in 2 genera, *Commiphora* and *Boswellia*.

In Asia two species *(Canarium indicum* and *C. ovatum)* are cultivated because of their valuable nuts.

In Ethiopia several species provide resins which are of considerable commercial value as raw material of balm, myrrh, incense and frankincense.

The *Burseraceae* are, in many cases, important bee plants of the vegetation in dry lowland areas. They are sometimes excellent pollen and nectar suppliers, for example, *Commiphora africana* and *Boswellia papyrifera*. They contribute not only to the bees surviving in dry habitats, but also in the production of aromatic mixed honey.

Cactaceae

Members of the family are spiny (seldom unarmed) stem-succulents, which usually have thick stems with scarcely developed leaves, or rarely with woody, scarcely succulent stems and well developed, succulent, alternate simple leaves and are as a whole green, sometimes flattened and with leaf-like branches and with groups of spines. The flowers are solitary, seldom in terminal cymes, often large and showy and pollinated by various pollinating agents like bees, hummingbirds, bats or moths.

The *Cactaceae* is a large family with about 30-200 genera and 1500 species which are endemic to South and North American deserts, except one species of the genus *Rhipsalis* which is a native of eastern Africa.

Cacti were introduced from Central America to Spain around 500 years ago. They were taken to North Africa by the "Moors" when these were finally expelled from Spain at the end of the 15th century. Cacti (mainly *Opuntia ficus-indica*) have become naturalized and multiplied by birds, especially in cliffs and other inaccessible places, and distributed by men in the semi-arid and sub-humid zones.

Nowadays many cacti are cultivated for living fences, erosion control and animal and human food. Spineless varieties of *Opuntia ficus-indica* are more and more widespread and also called "living fodder banks" for livestock in arid and semi-arid climates.

Campanulaceae

The *Campanulaceae* are a family of herbs, sometimes climbing or epiphytic. The flowers have the petals fused into a tube and borne at the top of the ovary. This family can be readily separated from most other groups of herbs by its white or yellow sap.

The *Campanulaceae* is a large cosmopolitan family with 70 genera and 2000 species. Members of the family are very widespread, especially in temperate regions. In Ethiopia 6 genera represent the family.

Members of the *Campanulaceae* are attractive to honeybees. In European countries *Campanula* pollen is always found in different honeys, especially in honeys from mountainous areas. *Campanula persicifolia* and *Campanula urticifolia* are reported to be important for beekeeping in Ethiopia. *Campanula edulis* is frequently visited by honeybees.

Capparaceae

Members of this family are tres, shrubs, herbs, or sometimes climbers. They have stiff, alternate and simple, trifoliate, or palmately compound leaves, some of them with extrafloral nectaries. The flowers are bisexual (rarely unisexual), regular or irregular and arranged solitary or in racemes. The petals are 4 (sometimes 5 or more or absent), free and often narrow at the base, equal or unequal in size.

The *Capparaceae* or also called *Capparidaceae* is a medium-small family with 800 species in 45 genera which are widespread in tropical and subtropical regions, with a few species occurring in temperate parts, but mostly in arid climates. This family is well represented in Ethiopia, with 8 genera and 77 species, where a great number of woody species form a conspicuous element in the dry-country vegetation.

Many species are attractive to honeybees and the African *Boscia angustifolia* is one of the most important trees for beekeeping representing this family.

Caricaceae

Members of the *Caricaceae* are soft-stemmed shrubs or trees usually with only one trunk and smooth stems. They are easily recognised by their single trunk, white sap, large deeply lobed leaves and unisexual flowers. The male and female flowers are rarely found on the same plant. They are arranged in cymose, axillary inflorescences or sometimes solitary in leaf axils and they are regular. The sepals 5, and the 5 petals form an elongate, slender corolla tube.

The *Caricaceae* is a very small family with 30 species in 4 genera, growing in tropical and subtropical America and Africa. In Ethiopia this family is represented by the widely cultivated papaya.

Of the various species of the genus *Carica* only *C. papaya* has an economic importance. For beekeepers it is also a very important nectar and pollen source because the flowering period is all year round. It seems that the juice of ripe damaged fruits contributes a lot to stored surplus of nectar.

Celastraceae

The family is composed of trees or shrubs, sometimes scandent, and sometimes with spines. Members of the family *Celastraceae* have opposite or alternate simple leaves. The flowers are arranged in terminal or axillary inflorescences, seldom solitary in the leaf axils, mostly rather small, commonly greenish or white. The sepals are small and the petals are overlapping. The stamens are on or outside the nectary-disk.

The *Celastraceae* is a large family with 50 genera and 800 species which are found throughout the tropics with some in temperate regions. In Ethiopia the family is represented by 6 genera *and 22 species.*

The most famous species of this family is *Catha edulis* which is cultivated in eastern African and some Arabian countries for its stimulative properties in fresh leaves which produces apathy. The usage is increasing in Northeast Africa and Yemen.

Combretaceae

The family is composed of trees, shrubs or sometimes climbers. Members of the family *Combretaceae* are important part of the vegetation in deciduous woodlands and thorn-scrub. Members of this family have alternate, opposite, or less often whorled, simple and entire leaves. The flowers are arranged in terminal and axillary racemes, spikes or heads, mostly rather small, bisexual or less often unisexual. The sepals are 4-5 and the small petals alternate with them. The stamens are commonly twice as many as the sepals.

The *Combretaceae* is a small family with 20 genera and 400 species which are found in tropical and subtropical regions, especially in Africa.

Members of the family are very attractive to honeybees for pollen and nectar; for example *Bucida buceras* and *Combretum fruticosum* from tropical America are known as major honey source, whereas in Asia different *Terminalia spp.* are reported as important honey trees.

In Africa the *Combretaceae* include several important bee trees and shrubs like *Combretum celastroides, C. platypetalum, C. imberbe, C. zeyheri, Guiera senegalensis* and *Terminalia brachystemma.*

In Ethiopia *Combretum molle* is known as an important nectar and pollen source and the climber *Combretum paniculatum* is the most valuable source of honey in the western and southwestern parts of the country. *Terminalia spp.* may also contribute to mixed honeys in deciduous woodlands.

Commelinaceae

The family *Commelinaceae* is composed of herbs with rather fleshy leaves, the base of which is wrapped around the stem to form a sheath. The flowers have commonly 3 blue petals which are very short-lived, appearing to melt away at the end of the day. The stamens are 6 which are either all fertile or only 3 of them are fertile, and are often very variable in size.

The *Commelinaceae* is a medium-small family with 700 species in 50 genera and are widespread in tropical and subtropical regions.

Several species are cultivated as ornamentals and pot plants. The best known is a group of species which are creeping or hanging herbs and known as Wandering Jew, *Tradescantia* spp. from Mexico.

Convolvulaceae

The *Convolvulaceae* include herbs, shrubs and, most commonly climbers with slender stems which trail on the ground or coil round available supports, and which often contain milky sap. The leaves are alternate and simple, rarely scale-like. The flowers are short-lived, fading rapidly after picking. The petals are fused to form a tube, usually funnel-shaped, folded and often spirally-twisted when in bud. All the petals lobes have the same size, so that the flower is radially symmetrical. The fruit is dry and globose, splitting to reveal small number of relatively hard, often hairy seeds. The climbing or trailing branches and the distinctively folded and twisted corolla of this family are characteristic.

The *Convolvulaceae* is a medium-large family with 1500 species in 50 genera, which are nearly cosmopolitan and widespread, especially in warmer parts of the New World.

Several species are cultivated as ornamentals and some species like the sweet potato, *Ipomoea batatas* and the water spinach, *Ipomoa aquatica* are grown as vegetables in many tropical and subtropical regions of the world.

Many species are very attractive to honeybees for rich nectar and some pollen supply and are also known throughout the world as important honey plants, for example *Ipomoea acuminata, I. nil, I. sidifolia, I. triloba, Jacquemontia nodiflora, Turbina corymbosa* and the important starch plant, *I. batatas.*

In Ethiopia the most important honey plant of the family *Convolvulaceae* is, of course, the widely cultivated SIKWAR DNCH *(Ipomoea batatas)*. In addition many other species of this family, often found as a weed, are visited by the bees for pollen and nectar.

Crassulaceae

The family *Crassulaceae* contains herbs or small shrubs with rather succulent stems. The leaves are simple and very fleshy. The inflorescence in most species is branched, with the oldest flowers in the centre being tough, and a few inconspicuous species have the flowers solitary or arranged along an unbranched stem. The fruit is made up of several distinct parts, equal in number to the petals, each part with the tip very pointed. The fruit splits along one side to release very many tiny seeds.

The *Crassulaceae* is a medium-large family with 35 genera and 1500 species some of which are cosmopolitan and widespread with major centres of diversity in South Africa, Mexico and eastern Asia and rare in wet tropics and absent from Australia and Polynesia.

Many species of the family are cultivated as ornamentals with increasing number all the time.

Many species of the genus *Sedum* are very valuable bee plants for pollen and nectar, while *Kalanchoe* spp. are much visited by butterflies throughout the day. These plants are also visited by honeybees, mainly during early mornings when the nectar level inside the corolla-tubes is very high.

Cucurbitaceae

Members of the family are climbers with almost always well-developed tendrils and with herbaceous or woody stems. They are easily recognized by the climbing habit, spirally coiled tendrils and simple and alternate palmately veined leaves. Stiff hairs are always present on various parts of the plant. The unisexual usually white or yellow, less often orange or green flowers have usually united stamens. The male flowers have a cluster of 3 to 5 orange or yellow stamens in the centre, while the female flowers, which are either solitary or in small, branched inflorescences, have a single orange or yellow stigma in the centre and a distinctly swollen ovary below the flowers as a whole. The fruits are fleshy and with many seeds.

The *Cucurbitaceae* is a medium-small family with 120 genera and 825 species which are widespread in tropical and subtropical regions, rarely in temperate or cool temperate climatic zones. In Ethiopia the family is represented by 24 genera and 71 species.

Several species are cultivated as ornamentals, as vegetable and for fibre. The cultivation of *Cucurbita spp.* in South America dates back 4000 years B.C.

In Ethiopia many species are cultivated because of their economic importance as sources of food (*Cucurbita* and *Coccinia*), medicine (*Cucumis*) and containers (*Lagenaria*).

Many species are very attractive to honeybees and provide good amounts of nectar which is produced by the female and male flowers. The pollen value is of minor importance and the bees face some difficulties to collect the coarse-grained pollen.

Dipsacaceae

Members of the family *Dipsacaceae* are herbs often with rosette leaves, or rarely small shrubs with opposite leaves. The flowers are arranged in dense heads, each with 4 (rarely 2 or 3) stamens quite separate from each other. The fruit has a single seed, with the dry calyx remaining at the top.

The *Dipsacaceae* is a small family with 10 genera and 270 species which are distributed in Eurasia and Africa, especially in the Mediterranean. In Ethiopia there are 5 genera.

Several species are cultivated as ornamentals mainly in temperate regions. Some species are attractive to honeybees and are known as important bee plants, like *Dipsacus fullonum* and *D. pilosus.*

In Ethiopia very important bee plants are *Dipsacus pinnatifidus* as well as *Pterocephalus frutescens*.

Ebenaceae

The family is composed of trees or shrubs. Members of the family are usually either male or female but not both. The wood is commonly hard, dark or black. The leaves are often alternately arranged and rarely oppositely, simple, entire and stiff. The flowers are unisexual and regular, mostly rather small, borne singly or in small cymose clusters in the axils of leaves.

The *Ebenaceae* is a small family with 5 genera and 450 species which are distributed throughout the tropical and subtropical regions with only a few species extending into temperate climates. In Ethiopia this family is represented by 2 genera.

The *Ebenaceae* include some excellent honey sources, like *Diospyros virginiana* in North America. This genus is also an important honey plant in Africa represented, for example, by *Diospyros batocana* in Zambia and *Diospyros mespeliformis* in Ethiopia. Further valuable bee trees might bee *Diospyros abyssinica*, *Euclea divinorum* and *E. schimperi*, but further research is needed.

Ericaceae

The family is composed of evergreen or sometimes deciduous shrubs or small trees or lianas. Members of the family *Ericaceae* are usually growing on acid soils. The leaves are alternate or sometimes opposite or even whorled, simple, often small and firm. The tubular flowers are arranged in racemes, sometimes solitary and terminal or axillary. The sepals and petals are 3 to 7, most often 5, less often 4.

The *Ericaceae* is a large family with 125 genera and 3500 species which are widespread in temperate, cool and subtropical regions as well as in montane tropical regions. In Ethiopia they are represented by four genera.

Many species belonging to the genera *Arbatus*, *Calluna*, *Epigaea*, *Erica*, *Kalmia*, *Oxydendrum*, *Pieris and Rhododendron* are cultivated as ornamentals. Several *Vaccinium* spp. are cultivated for their edible and tasty fruits.

The *Ericaceae* include excellent suppliers of pollen and nectar and some are famous world-wide as important honey sources, for example *Calluna vulgaris*, *Erica arborea*, *Erica cinerea*, *Erica herbacea*, *Oxydendron arboreum* and *Vaccinium uliginosum*.

In Ethiopia *Erica arborea* is the most important honeyplant of higher altitudes. Unfortunately, in most places *E. arborea* has been cut and burnt and small shrubs are left.

Euphorbiaceae

The family is composed of shrubs and trees, less often climbers or herbs. Members most often have simple alternate leaves which are occasionally opposite or absent. The flowers are extremely variable, always unisexual, often inconspicuous but sometimes gathered into complex inflorescences surrounded by conspicuous bracts or glands which are acting as nectaries.

The *Euphorbiaceae* is a very large a cosmopolitan family with 300 genera and 8000 to 10000 species. Members of the family are most numerous in tropical and subtropical regions. The family is represented in Ethiopia by 30 genera and 200 indigenous species which form an important element of the vegetation in many areas.

Several species of *Euphorbiaceae* are cultivated as ornamentals, for example, *Euphorbia pulcherima*, as oil crops, for example *Ricinus communis*, or as food crop, like *Manihot esculenta*. Others are known world-wide as major honey sources, *examples being Croton floribundus*, *Hevea brasiliensis*, *Euphorbia resiniera* and *Manihot glaziovii*.

In Ethiopia mainly *Euphorbia spp.* supply significant amounts of nectar for bees and even pure honeys are obtained. *Euphorbia abyssinica* honey are harvested in the southern parts and generally called as "hot". In the northern parts of the country, honeys from *Euphorbia candelabrum* are harvested but disliked because of their smell and being considered to be a little bit poisonous.

Croton macrostachys is in many parts of the country considered as an important tree for nectar and pollen supplies.

Flacourtiaceae

The family is composed of trees or shrubs. Members of this family have often spines. The leaves are alternate and simple, entire to serrate and often with glands along the edge. The flowers are bisexual or unisexual, regular and often borne on a joined stalk. The sepals are 3 to 6 or more, free or united at the base and usually persisting in fruit. The petals are 3 to 15 and free (absent in *Flacourtia* and *Dovyalis*). The stamens are many or less often 5 or more, free or united in groups.

The *Flacourtiaceae* is a family with 800 species distributed in 85 genera, which are widespread in tropical regions. In Ethiopia 6 genera represent the family.

In our area two species, the indigenous *Dovyalis abyssinica* and the introduced and more widespread *D. caffra* and commonly used as a hedge plant in many towns, are very important nectar and pollen suppliers.

Gentianaceae

Members of this family are herbs or rarely small shrubs or very rarely small trees. They have opposite, simple and entire or toothed leaves. The flowers are bisexual and regular and often showy. They have 4 to 6 free or united sepals (to form a short tube) and 4 to 6 petals (rarely up to 12) which are united to form a tube. The stamens are the same number as the corolla lobes and alternate with them.

The *Gentianaceae* is somewhat a large family with 1000 species in 75 genera which are cosmopolitan, and widespread, especially in temperate and subtropical regions and on tropical mountains. The family is represented by 5 genera in Ethiopia.

The *Gentianaceae* are attractive to honeybees for pollen supply and some are even yielding good amounts of nectar.

Geraniaceae

Members of this family are herbs or subshrubs or shrubs which are rarely woody and often have rather succulent stems. The leaves are usually divided or lobed, rarely almost entire or compound, with 3 or more large, separate veins running parallel to each other starting from the base of the leaf-blade. The flowers have 4 or 5 separate petals alternating with 5 glands and the stamens have fused filaments at the base. The fruit has a swollen, five-lobed base and a tapering beak, splitting from the base into 5 parts that often remain for a time attached at the tip to a central column.

The *Geraniaceae* is a medium sized family with 11 to 14 genera and 750 species. The family is best represented in drier temperate and subtropical regions. In Ethiopia 4 genera represent the family.

Several species are widely grown as ornamentals, while others are important sources of essential oils and many others are used locally as medicinal and dye plants.

Guttiferae

The *Guttiferae* are here considered to consist of two small families, the *Hypericaceae* and *Clusiaceae*. Members of the family include herbs, shrubs and trees. The leaves are simple, oppositely arranged or whorled, with gland dots which appear either dark or bright, if the leaf is seen against light. The flowers have 4 or 5 separate petals, usually bright yellow, sometimes white, often marked with red, and the stamens are numerous.

The *Guttiferae* is a large family with 1200 species in 50 genera which occur throughout moist tropical and north temperate regions. The Guttiferae is well represented in the North Temperate Zone, while it is represented in Ethiopia by the genera *Hypericum*, *Psorospermum*, *Garcinia* and *Calophyllum*.

Several species of the family *Guttiferae* are cultivated or economically used for their delicious fruits, for example, *Garcinia mangostana*, *Mammea americana*, *Patonia esculenta and Rheedia acuminata*. *Garcinia morella* is cultivated for its resins.

Members of the *Guttiferae* are considered to be pollen suppliers only. The tree *Hypericum revolutum* is exceptionally a very rich nectar and pollen source and is an important honey tree at higher altitudes.

Hydrophyllaceae

The family is composed of herbs or seldom shrubs. The leaves are alternate or sometimes partly or wholly opposite, simple to compound, entire or dissected, rarely palmately compound. The flowers are solitary or in cymes with a regular corolla. They usually have bluish flowers and are cultivated and introduced ornamentals.

The *Hydrophyllaceae* is a small family with 20 genera and 250 species. They are widespread especially in dry western United States.

Phacelia tanacetifolia is known world-wide as an important honey plant as well as for green manure. It seems that this species needs very humid conditions to produce sufficient nectar, and is therefore in Ethiopia considered to be a rich pollen source.

Icacinaceae

The family is composed of trees, shrubs or climbers. Members of the *Icacinaceae* have simple leaves which are usually alternate, with entire or toothed or lobed margins. The flowers are usually in axillary inforescences, arranged in spikes or cymes. They are regular, without sepals or with 4 to 5 and free or united sepals. The petals are 4 to 5, free or united and the 4 to 5 stamens alternate with the petals.

The *Icacinaceae* is a small family with 55 genera and 400 species which have a pantropical distribution and with relatively few species in temperate climates. In Ethiopia the family is represented by 3 genera, *Apodytes*, *Raphiostylis* and *Pyrenacantha*.

A few species are grown but of minor economic importance. The seeds and tubers of the African species *Icacina senegalensis* are used to make a starchy flour and species of the South American *Poraqueiba* are locally used for their edible fruits.

Lamiaceae

The family is composed of herbs or small shrubs that can be identified by their four-sided stems with oppositely arranged, simple leaves. The flower often has a conspicuous calyx and 2-lipped corolla which is well-designed for visits by bees. The flowers are usually found in clusters in the axils of the leaves or in whorls around the stem in terminal inflorescences.

All parts (stems, leaves and flowers) of members of this family give a strong, often spicy smell when crushed. The smell comes from ethereal oils in glands and special hairs.

The *Lamiaceae* is a large family with up to 5000 species in about 170 genera which are distributed throughout the world, but particularly common in countries with a

Mediterranean climate. In the Ethiopian flora there are 41 genera and 159 species.

Several members of the family, for example, *Ocimum basilicum*, SWEET BASIL (English) and BASOBLA (Amh), are important condiments and spices, while others are used in medicine and for the perfume industry.

All members of *Lamiaceae* are excellent suppliers of nectar and many of genera are famous world-wide as important honey sources, for example, *Rosmarinus*, *Lavendula*, *Salvia*, *Thymus* and *Mentha*.

In Ethiopia, plants belonging to *Plectranthus*, *Salvia*, *Thymus*, *Satureja* and *Ocimum* are important bee plants because of their widespread occurrence and long flowering periods. *Plectranthus spp.* are also important nectar suppliers for bees in a wide variety of habitats in medium elevations. *Thymus* gives a pure, aromatic, amber honey which is produced from higher areas, such as the Bale and Simien mountains. *Ocimum* honey is known from both dry and more humid parts; that from the eastern escarpment is almost pure white and is prized traditionally for its medicinal properties. *Salvia* spp. are found in large areas at higher altitudes and are therefore important honey sources for the beekeepers there.

Lauraceae

Members of this family are trees and shrubs which have stems and leaves usually with aromatic oil glands. They have mostly alternate leaves which are simple and usually entire with glandular dots. The flowers are regular and small with rarely 2 and often 3 sepals and petals.

The *Lauraceae* a medium-large family with 30-50 genera and 2000 species which are widespread in the tropical and subtropical regions. They are represented in Ethiopia by the herbaceous parasite *Cassytha filiformis* and the cultivated AVOCADO (*Persea americana*) and CINNAMON (*Cinamomum zyelanicum*).

Beside the economically very important world-wide cultivated AVOCADO, the Asian *Actinodaphne angustifolia*, *A. hookerii*, *Litsea stocksii* and *Machilus macrantha* are known as important sources for honey production.

Leguminosae

The family is composed of trees, shrubs, herbs or climbers. Members of the *Leguminosae/Fabaceae* can be identified by their alternate leaves which are often compound, and by their pea-like or bean-like fruits which typically splits along opposite sides into two separate halves to release several seeds.

The *Leguminosae* is one of the largest families of flowering plants with up to 590 genera and 17,000 species which are distributed throughout the world, especially in tropical and subtropical regions. They play a dominant role in the vegetation of large areas in tropical Africa.

The *Leguminosae* are divided into three sub-families: *Caesalpinioideae*, *Mimosoideae* and the *Papilionoideae*.

Members of the subfamily *Caesalpinioideae* are usually trees or shrubs, occasionally climbers, and rarely herbs. The subfamily consists of about 150 genera and 2200 species. Members of this subfamily bear sometimes root-nodules to harbour nitrogen-fixing bacteria, but more often not and seldom extrafloral nectaries are present. Flowers are arranged in racemes or spikes or sometimes in cymes and are large and showy with usually 5 petals.

The *Mimosoideae* is usually composed of trees or shrubs, sometimes climbers and rarely herbs and consist of about 3000 species in about 50 genera. Members of the subfamily commonly bear root-nodules to harbour nitrogen-fixing bacteria and frequently extrafloral nectaries are present. Flowers are arranged in racemes, spikes or heads and generally they are rather small with numerous stamens.

Members of the subfamily *Papilion-oideae* are usually herbs, less often shrubs, trees or climbers and seldom spiny and consist of about 12000 species in about 440 genera. They are commonly bearing root-nodules for harbouring nitrogen-fixing bacteria and sometimes extrafloral nectaries are present. Flowers are arranged mostly in racemes, spikes or heads, commonly more or less showy with 5 petals and sepals.

The *Leguminosae* is of particular importance, because in most cases members of this family contribute to soil improvement by fixing atmospheric nitrogen and they add nitrogen to the soil in which they grow.

This family contains many important food plants such as peas, important oilcrops like soya beans and RAPE and also contain many important fodder plants such as clover and ALFALFA.

Numerous members of *Leguminosae* are very important honey sources, like *Trifolium spp.*, *Acacia spp.*, *Medicago spp.* and *Melilotus spp.*

In African drylands many important bee trees are known to produce honey, to maintain bee colonies and to provide people with significant additional income and food, like *Brachystegia spp.*, *Parkia biglobosa*, *Peltophorum africanum*, *Julbernardia globiflora*, *J. paniculata* and *Dalium engleranum* and several introduced *Prosopis spp.*

In Ethiopia the species of *Trifolium* are very important bee plants in higher altitudes and in areas where trees have already virtually disappeared. Because of their widespread occurrence, particularly the Acacia spp. in drier habitats, and the Albizia spp. in more humid climates, and also Erythrina spp. are very important for beekeepers and their colonies.

Important "bee trees" like *Acacia mellifera* and *Tamarindus indica* may contribute locally a lot to bee colonies survival and for honey production.

It is interesting to note that *Acacia decurrens* is not visited by bees in Ethiopia and the *Flamboyant* is only occasionally visited for pollen only.

Liliaceae

Members of this family are herbs and shrubs or, rarely, climbers. They usually have a bulb, rhizome, corm or swollen roots. The leaves have parallel veins and no leaf stalk. Sometimes they are very fleshy and then the leaf margin is almost always toothed. The flowers are borne along the stem, each with its own bract and, rarely, they are arranged solitary. They have 6 similar petals and sepals, free or fused.

This large family includes small families like the *Alliaceae* and *Asparagaceae* with 280 genera and

4000 species which are very widespread, especially in dry temperate to subtropical regions and well represented in Ethiopia.

Several members of the *Liliaceae* are cultivated world-wide as ornamentals and *several Allium spp.* are cultivated as important easy-to-grow vegetables throughout the world.

Some species are considered as major honey sources like *Allium cepa, Allium fistolosum* and *Asparagus officinalis.*

Linaceae

The family is composed of herbs or small shrubs. They have alternate or opposite, simple and entire leaves. The flowers are arranged in small cymose, sometimes raceme-like or spike-like inflorescences. The sepals and petals are 5 and the carpels are united to form a compound ovary.

The *Linaceae* is a small family with 220 species in 6 genera which are widespread, especially in temperate and subtropical regions. In Ethiopia they are represented by 2 genera.

The most well-known species is *Linum usitatissimum* which is grown mostly for fibre, linseed meal, livestock feed, fibre, linen, other fibres and ropes in Asian countries, and with a strong recent recovery in Europe. In Ethiopia it is grown since ancient time for oil.

Loranthaceae

Members of this family are shrubs or rarely herbs, or seldom trees, semi-parasitic and growing upon the branches of trees and shrubs or they . are terrestrial. They have stems with usually thickened nodes. The leaves are opposite or whorled (rarely alternate), simple and entire. The flowers are bisexual or unisexual,

regular or somewhat irregular and are often arranged in groups of 3 or 2. The sepals are 4 to 6, free or united to form a tube. The petals are absent or the sepals are petal-like. The stamens are 4 to 6 and opposite the sepals.

The *Loranthaceae* is a medium-small family with 60 to 70 genera and 700 species which are widespread mostly in tropical and subtropical regions.

The mistletoes are chlorophyllous and due to the photosynthesis they are able to produce sugars and some are therefore providing some nectar and good pollen supplies to honeybees.

Lythraceae

The herbs or seldom shrubs or even trees composing the family *Lythraceae* have their simple and commonly entire leaves opposite or less often whorled, only seldom alternate. The bisexual flowers ar solitary or fascicled in the axils, or often in terminal racemes or spikes. The petals alternate with the sepals. Stamens are most commonly twice as many as the sepals or petals and solitary in *Rotala*.

The *Lythraceae* are a small plant family with 500 species in 24 genera and are widespread in tropical countries, with few species in temperate regions. In Ethiopia they are represented by 6 genera.

CUFFEA and the CRAPE-MYRTLE are widely cultivated as ornamental shrubs. Commercial henna dye is obtained from the dried leaves of the pantropical species *Lawsonia inermis*.

Malphigiaceae

The family is composed of woody climbers or sometimes trees or shrub. They have usually simple oppositely arranged leaves with unusual hairs.

The flowers are with glandular sepals and distinct petals. They are arranged in terminal or axillary racemes, panicles or cymes, bisexual or seldom unisexual.

The *Malphigiaceae* is a medium-large family with 1200 species in 60 genera which are distributed throughout the tropics and extending into the subtropics and are very abundant in the New World. In Ethiopia they are represented by 4 genera *Caucanthus, Triaspis, Tristellateia* and *Acridocarpus.*

In South America several species are cultivated for their vitamin-rich fruits like *Malphigia glabra* as well as species of *Bunchosia.* Several species of *Banisteriopsis* and related genera produce alkaloids which are used by local people as hallucinogens.

One species is recorded as an important honey plant, the Caribbean *Byrsonima crassifolia.*

Malvaceae

Members of the family are herbs, shrubs or, rarely, small trees. The have alternate and hairy leaves with three or more separate veins from the base of the leaf-blade. The leaves are often lobed in outline. The flowers have 5 separate petals, often with extra bracts immediately next to the flower and looking like an extra ring of sepals and sometimes known as epicalyx. The stamens are very numerous, with the filaments all fused to form a single column in the centre of the flower. The fruit is a capsule with two or more compartments, each containing several seeds or breaking up into 5 or more separate pieces, each containing one or two seeds.

The *Malvaceae* is a medium-large family with 90 genera and 2000 species. They are widespread throughout the world in all tropical, subtropical and temperate regions, but particularly numerous in tropical America and from Africa to India. In Ethiopia they are represented by 18 to 19 genera and 139 species.

Several members of the *Malvaceae* are cultivated for fibre which are similar to Jute like KENAF *(Hibiscus cannabinus)* and ROSELLE *(H. sabdariffa)* which is also produced for beverages. This family includes the MUSK MALLOW *(Abelmoschus moschatus)*, the cotton plant *(Gossypium)*, OKRA *(Hibiscus esculentum)*, the SUNSET hibiscus *(Hibiscus manihot)* and many garden ornamentals.

The very common but introduced *Hibiscus rosa-sinensis* is elsewhere known as a valuable honey plant, whereas the cultivated cotton plants, *Gossypium* spp., are known worldwide as major honey sources in countries such as Egypt, Russia and America, if pesticides would not kill the bees.

Melastomaceae

The family is composed of herbs, shrubs or trees, sometimes climbing or growing on other plants. They have opposite or sometimes whorled, simple and palmately veined, with 3 to 9 sub-parallel primary veins and many transverse secondary veins between them. The flowers are bisexual and regular or somewhat irregular and often showy. The sepals are 4- or 5- (rarely 3 or 6) lobed, united to form a tube and the petals are 4 or 5 (rarely 3 or 6), free and borne on the calyx-tube. The stamens are 8 or 10.

The *Melastomaceae* is a large family with 200 genera and 4000 species which are widespread in tropical and subtropical regions, especially in South America. In Ethiopia they are represented by 3 genera.

In East Africa *Memecylon sapini* and *M. flavovirens* are reported as valuable bee plants.

In Ethiopia the *Dissotis spp.* are reported to be visited by honeybees. Most members of the *Melastomaceae* are without nectar and only visited by pollen gathering insects.

Meliaceae

The family is composed of trees or shrubs, or rarely herbs. Members of *Meliaceae* have usually ethereal oils in the leaves and bark. The leaves are alternate or rarely opposite, very often clustered at the branch-tips, pinnately or bipinnately compound, sometimes trifoliolate, seldom unifoliolate or simple. The flowers are axillary, less often terminal, mostly small, bisexual or sometimes unisexual. The petals are as many as the sepals and alternate with them.

The *Meliaceae* consist 51 genera and 550 species which are widespread throughout tropical and subtropical regions, with some taxa in temperate habitats. In Ethiopia there are 7 genera and 15 species.

This family includes many important timber trees like *Swietenia mahogani*, the source of the mahogany wood and others like *Cedrela odorata*.

Several species are known world-wide as important bee trees for example *Azadirachta indica*, *Melia azedarach*, *Trichilia havanensis*, *Toona ciliata* and *Khaya senegalensis*.

In Ethiopia *Ekebergia capensis* and *Trichilia spp.* are known as important bee trees.

Melianthaceae

The *Melianthaceae* is composed of trees and shrubs which can be identified by their alternate and odd-pinnate leaves and their irregular flowers which are borne in racemes. They have 5 sepals, or 4 by fusion of 2 and 5 petals with well-developed nectary disks. The 4 or 5 stamens alternate with the petals.

The *Melianthaceae* contains 2 genera and 8 to 36 species all of which are restricted to Africa.

The genus *Melianthus* is sometimes cultivated as an ornamental and well known for its abundant nectar production.

The only genus represented in Ethiopia is *Bersama* which is very attractive to bees for pollen and nectar supplies.

Moraceae

Members of this family are trees, shrubs or perennial herbs, very often with milky latex. The leaves are alternately and simple or sometimes palmately compound. The flowers are unisexual and regular, often very small and crowded into condensed inflorescences or sometimes disc-shaped with flowers on one side or hollow receptacles with flowers on the inside.

The family is composed of about 53 genera and 1400 species which are distributed in the tropics, but this family is also represented in subtropical and warm temperate areas. They are represented in Ethiopia by 4 genera.

Several species of *Moraceae* are economically important for their tasty fruits like *Artocarpus heterophyllus, A. integer, A. odoratissima, Ficus carica* and *Morus nigra.* The widely cultivated *Morus alba* is the food plant of the silkworm *Bombyx mori.* Experiments on the rearing of silkworm in Nazret have shown good results and are worth to be expanded to other areas where *M. alba* is abundant.

For beekeepers only the juicy fruits of fig trees are important. Mostly in drier habitats they are helpful to supply the bees with supplementary feed whereas pollen of *Morus alba* has already found in honeys elsewhere.

Musaceae

The family is composed of herbs which are large or tree-like plants with unbranched stems or trunks that are made up of the sheathing leaf-bases. The leaves are very large and spirally arranged. The flowers are unisexual and irregular and strongly nectariferous and adapted to pollination by birds and bats.

Members of the family *Musaceae* include the widely cultivated bananas *(Musa spp.)* and the indigenous ENSET *(Ensete ventricosum)*, which is extensively cultivated in south-central Ethiopia.

The *Musaceae* consists of 2 genera and 42 species. In Ethiopia the family is represented by 2 genera and 2 species.

Several species are cultivated for a variety of reasons, for example *Musa textilis* as a source of fibre, the MANILA HEMP. The common cultivated banana *(Musa spp.)* is known world-wide not only for its delicious fruits but also as a very important honey plant. It is a sterile triploid that produces no seeds.

Myrsinaceae

The *Myrsinaceae* consists of mostly evergreen small trees and shrubs or sometimes woody vines. The leaves are alternate (rarely opposite) and simple, stiff or leathery. Usually glandular dots or streaks are seen along the edge of the leaf blade when viewed against light. The flowers are bisexual or unisexual and regular with 4 to 6 sepals, often with glandular dots, and 3 to 6 petals which are united at the base or free. The stamens are as many as the petals.

The *Myrsinaceae* consists of 30 genera and 1000 species which are wide spread in tropical and subtropical New World and Old World regions and also found in temperate Old World. In Ethiopia species of this family are only found in higher altitudes above 1500 m.

Some species are sometimes cultivated as ornamentals but without any great economic importance.

The river mangrove *(Aegiceras corniculatum)* in tropical Asia is known as an important honey source.

Myrtaceae

The family is composed of trees or shrubs, very often with aromatic oils in leaves or bark. Members of the *Myrtaceae* are recognized by their simple and entire gland-dotted leaves and their flowers with many stamens and inferior ovary with a single style and stigma.

The *Myrtaceae* is a large family with 140 genera and 3000 species which are widespread in tropical and subtropical regions and temperate

Australia. In Ethiopia they are represented by the genera *Myrtus, Syzygium, Eugenia* and the introduced and widely cultivated *Eucalyptus* and *Psidium*.

Several species of *Myrtaceae* are cultivated as spices like *Pimenta dioica* and *Syzygium aromaticum*, while several other *Syzygium spp.* and *Eugenia spp.* as well as GUAVA (*Psidium guajava*) are cultivated for their edible and tasty fruits.

Several other species like *Myrtus communis* and many species of the eucalypts are cultivated as ornamentals, and species of eucalypts are also grown for commercial timber and fuelwood production.

Members of the family *Myrtaceae* are very attractive to honeybees and numerous *Eucalyptus spp.* as well as many *Metrosideros spp.* are known word-wide as important honey sources.

In Ethiopia the *Syzygium* trees are very important nectar and honey sources. Where these trees are plentiful and where even *Syzygium* forest exists abundant honey can be harvested. *Myrtus communis* is considered also as a major honey source.

But the major honey producing trees of the country belong to the genus *Eucalyptus* which are grown throughout the country for fuel and construction purposes. They were introduced by the Emperor Menelik II. in 1895. A French railway engineer, M. Mondon-Vidaillet, who was studying Ethiopian languages, suggested the introduction of *Eucalyptus* to the cold highlands where natural fuelwood was already very scarce.

E. camaldulensis, E. citriodora, E. globulus, E. grandis, E. saligna, E.

ficifolia and *E. viminalis* are commonly grown at altitudes between 900 and 3300 m. Their prolonged flowering seasons and their widespread occurrence makes the eucalypts essential for beekeeping mainly in areas where indigenous trees have already virtually disappeared.

The eucalypts are usually regarded as Australian trees and over 100 different species are known. Nevertheless several eucalypts are native to Papua New Guinea and the Indonesian archipelago and one species extends even to southern Philippine islands.

It is interesting to note that these heavy nectar and pollen suppliers evolved on a continent where honeybee races were not known until the recent introduction in 19th century when *Apis m. nigra* and later on *Apis m. ligustica* were introduced. Within several decades Australia developed to one of the major honey-producing countries of the world due to the rich Australian honeybee flora mainly with eucalypts and due to the gentleness of the temperate-evolved bee races.

Warning: The Australian micro-organisms that help to break-down fallen gum leaves appear to be absent in Ethiopia and few indigenous plants can grow with them especially in the case of *E. camaldulensis*. This leaves the soil bare and vulnerable to erosion. Large trees near houses are considered dangerous as branches or even the whole tree may fall in storms.

Nyctaginaceae

Members of the family are herbs, shrubs, trees or woody climbers which have simple and entire leaves and bisexual and regular flowers. The sepals are 3- to 5-lobed, united and often forming a long petal-like tube.

The *Nyctaginaceae* is a small family with 30 genera and 300 species. Members of the family are most numerous in the New World tropics but also extending into temperate regions around the world. In Ethiopia 3 genera and 14 species are indigenous, while 2 other genera are introduced, one of which is well established in the wild and the other one is the widely cultivated BOUGAINVILLEA.

Nypmphaeaceae

The family is composed of herbs floating on the surface of fresh water with stems often rooted in muddy. The leaves are alternate and simple, floating on the water surface, entire and round or with deep sinus on one side and with the leaf-stalk attached near the centre of the blade. The flowers are bisexual and large and floating on water. The sepals 4 to many and are free and the petals are 5 to many and free with many stamens intergrading with the petals.

Members of the family are often cultivated as ornamentals throughout the world. The *Nymphaeaceae* is a small cosmopolitan family with 65 species in 7 genera. In Ethiopia there is one genus with two species.

Olacaceae

The *Olacaceae* consists mostly of evergreen trees, shrubs or climbers, very often hemi-parasitic, attaching to the roots of other plants. The leaves are alternate, simple and entire and pinnately veined. The flowers are mostly rather small and arranged in axillary clusters that may be elaborated into racemes or panicles and are regular, bisexual or rarely unisexual. The 3 to 6 petals alternate with the calyx teeth and are seldom forming a long tube. The stamens are as many as and opposite with the petals or 2 to 5 times as many.

The *Olacaceae* is a small family with 25 to 30 genera and 250 species which are widespread in tropical and subtropical regions. In Ethiopia the family is represented by 1 genus which has 2 species, one of these with 2 varieties.

Oleaceae

The *Oleaceae* is composed of trees, shrubs or woody climbers. The leaves of members of this family are oppositely arranged (rarely alternate, as in *Jasminum stans)*, and simple or compound. The flowers have only 2 stamens and the sepals and petals, which are all similar to each other and united to form a tube, are often arranged in multiples of 2, 4, 6 or 8.

The *Oleaceae* is a small family with 30 genera and 600 species which are nearly cosmopolitan widespread, especially in Asia and Malaysia. In Ethiopia they are represented by 4 genera.

Several species are cultivated as ornamentals and for perfumery, like *Jasminum officinale* or *J. sambac*. *Olea europea* is cultivated throughout the Mediterranean countries for its edible fruit and oil.

Several species are known world-wide as important honey sources, like the African wild olive *Olea europaea subsp. cuspidata* (widely known as O. africana) and the tropical Asian *Ligustrum walkeri* and the European *L. vulgare*.

Oliniaceae

The family is composed of species of small trees or shrubs which have quadrangular twigs and opposite and simple leaves which are stiff and entire. The flowers are bisexual and regular and borne in cymes. The 4 or 5 sepals are united below to form a small tube and they are petal-like and pinkish-white in colour. The very small petals are 4 to 5 and are borne on the rim of the calyx-tube. The 4 or 5 stamens are opposite the sepals and alternate with the petals.

The family *Oliniaceae* consists of the single genus *Olinia* with 8 species ranging from Ethiopia to South Africa and one is on the Island of St. Helena.

Onagraceae

The family consists of herbs and shrubs or even trees which have simple alternate, opposite or whorled leaves. The flowers are most often four-parted, with 4 sepals, and sometimes united to form a tube, arranged solitary in leaf axils, or naked spikes, racemes or panicles.

The *Onagraceae* is a small family with 675 species in 17 genera which are widespread in temperate and subtropical regions, especially in the New World. In Ethiopia the family is represented by 2 indigenous genera *Ludwigia* and *Epilobium*.

Several species of this family are cultivated as ornamentals in many parts of the world.

About half of the species are self-pollinated, while the others are pollinated by various insects including honeybees. Some taxa are known world-wide as important honey sources, like the cosmopolitan ROSEBAY WILLOW-HERB, *Epilobium*

angustifolium, the Asian *Fuchsia excorticata* and *the* tropical American *Ludwigia nervosa*.

Oxalidaceae

The *Oxalidaceae* is composed of herbs or sometimes subshrubs or shrubs, rarely small trees which have compound leaves that fold up at night. The flowers have 5 separate petals and the stamens are united at the base.

The *Oxalidaceae* consists of 7 genera and about 900 species which are widespread throughout tropical and subtropical regions with some species occurring in temperate region. In Ethiopia 3 genera have been reported.

Several species of *Oxalis* are common garden weeds in temperate regions. Other species are cultivated for their edible tubers, for example, *Oxalis tuberosa* in South America, or *Averrhoa bilimbi* and *A. carambola* for their rather acid fruits, mainly in Asia.

Papaveraceae

Members of this family are herbs which can be easily identified by their white or yellowish sap. The leaves are entire or more often lobed or dissected, alternate or almost whorled. The flowers are solitary or less often in cymes or umbels, generally rather large and perfect. The petals are usually twice as many as the 2 or 3 or 4 sepals which are falling off early.

The family consists of 25 genera and 200 species which are distributed in temperate and tropical Northern Hemisphere. They are not native in eastern Africa but some species have become widely established or are planted as ornamentals.

The family provides a number of showy garden ornamentals especially, *Eschscholzia* and *Papaver*. The widely cultivated *Papaver somniferum* is the species with the greatest economic importance as the source of opium.

The poppies are insect-pollinated plants but do not have nectaries except few taxa, like *Corydalis spp.* in Europe. The stamens supply abundant amounts of fine and protein-rich pollen which is considered to be most valuable for honeybees.

Passifloraceae

The family is composed of herbaceous or woody climbers. Members of the family *Passifloraceae* have a climbing habit, usually with tendrils arising from the leaf axils. The leaves are alternate, entire or often palmately lobed, seldom compound and very often with extra-floral nectaries on the leaf stalk. The bisexual or less often unisexual flowers are arranged in cymes, or seldom solitary. The petals are as many as the sepals.

The *Passifloraceae* consists of 16 genera and 650 species which are widespread throughout the tropics and extending into the subtropics, but best-developed in tropical America and Africa. In Ethiopia there are 3 genera: *Adenia, Carania* and *Passiflora.*

Almost all of the 500 species of the genus *Passiflora* are native to South America. Many are nowadays widely cultivated as ornamentals due to the fantastic shape and striking colouring of their flowers and their delicious fruits.

Pedaliaceae

The *Pedaliaceae* consists of herbs, occasionally shrubs or rarely aquatic, that can be distinguished by the presence of mucilage-glands that become slimy when wet, simple opposite, entire to toothed leaves and solitary flowers borne in leaf axils or terminally arranged in racemes, often with 1 or 2 characteristic extrafloral nectaries. The 4 to 5 sepals are often united to form a lobed calyx.

The *Pedaliaceae* is a very small family with 20 genera and 80 species. Members of this are found in tropical regions, with the greatest number in Africa with only a few species in temperate climates. In Ethiopian there are 6 genera.

Several species are cultivated, like *Proboscidea* or *Martynia* as well as the economically important *Sesamum indicum* for its aromatic oil seeds.

S. indicum is also known world-wide as an important honey plant.

Phytolaccaceae

The *Phytolaccaceae* is composed of herbs, shrubs and climbers or even small trees, and can easily be identified by their alternate simple and entire leaves and flowers with almost separate pistils and without petals.

The *Phytolaccaceae* is a small family with 125 species in 18 genera which are distributed in tropical and subtropical regions, especially in warm North and Central America. In Ethiopia it is represented by the genus *Phytolacca.*

A few members of the family are economically important, which include the American *Phytolacca americana* which provides the red pigment "Betanin". The Ethiopian species *Phytolacca dodecandra* contains a molluscicide which is toxic against snails that are the intermediate host for schistosomiasis (Bilharzia).

Pittosporaceae

The family is composed of trees, shrubs or sometimes woody climbers. It can be recognized by the simple alternate leaves and flowers with 5 sepals, petals and stamens. The seeds are often covered by a colourful resin.

This small family consists of 9 genera and 200 species which are found in the tropical and warm temperate Old World and especially in Australia. In Ethiopia this family is represented by one genus *Pittosporum*.

Few species of this family are cultivated for lumber or as ornamentals like the Australian LAUREL *(Pittosporum tobira)*.

Pittosporum species are attractive to honeybees which gather good quantities of nectar and some amounts of pollen.

Plantaginaceae

Members of the family are herbs (in Ethiopia) and sometimes shrubs. They have their leaves in basal rosettes or less often opposite or alternate, simple or lobed with parallel or less often palmate venation. The flowers are arranged in spikes or are solitary, small and wind-pollinated.

The *Plantaginaceae* is a small cosmopolitan family with 254 species in 3 genera and found throughout the world. They are represented in Ethiopia by the genus *Plantago*.

Plantago spp. are very valuable and rich pollen sources for honeybees and other insects. A single *Plantago* flower supplies about 1 mg of the light-yellow protein-rich pollen which is more valuable for bees compared with pollen from *Poaceae*. It is a very important pollen source during rains because the pollen-sacs remain closed to be protected from moisture.

Poaceae

The family is composed of herbs with stems (called culms) which are often hollow between the nodes and usually round in cross-section. The nodes are usually thickened and solid within. The leaves are alternate or basal, borne in 2 usually opposing ranks, simple and entire, often narrow with parallel venation. The leaf-base is clasping and enclosing the stem in a usually open sheath. The very small flowers are bisexual or sometimes unisexual and are lacking petals and are usually enclosed in a series of tiny bracts and called spikelet. The spikelet is the basic unit of the inflorescence of members of the *Poaceae*.

The *Poaceae* is one of the largest families of flowering plants with 500 genera and 8000 species. They are cosmopolitan and widespread, especially in tropical and north temperate semi-arid regions with seasonal rainfall. They are especially important in eastern Africa where a large portion of the vegetation is savanna and grassland.

The grasses are plants of greatest importance to man. They are used for the nourishment of the various domestic animals, which produce animal protein like meat, milk and eggs and which serve for draught and transport and which provide also clothes from wool and leather.

They provide staple foods for the human society. They include grain-crops such as millet species like *Eragrostis tef, finger millet, Barley,*

Wheat, Maize, Sorghum and others. In addition to the all-important grain crops, grasses provide sugar cane and bamboo.

In the south southern Ethiopia, for example in Sidamo, *Arundinaria alpina* is used for fences and house-construction. Sometimes houses are entirely made of this bamboo. The WASHINT, the Ethiopian flute sometimes played by shepherd-boys but also used in more sophisticated orchestras, is made from *Arundo donax.*

All the grasses are wind-pollinated and many are frequently visited by honeybees for pollen supply and are therefore important for brood rearing and bee colony development. The protein value of many *Poaceae* pollen is high especially that of maize. In addition some grasses will provide honey dew produced by aphids.

Polygalaceae

The family is composed of herbs and shrubs or woody vines or, rarely, small trees which usually have simple and entire alternate leaves, rarely opposite or whorled. The usually irregular flowers are arranged in terminal, axillary spikes, racemes, or panicles. The 8 or 10 stamens are united to form a split tube which resembles almost the flowers of the *Papilionoideae.*

The *Polygalaceae* is a family with 12 to 18 genera and 800 to 1000 species which are nearly cosmopolitan in distribution. In Ethiopia they are represented by 2 genera and 21 species.

The small tree *Securidaca longepedunculata* is very common in drier lowland areas and is the most important honey plant representing this family.

Polygonaceae

Members of this family are herbs, or shrubs, sometimes climbing, or even fairly large trees. They have simple and alternate leaves which are provided with stipules which form a thin sheath at the base that surrounds the stem. The flowers are rather small, but they sometimes form quite large, conspicuous inflorescences, each with 3 petals and 3-6 sepals, the outermost often persisting and becoming attached to the fruit.

The *Polygonaceae* is a large cosmopolitan family with about 1050 species in 50 genera which are largely concentrated to temperate areas of the northern Hemisphere and tropical and subtropical mountains. In Ethiopia they are represented by 5 genera.

Several species are cultivated as vegetables or as pseodocereals like buckwheat *Fagopyrum spp.*

Some species of this family are known world-wide as important honey sources like *Fagopyrum esculentum, Coccoloba belizensis, C. uvifera, Gymnopodium antigonoides* and *Triplaris surinamensis.*

Pontederiaceae

The family is composed of aquatic or semi-aquatic herbs which are free-floating or rooted to the soil beneath the water surface and are perennials or seldom annuals The leaves are alternate, opposite or whorled, usually in 2 opposite ranks, simple and entire and often cordate at the base. The venation is pinnate, palmate or subparallel and curved. The leaves are floating or more often growing upright out of the water. The flowers are arranged in terminal racemes or spikes or panicles, or solitary and terminal. They are bisexual and usually somewhat irregular, the inflorescence is subtended by a spathe-like bract. Sepals and petals are 6, equal in size and coloured or somewhat different, free or united and the stamens are 6, 3 or rarely 1.

The *Pontederiaceae* consists of 9 genera and 30 species which are widespread in tropical and subtropical regions with a few species extending into the north temperate zones. In Ethiopia they are represented by 3 genera, *Monochoria, Eichhornia* and *Heteranthera.* Except the *Heteranthera,* the *Pontederiaceae* have nectaries developed in the sepals and are often visited by honeybees.

Portulaccaceae

Members of this family are herbs or small shrubs which can be recognized by their usually fleshy leaves, their flowers with only 2 sepals and 4-6 petals. The leaves are alternate or opposite or less often whorled, simple and usually entire.

The *Portulacaceae* is a cosmopolitan family with 20 genera and 500 species which are widespread, especially in western North America and the Andes. The family is represented in Ethiopia by *Portulaca. Talinum, Calyptrotheca* and *Anacampseros.*

Few species are widely cultivated as ornamentals in gardens or as pot-herbs like *Portulacca grandiflora* or *P. oleracea.*

Primulaceae

The family is composed of herbs which often have all the leaves in rosette, borne at the ground level. The leaves are simple, often marked with small gland dots and the flowers have usually 5 petals, all similar to each other and joined together with a single stamen attached along the centre-line of each petal.

The *Primulaceae* is a family with 30 genera and 1000 species which are mostly found in temperate and cold Northern Hemisphere and on tropical mountains. In Ethiopia 7 genera are represented.

Several species, especially of the genera *Primula* and *Cyclamen* are world-wide cultivated as ornamentals in rock-gardens or as pot-plants. *Primula* causes allergic reactions to some people and is a frequent cause of dermatitis.

Proteaceae

The *Proteaceae* is a family composed of trees and shrubs with alternate leaves, rarely opposite or whorled, simple and entire or deeply pinnately divided. The flowers are solitary or paired, borne in racemes, umbels or cone-like inflorescences. They are pollinated by insects, birds or mice.

The *Proteaceae* is a family with 75 genera and 1000 species which are widespread in tropical and subtropical regions, especially in warmer Southern Hemisphere. In Ethiopia only two genera are indigenous *Faurea* and *Protea.*

The widely cultivated SILKY OAK *Grevillea robusta* is introduced from Australia.

MACADAMIA NUTS *(Macadamia integrifolia* and *M. tetraphylla)* have become an important economic value and are cultivated in southern and eastern Africa.

Several members of *Proteaceae* are known as important honey sources, like some of the Australian *Grevillea* spp., the PARROT BUSH *Dryandra sessilis* and *Knightia excelsa* from temperate Oceania as well as the RED HONEYSUCKLE *Banksia serrata*. *Faurea saligna* and *Faurea speciosa* are the most important species native to Africa known as important bee trees.

Punicaceae

Members of this family are shrubs or small trees which have simple and oppositely arranged or clustered leaves. The flowers are bisexual and regular, large and showy and usually red and the many stamens are borne on the calyx tube, the petals are crumpled in buds.

The *Punicaceae* is a very small family with 1 genus and 2 species. Members of the family are distributed from the Balkans to northern India and one species is found on the Island of Socotra. In Ethiopia they are represented by the widely cultivated *Punica granatum.*

Ranunculaceae

Members of this family are herbs or woody climbers which have leaves often deeply divided or compound, rarely only shallowly lobed. The sepals are 3 to many and are often petal-like, not much different from the true petals. The petals also are variable in number, 3 to many and in some species the petals are absent. The stamens are very numerous and they are arranged spirally.

The *Ranunculaceae* is a medium-large family with 50 genera and 2000 species which are distributed throughout the world with centres in temperate and cold regions of the Northern and Southern Hemispheres. In Ethiopia 7 genera and 20 species represent the family.

The *Ranunculaceae* includes many species of horticultural and medicinal importance. All of the genera found in Ethiopia also contain species found elsewhere which have been developed as horticultural plants and some of which can be found in gardens in Addis Ababa.

In general, all members of the *Ranunculaceae* are prolific pollen suppliers. Some species do not have nectaries and others are wind pollinated. But several members of the family are important for early development of bee colonies, flowering profusely during rains and many are flowering during times where other bee feed are scarce.

Resedaceae

The family *Resedaceae* is composed of herbs or sometimes shrubs which have alternate or closely grouped leaves, which are simple and entire to deeply lobed. The flowers are usually bisexual and irregular and arranged in racemes or spikes. The sepals are usually 6, seldom 4 or 8 and the 4 to 8, most often 6 petals are white to yellow.

The family consists of 6 genera and 70 species which are widespread in Northern Hemisphere, mostly in the old World, especially in Mediterranean countries. In Ethiopia 3 genera have been reported.

Members of the *Resedaceae* are attractive to bees and the cultivated garden ornamental *Reseda odorata* is a well known honey plant. In Ethiopia mainly *Caylusea abyssinica* is an important supplier of nectar and pollen, especially during times when other bee feed is scarce.

Rhamnaceae

Members of this family are trees, shrubs or climbers, or rarely even herbs. They have simple unlobed leaves, small and usually greenish flowers with 4-5 sepals and 4-5 petals. The fruits are usually berries or drupes.

The *Rhamnaceae* is a cosmopolitan family with 900 species in 55 genera which are widespread, especially in tropical and subtropical regions. In Ethiopian flora 8 genera represent the family.

This family provides the beekeepers world-wide with many valuable honey sources like the North American *Berchemia scandens,* the Central American *Gouania lupuloides* and *Gouania polygama,* the Mediterranean *Paliurus spina-christi,* the American *Rhamnidium glabrum* and the widespread tropical *Ziziphus jujuba, Ziziphus mauritiana, Ziziphus nummularia, Ziziphus oxyphylla* and *Ziziphus spina-christi.*

Rosaceae

The family consists of trees, shrubs, herbs and sometimes climbers which can be identified by the alternate stipulate leaves, which are compound in most Ethiopian species and flowers with a fusion of sepals, petals and usually many stamens being mounted on a raised disc.

The *Rosaceae* is a large family with 100 genera and 3000 species which are widespread throughout the world, especially in the temperate and subtropical Northern Hemisphere.

They include many cultivated crops like STRAWBERRY *(Fragaria),* RASPBERRY *(Rubus)* and PEACH *(Prunus sp.).* Many other genera are also cultivated for their tasty fruits or as ornamentals.

Beside some wind-pollinated species like those *Sanguisorba,* several genera do not produce nectar, for example, *Rosa* and *Potentilla.* But several genera are very potential nectar suppliers for honeybees, especially fruit trees and fruit bearing shrubs.

World-wide famous honey sources are *Malus sylvestris,* nowadays also cultivated in Ethiopia, and *Prunus spp.* and *Rubus spp.*

In Ethiopia *Hagenia abssynica* is the most important honey and pollen source in higher altitudes. In addition many different *Rubus spp.* supply abundant pollen and nectar, especially in forest clearings and in some areas *Prunus africana* is reported to be a valuable source for pollen and nectar.

Rubiaceae

The family *Rubiaceae* includes herbs, shrubs, trees and climbers. The leaves are always simple and usually entire and opposite, or whorled. The flowers are bisexual and regular and have 4 or 5 petals, rarely more, joined together to form a tube and mounted on the top of the ovary. They are usually in cymes but sometimes in heads. The 4 or 5 (to 12) stamens are often very short and attached to the tube formed by petals.

The *Rubiaceae* is a large family with 450 genera and 6500 species which are widespread, especially in tropical and subtropical regions. Members of the *Rubiaceae* are one of the most important families of tropical woody plants and it is the family to which the coffee tree belongs. Coffee is thought to have originated in Kefa or Illubabor province, and is found growing wild in the forests of south-west Ethiopia.

Many species are cultivated as very important medicinal plants like *Cinchona pubescens* and other *Cinchona spp.* which yield "Quinine" the only agent against Malaria until the 1930s.

Others are cultivated for dyes and colourings like *Morinda citrifolia* and *Rubia cordifolia* or are cultivated as stimulants or for beverages like *Borojoa patinoi* and *Uncaria gambir.*

Numerous species of this family are attractive to honeybees for pollen and nectar supplies. Several species are known world-wide as important honey sources like the Caribbean *Borreria verticilata* and *Calycophyllum candidissimum,* the Asian *Canthium coromandelicum, Catunaregam spinosa* and *Wendlandia notoniana* and the now pantropical *Coffea arabica.*

Rutaceae

The family is composed of trees or shrubs, very rarely herbs which have glandular-punctate leaves that are aromatic when crushed. The leaves are alternate, less often opposite, simple, trifoliate or pinnately or palmately compound. The flowers are regular and bisexual. The plants are either male or female, not both when the flowers are unisexual the sepals and petals are 4 to 5 and free and the stamens are 3 to 10. The fruits are usually fleshy with aromatic oils in their outer parts.

The *Rutaceae* is a large family with 150 genera and 1500 species. They are nearly cosmopolitan and widespread, especially in South Africa and Australia. In Ethiopia 8 genera are have been reported, including the widely cultivated fruit trees belonging to *Citrus*.

Many species are cultivated as spices, culinary herbs, for seasoning and as condiments, as medicinal plants and for their delicious fruits as in *Casimiroa* or *Citrus* which are producing juicy fruits prized for their flavour and their high vitamin C content.

The *Rutaceae* are very attractive to bees and especially *Citrus spp.* are known as very important bee plants as well as the Asian *Phellodendron amurense.* Insect pollination is often very beneficial for fruit setting in *Citrus* and *Casimiroa* and honeybees are the most important pollinators.

Salicaceae

The family is composed of trees and shrubs which bear female and male flowers on different trees and preferably waterside habitats.

The leaves are alternate, simple and deciduous. In *Salix* the flowers are generally pollinated by insects.

The *Salicaceae* consists of about 3 or 4 genera and 500 species which are very widespread in North temperate regions and also found in Australia, Malaya Archipelago and Africa. Only one genus, *Salix* is represented by indigenous species, *S. subserrata*, in Ethiopia.

Populus spp. are pollinated by wind and are considered as pollen suppliers only. However, the *Salix spp.* are valuable pollen and nectar suppliers for honeybees. Several species are world-wide famous honey sources for example *Salix alba, Salix caprea* and *Salix nigra.*

The nectaries of both the male and female flowers supply sufficient nectar for insects and the pollen value is high.

Santalaceae

Members of this family are small trees, shrubs, or perennial herbs which are green and photosynthetic, but hemi-parasitic, attaching themselves to the roots of other plants, or seldom attached to the branches of the host. The leaves are opposite or less commonly alternate, simple, entire and well developed or sometimes reduced to mere scales. The flowers are arranged in various sorts of inflorescences, small. often greenish, perfect or unisexual and regular. They have 3 to 6 sepals, free or united at the base and the petals are absent. The stamens are 3 to 6, as many as the sepals and opposite them.

The *Santalaceae* consists of 35 genera and 400 species with a nearly cosmopolitan distribution, but most common in tropical and subtropical, often arid climates. In Ethiopia they are represented by 3 genera.

In India and Indonesia the WHITE SANDALWOOD, a semi-parasitic species, is cultivated in nurseries on suitable host plants. The SANDALWOOD *(Santalum album)* and related species has long been used for ceremonial burning rites in some Asian societies and the yellow aromatic sandal oil, distiled from sandalwood, is ceremonially used as well as for perfumery and pharmacy.

Sapindaceae

The family is composed of trees, shrubs and woody climbers which have simple, trifoliate, biternate, pinnate or bipinnate and alternate leaves. The perfect or more often unisexual flowers are arranged in terminal or axillary, mostly cymose inflorescences, seldom solitary and axillary and have 4 to 5 sepals and petals.

This family consists of 150 genera and 2000 species which are widely distributed in all tropical and subtropical regions with relatively few members extending into temperate climates. In the Ethiopian flora 19 species are found in 14 genera.

In this family several valuable and economically important species are found. *Blighia sapida* is cultivated in West Africa for its fruits, the berries *of Sapindus saponaria* are used in tropical America as a soap and *Paullinia cupuna* is an important crop in Brazil

Some species of this family are known world-wide as important honey sources and are therefore recommended for planting, like the Asian *Euphoria longan, Litchi chinensis, Nephelium lappaceum, Sapindus emarginatus, S. laurifolius, S. mukorossi and S. trifoliatus* and the tropical American *S. saponaria* and *Serjania triqueta.*

Sapotaceae

The family is composed of trees or shrubs, mostly evergreen, with a white sap. Members of this family of woody plants can be recognized by their alternate leaves which are also sometimes clustered, but always entire and simple, often stiff and leathery. The flowers are solitary or in small inflorescences borne in leaf axils, with usually united petals.

The *Sapotaceae* consists of 70 genera and 800 species which are widespread in the tropics with a relatively few species extending into temperate regions. In Ethiopia they are represented by 5 genera.

Several species are economically important for their tasty fruits, like *Chrysophyllum cainito, Manilkara zapota* and *Pouteria sapota.* Many other members this family have edible fruits, but they are only locally commercial important or are not of noteworthy commercial importance.

The Caribbean *Mimusops elengi* is known world-wide as an important honey source as well as the tropical Asian *Madhuca longifolia.* The crushed flowers of the latter species are used as supplementary feed for bees.

In Ethiopia the two famous trees species of this family: *Aningeria adolfi-friederici* and *A. altissima* are known as the most important honey trees of evergreen forest or rainforests in the south and southwest. The honey from these tree species is highly priced in Addis Ababa by the international community because of its aromatic and fruity taste.

Scrophulariaceae

The *Scrophulariaceae* includes herbs or shrubs and rarely trees. The leaves are simple, often oppositely arranged or they are rosette, coming straight from the ground. They are sometimes very small and not green in certain parasitic species. The flowers have 4 to 5 petals and are united to form a tube and have 2 or 4 stamens or 5 in the genus *Verbascum.*

The *Scrophulariaceae* is a large family with 190 genera and 4000 species which have cosmopolitan distribution and very common in temperate regions and on tropical mountains. In Ethiopia they are represented by 37 genera.

Several species are known throughout the world as important honey sources, like *Scrophularia nodosa* and *S. vernalis.* All members of the *Scrophulariaceae* are insect pollinated and several species supply significant amounts of nectar and some pollen for visiting honeybees.

Simaroubaceae

The family is composed of trees, shrubs or seldom subshrubs. Members of this family have mostly very bitter bark, wood and seeds. The leaves are alternate and pinnately compound or simple. The flowers are usually unisexual or less often bisexual and regular. They have 3 to 5 sepals (rarely 2 to 9), free or united near the base. The petals are 4 or 5 (rarely 3 to 9) and free, or they are absent. The stamens are 4 to 10, usually as many or twice as many as the petals.

The *Simaroubaceae* consists of are 150 species in 25 genera which are pantropical in distribution, with some species extending into warm-temperate regions. In Ethiopia 3 genera are present.

Solanaceae

Members of this family are herbs, shrubs, small trees or, rarely, climbers which usually have alternate leaves, which are simple or sometimes pinnate and entire or lobed. The flowers have 5 petals (rarely 4-7), fused to form a tube, and have an equal number of stamens alternating with the petals, usually all with the same length, so that the flower is readily symmetrical, like a circle or star. The fruit is often very fleshy and usually has 2 compartments, each containing many small seeds.

The *Solanaceae* consists of 2800 species in 85 genera, which are nearly cosmopolitan in distribution, especially common in South America. In Ethiopia they are represented by 84 species.

Several species of this family are cultivated as ornamentals, vegetables, spices, stimulants and as starch plants. They include the POTATO *(Solanum tuberosum)* which is the only one of the many tuber-forming species of *Solanaceae* which has world-wide importance. The family includes the *Capsicum* pepper which was introduced by the Spanish from the New World to Europe towards the end of the 15th century and the plant spread within one century over the whole world and became an important dietary ingredient for many people in the tropics. Also the TOMATO plant originated in the New World and is nowadays cultivated in almost all parts of the world.

All Ethiopian cultivated *Capsicum* are belonging to one species: *Capsicum annuum L.* The Ethiopians distinguish three kinds of *Capsicum*: KARYA (immature green fruits), BERBERE (red mature fruit) and MITMITA (the small extremely pungent fruits).

Several species of the *Solanaceae* are visited by honeybees occasionally and then for pollen only. In times where other bee feed are scarce they contribute to maintain bee colonies by providing protein, and some species provide even good amounts of nectar, like the shrub or tree *Discopodium penninervium* or the climber *Solanum benderianum*, and the tobacco plant *(Nicotiana tabacum)* which is known world-wide as an important honey source.

Sterculiaceae

The family is composed of trees, shrubs or herbs which usually have simple alternate leaves with star-shaped hairs and flowers with united stamens with their anthers containing small smooth pollen which are not surrounded with fibres or powder.

The *Sterculiaceae* is a family with 65 genera and 1000 species which are widespread in tropical and subtropical regions. In Ethiopia they are represented by 8 genera.

Some species have an important economic value, like the South American *Theobroma cacao* for cocoa production and the rain-forest genus *Cola*, which is now widely cultivated for the stimulant in its seeds, which is the basis for a world-wide soft drink. Others have a big medicinal value, like *Sterculia urens* for "karaya" production.

Several species of this family are valuable bee trees, for example, the ornamental Australian Flame, *Brachychiton acerifolium*, is a rich pollen supplier.

The African *Dombeya spp.* are very valuable honey plants, especially *Dombeya rotundifolia*. In Ethiopia *Dombeya torrida* is known as a major honey source of the evergreen woodlands in the southwest.

Tiliaceae

Members of this family are herbs, shrubs or trees which often have star-shaped or branched hairs. The leaves are simple and alternate or rarely opposite, usually with palmate venation. They are toothed, lobed or less often entire. The flowers are borne in cymes that are often leaf-opposed. The flowers have usually 5 sepals and petals and many stamens which are often borne on a disc or short stalk.

The *Tiliaceae* is a small family with 50 genera and 450 species which are widespread in tropical and subtropical regions, with few species in northern hemisphere. In Ethiopia they are represented by 5 genera.

Many species are known world-wide as important honey sources, like the *Tilia spp.* which are very widespread in the northern hemisphere.

In Ethiopia *Sparmannia spp.* and *Triumfetta spp.* as well as several different *Grewia spp.* are important bee plants

Tropaeolaceae

A family of herbs whose members are annual, sometimes perennial dwarf or climbing herbs and more or less succulent and often scandent. The leaves are alternate (or the lower opposite), palmately veined, peltate or palmately lobed or cleft. The flowers are solitary or axillary, often on long stalks and showy, with 5 sepals which are prolonged backwards into a nectariferous spur and 5 distinct petals and 8 stamens in cycles of 4.

The *Tropaeolaceae* is a very small family with 93 species in 3 genera which are confined to Central and South America. Members of this family are not native to Africa, but are often planted as garden ornamentals.

The cultivated *Tropaeolum majus* is the gardeners' nasturtium.

Urticaceae

The family is composed of herbs or occasionally shrubs or rarely small, soft-wooded trees or very rarely lianas which are often provided with specialized stinging hairs. They are recognized by the very small flowers in axillary cymose inflorescences. The flowers are unsisexual and without petals, and the stamens are opposite the sepals.

The *Urticaceae* is a family with 50 genera and 1000 species which are widely distributed in tropical and subtropical regions. Relatively few species are growing in the cooler parts of the world. In Ethiopia they are represented by 12 genera.

Only few species are grown as ornamentals and one *Boehmeria nivea*, the China grass, is cultivated for fibre.

Verbenaceae

Members of the *Verbenaceae* are herbs, shrubs, lianas and trees that can be separated from other families by their square stems, opposite and usually simple leaves which contain often aromatic oils. They are closely related to the *Labiatae* family but differ in that the flowers are not deeply lobed and are arranged in cymes.

This medium sized family is composed of 100 genera and 2600 species with a pantropical distribution. Only a limited number of species, *(e.g. Verbena officinalis)* are found in temperate regions. In Ethiopia they are represented by 24 genera.

The TEAK, *Tectona grandis* is well known for its hard and valuable wood and it is widely cultivated.

Members of the family *Verbenaceae* are attractive for honeybees. *Vitex agnus-castus* of Mediterranean regions, *Aloysia spp.* and *Vitex cymosa* in tropical South America, and *Lippia spp.* in subtropical North America are reported to be important for beekeeping. The Asian *Gmelina arborea* is recommended for planting to increase honey production.

In Ethiopia members of *Verbenaceae* are important bee plants, providing stimulating nectar and pollen supplies, which result in an increase in brood-rearing and colony strengthening. Some of them like *Clerodendron spp.* are very useful bee plants, mainly in drier parts of the country, for example in burnt savanna.

Vitaceae

The family is composed of climbers or rarely succulent-stemmed shrubs which are recognized by their usually climbing habit and leaf-opposed tendrils, leaf-opposed inflorescences, stamens opposite the petals and by the fleshy fruits.

The *Vitaceae* consists of 12 genera and 900 species which are widely distributed in all tropical, subtropical and warm temperate regions. In Ethiopia they are represented by 6 genera and 41 species.

Some species are cultivated in temperate regions as ornamentals and *Vitis vinifera* is the most important cultivated species of this family, cultivated in most countries of the world. Several species are important honey sources, like the North American *Ampelopsis arborea* and *Parthenocissus quinquefolia*.

In Ethiopia *V. vinifera* is widely cultivated in homegardens and vineyards and very often bees are wrongly accused to spoil the grapes. But honeybees are only sucking the juice of fruits which were damaged by wasps and other insects or simply burst open. Several other species of this family are known as important nectar and pollen suppliers, like *Cyphostemma spp.* and *Rhoicissus spp.*

Zygophyllaceae

The family *Zygophyllaceae* consists of herbs and shrubs and less commonly even small trees. The leaves are usually opposite and often pinnately compound and stipules are present or represented by spines. The flowers are solitary with free petals.

The *Zygophyllaceae* is a small family with 30 genera and 250 species which are widespread in arid tropical and subtropical areas, sometimes in saline habitats. In Ethiopia it is represented by the genera *Fagonia, Zygophyllum, Kelleronia, Nitraria* and *Tribulus.*

Several species have some economic value like the American LIGNUM VITAE *(Guaiacum officinale)*, a tree with a very strong valuable wood and also cultivated for its resins In the arid zones in Asia and the Mediterranean region *Peganum harmala* is cultivated as a source of dye called TURKEY RED.

The tropical South American tree *Guaiacum officinale* is reported as an important source for nectar.

GLOSSARY OF SOME BOTANICAL TERMS AND ETHIOPIC NAMES

abortion - expulsion within the first three months of pregnancy.

acuminate - with a tip that becomes gradually narrower to a cylindrical point.

AJIL - an unspecified disease.

AKOSHITA - an unspecified disease.

anthelmintic - destroys or causes expulsion of worms.

apex - the tip or end-point of a surface.

areole - a space marked out on a surface.

axil - the upper angle made between a leaf attachment and a stem.

axillary - in or arising from an axil.

bi - a prefix meaning "two" or "twice".

bilharzia - a disease caused by trematode worms for which the intermediate host is a fresh water snail, also called Schistosomiasis.

bipinnate - twice pinnate, when the first divisions of a leaf are themselves pinnate.

BULLA - common foodstuff in southwestern parts made from *Enset ventricosum*.

carmative - curing flatulence.

carpel - the basic unit of the female part of the flower

chancer - a diseased growth.

cordate - when the base of the leaf is deeply notched.

coriaceous - leathery.

corymb - a panicle-like inflorescence in which the branches or flower-stalks start from different places on the stem but all the flower are born at about the same level.

crenate - the margin notched with rounded or broad and blunt teeth or projections.

cuneate - wedge-shaped, as when the base of the blade tapers gradually to the top of the petiole.

cyme - an inflorescence in which the central axis is terminated by a flower which opens first, this flower is subtended by two opposite branches each of which ends in a flower, these open next; this branching-pattern may be repeated many times.

cymose - cyme-like.

decumbent - lying on the ground but with the ends growing upwards.

dentate - with a toothed margin, the teeth pointing outwards, not forward.

dermatitis - any inflammation of skin.

dioecious - plants with unisexual flowers in which the male and female flowers are not found on the same plants.

dysentery - inflammation of the large intestine accompanied by diarrhoea.

elephantiasis - a persistent enlargement of the tissue immediately beneath the skin caused by worms or deposits of silica; the legs and arms becomes enormous and in the male, the scrotum may enlarge to the size of a papaya.

endemic - only found in the specified area - not found elsewhere.

epiphyte - a plant which grows on other plants for support and does not have its roots in the ground but is not a parasite.

fascicle - a close cluster of structures arising from about the same point but lacking a distinctive arrangement of parts.

fibrifuge - to reduce fever.

funicle - the stalk of the ovule which attaches it to the placenta.

gamete - the sex cell or nucleus which combines with another gamete to form the fertilized egg or zygote.

glaberescent - nearly hairless.

glabrous - without hairs.

globose - a spherical structure.

hemi - a prefix meaning "half" or "partly".

hilum - a scar left on the seed where it was attached to the funicle or placenta; the place where this scar is formed.

hispid - with a covering of stiff erect hairs.

HOT SIRAY - an unspecified disease.

hyperpigmentation - loss of pigment from the skin.

inflorescence - the flowering portion of a plant.

INJERA - a large pancake made from fermented dough with the flour from *Eragrostis tef* and/or other cereals.

juvenile - the youthful or early stage of growth.

KOCHO - common foodstuff in south-western parts, made from *Ensete ventricosum*.

lamina - the flat and broad part of a leaf, a sepal or petal.

lanceolate - with the shape of the end of a lance or spear.

leishmaniasis - a disease transmitted by sandflies.

lenticles - a channel filled with loosely packed cork cells allowing the diffusing of gases in and out of stems and sometimes also roots - also called breathing pores.

LIB DEKAM - any disorder associated with or emanating from the heart.

lobed - having lobes.

lymphadenopathy - a disease of lymph nodes.

MASESHA - oily substance used to polish the METAD.

METAD - a flat clay plate 50 cm or more in diameter which is used to bake INJERA.

midrib - the principal or central vein or rib of a leaf or other organ.

MISHIRO - an unspecified disease.

monocarpic - dying after the production of flowers and fruit.

nectar - a sugary liquid produced by flowers or other plant parts, the liquid on which insects and birds that visit the flower feed.

nectariferous - producing nectar.

nectary - a glandular structure which secrets a sugary liquid, the nectar; either associated with a flower (floral nectary) or elsewhere on the plant (extrafloral nectary).

NEKERSA - a growth often thought of as cancer; tuberculosis is also considered as NEKERSA.

node - the place on a stem where a leaf or bud is formed; a thickened area on a stem-like organ where other parts are attached.

ob - a prefix meaning "opposite", "inverse", or "against".

oblanceolate - with the shape of the end of a lance or spear but with the arrow end towards the base.

oblique - a leaf-base in which the two sides are unequal.

oblong - a plane shape longer than broad with nearly parallel sides, almost rectangular in outline but with rounded ends and with the length two or three times the width.

obovate - a plane shape with an egg-shaped outline but with the broadest part near the apex and the narrow part near the base.

orbicular - a flat structure with an almost circular outline.

ovate - a flat structure which is egg--shaped in outline with the broadest part near the base and the narrow part near the apex.

palmate - with three or more parts attached to a single point and radiating outward, as the finger of an open hand radiating outward from the palm of the hand.

panaceae - universal remedy.

panicle - an inflorescence with an indeterminate axis and many side branches each of which bears two or more flowers.

paniculate - panicle-like.

papillate - covered with many minute rounded gland-like structures or papillae.

parasite - a plant (animal) that lives upon another and takes nourishment from it.

pedicle - the stalk of a single flower within an inflorescence or group of flowers.

peduncle - the stalk that bears an inflorescence consisting of two or more flowers.

peltate - with the stalk attached near the centre of a more or less rounded shape and not at the edge.

perianth - the outer sterile whorls or envelopes of a flower, made up of identical perianth segments.

petiole - the stalk of a leaf on which the blade is borne.

pinna - the primary division of a pinnate leaf which can be a leaflet in simple pinnate leaves, or can be divided again into pinnules in a bipinnate leaf.

pinnate - when a compound leaf has its leaflets along an extension of the leaf-stalk or when leaflets are borne on divisions or branches of the axis of a compound leaf.

pinnatipartite - with the leaf divided almost to the midrib to the midvein or centre and forming pinnate lobes.

pinnatisect - with the leaf divided to the midrib or centre and forming pinnate lobes.

pollen - the powder-like grains produced in the anthers that will produce the male gametes necessary in fertilization.

pseudostem - false stem.

pubescent - with the covering of soft hairs.

rabies - a virus disease caused by the bite of infected animals mainly carried by dogs. It is fatal for man unless treated immediately after the dog bite.

RAS ANKER - an unspecific disease.

rhachis - the axis of a compound leaf; the axis of an inflorescence.

rhizome - a root-like stem on or beneath the ground with roots growing downwards and leaves and shoots upwards.

ringworm - the skin infection which causes red, itching rings, produced by certain fungi.

runcinate - a margin in which the lobes or teeth point backwards towards the base.

scabrid - rough or tough to feel, usually caused by the presence of very short stiff hairs which point backwards to the line of growth.

scandent - a general term for climbing.

scorpioid - a cymose inflorescence curved to one side and coiled like the tail on a scorpion.

serrulate - with teeth like that of a saw, the teeth more or less regular and pointing forward.

sessile - without a stalk.

SHINT MAT - any disorder associated with the urinary tract, especially the failure to urinate.

SILJO - a fasting food made from broad beans, mustard seed and other ingredients.

sinuate - when the margin is uneven or wavy by turning inwards or outwards but not deeply enough to be lobed.

spinescent - ending in a spine or in a very sharp hard point, or provided with spine-like teeth.

stipules - scale-like or bract-like appendages, usually found in pairs, at the base of the petiole.

stoloniferous - bearing branches which grow over the ground (runners) which produce adventitious roots, mainly at the nodes.

sub- - a prefix meaning "slightly", "somewhat", "almost" or "below".

tapeworm - long, flat, segmented worms that rare parasites in the intestines of man and animal.

TEJ - Ethiopian local beverage mainly made from honey, also called honeybeer or honeywine.

TELA - Ethiopian local beverage mainly made from barley.

tepal - used for the parts of the perianth where the sepals and petals cannot be readily distinguished.

ternate - arranged in a whorl or cluster of three.

tomentose - covered with soft, more or less appressed, hairs that are not straight; woolly.

trifoliate - with three leaflets.

ulcer - an excavated sore.

umbel - an inflorescence in which the pedicels of the flowers all arise from one point and the flowers are borne at one level.

uni - a prefix meaning "one" or "single".

vermifuge - expels intestinal worms.

BIBLIOGRAPHY

Addis Ababa University: "Proceedings on Man and his Biosphere" Addis Ababa 1988 (mimeographed).

Agnew, A.D.Q.: "Upland Kenya Wild Flowers", A Flora of the Ferns and Herbaceous Flowering Plants of Upland Kenya. Oxford University Press, 1974.

Aichele, Dietmar: "Was blüht denn da", Wildwachsende Blütenpflanzen Mitteleuropas. Kosmos Naturführer, Stuttgart, 1991

Anderson, R.H., Buys, B. and Johannsmeier, M.F.: "Beekeeping in South Africa". Department of Agricultural Technical Services, Pretoria, 1983.

Andrews, Jean: "Peppers - The Domesticated Capsicums" University of Texas Press, Austin, USA.

Azene Bekele-Tesemma: "Useful Trees and Shrubs for Ethiopia", Identification, Propagation and Management for Agricultural and Pastoral Communities. Handbook No 5, Regional Soil Conservation Unit/SIDA, RSCU, Nairobi, 1993.

Bärtels, Andreas: "Farbatlas Tropenpflanzen". Zier- und Nutzpflanzen, 2. verbesserte Auflage, Eugen Ulmer Verlag, Stuttgart, 1990.

Blundell, Michael: "Wild Flowers of East Africa" Collins Guide. Collins Sons & Co. Ltd., London 1987.

Börie, Svensson: "Bees and Trees". Swedish University of Agricultural Sciences, Uppsala 1991.

Breitenbach, Friederich von: "The Indigenous Trees of Ethiopia". Ethiopian Forestry Association, Addis Ababa, 1963.

Burger, W. C.: "Families of Flowering Plants in Ethiopia". College of Agriculture, Haile Selassie I. University, Dire Dawa, Ethiopia.

Burkill, H.M.: "The useful plants of west tropical Africa". Royal Botanic Gardens, Kew, 1985.

CFSCDD: "Soil Conservation in Ethiopia". MoA, Addis Ababa, 1986.

Clauss, Bernhard: "Bees and Beekeeping in the North Western Province of Zambia". Report on Beekeeping Survey, Forest Dept. - IRPD, Zambia, 1992.

Clauss, Bernhard and Renate: "Zambian Beekeeping Handbook". Beekeeping Division of the Forest Department, Zambia, 1991.

Clemson, Alan: "Honey and Pollen Flora". Department of Agriculture New South Wales, Inkata Press Melbourne, Australia, 1985.

Crane, E., Walker, P., & Day, Rosemary: "Directory of Important World Honey Sources". IBRA, London, 1984.

Crane, E., Walker, P.: "Pollination Directory for World Crops". IBRA, London, 1984.

Cronquist, Arthur: "An Integrated System of Classification of Flowering Plants". The New York Botanical Garden, Columbia University Press, New York, 1981

Cufodontis, Georg: "Enumeratio Plantarum Aethiopiae Spermatophyta". Fac-Simile 1974, 1 & 2, Jardin Botanique National De Belgique, 1953 - 1972.

Dale, and Greenway, P.: "Kenya Trees & Shrubs". Published by authority of the Government of the Colony and Protectorate of Kenya, Buchanan's Kenya Estates Limited, London 1961.

Drake, Ellen: "Simyen - the roof of Africa". Ethiopian Tourist Organization, Addis Ababa, 1977.

Dutta, A.C.: "Botany for Degree Students". Oxford University Press, Calcutta 1979.

Edwards, Sue & Zemede Asfaw (eds.): "Plants Used in African Traditional Medicine as Practiced in Ethiopia and Uganda. Botany 2000: East and Central Africa". NAPRECA Monograph Series No.5. Published by NAPRECA, Addis Ababa University, Addis Ababa, 1992.

Edwards, Sue & Zemede Asfaw (eds.): "The status of Some Plant Resources in Parts of Tropical Africa. Botany 2000: East and Central Africa. NAPRECA Monograph Series No.2. Published by NAPRECA, Addis Abeba University, Addis Abeba, 1992

Edwards, Sue: "Some Wild Flowering Plants of Ethiopia". Addis Ababa University Press, 1976.

Encke, Buchheim, & Seybold, : "Zander - Handwörterbuch der Pflanzennamen". Stuttgart: Ulmer Verlag, 1984.

Ensermu Kelbessa: "Justicia Sect. Ansellia (Acanthaceae)". Acta Universitatis Upsaliensis, Vol.: XXIX:2, Uppsala, 1990.

FAO: "A Weed Identification Guide for Ethiopia". FAO-TCP/ETH 4532, Rome 1989.

FAO: "Eucalypts for planting". FAO, Rome, 1981.

FAO: "Tropical and Sub-Tropical Apiculture". Agricultural Services Bulletin 68, Rome, 1986.

FAO: "Tropical forage legumes" second edition, by P.J. Skerman, D.G. Cameron, & F. Riveros, Rome, 1988.

Fichtl, Reinhard: "Bienenhaltung und Ressourcenschutz" in "Wüstenwind und Tropenregen". Dietrich Reimer Verlag, Berlin 1993.

Fichtl, Reinhard: "Chikka Hive - A Beekeeping Handbook". DED, Addis Ababa, 1994.

Fischer, E., & Hinkel, H.: "Natur Ruandas". Einführung in die Flora und Fauna Ruandas. Ministerium des Innern und für Sport, Rheinland-Pfalz, Schillerplatz 3-5, 6500 Mainz, Germany, 1992.

Free, John B.: "Insect Pollination of Crops". Academic Press London and New York, Harcourt Brace Jovanovich, Publishers, London 1993.

Fries, Ib: "Forests & Forest Trees of Northeast Tropical Africa" Their Natural Habitats and Distribution Patterns in Ethiopia, Djibouti and Somalia. Royal Botanic Gardens, Kew, Kew Bulletin Additional Series XV, London, 1992.

Fröman, Bengt & Persson, Sven: "An Illustrated Guide to the Grasses of Ethiopia". CADU, Asella, June 1974.

Gleim, Klaus-H.: "Die Blütentracht", Nahrungsquellen des Bienenvolkes (I), 3., verbesserte Auflage, Delta-Verlag GMBH, Sankt Augustin 3, Germany, 1985.

Göhl, Bo: "Tropical Feeds". International Foundation for Science, Stockholm, Sweden, FAO Animal Production and Health Series, FAO, Rome, 1981.

Groombridge, Brian (ed.): "Global Biodiversity - Status of the Earth's Living Resources". A Report compiled by World Conservation Monitoring Centre, Chapman & Hall, London, 1992.

Hamza Mohamed El Amin: "Trees & Shrubs of the Sudan", Ithaca Press, Exeter, 1990.

Hedberg, Inga & Edwards, Sue (eds.): "Flora of Ethiopia, Volume 3: Pittosporaceae to Araliaceae". Addis Ababa and Asmara, Ethiopia, Uppsala, Sweden, 1989.

IBRA: Proceedings of the Fourth International Conference on Apiculture in Tropical Climates, Cairo 1988, London, 1989.

IDRC: "Research - Knowledge in the pursuit of Change". IDRC, SAREC, Sweden 1991.

Jansen, P.C.M.: "Spices, condiments and medicinal plants in Ethiopia, their taxonomy and agricultural significance". Agricultural Research Reports 906, Centre for Agricultural Publishing and Documentation, Wageningen, Netherlands, 1981.

Knapp, Rüdiger: "The Vegetation of Africa" with References to Environment, Development, Economy, Agriculture and Forestry Geography. Gustav Fischer Verlag, Stuttgart, Germany, 1973.

Kokwaro, J.O: "Medicinal Plants of East Africa". East African Literature Bureau, Nairobi, Kampala, Dar es Salaam, 1976.

Kotb, Fawzy Dr.: "Medicinal Plants in Lybia". Arab Encyclopedia House, Beirut - Lebanon, 1985.

Le Houerou, H.N.: "Browse in Africa - The current State of Knowledge". ILCA, Addis Ababa, 1980.

Lind, E.M. & Tallantine, A.C.: "Some Common Flowering Plants of Uganda". Oxford Press, London, 1962.

Lötschert, W. & Beese G.: "Pflanzen der Tropen". BLV Bestimmungsbuch, BLV München Wien Zürich, München, 1981.

Mats Thulin: "Leguminosae of Ethiopia". Opera Botanica Number 68 - 1983, Copenhagen, 1983.

Maurizio, Anna & Ina, Grafl: "Das Trachtpflanzenbuch". Ehrenwirth Verlag München, 1980.

Maydell, H.J.: "Trees and Shrubs of the Sahel: their characteristics and uses". Schriftenreihe der GTZ, Nr. 196, 6236 Eschborn 1, Federal Republic of Germany, 1986.

Mesfin Tadesse: "Some endemic Plants of Ethiopia". Ethiopian Tourism Commission, Addis Ababa 1991.

Mesfin Tadesse: "An Illustrated Guide to the Trees and Shrubs in the Red Cross Project (UMCC-DPP) Areas in Wello, Ethiopia". The Ethiopian Red Cross Society, Addis Ababa, 1990.

Mooney, H.F.: "A Glossary of Ethiopian Plant Names". Dublin University Press Ltd., 1963.

Muschler, R.: "A Manual Flora of Egypt". Reprint 1970, Verlag von J.Cramer, 3301 Lehre, Germany, 1970.

Noad, Tim and Ann, Birne: "Trees of Kenya". Nairobi, Kenya, 1989.

Poschen-Eiche, Peter: "The Application of Farming Systems Research to Community Forestry". Triops Verlag, Langen, 1988.

Prain, David: "Flora of Tropical Africa" Vol. IX.-Part 2, L. Reeve & Co. Limited, London, 1918.

Rehm, Sigmund & Espig, Gustav: "The Cultivated Plants of the Tropics and Subtropics". Verlag Josef Margraf, Weikersheim, 1991.

Rocheleau, D., Weber, F. & Field-Juma, A.: "Agroforestry in Dryland Africa". ICRAF, Nairobi, 1988.

Ruttner, Friedrich: "Naturgeschichte der Honigbiene", Verlag Ehrenwirth, München 1992.

Schmutterer, H.: "Plants of East Africa". TZ-Verlagsgesellschaft MBH, Rossdorf, 1976.

Sebsebe Demissew: "The Genus *Maytenus* (Celastraceae) in Tropical Africa and Tropical Arabia". Acta Universitatis Upsaliensis, Vol.: XXV:2, Uppsala, 1985.

Seegeler, C.J.P.: "Oil plants in Ethiopia, their taxonomy and agricultural significance". Centre for Agricultural Publishing and Documentation, Wageningen, Netherlands, 1983.

SFCDD: "Ethiopian Forestry Manual". Ministry of Agriculture and GTZ Forestry Project and NRCD-MD, Addis Ababa, 1987.

Siegenthaler, I.E.: "Useful Plants Of Ethiopia". Imperial Ethiopian College of Agricultural and Mechanical Arts, Jima Experiment Station, Experiment Station Bulletin No 14, Volume 1, An Oklahoma State University-USAID Contract Publication, c/o American Embassy, Addis Ababa, Ethiopia, 1972.

Smith, Francis G.: "Beekeeping in the Tropics". Longmans, Green and Co LTD, London, 1960.

Snook, Laurence C.: "Tagasaste-Tree Lucerne". Night Owl Publishers Ltd, Shepparton, 1986.

Stoll, Gaby: "Natural Crop Protection" based on Local Farm Resources in the Topics and Subtropics. Josef Margraf Verlag, 1986.

Tadros, T.M.: "Atlas of the Common Grasses of Tanzania". Publication No:2, Publications of the Departmental Herbarium, Botany Department, University of Dar Es Salaam, 1973.

Tindall, H.D.: "Vegetables in the Tropics". Macmillan Education Ltd., Hampshire, 1986.

Tsedeke Abate: "Insect and Mite Pests of Horticultural and Miscellaneous Plants in Ethiopia". IAR Handbook No.1, Institute of Agricultural Research, Addis Ababa, Ethiopia, 1988.

Uphof, J.C.Th.: "Dictionary of Economic Plants". Cramer Verlag, Lehre 1980, Germany.

Wendelberger, Elfrune: "Heilpflanzen - Erkennen, sammeln, anwenden". BLV Naturführer, BLV München, Wien, Zürich 1990.

Wolde Michael Kelecha: "A Glossary of Ethiopian Plant Names". Addis Ababa, 1987.

Zerihun Woldu & Backeus, Ingvar: "The shrubland vegetation in western Shewa, Ethiopia and its possible recovery". Journal of Vegetation Science 2, 1991, Uppsala, 1991.

INDEX OF VERNACULAR NAMES

The languages in this list of vernacular names are as follows:
Ade - Aderienya
Afar - Afarinya
Agew - Agewinya
Amh - Amharinya
Anu - Anuwakinya
Bil - Bileninya
Dor - Dorzienya
Gam - Gamonya
Ge'ez - Ge'ez
Gim - Gimiranya
Gof - Gofanya
Gur - Guragenya
Had - Hadiyinya
Kef - Kefinya
Kem - Kembatinya
Kon - Konsonya
Kun - Kunaminya
Mes - Mesengonya
Mur - Mursinya
Or - Orominya
Saho - Sahoya
Sha - Shakoniya
Sid - Sidamonya
Som - Somalinya
Tre - Tigre
Tya - Tigrinya
Wel - Welaytinya

This index gives names from 27 Ethiopian languages. However, there are over 70 languages with 200 dialects, so this index does not claim to be comprehensive.

Names start with the nearest equivalent Roman letter to the sound in the language concerned, followed by the language, scientific name and page number where description and other information on the plant is found.

A'LLA (Tya) *Acacia tortilis* (312)

A'LQWAY (Tya) *Vicia faba* (149)

A'NGO-GUASOT (Tya) *Ajuga integrifolia* (106)

A'SHA-OM (Tya) *Bersama abyssinica* (348)

A'TER (Ge'ez & Tya) *Cicer arietinum* (129)

A'TER-BAHRI (Tya) *Vicia faba* (149)

A'YNI-A'TER (Tya) *Pisum sativum* (138)

AACHA (Or) *Syzygium guineense* subsp. *afromontanum* (368)

AAF (Kef) *Nigella sativa* (182)

ABABO (Or) *Celosia argentea* (25)

ABADABO (Amh) *Galinsoga parviflora* (50)

ABAK (Som) *Acacia tortilis* (312)

ABAK'E (Tya) *Trigonella foenum-graecum* (146)

ABAR (Or) *Allophyllus abyssinicus* (407)

ABARE (Or) *Bidens pilosa* (37)

ABATABO (Or) *Galinsoga parviflora* (50)

ABAYE (Or) *Maesa lanceolata* (165)

ABBAAHRAH (Tya) *Nepeta azurea* (110)

ABBADERA (Tya) *Salvia schimperi* (121)

ABEKA (Amh) *Clerodendron myricoides* (209)

ABELBILLA (Amh) *Kniphofia foliosa* (153)

ABERRA (Or) *Allophyllus abyssinicus* (407)

ABERRA (Or) *Polyscias fulva* (228)

ABETEYO (Amh) *Gynandropsis gynandra* (86)

ABI'KAYE (Afar) *Trigonella foenum-graecum* (146)

ABISH (Kef) *Trigonella foenum-graecum* (146)

ABISHE (Gur) *Trigonella foenum-graecum* (146)

ABISHI (Or) *Trigonella foenum-graecum* (146)

ABITEREK (Tya) *Jasminum abyssinicum* (165)

ABLALAT (Amh) *Pavonia urens* (161)

ABOKAR (Amh) *Casimiroa edulis* (399)

ABOSADA (Or) *Nigella sativa* (182)

ABRASA (Or) *Scadoxus multiflorus* (25)

ABSH (Amh) *Trigonella foenum-graecum* (146)

ABUTAYE (Or) *Arisaema enneaphyllum* (30)

ACHO (Kef) *Solanum nigrum* (205)

ACQ-GRAR (Amh) *Acacia pilispina* (303)

ADAD (Gam) *Acacia senegal* (307)

ADAD-MERU (Som) *Acacia senegal* (307)

ADADO (Or) *Buddleja polystachya* (251)

ADAHALAT (Saho) *Dodonea angustifolia* (408)

ADALKAT (Saho) *Dodonea angustifolia* (408)

ADAMI (Or) *Euphorbium candelabrum* (276)

ADAMO (Or) *Galineria saxifraga* (189)

ADDA (Or) *Ageratum conyzoides* (33)

ADELA (Kem) *Bidens pachyloma* (37)

ADELA (Kem) *Bidens prestinaria* (37)

ADER (Amh) *Dichrostachys cinera* (130)

ADESSA (Or) *Clausena anisata* (403)

ADESSA (Or) *Dichrostachys cinera* (130)

ADESSA (Or) *Rhus glutinosa* (220)

ADEY ABEBA (Amh) *Bidens macroptera* (34)

ADEY-ABEBA (Amh) *Bidens pachyloma* (37)

ADEY-ABEBA (Amh) *Bidens prestinaria* (37)

ADGUAR (Amh) *Malva verticillata* (161)

ADI-ZANA (Tya) *Stereospermum kunthianum* (240)

ADIQENTO (Afar) *Acacia seyal* (308)

ADIU (Anu) *Diospyros mespeliformis* (268)

ADJUBAN (Amh) *Ocimum basilicum* (110)

AF-A'NSTI (Tya) *Carthamus lanatus* (38)

AF-SCHOLLER (Tya) *Olea capensis subsp. hochstetteri* (375)

AFFAJESHN (Amh) *Bersama abyssinica* (348)

AFLO (Saho) *Acacia seyal* (308)

AFRARTU (Or) *Erythrina abyssinica* (323)

AFRARTU (Or) *Erythrina brucei* (324)

AGALO (Amh) *Combretum molle* (267)

AGAM (Amh & Tya) *Carissa edulis* (29)

AGAMSA (Or & Tya) *Carissa edulis* (29)

AGERGURI (Or) *Olea capensis subsp. hochstetteri* (375)

AGHIO (Kef) *Clerodendron myricoides* (209)

AHARAGU (Som) *Cussonia holstii* (227)

AHAYA (Amh) *Salix subserrata* (404)

AHO-GADMA (Tya) *Heliotropium cinerascens* (78)

AHOT (Amh) *Pittosporum abyssinicum* (170)

AJOFTU (Or) *Plectranthus assurgens* (113)

AKAB (Som) *Acacia tortilis* (312)

AKACHITTA (Or) *Eucalyptus globulus* (364)

AKADE (Anu) *Justitia ladanoides* (21)

AKAKILI (Or) *Eucalyptus globulus* (364)

AKAKILTI (Or) *Eucalyptus camaldulensis* (359)

AKAKIMA (Amh) *Oxygonum sinuatum* (177)

AKERMA (Or) *Eleusine floccifolia* (173)

AKIRSA (Or) *Euphorbium candelabrum* (276)

AKKORAGAG (Amh) *Verbena officinalis* (213)

AKKRSA (Gam) *Acacia senegal* (307)

AKRIMA (Or) *Eleusine floccifolia* (173)

AKSHET (Gur) *Galinsoga parviflora* (50)

AKSIRA (Or) *Milletia ferruginea* (331)

AKURI (Amh) *Glycine wightii longicauda* (130)

AKWRI-ATER (Amh) *Glycine max* (130)

ALA-SHIEN (Gur) *Sphaeranthus suaveolens* (66)

ALALETI (Or) *Salix subserrata* (404)

ALAMATI (Amh) *Piliostigma thonningii* (335)

ALAMATIE (Amh) *Piliostigma thonningii* (335)

ALANCA (Or) *Salix subserrata* (404)

ALAYA (Amh) *Clematis simensis* (181)

ALELTU (Or) *Salix subserrata* (404)

ALFALFA (Tya) *Medicago sativa* (137)

ALHEM (Tya) *Discopodium penninervium* (198)

ALLA (Tya) *Acacia abyssinica* (291)

ALMA (Amh) *Trifolium burchellianum* (141)

ALUMA (Amh) *Discopodium penninervium* (198)

ALWARO (Anu) *Lonchocarpus laxiflorus* (328)

AMAM-GEMEL (Tya) *Piliostigma thonningii* (335)

AMANGEMEL (Tya) *Heliotropium cinerascens* (78)

AMBABESSA (Or) *Albizia gummifera* (315)

AMBABESSA (Or) *Albizia schimperiana* (319)

AMBACEIO (Gur) *Commelina benghalensis* (89)

AMBARDA (Gur) *Piliostigma thonningii* (335)

AMBARUT (Amh) *Cyphomandra betacea* (197)

AMBILLSH (Gum) *Erythrina abyssinica* (323)

AMBL-BAY (Gur) *Pittosporum abyssinicum* (170)

AMBO (Or) *Acacia abyssinica* (291)

AMBOKANA (Or) *Verbascum sinaiticum* (194)

AMBUCH (Tya) *Croton macrostachys* (272)

AMDOHALE (Or) *Kalanchoe petitiana*

AMERA (Or) *Lonchocarpus laxiflorus* (328)

AMERARO (Amh) *Discopodium penninervium* (198)

AMEYKELA (Amh) *Hygrophila auriculata* (17)

AMFAR (Amh) *Buddleja polystachya* (251)

AMJA (Amh) *Hypericum quartinianum* (105)

AMJA (Amh) *Hypericum revolutum* (284)

AMLI (Tya) *Brassica nigra* (81)

AMSHIKA (Or) *Pittosporum abyssinicum* (170)

ANANA (Amh & Or) *Mentha spicata* (109)

ANANSA (Or) *Combretum molle* (267)

ANBESA (Tre) *Scadoxus multiflorus* (25)

ANCABI (Or) *Calpurnia aurea* (320)

ANCHOTE (Or) *Coccinia abyssinica* (94)

ANCIN (Or) *Sparmannia ricinocarpa* (205)

ANCORURA (Or) *Kalanchoe densiflora* (90)

ANCURA (Had) *Kalanchoe quartiniana* (93)

ANDALO (Or) *Polyscias fulva* (228)

ANDEROCCI (Or) *Cussonia holstii (227)*

ANDHO (Gur) *Kalanchoe densiflora* (90)

ANDOHAHELE (Or) *Kalanchoe petitiana*

ANDOJE (Or) *Polyscias fulva* (228)

ANFAR (Amh) *Buddleja polystachya* (251)

ANFARE (Or) *Nuxia congesta* (252)

ANFARFARO (Tya) *Combretum molle* (267)

ANGADA (Tya) *Sesamum indicum* (169)

ANGAFO (Or-Bale) *Echinops longisetus* (49)

ANGALLIT (Amh) *Pittosporum abyssinicum* (170)

ANGIABI (Or) *Ocimum urticifolium* (110)

ANGITO (Kef) *Maytenus obscura* (263)

ANKAKUTEH (Or) *Dovialis abyssinica*

ANKAKUTEH (Or) *Dovyalis caffra* (283)

ANKISSA (Or) *Polyscias fulva* (228)

ANQIEBA (Tya) *Acacia tortilis* (312)

ANTALLO (Or) *Polyscias fulva* (228)

ANTATE-WOLLAKHA (Tya) *Salvia nilotica* (121)

ANTATEH-WOLLAKHA (Tya) *Salvia merjamie* (118)

ANTROKOHELA (Tya) *Steganotaenia araliaceae* (29)

ANUGA (Wel) *Guizotia abyssinica* (53)

AQAQIMA (Amh) *Tribulus terrestris* (213)

AQBA (Tre) *Acacia albida* (292)

AQBA (Tre) *Acacia tortilis* (312)

AQOMA (Amh) *Prunus africana* (391)

ARA (Or) *Pittosporum abyssinicum* (170)

ARABE (Or) *Cucurbita pepo* (97)

ARAJE (Or) *Allophyllus abyssinicus* (407)

ARAMANDAWA (Or) *Gloriosa simplex* (153)

ARARA (Had) *Prunus africana* (391)

ARASHADIYE (Gur) *Sphaeranthus suaveolens* (66)

ARBEQ (Ge'ez) *Rosa abyssinica* (186)

ARBOCHE (Amh) *Sapium ellipticum* (280)

AREMA (Amh) *Ageratum conyzoides* (33)

AREMU-LAEZAB (Or) *Trichodesma zeyclanicum* (78)

ARFATTU (Or) *Cussonia holstii* (227)

ARFATTU (Or) *Schefflera abyssinica* (231)

ARFETU (Or) *Erythrina abyssinica* (323)

ARFETU (Or) *Erythrina brucei* (324)

ARGI (Gam) *Rubus apetalus* (186)

ARGI (Gam) *Rubus steudneri* (189)

ARGTI (Tre) *Maytenus senegalensis* (264)

ARGWDI (Tya) *Maytenus senegalensis* (264)

ARMAGUSA (Amh) *Ajuga integrifolia* (106)

ARORESHA (Or) *Grewia velutina* (415)

ARORIS (Or) *Grewia velutina* (415)

ARRANCHI (Or) *Caylusea abyssinica* (185)

ARSHA-MARSHA (Tya) *Dichrostachys cinera* (130)

ARSHE-MERSHA (Amh) *Dichrostachys cinera* (130)

ARZIMA (Wel) *Trifolium quartinianum* (142)

ARZIMA (Wel) *Trifolium simense* (145)

ARZIMA (Wel) *Trifolium steudneri* (146)

ASANGIRRA (Or) *Datura stramonium* (198)

ASASO (Or) *Osyris quadripartita* (190)

ASHENDA (Amh) *Kniphofia foliosa* (153)

ASHOALA (Had) *Pycnostachys eminii* (117)

ASHU (Gum) *Medicago polymorpha* (134)

ASRA (Or) *Milletia ferruginea* (331)

ASSERKUSH (Amh) *Cyphostemma adenocaule* (213)

ASTA (Amh) *Erica arborea* (271)

ASTENAGER (Amh) *Datura stramonium* (198)

ASTIE (Wel) *Ximenia americana* (372)

AT'E-FARIS (Amh) *Datura stramonium* (198)

AT'E-FARIS (Amh) *Nicandra physalodes* (198)

ATA (Ge'ez) *Salix subserrata* (404)

ATARA (Wel) *Pisum sativum* (138)

ATAT (Amh) *Maytenus gracilipes* (89)

ATAT (Amh) *Sideroxylon oxyacantha* (190)

ATAT (Amh, Gur & Tya) *Maytenus obscura* (263)

ATCHARO (Tya) *Nuxia congesta* (252)

ATER (Amh) *Pisum sativum* (138)

ATER-QEY'YH' (Tya) *Cicer arietinum* (129)

ATERA (Or) *Pisum sativum* (138)

ATERA-DONGOLO (Or) *Pisum sativum* (138)

ATERE (Gur & Gof) *Pisum sativum* (138)

ATERE (Gur) *Vicia faba* (149)

ATERIYYA (Wel) *Pisum sativum* (138)

ATERO (Had) *Pisum sativum* (138)

ATIR (Saho) *Cicer arietinum* (129)

ATKUAR (Amh) *Buddleja polystachya* (251)

ATTUCH (Amh) *Achyranthes aspera* (25)

ATTUCH (Amh) *Verbena officinalis* (213)

AUERA (Sid) *Aningeria altissima* (411)

AUHEH (Tya) *Cordia africana* (247)

AULI' (Tya) *Olea europaea subsp. cuspidata* (376)

AUTI (Or) *Physalis peruviana* (201)

AVALO (Amh) *Combretum molle* (267)

AVETIA (Tya) *Hypericum revolutum* (284)

AVOCADO (Amh) *Persea americana* (288)

AWETSCHA (Tya) *Hypericum quartinianum* (105)

AWHI (Tya) *Cordia africana* (247)

AWOSETTA (Tya) *Nigella sativa* (182)

AWRE-MUDUBE (Som) *Ximenia americana* (372)

AWTIEBEDL (Ge'ez) *Vicia faba* (149)

AWTT' (Amh) *Physalis peruviana* (201)

AYEH (Amh & Tya) *Diospyros mespeliformis* (268)

AYHADA (Tya) *Dovialis abyssinica* (283)

AYNEB (Ade) *Vitis vinifera* (213)

AZAMR (Amh) *Bersama abyssinica* (348)

AZANGIRA (Or) *Nicandra physalodes* (198)

AZMUD (Amh) *Nigella sativa* (182)

AZMUD (Tya) *Trachyspermum ammi* (29)

AZMUD-ADDI (Or) *Trachyspermum ammi* (29)

AZO HAREG (Amh) *Clematis hirsuta* (181)

BABUN (Amh) *Craterostigma plantagineum* (193)

BACHANGA (Sid) *Sorghum bicolor* (173)

BACHANKA (Sid) *Sorghum bicolor* (173)

BADDANNO (Or) *Balanites aegyptiaca* (236)

BADENA (Wel) *Balanites aegyptiaca* (236)

BADESSA (Or) *Syzygium guineense* subsp. *afromontanum* (368)

BAGANAPSI (Or) *Heliotropium cinerascens* (78)

BAHR-MASHLA (Amh) *Zea mays* (174)

BAHR-ZAF (Amh & Tya) *Eucalyptus globulus* (364)

BAIELA (Gur) *Vicia faba* (149)

BAKALO (Or) *Zea mays* (174)

BAKANICHA (Or) *Croton macrostachys* (272)

BAKANISSA (Or) *Croton macrostachys* (272)

BAL (Gim) *Sapium ellipticum* (280)

BALAMI (Or) *Andropogon abyssinicus* (170)

BALANDALECHA (Or) *Achyrospermum schimperi* (105)

BALATIMBO (Or) *Nicotiana tabacum* (201)

BALCHA (Amh) *Galinsoga parviflora* (50)

BALDENGWA (Tya) *Vicia faba* (149)

BALDER (Or) *Rumex nepalensis* (178)

BAMBA (Amh & Tya) *Adansonia digitata* (243)

BAQEL (Had) *Vicia faba* (149)

BAQELA (Or) *Vicia faba* (149)

BAQIELA (Ade, Afar, Amh, Kem & Wel) *Vicia faba* (149)

BARBARASH (Or) *Plectranthus punctatus edulis* (117)

BARO (Kef) *Zea mays* (174)

BARTU (Or) *Erythrina abyssinica* (323)

BARTU (Or) *Erythrina brucei* (324)

BARZAF (Ader) *Eucalyptus camaldulensis* (359)

BARZAFI-DIMA (Or) *Eucalyptus camaldulensis* (359)

BASOBILA (Amh) *Salvia nilotica* (121)

BATALLA (Gur) *Bersama abyssinica* (348)

BATE (Or) *Acacia persiciflora* (300)

BAZINJA (Amh) *Solanum melongena* (202)

BAZRA-GRAR (Amh) *Acacia abyssinica* (291)

BEDDENNA (Or & Wel) *Balanites aegyptiaca* (236)

BEDDENNO (Amh) *Balanites aegyptiaca* (236)

BEDL (Ge'ez) *Vicia faba* (149)

BEGE (Or) *Combretum paniculatum* (89)

BEHBEY (Afar) *Acacia tortilis* (312)

BEKANISA (Or) *Croton macrostachys* (272)

BELBATE (Or) *Nymphaea nouchali* (165)

BELBELTO (Amh) *Celosia argentea* (25)

BELEME (Amh) *Andropogon abyssinicus* (170)

BERBERE (Amh) *Capsicum annuum* (197)

BERBERE (Or) *Capsicum annuum* (197)

BERBERE-ABAKTA (Tya) *Acmella caulirhiza* (33)

BERBERE-ASLAMAY (Tya) *Sapium ellipticum* (280)

BERBERE-TSELIM (Tya) *Schinus molle* (223)

BERDE (Som) *Ficus vasta* (352)

BERDELE (Dor) *Apodytes dimidiata* (287)

BERO (Kef) *Erythrina brucei* (324)

BERU (Kef) *Erythrina abyssinica* (323)

BERU (Sha) *Prunus africana* (391)

BESHINGA (Kem) *Sorghum bicolor* (173)

BESO-BLA (Amh) *Ocimum basilicum* (110)

BESO-BLA (Amh) *Ocimum urticifolium* (110)

BESSO-AT'AL (Tya) *Pittosporum abyssinicum* (170)

BETUBA (Wel) *Acacia senegal* (307)

BEYE (Amh) *Olinia rochetiana* (379)

BIBERO (Kef) *Milletia ferruginea* (331)

BIBILE (Som) *Kalanchoe lanceolata* (93)

BIKA (Or) *Combretum molle* (267)

BIKILTU (Or) *Polygala persicariifolia* (174)

BILEWU-HAQA (Had) *Milletia ferruginea* (331)

BISI (Or) *Physalis peruviana* (201)

BITTE (Or) *Sideroxylon oxyacantha* (190)

BOBANKA (Had) *Pycnostachys abyssinica* (117)

BOBBA (Gam) *Ficus sur* (351)

BOBOLUHU (Som) *Schefflera abyssinica* (231)

BOCATTA (Kef) *Pterocephalus frutescens* (98)

BOCCU-FARDA (Or) *Leucas martinicensis* (109)

BODORO (Or) *Stereospermum kunthianum* (240)

BOEKBEHA (Tya) *Gynandropsis gynandra* (86)

BONCO (Or) *Pittosporum abyssinicum* (170)

BONGA (Amh) *Trichilia dregeana* (347)

BOQO (Or) *Bersama abyssinica* (348)

BORBORIS (Kon) *Ehretia cymosa* (248)

BORDA (Kon) *Carthamus tinctorius* (38)

BORODO (Or) *Salix subserrata* (404)

BORTO (Gam) *Erythrina brucei* (324)

BORTO (Or) *Erythrina abyssinica* (323)

BORTWA (Gof) *Erythrina brucei* (324)

BORTWA (Wel) *Erythrina abyssinica* (323)

BORTWA (Wel) *Erythrina brucei* (324)

BOSAKA (Or) *Sapium ellipticum* (280)

BOSOKE (Or) *Kalanchoe marmorata* (93)

BOSOQQE (Or) *Kalanchoe petitiana*

BOSOQQE (Or) *Kalanchoe quartiniana* (93)

BRBRRA (Amh, Gur & Tya) *Milletia ferruginea* (331)

BRSMA (Tya) *Bersama abyssinica* (348)

BSANNA (Amh) *Croton macrostachys* (272)

BSSANA (Am & Tya) *Ajuga integrifolia* (106)

BTREMUSEH (Amh) *Diospyros mespeliformis* (268)

BUN (Tya) *Coffea arabica* (396)

BUNA (Amh, Or, Afar, Sid, Gur & Tya) *Coffea arabica* (396)

BURKO (Tya) *Cyanotis barbata* (90)

BURO (Som) *Clausena anisata* (403)

BURO (Som) *Salix subserrata* (404)

BURQUQQE (Or) *Acacia lahai* (296)

BURQUQQE (Or) *Acacia sieberiana* (311)

BURTO (Dor) *Erythrina brucei* (324)

BURURI (Or) *Grewia ferruginea* (205)

BUSHA-DUBSIS (Amh) *Clerodendron myricoides* (209)

BUTLANSA (Amh) *Satureja abyssinica* (122)

BUTTANSA (Amh) *Satureja abyssinica* (122)

BYE-BYE (Anu) *Azadirachta indica* (340)

CAJJA (Amh) *Andropogon abyssinicus* (170)

CALENTA (Kon) *Dichrostachys cinera* (130)

CAMUN (Tya) *Trachyspermum ammi* (29)

CAQMOSH (Amh) *Cussonia holstii* (227)

CATA (Kem) *Catha edulis* (86)

CATI (Or) *Catha edulis* (86)

CATIYYA (Wel) *Catha edulis* (86)

CATTO (Kef & Or) *Albizia gummifera* (315)

CATTO (Or) *Albizia schimperiana* (319)

CAWICCO (Or) *Albizia gummifera* (315)

CAWICCO (Or) *Albizia schimperiana* (319)

CEKA (Or) *Calpurnia aurea* (320)

CEKA (Or) *Pittosporum abyssinicum* (170)

CEKA-QEMELE (Or) *Pterrolobium stellatum* (141)

CEKATA (Or) *Calpurnia aurea* (320)

CELEQLEQQA (Amh) *Apodytes dimidiata* (287)

CENGWEREFIA (Tya) *Lonchocarpus laxiflorus* (328)

CEQSA (Gam) *Calpurnia aurea* (320)

CERIN (Som) *Acacia sieberiana* (311)

CGINDA (Gam) *Acacia seyal* (308)

CH'ENA-ADDAM (Tya) *Ruta chalepensis* (190)

CH'EQENTE (Tya) *Pittosporum abyssinicum* (170)

CH'EW-MRA'KUT (Tya) *Oxygonum sinuatum* (177)

CH'FRI-DMU (Tya) *Acacia senegal* (307)

CH'IAQMAL (Amh) *Ricinus communis* (279)

CH'NDOG (Tya) *Otostegia integrifolia* (113)

CH'UGOGET (Amh) *Cynoglossum coeruleum* (78)

CHAT (Amh, Gur & Tya) *Catha edulis* (86)

CHE'A (Tya) *Acacia abyssinica* (291)

CHE'A (Tya) *Acacia pilispina* (303)

CHE'A' (Tya & Tre) *Acacia seyal* (308)

CHE'A' (Tya) *Acacia sieberiana* (311)

CHE'GOGIT (Amh) *Bidens pilosa* (37)

CHECHEYE (Had) *Nicandra physalodes* (198)

CHECHO (Amh) *Premna schimperi* (210)

CHIAI (Or) *Buddleja polystachya* (251)

CHIBO (Amh) *Vernonia leopoldii* (70)

CHIGAQWA'HIT (Tya) *Anagallis arvensis* (181)

CHIMKI (Amh) *Sparmannia ricinocarpa* (205)

CHINGERCH (Amh) *Justitia ladanoides* (21)

CHOCHA (Kem) *Acanthus eminens* (14)

CHOCHO (Amh) *Nuxia congesta* (252)

CHOWYEH (Amh) *Dracaena steudneri* (216)

CIKOTEN (Wel) *Clausena anisata* (403)

CILWIEDE (Anu) *Lonchocarpus laxiflorus* (328)

CIRAKOTA (Or) *Ruta chalepensis* (190)

CIRCUFA (Or) *Lepidium sativum* (82)

D'KA-NEKEL (Tya) *Flaveria trinervia* (50)

DA'RO (Ge'ez, Tre & Tya) *Ficus vasta* (352)

DAARO (Tya) *Triumfetta rhomboidea* (206)

DABAKADET (Amh) *Verbascum sinaiticum* (194)

DABDI (Amh) *Piliostigma thonningii* (335)

DADAMSA (Or) *Combretum molle* (267)

DADATU (Or) *Brucea antidysenterica* (197)

DADECCA (Or) *Acacia abyssinica* (291)

DAGNISA (Or) *Acacia abyssinica* (291)

DALECHO (Or) *Olinia rochetiana* (379)

DAMA-KESIE (Amh) *Ocimum lamiifolium* (110)

DAMACSE (Or) *Plectranthus lanunginosus* (114)

DAMAKA (Amh) *Nepeta azurea* (110)

DAMAKASE (Had) *Ocimum urticifolium* (110)

DAMAKESEH (Or) *Ocimum lamiifolium* (110)

DAMAKHER (Tya) *Ocimum lamiifolium* (110)

DAMAT-WEYRA (Amh) *Olea capensis subsp. hochstetteri* (375)

DAME (Amh) *Acmella caulirhiza* (33)

DANDER (Amh & Tya) *Cirsium dender* (41)

DANDER (Tya) *Carduus nyassanus* (38)

DANDER (Tya) *Echinops hispidus* (46)

DANDER-BEITA (Tya) *Carthamus lanatus* (38)

DANGEGO (Or) *Rumex nervosus* (178)

DANGIRATO (Kef) *Vernonia auriculifera* (69)

DANGULLE (Or) *Pisum sativum* (138)

DANISSA (Or) *Dombeya torrida* (412)

DANNISA (Or) *Apodytes dimidiata* (287)

DANNO (Som) *Euphorbia tirucalli* (101)

DARGU (Or) *Achyranthes aspera* (25)

DARGU (Or) *Brillantaisia madagascariensis* (17)

DARGU (Or) *Hypoestes forkaolii* (18)

DARGU (Or) *Hypoestes triflora* (18)

DARGU (Or) *Isoglossa laxa* (18)

DARGU (Or) *Isoglossa somalensis* (18)

DARGU (Or) *Ocimum lamiifolium* (110)

DARGU (Or) *Phaulopsis imbricata* (21)

DARGUNA (Bil) *Ficus vasta* (352)

DASHAN-MIREHAT (Tya) *Oxygonum sinuatum* (177)

DASHLOME (Wel) *Clausena anisata* (403)

DAYERO (Som) *Rosa abyssinica* (186)

DEBBI (Som) *Grewia velutina* (415)

DEBERJAN (Amh) *Solanum melongena* (202)

DEBO (Or) *Coriandrum sativum* (26)

DEDATU (Or) *Milletia ferruginea* (331)

DEDECCA (Or) *Acacia abyssinica* (291)

DEGMUT (Tya) *Maytenus gracilipes* (89)

DEGUSTA (Tya) *Girardinia bullosa* (206)

DEK'WA'TA (Tya) *Kalanchoe marmorata* (93)

DEKE-DAHRO (Tya) *Sida rhombifolia* (161)

DEMBI (Or) *Ficus vasta* (352)

DEN (Som) *Dodonea angustifolia* (408)

DENGYA-SEBBER (Amh) *Pittosporum abyssinicum* (170)

DERO (Afar) *Sorghum bicolor* (173)

DEROT (Or) *Acacia albida* (292)

DEROT (Or) *Acacia lahai* (296)

DESH (Gim) *Trichilia dregeana* (347)

DEWENI-BUNNA (Gur) *Acacia sieberiana* (311)

DGTA (Amh) *Syzygium guineense* subsp. *afromontanum* (368)

DGTTA (Amh & Gur) *Calpurnia aurea* (320)

DHA-NEQAY (Amh) *Galinsoga parviflora* (50)

DHAY-DHAY (Som) *Dichrostachys cinera* (130)

DHIGDAR (Som) *Dichrostachys cinera* (130)

DIDESSA (Or) *Combretum molle* (267)

DIDU (Or) *Galineria saxifraga* (189)

DIFU (Or) *Senecio ochrocarpus* (62)

DIKWALA (Tya) *Tapinanthus globiferus* (154)

DILISHA (Or) *Commelina benghalensis* (89)

DINICHA-SHEWA (Or) *Solanum tuberosum* (205)

DINKIA-SEBBER (Amh) *Crateva adansonii* (259)

DKA-NEQEL (Tya) *Galinsoga parviflora* (50)

DMBLAL (Amh) *Coriandrum sativum* (26)

DNCH (Amh) *Plectranthus punctatus edulis* (117)

DNCH (Amh) *Solanum tuberosum* (205)

DNGAY-SEBER (Amh) *Ritchiea albersii* (86)

DOBI (Or) *Urtica simensis* (209)

DOBI (Or) *Girardinia bullosa* (206)

DODET (Tya) *Achyranthes aspera* (25)

DOG (Amh & Tya) *Ferula communis* (29)

DOK (Gur) *Satureja punctata* (122)

DOKMA (Amh) *Syzygium guineense* subsp. *afromontanum* (368)

DOKMA (Amh) *Syzygium guineense* subsp. *guineense* (371)

DOKO (Kef) *Solanum tuberosum* (205)

DOKONNU (Or) *Grewia ferruginea* (205)

DOLKIISA (Or) *Bersama abyssinica* (348)

DOLMUNCHA (Had) *Glycine wightii petitiana* (130)

DOMAY (Gam) *Balanites aegyptiaca* (236)

DOMAYE (Gam) *Balanites aegyptiaca* (236)

DOMBRECCO (Kef) *Solanecio mannii* (65)

DOMOHO (Or) *Balanites aegyptiaca* (236)

DONGA (Amh) *Apodytes dimidiata* (287)

DONIKE (Or) *Plectranthus punctatus edulis* (117)

DONKIKO (Sid) *Apodytes dimidiata* (287)

DRUBA (Or) *Allophyllus abyssinicus* (407)

DUANDO (Sid) *Syzygium guineense* subsp. *afromontanum* (368)

DUBA (Amh) *Cucurbita pepo* (97)

DUBBA (Tya) *Triumfetta rhomboidea* (206)

DUBI (Or) *Helianthus annuus* (54)

DUBOBEIS (Som) *Maytenus gracilipes* (89)

DUCCA (Or) *Hagenia abyssinica* (388)

DUCYA (Gam) *Salix subserrata* (404)

DUDUNA (Amh) *Cussonia holstii* (227)

DUDUNA (Or) *Ekebergia capensis* (343)

DUM-DUM (Som) *Ceiba pentandra* (244)

DUMUGA (Or) *Justitia schimperana* (21)

DUS (Or) *Erythrina abyssinica* (323)

E'QA (Tya) *Agave sisalana* (22)

E'SHOCH'-GUASSA (Tya) *Hygrophila auriculata* (17)

EBERRAKO (Or) *Bersama abyssinica* (348)

EBICHA (Or) *Vernonia amygdalina* (235)

EDERA (Or) *Hypericum revolutum* (284)

EJERSA (Or) *Olea europaea subsp. cuspidata* (376)

ELAYDEEA (Amh) *Clematis simensis* (181)

ELESELOSEK (Gum) *Salix subserrata* (404)

ELKEMME (Or) *Jasminum abyssinicum* (165)

EMELA (Or) *Albizia gummifera* (315)

EMELA (Or) *Albizia schimperiana* (319)

ENDODI (Or) *Phytolacca dodecandra* (170)

ENDUGOKHILLA (Tya) *Steganotaenia araliaceae* (29)

ENTATIE-VALLAHA (Tya) *Salvia nilotica* (121)

ERENGA-QOLO (Amh) *Maesa lanceolata* (165)

ERTU (Or) *Tapinanthus globiferus* (154)

ERWE (Tya) *Scorpiurus muricatus* (141)

ETIBIRO (Or) *Bersama abyssinica* (348)

ETO (Or) *Hagenia abyssinica* (388)

ETSA (Dor) *Ficus sur* (351)

ETSE-YOHANNES (Ge'ez) *Plectocephalus varians* (61)

ETTECCA (Or) *Dodonea angustifolia* (408)

FARANJA-SHUFIYA (Wel) *Helianthus annuus* (54)

FATUQA (Agew) *Boswellia papyrifera* (255)

FECIO (Or) *Lepidium sativum* (82)

FERESHEI (Tya) *Salvia nilotica* (121)

FERISH-TENU (Amh) *Cynoglossum coeruleum* (78)

FETO (Amh & Or) *Lepidium sativum* (82)

FICO (Or) *Hagenia abyssinica* (388)

FIFO (Tya) *Argemone mexicana* (169)

FIHISO (Ge'ez) *Scadoxus multiflorus* (25)

FIRI DUBA (Or) *Cucurbita pepo* (97)

FORAKA (Or) *Bersama abyssinica* (348)

FOSI-ANQRBIT (Tya) *Craterostigma plantagineum* (193)

FOSI-MOSKOJEW (Tya) *Sonchus asper* (65)

FRQA (Agew) *Piliostigma thonningii* (335)

FUGAZERARO (Had) *Plectocephalus varians* (61)

FUGI-BATCHAW (Kem) *Arisaema enneaphyllum* (30)

FUJUL (Or) *Crambe hispanica* (81)

FUL (Ge'ez) *Vicia faba* (149)

FULAÄY (Som) *Acacia seyal* (308)

FULLSA (Or) *Acacia sieberiana* (311)

FURGUGE (Or) *Kalanchoe lanceolata* (93)

GABAI (Or) *Combretum paniculatum* (89)

GABTZE (Gam) *Schefflera abyssinica* (231)

GADAM (Tya) *Cussonia holstii* (227)

GAEJA (Gam) *Clausena anisata* (403)

GAGUME (Tya) *Oxygonum sinuatum* (177)

GALABA (Or) *Maesa lanceolata* (165)

GALGALAM (Or) *Boswellia papyrifera* (255)

GALIMA (Amh) *Helinus mystacinus* (185)

GALOÖL-SUR (Som) *Dichrostachys cinera* (130)

GAMBELA (Gam) *Plantago lanceolata* (170)

GAMCLE (Amh) *Clausena anisata* (403)

GAME (Amh) *Ehretia cymosa* (248)

GANCHO (Sid) *Sapium ellipticum* (280)

GAQA (Tya) *Rosa abyssinica* (186)

GARA (Wel) *Vernonia amygdalina* (235)

GARA (Wel) *Acacia sieberiana* (311)

GARAMBA (Or) *Hypericum quartinianum* (105)

GARAMBA (Or) *Hypericum revolutum* (284)

GARARABICHU (Sid) *Hypericum revolutum* (284)

GARBE (Wel) *Prunus africana* (391)

GARBI (Or) *Acacia abyssinica* (291)

GARBI (Or) *Acacia albida* (292)

GARBI (Or) *Prunus africana* (391)

GARBI (Or) *Acacia lahai* (296)

GARGAMMA (Tya) *Gynandropsis gynandra* (86)

GARGARU (Gam & Wel) *Dichrostachys cinera* (130)

GARMI (Amh) *Ehretia cymosa* (248)

GARSHA (Tya) *Acacia albida* (292)

GARU (Or) *Pterrolobium stellatum* (141)

GARUL (Or) *Pterrolobium stellatum* (141)

GATAMA (Or) *Schefflera abyssinica* (231)

GAYU (Or) *Lathyrus sativus* (133)

GAYYA (Gur & Or) *Lathyrus sativus* (133)

GBTO (Amh & Tya) *Lupinus albus* (134)

GDICCO (Or) *Milletia ferruginea* (331)

GECHA (Amh) *Maesa lanceolata* (165)

GEDDEM (Tya) *Cussonia holstii* (227)

GEDEL-AMUQ (Amh) *Delphinium dasycaulon* (182)

GEDEL-AMUQ (Amh) *Delphinium wellbyi* (182)

GEDETAMO (Amh) *Cussonia holstii* (227)

GEDIL (Tre) *Kalanchoe lanceolata* (93)

GEDIL (Tre) *Kalanchoe quartiniana* (93)

GEENDA'I (Tya) *Calotropis procera* (30)

GEGHO (Agew) *Rhamnus prinoides* (384)

GELE-ILA (Afar) *Nymphaea nouchali* (165)

GELGELE MESKEL (Tya) *Bidens pachyloma* (37)

GELGELE-MESKEL (Tya) *Bidens prestinaria* (37)

GELGELLE-MESKEL (Tya) *Bidens macroptera* (34)

GEMMA-HASHISH (Amh) *Tagetes minuta* (66)

GENH (Tre) *Pittosporum abyssinicum* (170)

GERBI (Amh & Gur) *Acacia albida* (292)

GERENGA (Bil) *Lablab purpureus* (133)

GERENGERE (Amh) *Argyrolobium ramosissimum* (126)

GERGETWA (Wel) *Dodonea angustifolia* (408)

GESHA (Kem & Saho) *Rhamnus prinoides* (384)

GESHI (Or) *Maesa lanceolata* (165)

GESSA (Or) *Bersama abyssinica* (348)

GESWA (Wel) *Rhamnus prinoides* (384)

GETCHAE (Tya) *Triumfetta pilosa* (206)

GET'EM (Tya) *Schefflera abyssinica* (231)

GETEM (Had & Sid) *Schefflera abyssinica* (231)

GETEMI (Or) *Cussonia holstii* (227)

GETIN (Amh) *Haplocarpha schimperi* (54)

GETO (Or) *Dichrostachys cinera* (130)

GHECCIE (Tya) *Triumfetta pilosa* (206)

GHERACCIA (Tya) *Nicandra physalodes* (198)

GIESHO (Amh, Ade & Gam) *Rhamnus prinoides* (384)

GIESHO (Had, Or & Tya) *Rhamnus prinoides* (384)

GIESO (Tya) *Rhamnus prinoides* (384)

GIRBI (Or) *Gossypium hirsutum* (157)

GIRMI (Or) *Dichrostachys cinera* (130)

GISHE (Gur) *Rhamnus prinoides* (384)

GISHI-SHAATO (Kef) *Pisum sativum* (138)

GITEE (Had) *Pisum sativum* (138)

GMARDA (Amh) *Acacia polyacantha* (304)

GOD-HAW-TORLE (Som) *Dichrostachys cinera* (130)

GODA (Or) *Rubus apetalus* (186)

GODA (Or) *Rubus steudneri* (189)

GOETOEB (Amh & Tre) *Plantago lanceolata* (170)

GOFA JIMA' (Or) *Catha edulis* (86)

'GOFT (Amh) *Erythrina abyssinica* (323)

GOMANZA (Or) *Erucastrum abyssinicum* (82)

GOMBOCERIE (Amh) *Cussonia holstii* (227)

GOMENA-GURAGE (Or) *Brassica carinata* (81)

GOMÖRYYA (Wel) *Pterrolobium stellatum* (141)

GORA (Had) *Rubus steudneri* (189)

GORA (Or) *Pterrolobium stellatum* (141)

GORA (Or) *Rosa abyssinica* (186)

GORA-GORA (Agew) *Hagenia abyssinica* (388)

GORAN-MEDU (Som) *Dichrostachys cinera* (130)

GORBE (Or) *Albizia gummifera* (315)

GORBE (Or) *Albizia schimperiana* (319)

GORCO (Or) *Rubus apetalus* (186)

GORCO (Or) *Rubus steudneri* (189)

GORGORO (Or) *Hypericum quartinianum* (105)

GORGORO (Or) *Hypericum revolutum* (284)

GORJEJIT (Amh) *Sida schimperiana* (162)

GOROSEZA (Or) *Flaveria trinervia* (50)

GOROSITU (Amh) *Galinsoga parviflora* (50)

GORTA (Or) *Pterrolobium stellatum* (141)

GOT (Som) *Balanites aegyptiaca* (236)

GOTBUYA (Had) *Crinum ornatum*

GRARO (Kef) *Trigonella foenum-graecum* (146)

GRAWA (Amh) *Vernonia amygdalina* (235)

GRBIA (Tya) *Asystasia gangetica* (14)

GRMA (Or) *Dichrostachys cinera* (130)

GRMO (Tya) *Acacia sieberiana* (311)

GRUMBA (Tya) *Brassica carinata* (81)

GRUMBA (Tya) *Brassica nigra* (81)

GUDUBA (Or) *Aningeria altissima* (411)

GUDUBA (Or) *Polyscias fulva* (228)

GUDUBO (Sid) *Aningeria altissima* (411)

GUFTEH (Or) *Sida schimperiana* (162)

GUGANTA (Wel) *Acacia dolichocephala* (295)

GUGANTA (Wel) *Acacia lahai* (296)

GUJO (Amh) *Vernonia auriculifera* (69)

GUL'I (Tya) *Ricinus communis* (279)

GULO (Amh) *Ricinus communis* (279)

GULO-KOKKOBA (Amh) *Maytenus senegalensis* (264)

GUMERE (Or) *Rubus apetalus* (186)

GUMERE (Or) *Rubus steudneri* (189)

GUMMUR-HURTUI (Som) *Trachyspermum ammi* (29)

GUNA (Or) *Olinia rochetiana* (379)

GUNK'I (Tya) *Stereospermum kunthianum* (240)

GUNYATO (Gur) *Ageratum conyzoides* (33)

GURA (Or) *Opuntia ficus-indica* (256)

GURATI (Or) *Nigella sativa* (182)

GURAYU (Or) *Prunus africana* (391)

GURHA-DARUYE (Som) *Acacia tortilis* (312)

GURRA-HARRE (Or) *Verbascum sinaiticum* (194)

GURSHT (Amh) *Impatiens rothii* (74)

GUT (Som) *Balanites aegyptiaca* (236)

GUZA (Amh) *Balanites aegyptiaca* (236)

GWAYYA (Amh) *Lathyrus sativus* (133)

GWENEQW (Tya) *Dichrostachys cinera* (130)

GWEZA (Tya) *Balanites aegyptiaca* (236)

GWMERO (Tya) *Acacia polyacantha* (304)

GWRDMAKWYO (Tya) *Trifolium quartinianum* (142)

GWRDMAKWYO (Tya) *Trifolium steudneri* (146)

GWSSA'MAI (Tya) *Trifolium schimperi* (145)

H'ABBI (Tya) *Hagenia abyssinica* (388)

H'AMAT-KAKI'TO (Tya) *Astralagus atropilosulus* (126)

H'AMLI-GILA (Tya) *Commicarpus plumbagineus* (165)

H'AREG (Tya) *Clematis simensis* (181)

H'AREG-TEMEN (Tya) *Cyphostemma adenocaule* (213)

H'EH'OT (Tya) *Rumex nervosus* (178)

HABASUDU (Or) *Nigella sativa* (182)

HABBI-SELIM (Tya) *Jasminum abyssinicum* (165)

HABLALIT (Amh) *Ricinus communis* (279)

HABRU (Or) *Ficus sur* (351)

HACAT (Agew) *Maytenus obscura* (263)

HACAT (Tya) *Maytenus obscura* (263)

HADA (Or) *Guizotia scabra scabra* (53)

HADAMI (Or) *Euphorbia abyssinica* (275)

HADAMI (Or) *Euphorbium candelabrum* (276)

HADAWI (Som) *Brucea antidysenterica* (197)

HADE (Or) *Guizotia scabra schimperi* (53)

HALTUFA (Or) *Rubus apetalus* (186)

HALTUFA (Or) *Rubus steudneri* (189)

HALUTA (Had) *Echinops longisetus* (49)

HAMAQITA (Or) *Medicago polymorpha* (134)

HAMARARA (Amh) *Maesa lanceolata* (165)

HAMAROO (Kem) *Rubus apetalus* (186)

HAMAROO (Kem) *Rubus steudneri* (189)

HAMBAGWITA (Tya) *Arisaema enneaphyllum* (30)

HAMS (Tre) *Rhus glutinosa* (220)

HAMSHIKA (Or) *Pittosporum abyssinicum* (170)

HANCUCU (Or) *Solanum indicum* (202)

HANCURA (Or) *Kalanchoe petitiana* (93)

HARAH (Som) *Acacia tortilis* (312)

HARANGA (Or) *Phytolacca dodecandra* (170)

HARANGAMA (Or) *Pterrolobium stellatum* (141)

HARBU (Or) *Ficus sur* (351)

HAREG (Amh) *Microglossa pyrifolia* (58)

HAREG (Amh) *Mikaniopsis clematoides* (58)

HAREG (Amh) *Solanecio angelatus* (65)

HARFAT (Or) *Cussonia holstii* (227)

HARFATU (Or) *Schefflera abyssinica* (231)

HARMAL-ADI (Or) *Clerodendron myricoides* (209)

HASO (Amh) *Clematis hirsuta* (181)

HASO (Amh) *Clematis simensis* (181)

HASSAB (Amh) *Origanum majorana* (113)

HATCHAT (Tya) *Maytenus gracilipes* (89)

HATTE (Or) *Dichrostachys cinera* (130)

HAWAUTI (Tya) *Grewia velutina* (415)

HAYA (Amh) *Salix subserrata* (404)

HAYRAMAT (Som) *Dodonea angustifolia* (408)

HAZIBA (Tya) *Combretum molle* (267)

HAZTE (Gam) *Ximenia americana* (372)

HBRE-MESRY (Ge'ez) *Rosa x richardii* (186)

HEBA (Kem) *Vernonia amygdalina* (235)

HERMER BANBA (Tya) *Adansonia digitata* (243)

HENDI (Or) *Hypericum revolutum* (284)

HENJORIYA (Wel) *Rubus apetalus* (186)

HENJORIYA (Wel) *Rubus steudneri* (189)

HENSERASE (Amh) *Pterocephalus frutescens* (98)

HETO (Or) *Hagenia abyssinica* (388)

HETOT (Sid) *Hagenia abyssinica* (388)

HIDAN-HIDO (Or.-Bale) *Alchemilla haumannii*

HIDDA (Or) *Clematis hirsuta* (181)

HIDDEE (Or) *Solanum incanum* (202)

HILLO (Kef) *Pterocephalus frutescens* (98)

HIMFIDE AS (Som) *Erucastrum abyssinicum* (82)

HINJARO (Had) *Rubus apetalus* (186)

HINJARO (Had) *Rubus steudneri* (189)

HINNEH (Or) *Hypericum quartinianum* (105)

HIRKAMO (Or) *Allophyllus abyssinicus* (407)

HIRKUM (Or) *Allophyllus abyssinicus* (407)

HLBET (Ade) *Trigonella foenum-graecum* (146)

HOGIO (Kef) *Ranunculus multifidus* (182)

HOH (Ge'ez) *Prunus persica* (395)

HOLAGABIS (Gur) *Sphaeranthus suaveolens* (66)

HOLAGABIS (Or) *Sphaeranthus suaveolens* (66)

HOLEGEBIS (Or) *Commelina benghalensis* (89)

HOMER (Tya) *Hibiscus calyphyllus* (157)

HOMI (Or) *Prunus africana* (391)

HORAQQA (Or) *Bersama abyssinica* (348)

HOSANA (Amh) *Phoenix reclinata* (232)

HRGTE (Tre) *Maytenus senegalensis* (264)

HTSAWTS (Tya) *Calpurnia aurea* (320)

HUDA (Or) *Polyscias fulva* (228)

HUDA (Or) *Ximenia americana* (372)

HUDI (Or) *Ximenia americana* (372)

HULAGA (Amh) *Ehretia cymosa* (248)

HULBATA (Or) *Trigonella foenum-graecum* (146)

HULKOT (Amh) *Ocimum basilicum* (110)

HUMER (Amh) *Tamarindus indica* (339)

HUMER (Som & Tya) *Tamarindus indica* (339)

IDADO (Or) *Acacia senegal* (307)

IDEFETI (Or) *Clematis simensis* (181)

IHIY (Ade) *Sorghum bicolor* (173)

ILILI ADDI (Or) *Otostegia tomentosa* (113)

ILILI-HURDY (Or) *Delphinium dasycaulon* (182)

IM'BWACH'O (Amh) *Rumex nervosus* (178)

IMBIS (Gur) *Maesa lanceolata* (165)

IMBWAY (Amh) *Solanum indicum* (202)

INBOBA (Tre) *Scadoxus multiflorus* (25)

INCHINI (Or) *Pavonia urens* (161)

INDEFDELE (Tre) *Plectranthus ornatus* (114)

INTABUYE (Or) *Jasminum stans* (166)

INTANCA (Sid) *Dodonea angustifolia* (408)

IRBA (Or) *Nuxia congesta* (252)

IRE (Tya) *Aloe berhana* (22)

IRET (Amh) *Aloe berhana* (22)

ISKEE (Tre) *Becium grandiflorum* (106)

ITTICCA (Or) *Dodonea angustifolia* (408)

JEGALLATIIT (Amh) *Crassocephalum vitellinum* (45)

JELA (Had) *Guizotia scabra schimperi* (53)

JELOMISCET (Amh) *Satureja abyssinica* (122)

JEMO (Amh) *Balanites aegyptiaca* (236)

JEREMME (Or) *Dichrostachys cinera* (130)

JERENCHI (Or) *Caylusea abyssinica* (185)

JERIN (Som) *Acacia sieberiana* (311)

JIABARA (Tya) *Portulacca quadrifida* (178)

JIIQ (Som) *Acacia seyal* (308)

JIMAERTU (Or) *Leucas martinicensis* (109)

JIRMA-JALESA (Or) *Steganotaenia araliaceae* (29)

JIMA'-HARRE (Or) *Maytenus senegalensis* (264)

JOLIYA-MITA (Wel) *Hagenia abyssinica* (388)

'JORE (Gur) *Rubus apetalus* (186)

'JORE (Gur) *Rubus steudneri* (189)

JULI (Kun) *Balanites aegyptiaca* (236)

JUMEFOK (Or) *Bersama abyssinica* (348)

KACHA (Amh & Ade) *Agave sisalana* (22)

KACHABA (Had) *Achyranthes aspera* (25)

KACHEBA (Had) *Cynoglossum coeruleum* (78)

KACHIYA (Wel) *Agave sisalana* (22)

KADDO (Or) *Trifolium rueppellianum* (145)

KAFAL (Or) *Boswellia papyrifera* (255)

KAFO-DREGANTA (Wel) *Brassica nigra* (81)

KAJIMA (Or) *Pterrolobium stellatum* (141)

KAKERO (Amh) *Brucea antidysenterica* (197)

KAKITE-HARMATH (Tya) *Tribulus terrestris* (213)

KALABA (Or) *Sida rhombifolia* (161)

KALANICA (Kef) *Erythrina abyssinica* (323)

KALAWA (Amh) *Maesa lanceolata* (165)

KALKWOL (Tya) *Euphorbium candelabrum* (276)

KAMON (Or) *Trachyspermum ammi* (29)

KAMU (Amh) *Maytenus gracilipes* (89)

KAMUN (Amh) *Anethum foeniculum* (26)

KAMUNI (Or) *Anethum foeniculum* (26)

KAMUNI (Or) *Anethum graveolens* (26)

KAMUNI (Or) *Trachyspermum ammi* (29)

KANKAMO (Wel) *Echinops giganteus* (46)

KARACO (Kef) *Polyscias fulva* (228)

KARAMUT (Tya) *Sphaeranthus suaveolens* (66)

KARARO (Or) *Aningeria altissima* (411)

KARASHO (Or) *Polyscias fulva* (228)

KARCECCE (Or) *Milletia ferruginea* (331)

KARCHABA (Or) *Pavonia urens* (161)

KARCOFFE (Or) *Albizia gummifera* (315)

KARCOFFE (Or) *Albizia schimperiana* (319)

KARO (Gur) *Osyris quadripartita* (190)

KARRO (Kef) *Ficus sur* (351)

KARUAK (Tya) *Ehretia cymosa* (248)

KASEY (Or) *Lippia adoensis* (210)

KASSE (Or) *Ocimum basilicum* (110)

KASSY (Or) *Pentas schimperiana* (189)

KASTA ANSITEE (Tya) *Asparagus africanus* (150)

KATABIR (Som) *Dichrostachys cinera* (130)

KATATR (Tya) *Leucas martinicensis* (109)

KATEKATE (Or) *Lantana camera* (210)

KATHI (Mur) *Triumfetta rhomboidea* (206)

KAYA (Nuw) *Brassica carinata* (81)

KAZAMORA (Amh) *Casimiroa edulis* (399)

KAZMIER (Tya) *Casimiroa edulis* (399)

KEBSE (Gur) *Hagenia abyssinica* (388)

KEFO (Or) *Ocimum basilicum* (110)

KEKAYI (Or) *Allophyllus abyssinicus* (407)

KELLA (Tre) *Ricinus communis* (279)

KELO (Or) *Bidens ghedoensis* (34)

KELO (Or) *Bidens macroptera* (34)

KELO (Or) *Bidens pachyloma* (37)

KELO (Or) *Bidens prestinaria* (37)

KENDAMA (Or) *Ocimum basilicum* (110)

KENEY (Tya) *Dichrostachys cinera* (130)

KERARA (Agew) *Dodonea angustifolia* (408)

KERBONI (Sid) *Polyscias fulva* (228)

KES-KESA (Amh) *Laggera pterodonata* (58)

KESHESHLLA (Tya) *Rubus steudneri* (189)

KESSIE (Amh) *Lantana trifolia* (210)

KESSIE (Amh) *Lippia adoensis* (210)

KESTENNICHA (Amh) *Asparagus africanus* (150)

KETEME (Amh) *Schefflera abyssinica* (231)

KETETINNA (Amh) *Verbascum sinaiticum* (194)

KIAFREG *Sida schimperiana* (162)

KIBIRU (Or) *Bersama abyssinica* (348)

KIMATARI (Or) *Datura stramonium* (198)

KIMBO (Or) *Calotropis procera* (30)

KINCHIBA (Kef) *Euphorbia tirucalli* (101)

KIRNCHIT (Amh) *Oxygonum sinuatum* (177)

KIYARE (Amh) *Cucumis sativus* (97)

KODO (Tya) *Ficus sur* (351)

KOH' (Tya) *Prunus persica* (395)

KOILO (Amh) *Echinops ellenbeckii* (46)

KOK (Amh, Ge'ez & Gur) *Prunus persica* (395)

KOKI (Or) *Prunus persica* (395)

KOL (Amh) *Ximenia americana* (372)

KOLANCU (Kef) *Erythrina abyssinica* (323)

KOLANCU (Kef) *Erythrina brucei* (324)

KOLANICA (Kef) *Erythrina brucei* (324)

KOLQUAL (Amh) *Euphorbia abyssinica* (275)

KOMBOLCA (Or) *Maytenus obscura* (263)

KOMBOLCA (Or) *Maytenus senegalensis* (264)

KOMBOLCHA (Or) *Maytenus gracilipes* (89)

KOMBORRE (Or) *Echinops longisetus* (49)

KOMMER (Tya) *Adansonia digitata* (243)

KONTER (Or) *Linum usitatissimum* (153)

KONU (Or) *Trichilia dregeana* (347)

KOOMUTO (Gur) *Oxygonum sinuatum* (177)

KORA (Or) *Piliostigma thonningii* (335)

KORA (Or) *Rosmarinus officinalis* (118)

KORAKA (Or) *Bersama abyssinica* (348)

KORATTI-SARE (Or) *Hygrophila auriculata* (17)

KORE-ADI (Or-Harerge) *Echinops longisetus* (49)

KORE-BUSE (Or) *Xanthium spinosum* (73)

KORIBA (Or) *Polyscias fulva* (228)

KORISSA (Or) *Plantago lanceolata* (170)

KOROMO (Tya) *Maerua angolensis* (86)

KORTOBI (Gur) *Plantago lanceolata* (170)

KOSERET (Amh) *Lippia adoensis* (210)

KOSHESHLA (Amh) *Acanthus sennii* (14)

KOSHESHLA (Amh) *Carduus camaecephalus* (38)

KOSHESHLA (Amh) *Carduus nyassanus* (38)

KOSHESHLA (Amh) *Cirsium englerianum* (41)

KOSHESHLA (Amh) *Cirsium schimperi* (42)

KOSHESHLA (Amh) *Echinops ellenbeckii* (46)

KOSHESHLA (Amh) *Echinops giganteus* (46)

KOSHESHLA (Amh) *Echinops hispidus* (46)

KOSHESHLA (Amh) *Echinops macrochaetus* (49)

KOSHESHLA (Amh) *Xanthium spinosum* (73)

KOSHESHLLA (Tya) *Rubus apetalus* (186)

KOSHM (Amh) *Dovyalis caffra* (283)

KOSHM (Amh) *Dovyalis abyssinica*

KOSKUS (Amh) *Trichodesma zeylanicum* (78)

KOSO (Amh) *Hagenia abyssinica* (388)

KOSORU (Or) *Acanthus sennii* (14)

KOSORU (Or) *Echinops longisetus* (49)

KOSUWA (Wel) *Hagenia abyssinica* (388)

KOTEBAY (Or) *Scorpiurus muricatus* (141)

KOTELLU (Or) *Milletia ferruginea* (331)

KOTTO (Tya) *Lepidium sativum* (82)

KTKTTA (Amh, Gur, Kem & Saho) *Dodonea angustifolia* (408)

KUDKUDDA (Amh) *Balanites aegyptiaca* (236)

KUL (Amh) *Lagenaria abyssinica* (97)

KUMUTO (Or) *Medicago polymorpha* (134)

KURAVA (Amh) *Maytenus gracilipes* (89)

KUREMEHIT (Tya) *Tribulus terrestris* (213)

KURNCHT (Amh) *Medicago polymorpha* (134)

KURO (Or) *Aningeria altissima* (411)

KURRUNFULI (Or) *Syzygium guineense* subsp. *afromontanum* (368)

KURUMSHIT (Or) *Tribulus terrestris* (213)

KUSAY (Tya) *Lippia adoensis* (210)

KWA'K'ITO (Tya) *Tribulus terrestris* (213)

KWA'KITO (Tya) *Medicago polymorpha* (134)

KWI'HA (Ge'ez & Tya) *Salix subserrata* (404)

LA'HAM (Tya) *Syzygium guineense* subsp. *afromontanum* (368)

DOKMA (Amh) *Syzygium guineense* subsp. *guineense* (371)

LABUNCHE (Or) *Commelina benghalensis* (89)

LAFTO (Or) *Acacia abyssinica* (291)

LAFTO (Or) *Acacia dolichocephala* (295)

LAFTO (Or) *Acacia pilispina* (303)

LAFTO (Or) *Acacia sieberiana* (311)

LAFTO (Or) *Acacia lahai* (296)

LAFTO-ADI (Or) *Acacia sieberiana* (311)

LAHAY (Tya) *Acacia lahai* (296)

LALATO (Or) *Acacia sieberiana* (311)

LALUNTYE (Gur) *Commelina benghalensis* (89)

LANKUSO (Or) *Dracaena steudneri* (216)

LANSO (Gam) *Salix subserrata* (404)

LEBBEK (Amh) *Albizia lebbek* (316)

LELDA (Or-Bale) *Kniphofia foliosa* (153)

LEMIN (Tya) *Citrus aurantifolia* (400)

LEMUN (Tre) *Citrus aurantifolia* (400)

LENQUATA (Amh) *Dombeya torrida* (412)

LEYEKWA-RIBA (Tya) *Persicaria setosula* (177)

LIBAH-HALALALIS (Som) *Pterrolobium stellatum* (141)

LIBANAT (Ade & Or) *Boswellia papyrifera* (255)

LILU (Or) *Piliostigma thonningii* (335)

LITA (Or) *Pavonia urens* (161)

LITI (Or) *Malva verticillata* (161)

LMMCH (Amh) *Clausena anisata* (403)

LOL (Amh) *Ekebergia capensis* (343)

LOLA (Amh) *Pittosporum abyssinicum* (170)

LOLCISA (Or) *Bersama abyssinica* (348)

LOMI (Amh) *Citrus aurantifolia* (400)

LOMI (Or) *Citrus aurantifolia* (400)

LONGATA (Amh) *Grewia ferruginea* (205)

LOTTOBA (Or) *Acacia tortilis* (312)

LT'-MAREFYA (Amh) *Crassocephalum vitellinum* (45)

LUGO (Or) *Kalanchoe quartiniana* (93)

LUIYA (Kef) *Trichilia dregeana* (347)

LUKINA (Amh, Or & Tya) *Leucena leucocephala* (327)

LUYA (Or) *Trichilia dregeana* (347)

MACCA (Kef) *Dodonea angustifolia* (408)

MAGALA (Or) *Ximenia americana* (372)

MAGET (Amh) all *Trifolium* spp. (141-146)

MAGOSHIMO (Kef) *Trifolium burchellianum* (141)

MAHARA (Kun) *Acacia senegal* (307)

MAJITE (Amh) *Grewia velutina* (415)

MAKANI (Afar) *Acacia seyal* (308)

MAKOTA (Wel) *Sorghum bicolor* (173)

MAKRUS (Tre) *Ranunculus multifidus* (182)

MAMAN (Saho) *Acacia albida* (292)

MANDARA (Bur) *Dodonea angustifolia* (408)

MANDELDO (Tya) *Plantago lanceolata* (170)

MANDURAT (Som) *Ximenia americana* (372)

MANGO (Amh, Or & Tya) *Mangifera indica* (219)

MANJI (Or) *Datura stramonium* (198)

MARARAJA (Amh & Tya) *Otostegia integrifolia* (113)

MARARO (Or) *Discopodium penninervium* (198)

MAREYTA (Kon) *Dodonea angustifolia* (408)

MARFATU (Or) *Schefflera abyssinica* (231)

MARRAT (Tya) *Vernonia leopoldii* (70)

MASCHILL (Tya) *Commelina benghalensis* (89)

MASHASHE (Amh) *Brassica carinata* (81)

MASHLA (Amh & Or) *Sorghum bicolor* (173)

MASSAGANTA (Kon) *Croton macrostachys* (272)

MATANE-CHATI (Or) *Cynoglossum coeruleum* (78)

MATANNE (Or) *Achyranthes aspera* (25)

MATENEH (Sid) *Achyranthes aspera* (25)

MATOSCH (Amh) *Becium grandiflorum* (106)

MATTERI (Tya) *Buddleja polystachya* (251)

MAWORDI (Ade) *Rosa abyssinica* (186)

'MBRITTO (Kef) *Clausena anisata* (403)

'MBS (Amh) *Allophyllus abyssinicus* (407)

'MBS (Amh) *Rhus glutinosa* (220)

MBWAI(Amh) *Solanum giganteum* (202)

MECECO (Tre) *Rhus glutinosa* (220)

MECH' (Amh) *Guizotia scabra schimperi* (53)

MECHELO (Tya) *Achyranthes aspera* (25)

MEDAFE (Amh) *Argemone mexicana* (169)

MEDAFE-T'LYAN (Tya) *Argemone mexicana* (169)

MEDALLE (Or) *Ficus sur* (351)

MEDANIT (Amh) *Ajuga integrifolia* (106)

MEDER (Tya) *Triumfetta rhomboidea* (206)

MEDISSA (Sid) *Clerodendron myricoides* (209)

MEI (Or) *Apodytes dimidiata* (287)

MEKICHU (Sid) *Olea europaea subsp. cuspidata* (376)

MELAKO (Or) *Erythrina abyssinica* (323)

MELAKO (Or) *Erythrina brucei* (324)

MELITA (Tya) *Brucea antidysenterica* (197)

MELKHENA (Tya) *Portulacca quadrifida* (178)

MELLITANO (Gam) *Rubus apetalus* (186)

MELLITANO (Gam) *Rubus steudneri* (189)

MENCHA (Amh) *Sesamum indicum* (169)

MENGI (Tya) *Rhus glutinosa* (220)

MEQER (Tya) *Boswellia papyrifera* (255)

MEQI (Tya) *Balanites aegyptiaca* (236)

MERE (Tya) *Maerua angolensis* (86)

MERKO (Or) *Dracaena steudneri* (216)

MERRERET (Tre) *Caylusea abyssinica* (185)

MESERBA' (Tya) *Datura stramonium* (198)

MESI (Tya) *Trifolium acaule* (141)

MESI (Tya) *Trifolium decorum* (142)

MESI (Tya) *Trifolium quartinianum* (142)

MESI (Tya) *Trifolium rueppellianum* (145)

MESI (Tya) *Trifolium schimperi* (145)

MESI (Tya) *Trifolium steudneri* (146)

MESRY (Ge'ez) *Rosa x richardii* (186)

MESSERIK (Amh) *Jasminum abyssinicum* (165)

MESSI (Tya) *Trifolium simense* (145)

METMETI (Tya) *Ranunculus multifidus* (182)

METTI (Or) *Phoenix reclinata* (232)

MICIKKO (Sid) *Prunus africana* (391)

MIDAN-RAFU (Or) *Brassica carinata* (81)

MIDANI-BERA (Or) *Lantana trifolia* (210)

MIELO (Kef) *Ficus vasta* (352)

MIERSENS (Ge'ez) *Rosa abyssinica* (186)

MIESSA (Or) *Prunus africana* (391)

MIKICCO (Or) *Prunus africana* (391)

MIRSENS (Ge'ez) *Rosa abyssinica* (186)

MIRSNS (Ge'ez) *Rosa abyssinica* (186)

MISH-MISH (Or) *Tagetes minuta* (66)

MISINGA (Kef, Or & Som) *Sorghum bicolor* (173)

MISSIRICH (Amh) *Clerodendron cordifolium* (209)

MISSIRICH (Amh) *Clerodendron myricoides* (209)

MIT'MIT'A (Amh) *Capsicum annuum* (197)

MITESHIYYE (Wel) *Pittosporum abyssinicum* (170)

MITO (Or) *Galineria saxifraga* (189)

MITO (Or) *Hypericum quartinianum* (105)

MKOKO (Amh) *Solanum indicum* (202)

ML'O (Tya) *Ximenia americana* (372)

MLHTTA (Tre) *Ximenia americana* (372)

MOAD (Tya) *Steganotaenia araliaceae* (29)

MOKONISSA (Or) *Croton macrostachys* (272)

MOKOTO (Or) *Cordia africana* (247)

MOMONA (Tya) *Acacia albida* (292)

MOMRET (Tya) *Adansonia digitata* (243)

MONDRUK (Som) *Ximenia americana* (372)

MORHOD (Som) *Ximenia americana* (372)

MRSENIEN (Ge'ez) *Rosa abyssinica* (186)

MUCA-MICHIANCHABI (Or) *Ocimum lamiifolium* (110)

MUCHA-ARAB (Or) *Rumex nepalensis* (178)

MUDA (Gam) *Kalanchoe petitiana* (93)

MUDA (Gam) *Kalanchoe quartiniana* (93)

MUGAN (Or) *Rhus glutinosa* (220)

MUKA AJAYA (Or) *Tagetes minuta* (66)

MUKERBA (Amh) *Ehretia cymosa* (248)

MUKKA-ARBA (Or) *Albizia gummifera* (315)

MUKKA-ARBA (Or) *Albizia schimperiana* (319)

MUKKA-DIMA (Or) *Prunus africana* (391)

MUKKA-RAJA (Or) *Prunus africana* (391)

MUKOFONI (Or) *Hypericum quartinianum* (105)

MUSERICH (Or) *Clerodendron myricoides* (209)

MUTANSA (Amh) *Satureja abyssinica* (122)

MUTCHULO (Tya) *Achyranthes aspera* (25)

MUTE (Had) *Bidens pilosa* (37)

MUTTO (Kef) *Linum usitatissimum* (153)

MUZ (Amh & Or) *Musa x paradisiaca* (355)

N'CHET (Amh) *Pithecellobium dulce* (336)

'NABA (Or) *Vitis vinifera* (213)

NADDO (Amh) *Satureja paradoxa* (122)

NADDO (Kef) *Trifolium quartinianum* (142)

NADDO (Kef) *Trifolium rueppellianum* (145)

NADDO (Kef) *Trifolium steudneri* (146)

NEC-ATAT (Amh) *Maytenus senegalensis* (264)

'NDAARO (Saho) *Ficus vasta* (352)

'NDAHULLA (Amh) *Kalanchoe densiflora* (90)

'NDAHULLA (Amh) *Kalanchoe marmorata* (93)

'NDAHULLA (Amh) *Kalanchoe quartiniana* (93)

NDOD (Amh) *Phytolacca dodecandra* (170)

NECH'-AZMUD (Amh) *Trachyspermum ammi* (29)

NEHUKAS (Tya) *Guizotia scabra schimperi* (53)

NEKELKEGNE (Amh) *Galinsoga parviflora* (50)

'NGEDICCO (Sid) *Milletia ferruginea* (331)

'NGOCA (Gur) *Rosa abyssinica* (186)

'NGULE (Tya) *Solanum incanum* (202)

NIHUK (Tya) *Guizotia abyssinica* (53)

NIM (Tya, Tre & Saho) *Azadirachta indica* (340)

'NJORIE *(Amh) Morus alba* (162)

'NJORIE (Amh) *Rubus apetalus* (186)

'NJORIE (Amh) *Rubus rosifolius* (186)

'NJORIE (Amh) *Rubus steudneri* (189)

'NKOY (Amh) *Ximenia americana* (372)

'NKUTI (Ge'ez) *Vitis vinifera* (213)

NOBE (Kef) *Solanecio gigas* (65)

NOLLE (Or) *Olinia rochetiana* (379)

'NQOTO (Or) *Rosa abyssinica* (186)

'NQWI-HBEY (Tya) *Erythrina abyssinica* (323)

'NQWI-ZBI (Tya) *Erythrina abyssinica* (323)

'NSLAL (Amh & Tya) *Anethum foeniculum* (26)

'NSLAL (Amh) *Anethum graveolens* (26)

'NSLAL (Amh & Tya) *Ferula communis* (29)

NT'AT'I (Tya) *Linum usitatissimum* (153)

NUG (Amh) *Guizotia abyssinica* (53)

NUGA (Had & Kem) *Guizotia abyssinica* (53)

NUGHIO (Kef) *Guizotia abyssinica* (53)

NUGI (Afar & Or) *Guizotia abyssinica* (53)

NUGI ADI (Or) *Helianthus annuus* (54)

NUGI GURACHA (Or) *Nigella sativa* (182)

NUHUK (Tre) *Guizotia abyssinica* (53)

OBAH (Som) *Combretum molle* (267)

OCHA (Or) *Syzygium guineense* subsp. *afromontanum* (368)

ODA (Or) *Apodytes dimidiata* (287)

ODA-BADA (Or) *Apodytes dimidiata* (287)

ODABEDDA (Or) *Ficus sur* (351)

ODA-KIYET (Or) *Apodytes dimidiata* (287)

ODARA (Kem) *Acacia abyssinica* (291)

ODA-SEDA (Or) *Apodytes dimidiata* (287)

ODORO (Wel) *Acacia abyssinica* (291)

ODORWA (Wel) *Acacia abyssinica* (291)

ODORWA (Wel) *Acacia sieberiana* (311)

OKALA (Kon) *Lablab purpureus* (133)

OKOLE (Sid) *Acanthus sennii* (14)

OLEÄMO (Anu) *Ximenia americana* (372)

OLOLA (Had) *Ficus vasta* (352)

OLOMO (Wel) *Pycnostachys abyssinica* (117)

OMBI (Som) *Adenium obesum* (224)

ONSA (Wel) *Prunus africana* (391)

ORA (Som) *Acacia tortilis* (312)

ORGEESA (Or) *Aloe berhana* (22)

ORKETA (Gam) *Adenium obesum* (224)

ORONCE (Sid) *Schefflera abyssinica* (231)

PAPAYA (Amh) *Carica papaya* (260)

PRUN (Amh) *Prunus x domestica* (392)

PULLIESA (Wel) *Acacia sieberiana* (311)

QA'CHA (Amh) *Agave americana* (22)

QACONA (Amh) *Balanites aegyptiaca* (236)

QALQALLA (Wel) *Piliostigma thonningii* (335)

QALQALLO (Wel) *Piliostigma thonningii* (335)

QAMSHI (Tre & Tya) *Allophyllus abyssinicus* (407)

QANQALSHA (Or) *Lonchocarpus laxiflorus* (328)

QAQ (Tre) *Balanites aegyptiaca* (236)

QAQAWWE (Or) *Rosa abyssinica* (186)

QARACCA (Or) *Bersama abyssinica* (348)

QARYA (Amh) *Capsicum annuum* (197)

QATTATO (Tya) *Bidens pilosa* (37)

QEBQEB (Tya) *Maytenus senegalensis* (264)

QEGA (Amh & Or) *Rosa abyssinica* (186)

QEMIDA (Tya) *Clematis hirsuta* (181)

QENT'AFFA (Amh) *Pterrolobium stellatum* (141)

QENTB (Tya) *Acacia senegal* (307)

QENTBI (Tya) *Acacia senegal* (307)

QENTETEFE (Tre) *Pterrolobium stellatum* (141)

QENTIBA (Tya) *Acacia senegal* (307)

QEQEWWI (Or) *Pterrolobium stellatum* (141)

QEQEWWI (Or) *Rosa abyssinica* (186)

QERERO (Amh) *Aningeria altissima* (411)

QERERRIE (Amh) *Boswellia papyrifera* (255)

QERES (Amh, Tre & Tya) *Osyris quadripartita* (190)

QERES (Tya) *Osyris quadripartita* (190)

QERETOR (Gam) *Acacia albida* (292)

QERETOR (Gam) *Acacia lahai* (296)

QEY-BARZAF (Amh) *Eucalyptus camaldulensis* (359)

QEY-SHNKURT (Amh) *Allium cepa* (150)

QEYYH'-CHE'A' (Tya) *Acacia seyal* (308)

QILTU (Or) *Ficus vasta* (352)

QISHEWE (Gur) *Pisum sativum* (138)

QMMO (Amh) *Rhus glutinosa* (220)

QN'CHB (Amh & Tya) *Euphorbium candelabrum* (276)

QN'CHB (Amh) *Euphorbia tirucalli* (101)

QOG (Tre) *Balanites aegyptiaca* (236)

QOLOSHM (Tre) *Rosa abyssinica* (186)

QOLQWAL (Amh) *Euphorbium candelabrum* (276)

QOMOLO (Gam) *Vicia faba* (149)

QONDE (Had) *Calpurnia aurea* (320)

QONT'EFT'EFE (Tya) *Pterrolobium stellatum* (141)

QONT'R (Amh & Gur) *Pterrolobium stellatum* (141)

QONT'R (Amh) *Acacia senegal* (307)

QONT'R (Amh) *Caesalpina decapetala* (126)

QONT'R (Amh) *Caesalpina spinosa* (126)

QONTOMA (Or) *Kalanchoe lanceolata* (93)

QOQQOBA (Amh) *Maytenus senegalensis* (264)

QORCH (Amh) *Erythrina brucei* (324)

QORCH (Amh) *Erythrina abyssinica* (323)

QOTTBET (Tya) *Tribulus terrestris* (213)

QRUBITA-ARAZ (Saho) *Osyris quadripartita* (190)

QSLTO (Afar) *Acacia abyssinica* (291)

QTELE-REJIM (Amh) *Rumex nepalensis* (178)

QUERERET (Gur) *Lippia adoensis* (210)

QUERET (Amh) *Osyris quadripartita* (190)

QULQWAL (Amh) *Euphorbium candelabrum* (276)

QULQWAL (Amh) *Opuntia ficus-indica* (256)

QUMBALA (Or) *Apodytes dimidiata* (287)

QUSSA (Agew) *Balanites aegyptiaca* (236)

QUSTYA (Amh) *Schefflera abyssinica* (231)

QUTTA (Agew) *Balanites aegyptiaca* (236)

QWARA (Agew & Amh) *Erythrina brucei* (324)

QWARA (Agew, Amh, Bil & Tya)*Erythrina abyssinica* (323)

QWET (Tya) *Ekebergia capensis* (343)

QWRHO (Tya) *Cyphostemma adenocaule* (213)

RAHA (Or)*Rhamnus prinoides* (384)

RAHA (Or) *Pittosporum abyssinicum* (170)

RAQAKA (Ge'ez) *Ximenia americana* (372)

RARAWAYE (Mes) *Lonchocarpus laxiflorus* (328)

RAS KMR (Amh) *Leonotis ocymifolia* (109)

RAS KMR (Amh) *Leucas martinicensis* (109)

REGA (Or) *Osyris quadripartita* (190)

REGI (Amh & Sid) *Vernonia auriculifera* (69)

RENDI (Or) *Caylusea abyssinica* (185)

RENGAZENA (Kem) *Milletia ferruginea* (331)

RIGA (Amh) *Salix subserrata* (404)

RODUT (Tya) *Achyranthes aspera* (25)

ROHAZ (Tya) *Syzygium guineense* subsp. *afromontanum* (368)

ROOMA (Amh) *Punica granatum* (181)

ROQA (Amh, Or & Som) *Tamarindus indica* (339)

ROSMARINO (Amh) *Rosmarinus officinalis* (118)

RUAYNI (Nuw) *Sorghum bicolor* (173)

RUMANA (Kef) *Punica granatum* (181)

SA'DA-CHE'A' (Tya) *Acacia seyal* (308)

SA'DA-CHE'A' (Tya) *Acacia sieberiana* (311)

SA-TO (Or) *Erica arborea* (271)

SABANSA-DIMA (Or) *Acacia senegal* (307)

SACHAB (Kef) *Brassica carinata* (81)

SALADO (Gam) *Ruta chalepensis* (190)

SAMAREYE (Or) *Solanum nigrum* (205)

SAMIE (Or) *Bidens pilosa* (37)

SAMMA (Amh & Tya) *Urtica simensis* (209)

SAMO (Gam) *Rhus glutinosa* (220)

SANAVI (Or) *Brassica nigra* (81)

SANDAN-SHOA (Tya) *Anethum graveolens* (26)

SANKILE (Or) *Albizia schimperiana* (319)

SANKILE (Or) *Albizia gummifera* (315)

SANT (Ge'ez) *Cicer arietinum* (129)

SAPESSA (Or) *Acacia senegal* (307)

SARAGI (Or) *Allophyllus abyssinicus* (407)

SARARA (Or) *Allophyllus abyssinicus* (407)

SARI (Or) *Milletia ferruginea* (331)

SASA (Amh & Or) *Albizia schimperiana* (319)

SASA (Amh & Or) *Albizia gummifera* (315)

SASAT (Saho) *Dodonea angustifolia* (408)

SASSAG-WUCHARIA (Amh) *Satureja abyssinica* (122)

SATAWEE (Or) *Persicaria setosula* (177)

SAUMAH (Tya) *Grewia ferruginea* (205)

SBANSA-GRAR (Amh) *Acacia senegal* (307)

SCHIRBA (Amh) *Capsicum annuum* (197)

SCIAMHEGIT (Amh) *Triumfetta pilosa* (206)

SEBBERE (Tya & Saho) *Lathyrus sativus* (133)

SEBBERE-ANCH'WA (Tya) *Vicia sativa* (149)

SEBBERE-GWASOT (Tya) *Vicia sativa* (149)

SEEDDEESA (Kef) *Trifolium acaule* (141)

SEGO (Had) *Rosa abyssinica* (186)

SEKENDER (Tya) *Carthamus lanatus* (38)

SEKORRU (Kef) *Gloriosa simplex* (153)

SEKORU (Or) *Echinops longisetus* (49)

SELAN (Amh) *Anethum graveolens* (26)

SELIBATIQO (Bil) *Balanites aegyptiaca* (236)

SELIEN (Amh) *Phoenix reclinata* (232)

SELIT' (Amh) *Sesamum indicum* (169)

SELOTIE (Gam) *Ruta chalepensis* (190)

SEMBO (Amh & Or) *Ekebergia capensis* (343)

SENAFCH' (Amh & Tre) *Sinapis alba* (85)

SENAFCH' (Amh & Tya) *Brassica nigra* (81)

SENAFICCIA (Or) *Brassica nigra* (81)

SENATAM (Ge'ez) *Ruta chalepensis* (190)

SENGWEREFYA (Tya) *Lonchocarpus laxiflorus* (328)

SENKARA (Wel) *Dodonea angustifolia* (408)

SENSEL (Amh) *Justitia schimperana* (21)

SEÖ (Or) *Allophyllus abyssinicus* (407)

SEQUINON (Ge'ez) *Prunus persica* (395)

SERDO (Amh) *Eleusine floccifolia* (173)

SERREETTEE (Or) *Asparagus africanus* (150)

SERREROT (Tya) *Sideroxylon oxyacantha* (190)

SERRUFIT (Tya) *Verbena officinalis* (213)

SESA (Amh) *Albizia schimperiana* (319)

SESA (Amh) *Albizia gummifera* (315)

SESA (Or) *Bersama abyssinica* (348)

SESEG (Tya) *Ocimum basilicum* (110)

SESHA-A (Kem) *Guizotia scabra schimperi* (53)

SESSEG-GOLLA (Tya) *Satureja abyssinica* (122)

SESSEG-WU'KARIA (Tya) *Satureja simensis* (122)

SGIE-REDA-CISHA (Wel) *Rosa abyssinica* (186)

SHAFA (Tya) *Ficus sur* (351)

SHAGA (Or) *Combretum paniculatum* (89)

SHAKTO (Tya) *Erica arborea* (271)

SHAL (Amh) *Trifolium polystachyum* (142)

SHANGO (Or) *Sorghum bicolor* (173)

SHASHO (Wel) *Albizia lebbek* (316)

SHATO (Kef) *Commelina benghalensis* (89)

SHBT'I (Tya) *Phytolacca dodecandra* (170)

SHEBBO (Kef) *Vernonia thomsoniana* (73)

SHEDO (Kef) *Sapium ellipticum* (280)

SHEGO (Or) *Trichilia dregeana* (347)

SHEKO (Amh) *Heliotropium cinerascens* (78)

SHEMET'MAT' (Amh) *Kniphofia foliosa* (153)

SHEMUT (Tre) *Rhus glutinosa* (220)

SHEMUT-EFRUS (Tre) *Rhus glutinosa* (220)

SHEÖ (Kef) *Allophyllus abyssinicus* (407)

SHERA (Gam) *Acacia tortilis* (312)

SHETTO (Kef) *Bothriocline schimperi* (37)

SHIGURTI (Tya) *Allium cepa* (150)

SHILAN (Tya) *Anethum graveolens* (26)

SHIMBERO (Or) *Lantana camera* (210)

SHIMFA (Tya) *Justitia schimperana* (21)

SHIMFA (Tya) *Lepidium sativum* (82)

SHIMFI (Or) *Lepidium sativum* (82)

SHIMORO (Or) *Albizia schimperiana* (319)

SHIMORO (Or) *Albizia gummifera* (315)

SHIMP (Kef) *Lepidium sativum* (82)

SHINKUR-AGEDA (Amh)*Saccharum officinarum* (173)

SHINUR (Afar & Som) *Pittosporum abyssinicum* (170)

SHIQOTA (Had) *Trigonella foenum-graecum* (146)

SHISHIE (Som) *Maerua angolensis* (86)

SHIT (Ge'ez) *Calpurnia aurea* (320)

SHITO-BAHR-ZAF (Amh) *Eucalyptus citriodora* (360)

SHMBRA (Amh, Tya & Tre) *Cicer arietinum* (129)

SHNKORA (Amh & Or) *Saccharum officinarum* (173)

SHNQAQ (Amh) *Kalanchoe quartiniana* (93)

SHOFNA (Agew) *Carthamus lanatus* (38)

SHOK' (Amh) *Echinops giganteus* (46)

SHOLA (Amh) *Ficus sur* (351)

SHOLIE (Afar & Som) *Pittosporum abyssinicum* (170)

SHOLO (Or) *Pittosporum abyssinicum* (170)

SHOWYE (Or) *Dracaena steudneri* (216)

SHUCAR (Or) *Coriandrum sativum* (26)

SHUMBURA (Gur, Had, Or, Wel & Gam) *Cicer arietinum* (129)

SHUNKWORI (Amh) *Steganotaenia araliaceae* (29)

SHUÖ (Kem) *Trigonella foenum-graecum* (146)

SHUQO (Gamo) *Trigonella foenum-graecum* (146)

SHUQWA (Wel) *Trigonella foenum-graecum* (146)

SIDDISA (Or) *Trifolium quartinianum* (142)

SIDDISA (Or) *Trifolium simense* (145)

SIDDISA (Or) *Trifolium steudneri* (146)

SIDISSA (Gur) *Trifolium rueppellianum* (145)

SIEWA (Ge'ez) *Rhamnus prinoides* (384)

SILAN (Ge'ez) *Trigonella foenum-graecum* (146)

SINKHE (Tya) *Nicotiana tabacum* (201)

SINQO (Or) *Trigonella foenum-graecum* (146)

SISA (Or) *Albizia schimperiana* (319)

SISA (Or) *Albizia gummifera* (315)

SITAMO (Sid) *Olea capensis subsp. hochstetteri* (375)

SKINON (Ge'ez) *Prunus persica* (395)

SL'LO (Tya) *Maytenus obscura* (263)

SNDUQO (Gam) *Pterrolobium stellatum* (141)

SNFKO (Gur) *Clausena anisata* (403)

SOBERT (Ge'ez) *Hagenia abyssinica* (388)

SOBIEQAKA (Ge'ez) *Ximenia americana* (372)

SODA (Or) *Justitia schimperana* (21)

SOGDO (Or) *Oxygonum sinuatum* (177)

SOGIDAREA (Or) *Oxalis corniculata* (166)

SOKOKSA (Or) *Salvia nilotica* (121)

SOKORU (Or) *Acanthus sennii* (14)

SOLA (Afar & Som) *Pittosporum abyssinicum* (170)

SOLIE (Amh) *Galineria saxifraga* (189)

SOLITU (Or) *Calpurnia aurea* (320)

SOLLE (Or) *Olinia rochetiana* (379)

SOMBO (Or) *Ekebergia capensis* (343)

SONDI (Or) *Acacia lahai* (296)

SONDI (Or) *Acacia abyssinica* (291)

SONKUAH (Tya) *Dombeya torrida* (412)

SONO (Tya) *Hagenia abyssinica* (388)

SOSEN (Ge'ez) *Hagenia abyssinica* (388)

SOSHE (Or) *Prunus africana* (391)

SOTALLO (Or) *Milletia ferruginea* (331)

SOTELLI (Mes) *Milletia ferruginea* (331)

SOYAMA (Or) *Vernonia thomsoniana* (73)

SOYYOMA (Or) *Clerodendron myricoides* (209)

SQINON (Ge'ez) *Prunus persica* (395)

STRA (Tre) *Calpurnia aurea* (320)

SUF (Amh & Tya) *Carthamus tinctorius* (38)

SUF (Amh) *Helianthus annuus* (54)

SUFI (Or) *Carthamus tinctorius* (38)

SUFI-FERENJI (Or) *Helianthus annuus* (54)

SUKE (Or) *Lantana trifolia* (210)

SUKOT (Tya) *Hibiscus ludwigii* (158)

SUKUALE (Tya) *Vernonia leopoldii* (70)

SULTHE (Amh) *Clerodendron myricoides* (209)

SUMBURA (Ade & Afar) *Cicer arietinum* (129)

SUMBURO (Kem) *Cicer arietinum* (129)

SUMFA (Tya) *Lepidium sativum* (82)

SUNQO (Or) *Trigonella foenum-graecum* (146)

SUQQE (Or) *Prunus africana* (391)

SURBATRI (Tya) *Clerodendron myricoides* (209)

SUTO (Had) *Hagenia abyssinica* (388)

SWARYA (Tre & Tya) *Allophyllus abyssinicus* (407)

T'EF'RERIA (Tya) *Sida schimperiana* (162)

T'ELENJ (Amh) *Achyranthes aspera* (25)

T'EMBELAL (Amh) *Jasminum abyssinicum* (165)

T'ET'EM-AGAZEN (Tya) *Astralagus atropilosulus* (126)

T'IENA-ADDAM (Amh) *Ruta chalepensis* (190)

T'IFT'IRRIE (Amh & Or) *Gossypium hirsutum* (157)

T'KUR-AWTT' (Amh) *Solanum nigrum* (205)

T'KUR-AZMUD (Amh) *Nigella sativa* (182)

T'NJUT (Amh & Tya) *Otostegia integrifolia* (113)

T'NQSH (Amh) *Saccharum officinarum* (173)

T'QUR-BERBERE (Tya) *Schinus molle* (223)

T'QUR-BERBERIE (Amh) *Schinus molle* (223)

T'UT' (Tya) *Gossypium hirsutum* (157)

TABATOS (Amh) *Dracaena steudneri* (216)

TADO (Or) *Rhamnus prinoides* (384)

TAIFARETH (Tya) *Senecio hadiensis* (61)

TALAÖ (Or) *Polyscias fulva* (228)

TALATAM (Or) *Ruta chalepensis* (190)

TALBA (Amh) *Linum usitatissimum* (153)

TALE (Wel) *Ajuga integrifolia* (106)

TALIYA (Wel) *Hagenia abyssinica* (388)

TALO (Amh) *Maytenus gracilipes* (89)

TAMBO (Or) *Nicotiana rustica* (201)

TAMBUCH (Tre) *Croton macrostachys* (272)

TAMIGGIA (Or) *Brucea antidysenterica* (197)

TANDO (Wel) *Rhamnus prinoides* (384)

TASES (Bil) *Dodonea angustifolia* (408)

TASHES (Tre & Tya) *Dodonea angustifolia* (408)

TATESSA (Or) *Rhus glutinosa* (220)

TCHEMA (Gur) *Hagenia abyssinica* (388)

TEBEB (Tya) *Becium grandiflorum* (106)

TEBERAKO (Sid) *Bersama abyssinica* (348)

TEBERQO (Or) *Bersama abyssinica* (348)

TEDDECCA (Or) *Dodonea angustifolia* (408)

TEDDECCA (Or) *Acacia tortilis* (312)

TEDDECCA (Or) *Acacia negrii* (299)

TEKATILLA (Amh) *Tapinanthus globiferus* (154)

TELALO (Amh) *Maytenus gracilipes* (89)

TELBA (Amh) *Linum usitatissimum* (153)

TELENGE (Amh) *Justitia ladanoides* (21)

TEMBELEL-BILU (Or) *Jasminum abyssinicum* (165)

TENADDAM (Or) *Satureja paradoxa* (122)

TENAKA (Ge'ez) *Ficus vasta* (352)

TEO (Or) *Jasminum abyssinicum* (165)

TERBIENTO (Ge'ez) *Ficus vasta* (352)

TERERAK (Amh) *Jasminum abyssinicum* (165)

TERMIEN (Ge'ez) *Dodonea angustifolia* (408)

TESTES (Gum) *Allophyllus abyssinicus* (407)

TETA'LO (Tya) *Rhus glutinosa* (220)

TFIE (Amh) *Olinia rochetiana* (379)

THEIABI (Tya) *Scabiosa columbaria* (98)

THRIFRA (Tya) *Datura stramonium* (198)

TIBIRA (Or) *Bersama abyssinica* (348)

TIEMA (Kem) *Hagenia abyssinica* (388)

TIFFE (Amh) *Sideroxylon oxyacantha* (190)

TIKWA (Amh) *Vernonia adoensis* (69)

TILLO (Amh) *Clematis simensis* (181)

TIMAD (Som) *Acacia tortilis* (312)

TIMATIM (Amh) *Lycopersicon esculentum* (198)

TIMBO (Or) *Nicotiana tabacum* (201)

TINI (Or) *Opuntia ficus-indica* (256)

TIRNAHA (Tya) *Verbascum sinaiticum* (194)

TIRRO (Or) *Clerodendron myricoides* (209)

TITAKO (Or) *Melilotus suaveolens* (137)

TITO (Gam) *Dodonea angustifolia* (408)

TKUR GRAR (Amh) *Acacia lahai* (296)

TLEM (Or) *Dodonea angustifolia* (408)

TMBAHO (Amh) *Nicotiana tabacum* (201)

TOBBIYA (Amh) *Calotropis procera* (30)

TOLLO (Or) *Brucea antidysenterica* (197)

TOLOLAT (Amh) *Caylusea abyssinica* (185)

TONTAN (Amh) *Pycnostachys abyssinica* (117)

TORSERAWIT (Amh) *Xanthium spinosum* (73)

TOSGN (Amh) *Satureja paradoxa* (122)

TOSGN (Amh) *Satureja punctata* (122)

TOSGN (Amh) *Thymus schimperi* (125)

TOSSINGO (Or) *Satureja punctata* (122)

TOSSU (Or) *Pittosporum abyssinicum* (170)

TOTAKOLLA (Amh) *Galineria saxifraga* (189)

TOTOKE (Or) *Premna schimperi* (210)

TOW (Anu) *Balanites aegyptiaca* (236)

TQUR-N'CHET (Amh) *Prunus africana* (391)

TQUR-T'ELENG (Amh) *Hypoestes triflora* (18)

TSA'DA-AQBA (Tre) *Acacia tortilis* (312)

TSA'DA-DEKWA'TA (Tya) *Kalanchoe quartiniana* (93)

TSAGHA (Tya) *Coriandrum sativum* (26)

TSELLIM-DEBBESOM (Tre & Tya) *Delphinium dasycaulon* (182)

TSELLIM-DEBBESOM (Tre & Tya) *Delphinium wellbyi* (182)

TSGIE-REDA (Amh) *Rosa x richardii* (186)

TSILAL-A'NOY-MARYAM (Tya & Tre) *Gloriosa simplex* (153)

TUFO (Or) *Ageratum conyzoides* (33)

TUFO (Or) *Guizotia scabra scabra* (53)

TULU (Or) *Euphorbia abyssinica* (275)

TUMOGA (Kef) *Justitia schimperana* (21)

TUMUGA (Or) *Justitia schimperana* (21)

TUNGIT (Or) *Otostegia integrifolia* (113)

TUNJIT (Or) *Otostegia integrifolia* (113)

TUTTO (Or) *Citrus aurantifolia* (400)

TUTU (Amh) *Canarina abyssinica* (85)

TUTUQA (Agew) *Ximenia americana* (372)

TUTWA (Wel) *Maytenus obscura* (263)

UBEL (Tre) *Tamarindus indica* (339)

UDSHENA (Tya) *Erica arborea* (271)

ULIFONI (Or) *Apodytes dimidiata* (287)

ULUMAY (Or) *Clausena anisata* (403)

ULWIETO (Anu) *Lonchocarpus laxiflorus* (328)

URAGA (Or) *Ehretia cymosa* (248)

URAO (Anu) *Securidaca longepedunculata* (380)

URGESA (Or) *Premna schimperi* (210)

URGO Or) *Ocimum basilicum* (110)

URMAYA (Or) *Clausena anisata* (403)

UTORO (Or) *Stereospermum kunthianum* (240)

UTSHENA (Tya) *Erica arborea* (271)

WACU (Or) *Acacia seyal* (308)

WADESSA (Or) *Cordia africana* (247)

WADICHO (Sid) *Cordia africana* (247)

WAGAMO (Kef) *Ehretia cymosa* (248)

WAGGMA (Amh) *Trifolium acaule* (141)

WAGI (Or) *Ehretia cymosa* (248)

WAGINOS (Amh) *Brucea antidysenterica* (197)

WAGO (Kef) *Croton macrostachys* (272)

WAJEMA (Amh) *Medicago polymorpha* (134)

WAJJI (Or) *Acacia seyal* (308)

WAKKO-DIMO (Or) *Acacia seyal* (308)

WALAYA (Or) *Clausena anisata* (403)

WALBA (Tya) *Boswellia papyrifera* (255)

WALWAL (Bil) *Boswellia papyrifera* (255)

WANZA (Amh) *Cordia africana* (247)

WARKA (Amh) *Ficus vasta* (352)

WASHNT (Amh) *Stereospermum kunthianum* (240)

WASIYA (Or) *Acacia seyal* (308)

WATATE (Tya) *Launaea cornuta* (58)

WATO (Or) *Osyris quadripartita* (190)

WAZMA (Amh) *Trifolium quartinianum* (142)

WAZMA (Amh) *Trifolium steudneri* (146)

WAZO (Or) *Erythrina brucei* (324)

WAZO (Or) *Erythrina abyssinica* (323)

WCQA (Agew) *Calpurnia aurea* (320)

WEEO (Anu) *Triumfetta rhomboidea* (206)

WEIBA (Tya) *Combretum molle* (267)

WELA (Gam) *Ficus vasta* (352)

WELECCO (Kem) *Erythrina abyssinica* (323)

WELECO (Kem) *Erythrina brucei* (324)

WELENA (Or) *Erythrina abyssinica* (323)

WELENSU (Or) *Erythrina brucei* (324)

WELENSU (Or) *Erythrina abyssinica* (323)

WELESSIENU (Wel) *Bersama abyssinica* (348)

WELKA (Ge'ez) *Ficus vasta* (352)

WEMBELEL (Amh) *Jasminum abyssinicum* (165)

WENDEBYO (Or) *Apodytes dimidiata* (287)

WENQOQO (Gam) *Hagenia abyssinica* (388)

WERA (Had) *Erythrina brucei* (324)

WERA (Had) *Erythrina abyssinica* (323)

WERKELLO (Gam) *Rhus glutinosa* (220)

WESHMELLA (Amh) *Eriobotrya jabonica* (387)

WEYELO (Tya) *Pittosporum abyssinicum* (170)

WEYINAGIFT (Amh) *Pentas schimperiana* (189)

WEYL (Afar & Som) *Pittosporum abyssinicum* (170)

WEYN (Amh) *Vitis vinifera* (213)

WEYNI (Gur & Tya) *Vitis vinifera* (213)

WEYNIYYA (Wel) *Vitis vinifera* (213)

WEYRA (Amh) *Olea europaea subsp. cuspidata* (376)

WIGHIR (Som) *Olea europaea subsp. cuspidata* (376)

WITU (Or) *Kalanchoe quartiniana* (93)

WOF-ANQUR (Amh) *Commelina benghalensis* (89)

WOGRET (Tya) *Olea europaea subsp. cuspidata* (376)

WOLA (Wel) *Ficus vasta* (352)

WORARIKO (Sid) *Syzygium guineense* subsp. *afromontanum* (368)

WOSANGA (Or) *Sapium ellipticum* (280)

WRAFUTO (Wel) *Allophyllus abyssinicus* (407)

WTTIE (Amh) *Acacia lahai* (296)

WTTO (Kef) *Schefflera abyssinica* (231)

WUCHIU (Tya) *Erica arborea* (271)

WULKEFA (Amh) *Sparmannia ricinocarpa* (205)

WULQEFA (Amh) *Dombeya torrida* (412)

WURUGU (Or) *Ehretia cymosa* (248)

YA-A (Afar) *Agave sisalana* (22)

YAGO (Kef) *Milletia ferruginea* (331)

YAGO (Or) *Milletia ferruginea* (331)

YAGOY (Mes) *Milletia ferruginea* (331)

YAHIYASHITO (Amh) *Tagetes minuta* (66)

YAHYA-SUF (Amh) *Carthamus tinctorius* (38)

YAYT'-AREG (Amh) *Ipomoea tenuirostris* (90)

YE'SEY'TAN-GOMEN (Tya) *Launaea cornuta* (58)

YE'TAN-ZAF (Amh) *Boswellia papyrifera* (255)

YE'TBS-QTEL (Amh) *Rosmarinus officinalis* (118)

YE'TIT'-ZAF (Amh) *Ceiba pentandra* (244)

YE-AHIYA-SUF (Amh) *Carthamus lanatus* (38)

YE-FIYEL-DOKA (Amh) *Plectranthus barbatus* (114)

YEAHYA-JERO (Amh) *Verbascum sinaiticum* (194)

YEÄMORA-GWAYA (Amh) *Lablab purpureus* (133)

YEBAHR-MASHLA (Amh) *Zea mays* (174)

YEBEG-LAT (Amh) *Scorpiurus muricatus* (141)

YEBEG-LAT (Amh) *Trifolium quartinianum* (142)

YEBEG-LAT (Amh) *Trifolium steudneri* (146)

YEBERE CHEW (Amh) *Oxalis obliquifolia* (169)

YEBERE CHEW (Amh) *Oxalis corniculata* (166)

YEDJIB AGEDA (Amh) *Scadoxus multiflorus* (25)

YEFERENJ-KTKTTA (Amh) *Caesalpina decapetala* (126)

YEFERENJ-SUF (Amh) *Helianthus annuus* (54)

YEFERENJI-'NJORIE (Amh) *Morus alba* (162)

YEFERES-ZENG (Amh) *Vernonia adoensis* (69)

YEFERES-ZENG (Amh) *Otostegia tomentosa* (113)

YEFYEL WETET (Amh) *Crepis rueppellii* (45)

YEFYEL-GOMEN (Amh) *Isodon schimperi* (106)

YEGURAGHE-GOMMEN (Amh) *Brassica carinata* (81)

YEJB-ATER (Amh) *Tylosema fassoglensis* (146)

YEJB-DNCH (Amh) *Cyanotis barbata* (90)

YEKBRITT-N'CHET (Amh) *Ceiba pentandra* (244)

YELAM CHEW (Amh) *Epilobium hirsutum* (166)

YELOSKIT (Amh) *Satureja punctata* (122)

YELREGNOCH-TILA (Amh) *Arisaema enneaphyllum* (30)

YEMARYAM-WEHA-QEJI (Amh) *Plectranthus barbatus* (114)

YEMDR-'NJORIE (Amh) *Fragaria x ananassa* (185)

YEMDR-BERBERIE (Amh) *Acmella caulirhiza* (33)

YEMDR-BERHERU (Amh) *Galinsoga parviflora* (50)

YEMDR-KOSO (Amh) *Parochaetus communis* (138)

YEMESKEL-ABEBA (Amh) *Bidens pachyloma* (37)

YEMESKEL-ABEBA (Amh) *Bidens prestinaria* (37)

YEOROMO-DNCH (Amh) *Plectranthus punctatus edulis* (117)

YEQOLLA-WANZA (Amh) *Piliostigma thonningii* (335)

YEQQOLLA-'NDAHULLA (Amh) *Kalanchoe lanceolata* (93)

YEQUOLLA-'NDAHULLA (Amh) *Kalanchoe petitiana* (93)

YEREGNA-MSA (Amh) *Campanula edulis* (85)

YEREGNA-QOLO (Amh) *Lantana trifolia* (210)

YERENCHI (Amh) *Caylusea abyssinica* (185)

YESET-MLAS (Amh) *Xanthium spinosum* (73)

YESHEWA-AREM (Amh) *Galinsoga parviflora* (50)

YESIET-MLAS (Amh) *Hygrophila auriculata* (17)

YESKKOKO-GOMEN (Amh) *Solanecio gigas* (65)

YET'RUMBA-ABEBA (Amh) *Zantedeschia aethiopica* (30)

YETEBMENJA-ZAF (Amh) *Jacaranda mimosifolia* (239)

YETJA-SGA (Amh) *Persicaria nepalense* (177)

YEWHA-ANQUR (Amh) *Commelina benghalensis* (89)

YEWOF-QOLO (Amh) *Lantana camera* (210)

YEWOLLAMO-DNCH (Amh) *Plectranthus punctatus edulis* (117)

YEWOT'-QOLO (Amh) *Cyanotis barbata* (90)

YEZNJERO-GOMMEN (Amh) *Cussonia holstii* (227)

YEZNJERO-WENBER (Amh) *Polyscias fulva* (228)

YOKE (Gim) *Albizia lebbek* (316)

YUDO (Kef) *Dracaena steudneri* (216)

YUNGO (Or) *Albizia schimperiana* (319)

YUNGO (Or) *Albizia gummifera* (315)

ZADYA (Gof) *Milletia ferruginea* (331)

ZAGDA (Tya) *Coriandrum sativum* (26)

ZAGEZELA (Tya) *Laggera pterodonata* (58)

ZAGIE (Gam) *Bersama abyssinica* (348)

ZAGIE (Wel) *Milletia ferruginea* (331)

ZAGOGO (Tya) *Bidens pilosa* (37)

ZAHAHENE (Or) *Ocimum basilicum* (110)

ZAKAKEWE (Amh) *Ocimum basilicum* (110)

ZAKDI (Tya) *Erica arborea* (271)

ZANA (Amh) *Stereospermum kunthianum* (240)

ZEDI (Or) *Sesamum indicum* (169)

ZENADDAM (Amh) *Satureja paradoxa* (122)

ZENQILA (Amh) *Berberis holstii* (77)

ZEYITON (Ade) *Psidium guajava* (367)

ZEYTUN (Amh & Or) *Psidium guajava* (367)

ZEYITUNA (Amh, Or & Afar) Psidium guajava (367)

ZIFAL (Ge'ez) *Cicer arietinum* (129)

ZIYAG (Sha) *Milletia ferruginea* (331)

ZIYAGU (Sha) *Milletia ferruginea* (331)

ZMBABA (Amh) *Phoenix reclinata* (232)

ZOHUN-KACHAMO (Amh) *Jasminum abyssinicum* (165)

ZOMMER (Tya) *Plectranthus lanunginosus* (114)

ZUNGUAH (Tya) *Grewia ferruginea* (205)

ZWAW' (Tya) *Erythrina abyssinica* (323)

INDEX OF SCIENTIFIC NAMES